PHOTO
JOURNALISM
THE PROFESSIONALS' APPROACH

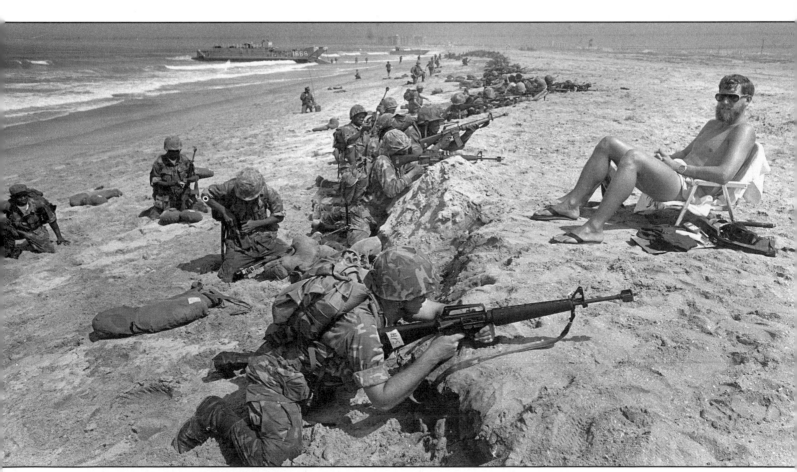

When the Marines landed in San Diego, the sunbather was unfazed because he was a demolitions expert who helped plan the landing. (Photo by Robert Lachman, *Los Angeles Times*.)

Firefighters snuff an electrical fire aboard an airplane parked on a Boston runway. (Photo by George Rizer, the *Boston Globe*.)

PHOTO
JOURNALISM
THE PROFESSIONALS' APPROACH

Kenneth Kobré
Editing & Design by Betsy Brill

FOCAL PRESS
Boston Oxford Melbourne Singapore Toronto Munich New Delhi Tokyo

Focal Press is an imprint of Butterworth–Heinemann

Cover design and interior design: Betsy Brill, San Francisco
Cover photograph: Dan Poush, The *Salem Oregonian*
(Five people were injured in this car accident. All lived. As the rescue team removed the passengers, the mother asked for her baby.)

Illustrations: Ben Barbante, San Mateo, Calif.

Library of Congress Cataloging-in-Publication Data

Kobré, Kenneth, 1946-
    Photojournalism : the professionals' approach / Kenneth Kobré ;
    editing & design by Betsy Brill. — 3rd ed.
        p.   cm.
    Includes bibliographical references (p.   ) and index.
    ISBN 0-240-80240-3 (pbk.)
    1. Photojournalism.   I. Brill, Betsy.   II. Title.
    TR820.K75   1995
    778.9'07049—dc20   95-20883
                                                            CIP

British Library Cataloguing-in-Publication Data
A catalogue record for this book is available from the British Library.

The publisher offers discounts on bulk orders of this book.
For information, please write:

Manager of Special Sales
Butterworth–Heinemann
313 Washington Street
Newton, MA 02158–1626

10 9 8 7 6 5 4 3 2 1

Printed in Canada.

Dedication

This book is dedicated to my parents, Reva and Sidney Kobre.

A combination of strobe and available light makes this portrait dramatic and memorable. (Photo by Greg Lehman, *Walla Walla* (Wash.) *Union-Bulletin.)*

Contents

A Florida state trooper tried to block the cameras of two *Palm Beach Post* photographers who were covering the arrest of an armed robbery suspect. See page 275. (Photo by C.J. Walker, the *Palm Beach Post*.)

Preface

Only twelve percent of the people who pick up a newspaper read a story on the front page if no picture accompanies the story. Add a photograph—any photograph—and the readership of that story zooms up to forty-two percent. Increase the size of the picture to four columns, and the readership of the story shoots up even higher. Journalism needs pictures.

In this era of the Internet and CD-ROMs, and with the disappearance of competitive daily newspapers, some pessimists predict the demise of photojournalism. We will receive all of our information from computers and TV, they say, and therefore newspapers and magazines will die out—and with them photojournalism.

Not true.

In fact, computers provide a new lease on life for photojournalism. While the Internet until recently carried printed information in only dull typographic form, the World Wide Web features clear graphics and crisp full-color photographs, as well. Soon, you'll get high-resolution color pictures on your computer as easily and as quickly as you get your daily newspaper or weekly magazine.

It won't be long before the marriage of words and pictures that now exists in print will be transposed to this new electronic medium. News stories, feature articles, and exposés alike will attract and hold readers better when the text on the computer screen is associated with hard-hitting photojournalism. Photographers won't be limited to one or two

pictures per story (as they now are in print) but will be able to offer up ten or even 100 pictures of a flood in Bangladesh or the Super Bowl playoffs in Buffalo.

Computer screens are starting to look like glossy magazine spreads—without the severe limitations of space now imposed on print. Thanks to the growing ease of access to the World Wide Web, millions of people around the world will be stimulated by the massive databank of powerful images electronically transmitted to their computer screens—images not always pre-selected or filtered by conventional news agencies. Far from being an outmoded form of communication, quality photojournalism will be in demand now more than ever.

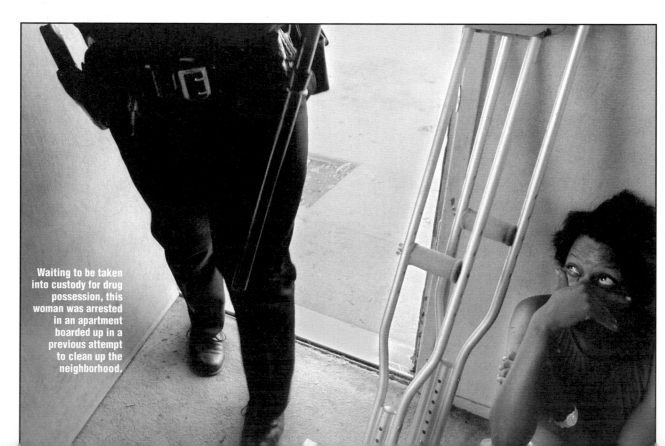

Waiting to be taken into custody for drug possession, this woman was arrested in an apartment boarded up in a previous attempt to clean up the neighborhood.

(Photo by Carolyn Cole, the *Sacramento Bee*.)

Acknowledgments

I would like to thank my parents, Dr. and Mrs. Sidney Kobre. Without their advice and guidance, I would never have written this book. My father, who died during production of this edition, was a reporter, editor, and professor of journalism for many years. He helped give the original book its clear journalistic focus. My mother, who also is a writer, suggested many improvements in the prose style of the original manuscript.

This edition of the book would never have been completed nor obtained its look without the devotion and love of Betsy Brill, my wife. For nearly a year, through many alterations and changes, she helped guide the project from initial idea to the final design of the printed page. Her experience as a professional photojournalist, editor, and designer helped bring my abstract ideas into reality on the page.

For some books, the author goes to the mountain top and writes. That is not how the original book nor its revisions have been produced. This text is based on interviews—both formal and informal—with working pros on newspapers, magazines, and wire services. I have mentioned their names in the text whenever possible. Their generosity with their expertise and their time makes this book unique.

In addition, a veritable platoon of photographers, photo editors, editors, academics, and lawyers have read parts of this revision. I greatly appreciate their time and efforts: Barbara London, editor of this book's original manuscript and co-author of *Photography*, by London and Upton; Michael Sherer, associate professor of journalism, University of Nebraska at Omaha; Cindy Russell, researcher; Jessica Lorber and Cammie, Max, and Ziggy Kotchetkov, photo assistants; Steven Blake Heiner, Nikon representative; Jay Koelzer, *Rocky Mountain News*; and Jim Johnson, *Muskegon Chronicle*.

A second wave of people helped give the book its wide diversity of images. For their help in picture research, I'd like to thank Hal Buell, Vin Alabiso, Michael Martinez, and David Breslauer of the Associated Press; Ken Irby, *Newsday*; Jim Gordon, *News Photographer* magazine; Nick Didlick, *Vancouver Sun*; and Rob Shields, Mercury Pictures.

Almost all of this book's photos have been lent to me by photographers, some of whom I know and others I've not had the opportunity to meet; some former students and some present ones. Their credits appear next to their pictures. I would like to thank all of them for their generous contribution to this project. A book of this scope would be impossible without their help.

One photographer wrote to tell me that he used the original book when he was a student. After a number of years in the profession, he began to teach part-time. Now he assigns the book to his students. His photo, in this edition, will help a third generation of future photojournalists.

This revision includes many more demonstration pictures and drawings than the original book. Daryl Wong and Sarah Prall shot many of these clear and accurate demonstration photos. Ben Barbante prepared all the explanatory drawings and sketches. Jerry Wolford, *Greensboro* (N.C.) *News and Record*, produced a number of the digital demonstration images. Freelancer Keith Philpott willingly exposed his camera bag.

Much of the book's information is based on the latest research in the field. Barbara Taber undertook the extensive, computer-assisted bibliographical searches. Cindy Russell helped locate a number of periodicals and manuscripts.

Marie Lee at Butterworth/Focal Press encouraged me to undertake this revision and has chaperoned the project to its publication.

Finally, like a chemist's research lab, my classes at San Francisco State University have allowed me the opportunity to experiment on new approaches to photojournalism, particularly the picture story and the portrait. I thank my students for undergoing the trials and tribulations of trying new ways to tell stories photographically.

Erna Smith, chair of the journalism department at SFSU, has co-taught a photo story class with me and continues today as a solid supporter of photojournalism in our department.

Assignment

Steve Linsenmayer, of the Fort Wayne, Indiana, *News-Sentinel* heard the darkroom's emergency band scanner cackle, "Structure fire." Looking out the window, he saw black rain clouds covering a sky broken by distant lightning. Linsenmayer hesitated to race out into the storm until his boss, Keith Hitchens, came running down the hall yelling "church fire." Hitchens had heard the second call on the radio asking for additional fire companies and identifying the burning structure as St. Mary's Church.

"Oh shit," Linsenmayer gasped as he raced by the

The photographer heard about this fire at a church by monitoring the emergency scanner radio. (Photo by Steve Linsenmayer, the *News-Sentinel*, Fort Wayne, Indiana.)

darkroom to grab his camera bag on the way to his car.

When he got to St. Mary's, the lightning storm that had started the blaze was still in full glory. Within minutes of starting to shoot, Linsenmayer's umbrella blew out, so he radioed back to the office to send more film, more photographers—and dry towels.

About an hour into the fire, heavy smoke started to billow out of the rear steeple. Linsenmayer kept shooting as he captured the shot of the church's crosses enveloped by smoke. The photo filled nearly the entire front page of the next day's edition. (See page 2.)

SCANNER RADIO SIGNALS FIRES AND ACCIDENTS

Only rarely will you stumble over a big, breaking news story. "Anticipating spot news is like trying to predict where lightning will strike," says Robert Bowden of the *St. Petersburg* (Fla.) *Times*.

How does a news photographer know when a story is breaking? One way is to monitor the emergency-band radio frequencies for a tip-off on a major spot news break. Most newspaper photographers monitor the police band because cops are usually the first ones called to a murder, robbery, or accident.

Police use three bands: low (35–50), very high (VHF) (152–174), and ultra high (UHF) (450–70). You can find the exact frequency by asking your local police department, or by obtaining from a local electronics store a directory that lists all emergency frequencies in the region.

To learn quickly about a major transportation disaster, you can monitor the international frequency for airplanes (121.5) or marine frequency (156.8) for distress calls at sea. Additional frequencies that enable you to get a jump on fast-breaking events include those of the state police, county sheriff, and fire department. Also, consider monitoring the national weather alert and civil defense.

Normally the police talk in codes. For instance, 10-42 means traffic accident at . . . 10-70 means fire at . . . The codes are published, but sometimes the police broadcast their calls through a scrambler, so you might have to purchase an unscrambler to understand what is being said.

News Radio Good in a Pinch

What else do photographers use to keep in touch with the news pulse of the city, especially when they can't afford a monitor? One alternative is an all-news radio station or a station that specializes in frequent news or

Political groups like this one demonstrating in front of an abortion clinic in Wichita, Kansas, often tip off the media about the time and place of their protests.
(Photo by Kim Johnson for the *Wichita* (Kansas) *Eagle.*)

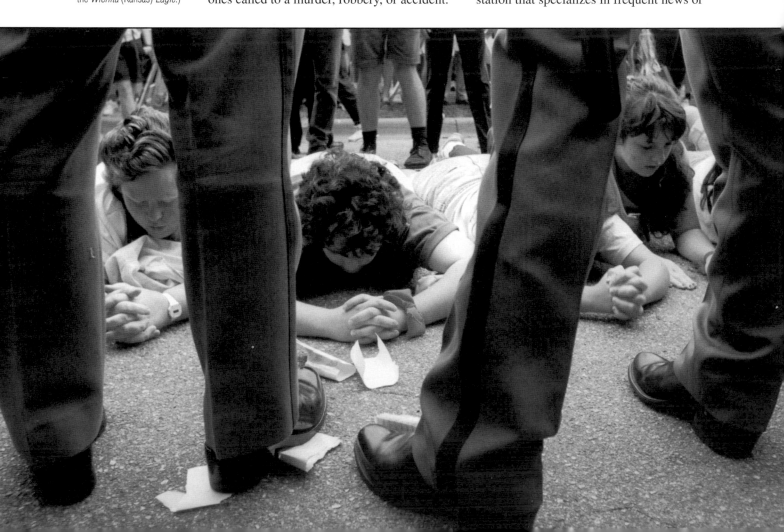

updated news reports. A station with an all-news format interrupts any in-progress programming immediately if an emergency arises. These stations monitor several scanner channels, including the fire and police departments, and will announce over the air any time a major fire alarm or multicar accident occurs. The all-news station also has its own reporters who cover breaking stories and give live updates. The radio's weather forecaster will predict a natural disaster such as a hurricane or tornado, and a reporter will describe the damage when the disaster hits. News radio does not provide as immediate information as the scanner, but the radio often will suffice.

Tips Help

Newspapers often get leads on top news stories when people call the city desk with tips. Some newspapers, in fact, offer monetary rewards for tips. The city desk sizes up the event. Then, if the decision is to respond, the city editor or an assistant may send out a reporter and photographer.

Special interest groups call in tips to the newspapers if the members think publicity will do them some good. If minorities, welfare mothers, gays, or anti-nuclear groups, for example, are going to stage a protest for which they want coverage, they might telephone the newspaper with the time and place of their planned demonstration.

Beat Reporter Knows the Territory

Most newspapers assign reporters to cover a certain beat: city hall, hospitals, police headquarters. Beat reporters keep up with the news and events in their specialty; consequently, these reporters know when to expect a major story to break. The city hall beat reporter may call in to the city desk and say, "The mayor is greeting some astronauts today. It will be worth a good picture." The editor agrees and assigns a photographer.

Whether a photographer stumbles into an event in progress, finds out about it from a scanner radio, or gets a tip, he or she still must evaluate its news and picture worthiness, photograph the activity, and rush the picture to a media outlet in time for the next deadline.

Making Contacts

Michael Meinhardt, of the *Chicago Tribune,* has developed his own system of finding out about spot news as it happens. Using a system of pagers, two-way radios, cellular phones, and a network of sources and contacts, he stays abreast of news as it breaks in the Chicago and greater-Chicago area.

Firefighters, police officers, dispatchers, and even air traffic controllers at surrounding airports notify Meinhardt of news events via a voice-message pager that he carries twenty-four hours a day. He has befriended these contacts at other news events, where he introduced himself, left a business card, and followed-up by giving them photographs of themselves at work.

"You'd be surprised how many of them remember me when the news breaks," he says.

"Additionally," he explains, "I belong to a network of contacts led by a local radio news reporter who is considered the dean of spot news. . . . We all have two-way radios on our own frequency that we monitor around the clock. . . . Once the closest person arrives on the scene, I can usually ascertain whether it's worth traveling to shoot pictures. They can also let me know how urgently I need to get there before the scene clears up."

Not surprisingly, Meinhardt is considered a great source of information by his colleagues in the newsroom and by the newspaper's city desk.

PR Office is There to Aid You

The mayor will arrive at his office at 9 A.M. He leaves for the airport at 10:15 A.M. to dedicate a new runway. He will be at the Golden Age Senior Citizens home from 11:30 A.M. to 12:30 P.M. Then, during a 1 P.M. lunch at the Parker House, the mayor will meet with the Committee for City Beautification.

If you want to know the whereabouts of the mayor practically every minute of the day, just consult the schedule. The mayor's personal or press secretary arranges the itinerary weeks in advance. Mayors, congressional representatives, senators, and the president of the United States have carefully planned schedules, available through their press officers.

Companies, schools, hospitals, prisons, and governmental departments also have press or public relations offices. These offices, sometimes called public affairs or public information departments, generate a steady stream of news releases announcing the opening of a new college campus, the invention of a long-lasting lightbulb, or the start of a new special education teaching program. Many of these PR releases suggest good picture possibilities.

Paper Prints Schedules

Another source for upcoming news events comes daily to your doorstep rolled and held with a rubber band. The daily paper carries birth, wedding, and death announcements. The paper prints schedules of local theaters, sports events, parades, and festivals. When the circus arrives in your town, the paper will list the time and place of the big top show.

Trade Magazines Supply Unusual Leads

For more unusual activities, check special interest newspapers, magazines, or your on-line computer service. Dog and cat lovers, cyclists, plumbers, skateboarders, mental health professionals, and environmental groups all publish magazines and newsletters that announce special events.

To keep track of upcoming happenings with visual possibilities, newspapers and wire services maintain a log book listing the time, place, and date of each future activity. The notation in the book includes a telephone number for the sponsoring organization in case the photographer needs more information. The log book idea also works well for freelancers.

WORKING WITH REPORTERS
■ WHEN CLICKERS MEET SCRIBBLERS
Photo Request Starts the Process

Most news publications have many more staff reporters than photographers. From their sources, these news-hounds generate potential stories. When an editor approves a story proposal, the reporter makes out a photo request.

For the photographer, the key to great photo coverage depends on the information and arrangements on the photo request. Typical assignment requests include the name of the person or event to be photographed, the time, date, and place. Usually, the editor has assigned a slug—a one- or two-word designation for the story that serves as the story's name until the copy desk writes a final headline. Usually the assignment sheet includes a brief description of the proposed article as well as a telephone number with which to contact the key subject if anything needs to be changed.

Photographer and Reporter Meet Ahead of Time

Under the best of circumstances, the reporter, photographer, and assigning editors meet at this point in the story's development to discuss the team's approach. The group tries to define the story's thrust and news. Here, the photojournalist can suggest visual ways to tell the story that correspond to the reporter's written approach. The photographer can recommend a candid approach, a portrait, or a photo illustration—and also can estimate the amount of time needed for the shoot, or identify props and necessary clearances.

On some publications, unfortunately, the photographer never meets with the reporter and assigning editor. Rather, the shooter receives the information from an intermediary editor, or is briefed by notes on the assignment sheet. In these circumstances the photographer plays a reduced role in determining the story's final outcome. Located at the end of the assigning chain, the photographer has little say in determining the best approach to the story.

Best Time for an Assignment

On many newspapers and magazines, the reporter calls the subject and makes the shooting arrangements for the photographer. Sometimes this saves the photographer time. In most cases, though, the reporter can inadvertently overlook great picture opportunities. The reporter, for example, may decide to do a story about the new principal at Lincoln High. The writer phones to ask when the principal is free for an interview and pictures. The principal responds: "Well, I'm busy all day. I greet the kids as they get off the bus. Then I meet with parents and teachers. Next I observe classes and eat lunch with the kids. Then I usually work with student discipline problems in the afternoon. All the teachers and students are gone by four. How about meeting me in my office after four?"

From the reporter's point of view, four o'clock would be fine. The principal is free to answer questions and chat in a quiet environment in her office. From the photojournalist's perspective, four o'clock would be okay if formal portraits or head shots are all that are sought. But four o'clock would be a disaster if the photojournalist wants to shoot honest, revealing candids.

The shooter should be at school at 7:30 A.M., as the principal greets the kids, again at noon when she eats with her teachers and students. Hopefully, the photographer could get access later to observe the principal's work with disciplinary problems. These pictures would show whether the principal is stern or kind, friendly or tough, or a little of each. Were the photographer to shoot when the writer originally planned, the resulting pictures would probably be of the subject standing in front of the building, in a hallway, or inside a classroom. The environmental portrait would show what the principal looked like but would hardly reveal her character.

Photographers Make Their Own Arrangements

When reporters and editors fill out assignment sheets, they do not always take into account the special needs of photographers. While reporters can hold a telephone inter-

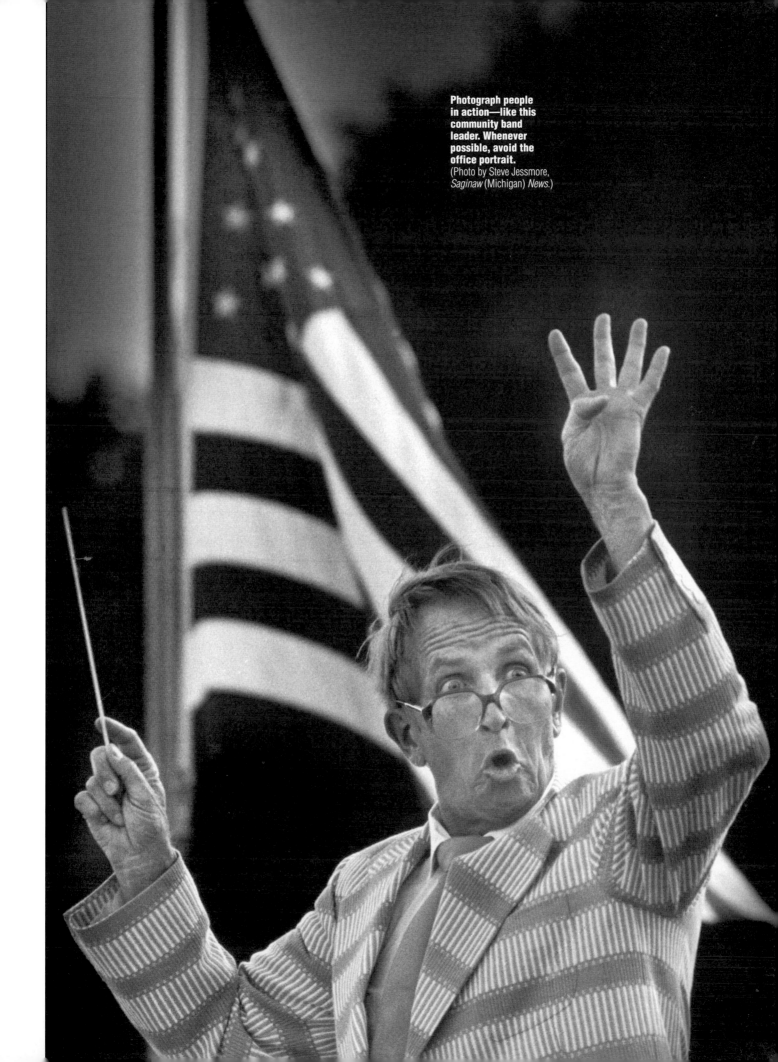

Photograph people in action—like this community band leader. Whenever possible, avoid the office portrait. (Photo by Steve Jessmore, *Saginaw* (Michigan) *News.*)

To avoid being attacked during his forays into San Francisco's Tenderloin neighborhood, *San Francisco Chronicle* staffer Fred Larson dressed unobtrusively and hid his camera inside a portable stereo.
(Photo by Scott Sommerdorf, *San Francisco Chronicle*.)

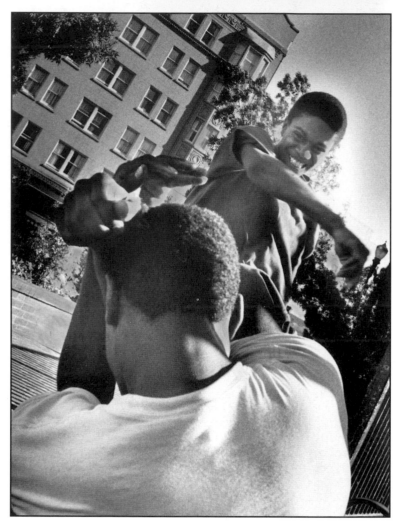

Street fighters continued their battle while an unobtrusive Larson moved in close with his camera-in-a-boombox.
(Photo by Frederic Larson, *San Francisco Chronicle*.)

appointment, or decide what other pictures might go with the story. While the reporters might tape the interview at four o'clock, the photographer might shoot the subject from dawn until dusk on a different day.

When arranging the shooting schedule with a subject, a good question for photographers to ask is, "What is your typical day like?" As the subject goes through a normal day's activities, the photographer keeps in mind which hours the person is just sitting behind a desk talking and which hours he or she is doing something active and therefore photogenic. The photographer also should find out if anything unusual is coming up that would lend itself to revealing photos.

On the Scene: Working in Tandem

For some types of news, the photographer and reporter must cover the event together. Sometimes it's the reporter who knows the important players. Sometimes the photographer needs a second set of eyes to help provide protection, such as at a violent street protest. However, even at these kinds of news events, the photographer and reporter should not become wedded at the hip. Each has different needs. One is following the action as it flows down a street, while the other is checking a quote and making sure the name is spelled correctly.

Even so, while both the photographer and reporter need independence, the two also need to reconnect every once in a while to confirm they are developing the story in parallel ways.

Although the photographer and writer don't shoot and interview at the same moment, they should coordinate the message of their words and pictures. Photographers should pass on their observations about the subject or event to the writers. Writers can explain to photographers the gist of their leads.

In the end, the reader will be looking at both the picture on the page and the accompanying story. If the writer describes the subject as drab, yet the picture shows a smiling person wearing a peacock-colored shirt, the reader is left trying to resolve the conflict. Writers and photographers should resolve any conflict between words and pictures before the story goes to press.

■ PICTURE POLITICS

With good planning, ideally, media management avoids poor use of photo resources. However, many newspapers and magazines continue to operate in a traditional structure long unfriendly to the effective use of photography.

Traditionally, management organized

view or call back later for more facts, the photographer needs to be present when the subject is engaged in work. Photographers and photo editors need to educate those who report, or assign reporting, because lack of such a mutual understanding leads all too predictably to just a routine picture.

Often photographers find that, because they know the kinds of pictures they are looking for, they can make arrangements better than the beat reporter or supervising editor. On some publications, photographers get names and phone numbers and then initiate the newsrooms to handle assignments proposed by either reporters or editors. In these newsrooms, photographers rarely originated story ideas. And even if they did, the photo-reporters received little in the way of picture play for their efforts.

The old-style process (still widely used today) works this way: once the reporter gets the green light, research begins. The reporter might interview subjects, check the newspaper's morgue for related articles, call authorities on the issue, and finally write the copy over a period of days or even weeks. Only when the story is nearly completed and ready for publication does the reporter fill out a photo request. Finally, the photo department becomes aware of the issue.

With the story written and the publication date set, the photographer has little room to maneuver. While the reporter took days and weeks to develop the story, the photographer might have just hours to produce accompanying photos. The photographer might have to squeeze the assignment in with three or four others that day. The photojournalist might have no choice about when to shoot for the best light. The deadline might not allow enough time to hang around for a candid look at the subject.

The Budget Meeting

On most publications, the managing editor, at a daily, weekly, or monthly story conference often referred to as a budget meeting, decides how much space to allocate for a story and where that story will play. Representing each section of the publication, the different editors gather around a conference table to pitch their best stories to the managing editor, who ultimately decides which stories get front-page display and which are buried inside. While the photo editor speaks up for pictures at this meeting, the word editors always outnumber the lonely representative from the photography department. (See Chapter 10, "Editing.")

Here, each editor represents a part of the paper or magazine. Individual editors defend their turf. On a large newspaper, the sports editor, fashion editor, city editor, and foreign desk editor might each have their own section fronts and inside pages. On a weekly news magazine, the national editor, political editor, and music editor each might have a minimum number of pages to cover the most important topics in a specific area. Too often, the photo editor has no designated turf: no space assigned solely to photo stories. While the photo editor might sit at the table with other decision makers, he or she has no formally reserved space in the publication.

Furthermore, the picture editor is up against colleagues who think their sections cover the most important news, contain the best writers, and ought to have the most space. And, because more and bigger photos mean fewer words, few section editors see the advantages of story-telling pictures eclipsing longer stories. Furthermore, managing editors, most of whom graduate from the writing rather than the visual side of the publication, make the final decisions about the use of space. The upshot at most publications: even a very outspoken photo editor can rarely counterbalance these inherent structural biases toward words.

Take a Reporter to Lunch

To avoid the trap of being the last one to know about important stories—and having your pictures played poorly—try this: if you are new on a paper, ask the managing editor which reporter stands out in the newsroom. If you have worked at a paper for a while, you probably already know the names of the best writers. Start by introducing yourself to one reporter. Ask what the writer is working on. If the story sounds interesting, talk about picture possibilities. If you know that an event is coming up that would help explain the story, suggest to your photo editor or managing editor an assignment that will help illustrate the story. On your own, start reading about the issue. If you notice a picture that might support the story, shoot it. Look for as many ways as you can to photograph the writer's story even before the wordsmith has finished the masterpiece.

When the story results in a formal photo request, your editor will likely assign the job to you because you have already started on the photos. By now you have a clear idea of the possible pictures that would help the story. Also, you know that, because the story was written by a top writer, it will probably get prominent display.

If you continue to cruise the newsroom looking for good writers, anticipating photo requests, and building alliances with the word side, you will probably find writers agreeable to listening to your story ideas. A writing/photography partnership will probably garner more newsprint than your proposal alone.

■ SELF-GENERATED ASSIGNMENTS

Sometimes a photographer pulls over next to an overturned car, jumps out, and shoots. No written assignment needed here. Most often, a photographer receives a verbal or written assignment from an editor. But many photographers report that their best assignments are those they proposed themselves. Self-generated assignments allow the photographer to pick exciting topics that lend themselves to visuals. When a photographer has researched a good story, the next step is to request a reporter to provide the needed text. The more stories photographers propose, the more control they will have over their work.

Fred Larson, of the *San Francisco Chronicle,* assigned himself to photograph a city neighborhood called the Tenderloin. The area got its nickname because, in the old days, a cop on the beat was assured enough under-the-table money to guarantee beef tenderloin chops on his dinner table every night. To this day, the Tenderloin is a crime-ridden area.

Because of the very real danger of being attacked in this part of town, Larson shot many pictures for his story from his car window. He also replaced the speaker in a "boom box" portable stereo with a camera. This subterfuge provided cover so that Larson could shoot easily and unobtrusively with the hidden camera. After four months of street shooting, Larson had enough revealing pictures to show a reporter how the story could develop. Only at this stage did the reporter come aboard the project and begin interviewing and writing.

Hal Wells was working for the *Lewisville Daily Leader,* in Texas, when he shot photos of illegal aliens crossing the Mexico/U.S. border. Later, he arranged with a reporter to provide a local angle, showing the influx of laborers into the Lewisville area. The final story and pictures were a result of Wells' initiative. (See page 133.)

When, a number of years after the war ended, Vietnam began allowing Americans into the country, the *Hartford Courant*'s Michael Kodas wanted to follow a veteran returning to the old battlefields. Kodas researched the story and even made the arrangements before proposing the idea to his editors. Not only did the editors agree to the story and underwrite the trip, but they also assigned one of the paper's top reporters to accompany Kodas on the assignment.

In each of these instances, the photographer originated the story, researched it, and then connected with a reporter. Because the photographer in each situation had selected the story topic, the subject lent itself to pictures. Working with a reporter helped assure that the stories received careful attention in the newsroom. (See "Developing a feature beat" in Chapter 4.)

INTERNATIONAL ASSIGNMENTS

Many of today's newspapers have expanded their beats to include the world. From covering earthquakes in India to uprisings in Rwanda, newspaper photographers are literally on the move. Photographers who covered high school football on Friday night may find themselves boarding a plane for Bosnia on Sunday morning. Never has the mastery of foreign languages or knowledge of international affairs been more important to photojournalists.

Kodas, of the *Hartford Courant,* who initiated his own international assignment, reads voraciously: the *Wall Street Journal,* the *Christian Science Monitor,* and the *New York Times,* among others.

National Public Radio is also a good source of international news for car-bound photographers. And, if an intensive language course is out of your budget, try substituting language tapes for your favorite rock 'n roll groups when you're stuck in traffic.

Finally, photographers can follow the most basic preparations recommended by free-lancer Keith Philpott: pack an up-to-date passport in your camera bag at all times. And make sure your inoculations are current for travel in Third World countries. (See page 212, "Inside a photographer's camera bag.")

Pack light for international assignments, says Carol Guzy, who covered the Ethiopian famine for the *Miami Herald* and the tumbling of the Berlin Wall for the *Washington Post.* She carries as little photo gear as she feels she can get away with but does bring an extra camera body, she says, and film—lots of film.

Kari René Hall carried 300 rolls of film when she photographed a large Cambodian refugee camp on the Thailand/Cambodian border. Her original assignment for the *Los Angeles Times, Orange County Edition,* was to follow politicians on a junket to Thailand. Wandering away from the planned PR events on the Cambodian border, she discovered a camp the size of a small city that contained refugees who had lived there for 17 years. Hall returned to Cambodia twice, using her own money to document the camp's conditions. She eventually published some of the pictures in the *Times* and produced a book, called ***Beyond the Killing Field***s, which was published by Aperture. (See opposite page.)

ASSURING VISUAL VARIETY
■ OVERALL SHOT SETS THE SCENE

If newspaper readers came to a news event, they would stand in the crowd and move their eyes from side to side to survey the entire panorama. The overall photo gives viewers at home this same kind of perspective. The overall allows viewers to orient themselves to the scene.

For some stories, an overall might include just a long shot of a room. For others, the overall might cover a city block, a neighborhood, or even a whole town. The scope of the shot depends on the size of the event. The overall shows where the event took place: inside, outside, country, city, land, sea, day, night, and so on. The shot defines the relative position of the participants. In a confrontation, for example, the overall angle would show whether the demonstrators and police were a block apart, or across the street from one another. The overall shot also allows the reader, by judging crowd size, to evaluate the magnitude of the event.

Margaret Bourke-White, a member of the original *Life* magazine staff, always shot overalls on each assignment, even if she didn't think they would be published. She explained that she wanted her New York editor to see the shooting location so that he could interpret the rest of the pictures she had taken.

Generally the overall requires a high angle. Rick Ferro knew this when he was flown in by the *St. Petersburg* (Florida) *Times* to cover the earthquake of 1989 in the San Francisco Bay Area. After renting a car, his first stop was at a large hardware store, where he purchased a thirty-foot ladder in anticipation of photographing an overall of the collapsed I-880 freeway in Oakland. The ladder came in handy, as Ferro was able to climb it to the top of the wreckage and shoot photos of the ongoing rescue.

When you arrive at a news event, quickly survey the scene to determine what is happening. Then search for a way to elevate yourself above the crowd. In a room, a chair will suffice.

But outside, a telephone pole, a leafless tree, or a nearby building will give you the high vantage point you need for an effective overall. When caught in a flat area, even the roof of your car will add some height to your view.

The wider angle lens you have, obviously, the less distance from the scene you will need. However, on a major news story that encompasses a vast area, such as a flood, hurricane, or conflagration, you may need to rent a helicopter or small airplane to get high enough to capture the dimensions of the destruction.

The photographer turned a routine assignment to Thailand, which included a side trip to a refugee camp on the Cambodian border, into a book-length project about the devastating conditions in the camps. (Photo by Kari René Hall, *Los Angeles Times, Orange County Edition.*)

■ MEDIUM SHOT TELLS THE STORY

The medium shot should "tell the story" in one photograph. Shoot the picture close enough to see the participants' action, yet far enough away to show their relationship to one another and to the environment. The medium shot contains all the story-telling elements of the scene. Like a news story lead, the photo must tell the whole story quickly by compressing the important elements into one image. The medium shot is the story's summary.

An accident photo might show the victims in the foreground, the wrecked car in the background. Without the car, the photo would omit an essential detail—the cause of the victims' injuries. With only the crumpled car, the reader would wonder if anyone had been hurt. The combination of elements—car plus victims—briefly tells the basic story.

A medium shot gains dramatic impact when the photograph captures action. Although the camera can catch fast action on film, you may still have difficulty: action often happens so quickly that you have no time to prepare. Shooting news action is like shoot-

ing sports action (see Chapter 6, "Sports"). For both, you must anticipate when and where the action will take place. If a man starts a heated argument with a police officer, you might predict that fists will fly and an arrest follow. You must aim your camera when the argument starts and not wait until a punch is thrown. If you hesitate, the quarrel might end while you're still fiddling with your equipment.

When published alone, a medium shot must tell a complete story. Had this couple not been carrying their belongings, readers wouldn't have known the two had been displaced by a flood.
(Photo by Dan White, the *Daily Herald*.)

The overall shot of the Thunderguard Bike Club establishes for the viewer the size of the motorcycle gang.
(Photo by Fred Comegys, *Wilmington* (Delaware) *News Journal*.)

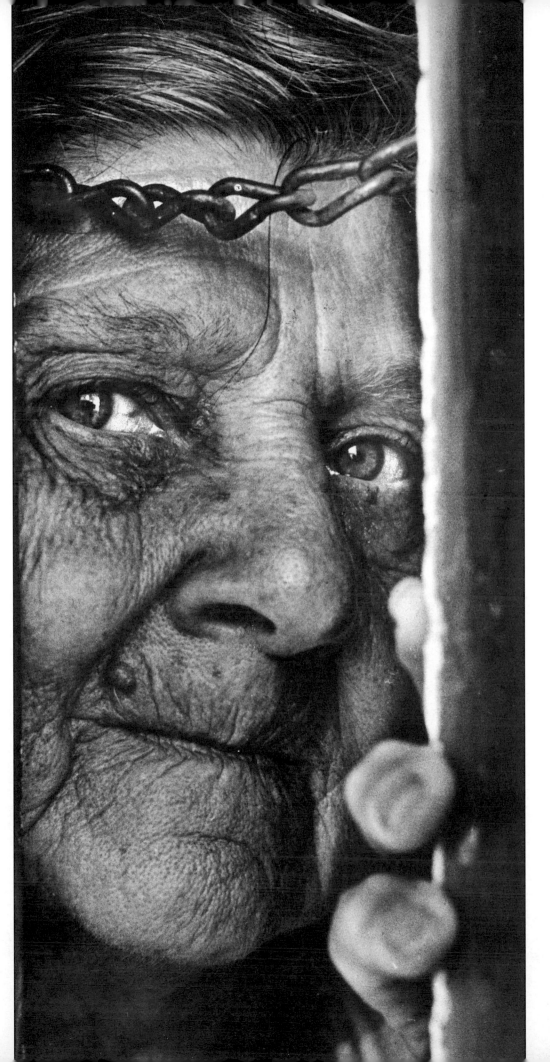

Nothing beats a close-up for drama. With the chain across her door, this woman's fear of outsiders is clear to the reader.
(Photo by Bruce Gilbert, *New York Newsday*.)

For the medium shot, a wide-angle lens, such as a 24mm or 28mm works well, although a normal 50mm will do.

Walter Green, a top photographer who worked for the Associated Press for many years, notes that he takes most medium shots with his 24mm lens. With this lens, Green gets extremely close to the subject and fills the entire negative area. The resulting pictures, says Green, tend to project a more intimate feeling between the subject and the viewer.

Because Green works close to the subject, few distracting elements intervene in front of his camera. Also, at this close distance, Green can emphasize the subject. Finally, Green's wide-angle takes in a large area of the background, thus establishing the relationship of the subject to his surroundings.

Wide-Angle Distortion

Buying a wide-angle lens, however, is not a photographer's panacea. The wider the angle of the lens, the greater the chance for apparent distortion. This is because you can focus very close to a subject with a wide-angle lens. And the closer any part of a subject is to the lens, the bigger it will appear in the picture. For example, if you stand relatively close to and above a person, and tilt the camera down to include the subject's full length, head to feet, the subject's head will appear to be the size of a basketball, while the feet will seem small enough to fit into baby shoes.

High angles such as this shot of construction in downtown Los Angeles help to give the reader perspective on the story.
(Photo by Paul Chinn, *San Francisco Examiner*.)

If you stand at the base of a building and point your wide-angle lens up to include the structure's whole height, the resulting pictures will look as if the building is falling over backwards. This happens with any lens, but particularly so with a wide-angle lens used close to the building.

To avoid distortion with the wide-angle lens, you must keep the back of the camera parallel to the subject. When shooting a building, you must either get far enough away or high enough that the back of your camera is perpendicular to the ground and therefore parallel to the structure.

■ CLOSE-UP ADDS DRAMA

Nothing beats a close-up for drama. The close-up slams the reader into eyeball-to-eyeball contact with the subject. At this intimate distance, a subject's face, contorted in pain or beaming in happiness, elicits empathy in the reader. (See page 13.)

How close is close? A close-up should isolate one element and emphasize it. All close-ups include a person's face. Sometimes objects can tell the story even when the story involves human tragedy. A close-up of a child's doll covered with mud might tell the story of a flood better than an aerial picture of the entire disaster.

Longer lenses enable the photographer to be less conspicuous when shooting close-ups. With a 200mm lens, a photographer standing ten feet away can still get a tight facial close-up. The telephoto lens decreases the depth-of-field, blurring the foreground and background, thereby isolating the subject from unwanted distractions.

Rather than a telephoto for close-up work, the photographer can employ a macro lens or a standard lens with an extension tube. With either of these lenses, the camera can take a picture of a small object such as a contact lens and enlarge it until it is easily seen.

■ HIGH/LOW ANGLES BRING NEW PERSPECTIVE

Since most people see the world from a sitting or standing vantage point, a photojournalist can add instant interest to a set of pictures simply by shooting from a unique elevation. Shoot down from a thirty-story building or up from a manhole cover. Either way, the viewer will get a new, sometimes jarring, but almost always refreshing look at a subject. Even when covering a meeting in a standard-sized room, just shooting from the height of a chair or taking pictures while sitting on the floor can add interest to your pictures.

Avoid the 5'7" syndrome. On every assignment, avoid taking all your pictures at eye level. When you start shooting, look around for ways to take the high ground.

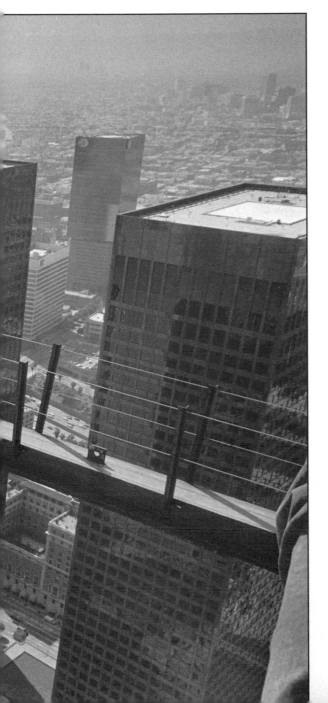

The photographer's low-angle perspective turned a routine golf shot into a more interesting image. Caution, however. During a golf game, never shoot when the golfer is stroking the ball. And turn off your motor drive, as well. (Photo by Robert Cohen, the (Memphis, Tenn.) *Commercial Appeal*.)

Whether going out on a catwalk or shooting from the balcony, find some way to look down on the scene you are shooting. For a low perspective, some 35mm cameras allow the photographer to remove their pentaprism housings, which allows the photographer to shoot—literally—from ground zero.

■ SATURATION METHOD INCREASES YOUR CHANCES

When on assignment, take several frames from each vantage point. Milton Feinberg, the author of *Techniques of Photo-journalism*, calls this approach the saturation method. He recommends taking at least six shots from each position. Then move over a few feet and shoot more frames. A slight change in perspective can bring important elements in the scene together to make the picture more visual. Keep shooting, Feinberg counsels. A minor change in a person's facial expression or body language can turn a routine picture into an eye-catcher. Don Robinson, who worked for United Press International wire service, describes his shooting approach this way: "I shoot one frame, then another and another. I am trying to improve each picture. I may be looking for a certain expression or gesture, or watching for something to happen. I may get something that is unusual, but in the next frame, I might get something much better."

Photographers stay on location until they get the best picture possible within their time limits. Amateurs take a few snapshots and hope for the best. Professionals, by contrast, search for the decisive moment and know when they get it. The pro might have to take a hundred or even a thousand frames to get the perfect moment, but, luckily, 35mm film is cheap. Even a newspaper publisher knows that film is the least expensive budget item.

Said George Tames, a former *New York Times* photographer, "If you see a picture, you should take it—period. It is difficult, if not impossible, to re-create a picture, so do not wait for it to improve. Sometimes it's better, and you will take that picture also, but if you hesitate and don't click the shutter, you've lost the moment, and you can't go back."

■ SAVE THE LAST FRAME

Many photographers stop shooting before the end of the roll. They have been caught with only one frame left just as something spectacular takes place—such as a person leaping out of a building. They raised their cameras and ran out of film. By changing film without waiting for the last frame, photographers build in some insurance. Having blank film

at the end of the roll is like having money in the bank. You might not ever need it, but it might save you in an emergency. Leaving film at the end of the roll will also reduce your own anxiety.

CATCHING CANDIDS

What sets photojournalistic pictures apart from other types of photography? The photojournalistic style depends on catching candids. The good photojournalist has developed the instinct to be at the right place, at the right time, with the right lens and camera. Often, the photojournalist can steal images like a pickpocket, without anyone realizing the sleight-of-hand of the photographer who grabbed the shot.

The photojournalist must catch the subject as unaware as possible to record real emotions. Rather than stage-managing pictures, the news photographer records the event as if it were an unfolding play. The photographer observes but does not direct. The results depend on the photojournalist's ability to capture these moments without interrupting.

With good candid pictures, subjects never stare at the camera. Eye contact would tip off the reader that the picture is not candid and suggests that the subject was at least aware of the photographer and might even be performing for the lens.

■ THREE APPROACHES TO CANDIDS
Big Game Hunter

Like a hunter stalking prey, the photojournalist studies the subject. Sighting through a rifle-like telephoto lens 100mm to 300mm long, the photojournalist stands across the room or across the street. The photographer watches, waits, and tries to anticipate what might happen next.

Patience. Patience. Patience.

On a tip from a local pet hospital, the *Boston Herald*'s George Martell waited for the right moment to photograph a man and his injured 5-year-old Brittany Spaniel, Yowser. Using a baby stroller to transport the dog, the man brought Yowser to Angel Memorial every day for treatment. The dog had been hit by a tractor-trailer, and his owner, who suffered a heart condition, was unable to carry the dog himself.

With a 300mm telephoto lens, Martell was able to shoot without distracting the man upon his arrival. The photographer caught a tender moment as the owner hugged the injured dog before taking him out of the stroller. The long lens and wide aperture provided an additional advantage for the picture. At f/4 with a 300mm lens, distracting background elements went out of focus and left just the owner and his on-the-mend friend isolated in the frame. When feature hunting, Martell carries a 300mm, an 80–200mm and a 20–35mm zoom lens.

Hit and Run

Rather than trying to operate unobserved, some photographers use the hit-and-run approach. They catch candids by walking past the subject, shooting quickly with a wide-angle lens, and then moving on. Observers have described Henri Cartier-Bresson's technique that way. The outstanding French candid-catcher pauses in front of his subject and, with one fluid motion, raises his Leica, focuses, and clicks several frames. By the time the subject turns toward the photographer, Cartier-Bresson has already gone his way. This type of hit-and-run photography leaves subjects unaware they have been photographed.

Norm Shafer of the *Fredericksburg* (Virginia) *Free-Lance Star* was shooting the King George Fall Festival parade when he noticed two young drummers getting bored with the marching. Realizing that he might have a potential feature, Shafer got in step with the young marchers. One drummer started to tease the other with his stick. Shafer moved in, shooting with his 24mm wide-angle lens focused at about ten feet. Just as one drummer selected the other fellow's head for a practice timpani, Shafer began to shoot. Engrossed in their own rhythms, the two drummer boys never noticed Shafer and his camera. As the embarrassed mother of one of the misbehaving boys pulled her son out of the parade, Shafer continued to record the incident because, as he explained later, "you never know till you see the film if you have the exact moment."

Shafer had caught the moment.

Out-in-the-Open

Sometimes the photojournalist doesn't have to use any subterfuge to catch a candid. The out-in-the-open approach works when the subject, engaged in an activity that is so engrossing, forgets for a moment the photographer's presence. For example, Ron Cortes was doing a picture story for the *Philadelphia Inquirer* about a 72-year-old woman returning to high school to finish her

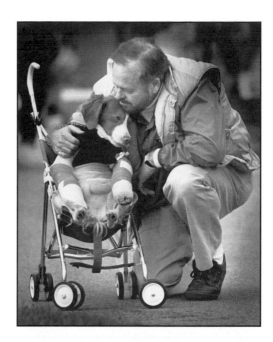

Using a 300mm f/2.8 telephoto lens, the photographer was able to remain in the distance. With a long lens, a photographer can often shoot pictures without being observed.
(© Photo by George Martell, the *Boston Herald*.)

The photographer snapped this candid by moving in quickly with a wide-angle lens.
(Photo by Norm Shafer, the *Fredericksburg* (Virginia) *Free Lance-Star*.)

Although both women were aware of the photographer, he was still able to capture this candid interaction between a 72-year-old high school student and her classmate. The women were more fascinated by one another than they were by the photographer's presence.
(Photo by Ronald Cortes, the *Philadelphia Inquirer*)

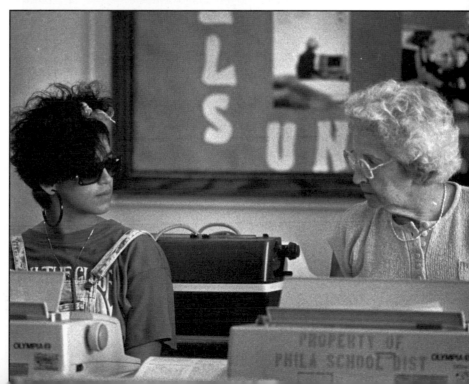

degree. The senior scholar took everything from math to typing. In the typing class, Cortes snapped a picture of a more typical student giving the older woman the once-over. Although the subjects knew Cortes was there to take pictures, they became so involved in their own activities after awhile that they paid no attention to him—and he was able to catch candid moments.

■ PRESET YOUR CAMERA

Unless your camera is automatic, set its aperture and shutter speed before you point the camera. If you're fiddling with the camera's dials, you might catch the subject's attention and lose the candid moment. To take your light meter reading without the subject being aware, point your camera toward an area that is receiving the same amount of light as the subject, then adjust your f-stop/shutter speed combination accordingly.

Select the appropriate lens before you bring the camera to your eye. Swing the lens once by the subject and stop just long enough to focus. As an alternative, you might focus on an object exactly the same distance away as your subject. The telephoto requires critical focusing. For that reason, some photographers prefer the wide-angle lens for candids, even though they must come closer to the subject. Prefocused at ten feet with a small aperture of f/16, a photographer with a 28mm lens can snap away happily without ever touching the focusing ring.

Now, watch your subject. The camera is set, hence, all you must do is concentrate on the subject's expression and, when it's right, swing up the lens, frame, and snap away.

Alternatively, use your camera's autofocus option: with autofocus selected, you are free to concentrate on action not hardware. (See pages 103–104 and 212–213 for more about autofocus.)

■ ANTICIPATION AND TIMING

Catching candids requires the photographer to have the skills of a weather forecaster. The photographer must guess what is going to happen based on how he or she sees the situation developing. If two kids in the street have their fists up, they are likely to fight. A couple holding hands might kiss. Sometimes the photographer, like the meteorologist, judges the evidence correctly and is prepared with the right lens, film, shutter speed, and f-stop. At other times, like the weatherperson, the photographer misinterprets the data.

As important as anticipation is the photographer's timing to release the shutter at the optimum moment. Even with motor drives, this skill requires photographers to "get into

the flow of the action." Most action builds to a peak and then settles down again. And almost every event has a crucial moment.

■ CANDIDS WHEN THEY KNOW YOU'RE THERE

The photographer often faces the problem of taking a subject's picture, even though the subject is aware of the photographer's presence. "In most of the photo stories in *People* magazine, the subject knows ahead of time when we're coming, so the portraits are not truly candid," says John Dominis, who was the magazine's first picture editor. "If the subject has a trade like a blacksmith or fisherman, *People* photographers try to coax the subject to do what he normally does. When the worker goes back to his daily routine, he tends to get lost in his work, and the photographer can produce story-telling candids."

WHEN AND WHERE TO SELL NEWS PHOTOS
■ STAFF PHOTOGRAPHER VS. FREELANCER

What should you do when you've snapped a good spot news picture?

The answer depends on whether you are a staffer or a freelancer. If you are a staff photographer for a paper and you've stumbled on a major train disaster, you should shoot your pictures, then get to the nearest phone and call your editor. Provide a brief description of the accident and your photos. Your editor will weigh the importance of the train wreck story against other news of the day, and will decide whether you should remain at the scene and send in your film by messenger or return to the office to process your photos before deadline. If you are a freelance photographer and you have a good spot news photo, you have, under the same circumstances, many more options for your pictures.

■ MARKETING SPOT NEWS: A CASE STUDY

After the earthquake that rocked San Francisco in October 1989, journalism student Kaia Means was one of thousands who initially thought the shaker was "just another" earthquake. Visiting friends atop Russian Hill, however, the San Francisco State University student noted, moments after the quake, a huge cloud of dust rising above the Marina District. She said her good-byes and left for a 5:30 P.M. meeting—thinking she'd drive by the Marina first to see what the dust was all about.

"I knew I had to turn in a spot news assignment sometime during the semester," recalls Means, a news-editorial major taking her second semester of photography. "So I thought I'd drive by to see if there was anything to take a picture of."

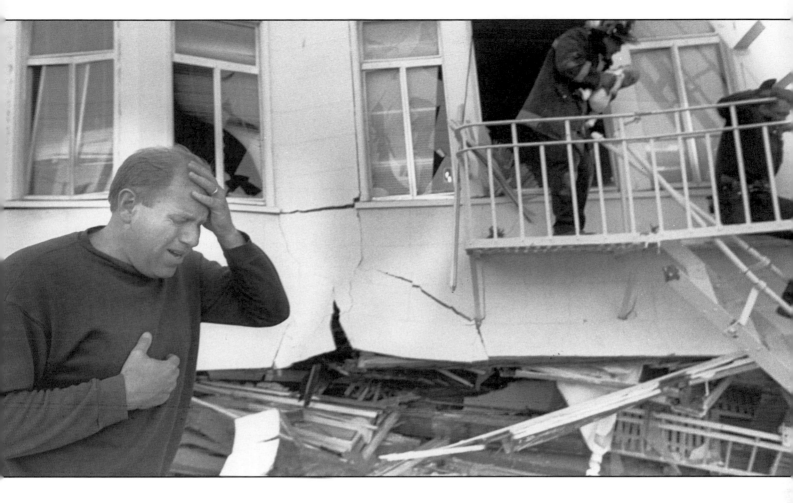

What Means found in the Marina was more than fallen bricks and broken glass. The first photographer on the scene, the 22-year-old student from Norway photographed a distraught father awaiting the rescue of his wife and baby. Standing beside the father in the crowd, she photographed firefighters carrying the baby from the building, the father grieving in the foreground. Later, herself crying upon the realization that the baby was dead, Means photographed the mother's rescue and reunion with her husband.

Although Means was "shaking all over" by the time she finished shooting the tragedy in the Marina, the young photojournalist's real-life mid-term exam was just beginning.

Determining Possible Outlets

The photo student's pictures certainly had wide local and national interest. And Means was in a good bargaining position because she had exclusive images. However, the earthquake had shaken local news outlets as well as buildings and bridges.

Means took the film to the *San Francisco Examiner*, which had lost all electricity and phone capabilities and was conducting its photo operation out of a van in the paper's parking lot. Having told the photo chief about the pictures, she helped out for a while and then left the film, marked "DEAD BABY" on the canister.

In less chaotic circumstances, Means could have bargained for the sale of the pictures. Having gotten a bid from the *Examiner*, she could have contacted local TV stations to see how much they would offer for rights to the photos. With the story's national impact, she could have offered the film to the wire services, either the Associated Press (AP), Agence France-Presse (AFP), or Reuters—all of which depend a great deal on stringers and free-lancers. None of the services maintains a large enough photo staff to cover the country—or the world—thoroughly. Many photos appearing in print and carrying the AP, AFP, or Reuters credit line are taken by independent photographers.

Alternatively, on a big disaster like this earthquake or perhaps a tornado, Means could have called other large dailies around the country.

Today, newspapers want their own photos of a major story to augment those supplied by the wires, and many send staff

A few minutes after the 1989 San Francisco earthquake, a father watches as his dead baby is removed from a collapsed apartment building. The photographer sold the picture to *Life* magazine.
(Photo by Kaia Means.)

photographers. However, none would have had this series of pictures.

But with phone lines down and chaos around her, Means left the film with the *Examiner*. Naturally, she was surprised when she opened the paper the following day and did not see the dramatic pictures. She called to see what had happened and learned that, in the confusion, the film had never been processed.

Following more confusion at the *Examiner*, the young photojournalist finally got her film back—still unprocessed two days after the event. Under normal circumstances, this series of faux pas would have spelled photographic disaster for the fledgling photojournalist. The pictures' timeliness would have dissipated long before.

However, once the film was processed, it was easy to see that these were no ordinary pictures. It was time to seek a national market. The news magazines were already closing by the time the film had finally been processed. And, besides, they rarely buy anything but color these days.

I gave the student the number of Peter Howe, who, at the time, was picture editor at *Life* magazine, and she took over from there. Howe was out of town, but editors at *Life* wanted to see the prints.

After viewing the pictures, *Life* editors not only purchased first North American rights for six months but also sent a reporter to San Francisco to interview Means and the parents she had photographed. When an order for a follow-up story came in, the second-semester photo student received the five-day *Life* assignment. In the 1989 year-end issue of *Life* magazine, Means' photo of the distraught father ran as a double-truck in addition to two of the follow-up pictures she shot on assignment.

Time Element is Crucial

Don't underestimate the value of your pictures, and don't wait too long to find a buyer for them.

As a student, Means could have assumed that professional photographers would have had more dramatic pictures than hers. However, while the *Examiner* missed its chance with the pictures, Means' photos turned out to be some of the most moving images to come out of the disaster.

In any news event, even if other photographers are present at the scene of an accident or fire, their equipment might fail, or you might have a shot from a better angle. For the price of a telephone call, you can find out if an editor is interested and would like to see your film.

Because of the time element, the best market for spot news is a newspaper or wire service. Means' instincts in taking the film to one of the city's major dailies was right on. However, it was the national interest in the quake that gave the photos an unusual second chance with *Life*. Editors have called the earthquake of 1989 the top news story of that decade. Certainly, *Life* magazine recognized its importance in 1989 by including Means' coverage in its wrap-up issue that year.

If you have a timely fire, accident, or crime picture, the curious editor will usually ask you to bring the raw film to the newspaper or have it picked up by cab. A lab technician will develop the film, and an editor will quickly scan the negatives to determine if the photo has news value. If the story has significant national appeal, a news magazine like *Time*, *Newsweek*, or *U.S. News & World Report* might buy the photo, if it's in color. These magazines maintain very small full-time photo staffs, so they also buy outside photos. Good editors don't mind a quick telephone call on a spot news story because they can't afford to ignore you and possibly miss the chance of publishing a Pulitzer Prize-winning picture.

What newspapers, magazines, or wire services pay for a picture depends on the value of the photo at the time of publication. *Life* magazine paid Abraham Zapruder between $25,000 and $40,000, according to the *New York Times*, for his 8mm movie film of President John F. Kennedy's assassination. In contrast, the Associated Press (AP), Reuters, and Agence France-Presse (AFP) pay a standard rate of less than $100 for most pictures they buy from freelancers. Still, each photo is unique, and its value must be dealt with on a case-by-case basis. If the story has national significance, you might call a picture agency like Mercury Pictures or Black Star. If you turn your pictures over to a photo agency, its representatives will handle the negotiations with domestic and foreign magazines but will usually split the profit with you. ∎

Making the Most of an Assignment
PHILADELPHIA'S HOMELESS: HOW THEY SURVIVE

Tom Gralish of the *Philadelphia Inquirer* recalls that when he received an assignment to photograph the homeless, editors suggested he "might do portraits of the street people, each standing in front of their grates or cardboard boxes or whatever else they called home. At that point, I wasn't sure what I would do, but I decided then and there that whatever it was, it would be the most honest photography I'd ever done. I was determined to do something as true as possible to the traditional ideals of documentary photojournalism."

Consequently, Gralish did not set up portraits.

Instead, he followed street people with names like Hammerman, Spoon, and Redbeard through the ups and downs of their barren, subsistence lives. He photographed them staying warm atop steam grates on a frozen street, drinking wine, and panhandling. He showed them sleeping in boxes. Rather than a series of formulated, posed portraits, Gralish photographed the nitty gritty of these men's lives. For his efforts, he won both the Pulitzer Prize and the Robert F. Kennedy Memorial Prize.

(Photos by Tom Gralish, the *Philadelphia Inquirer*.)

Spot News

At home early one morning, *Fort Worth Star-Telegram* staffer Joyce Marshall received a call from her paper's city desk. Her editor said that a man was holding his wife hostage at a 7–11 convenience store in nearby Arlington, Texas. Joyce threw on her clothes and, without brushing her teeth or combing her hair, jumped into her car, thinking, "This is probably a false alarm. Most of them are." With her cameras already in the trunk, she sped the five miles to the store in her two-door Subaru. As soon as she pulled to a stop, she got

From daylight until dark, Joyce Marshall waited seven hours while the tense hostage situation played itself out. The stand-off finally ended (LEFT) when the man took his own life. His wife, whom he had been holding hostage, escaped (RIGHT).
(Photos by Joyce Marshall, *Fort Worth Star-Telegram.*)

out of her car, grabbed her gear, and checked with the police officer in charge for an update on the situation. After determining that this stand-off was no false alarm, she called her office for backup equipment, including a 600mm lens and a two-way portable radio.

She knew that already the man had shot and possibly killed someone in the store. Later, she found out that the gunman's name was Thomas Stephens. His wife had left him because of his continued physical abuse during their seventeen-year marriage. When the divorce papers had finally come through the day before, he snapped. He left the drug treatment center he was in and tracked down his wife, who was working at the store. In the process of taking her hostage, he killed several of her co-workers.

Knowing there had already been gunfire at the store, Marshall used a car in a nearby driveway as protection. She had a clear view of the store window. Her telephoto lens and radio arrived via another staffer who took up a position behind the store.

"I was inside the police barrier," Marshall recalls. "The area was cordoned off. The time dragged on interminably. I had not eaten, I could not get a drink of water. I had not brushed my teeth or my hair, and there was no bathroom available."

Marshall knew, however, that if she left she would not be able to get across the police barrier again. "I had to stay," she recalls.

As the sun was setting directly into Marshall's camera, police went in to take out the victims.

With some cardboard she found nearby and tape she kept wrapped around the leg of her tripod, Marshall constructed a homemade sunshade on her lens barrel.

When police took the victims out of the store, the officers left the front door open. With her eye glued to her viewfinder, Marshall noticed Stephens coming to the front of the store while holding a gun to his wife's head. Marshall snapped off several frames.

By this time, a crowd had gathered behind the police lines. The neighborhood audience drank pop and beer and watched the situation in the 7-11 unfold in front of them like a movie playing in a theater. When the SWAT team arrived, the crowd started to yell, "Shoot them, shoot them. Hurry up and get this thing over with."

As the sun dropped in the late afternoon sky, Marshall began switching to more sensitive film. She went from color print film rated at ISO 200 to 400 then to 800. When Marshall could see no color at all in the scene, she threaded in a roll of ISO 400 black-and-white, which she rated at 1600.

Soon after the photographer loaded her camera with black-and-white film, the sun dropped behind the horizon, leaving only the lights in the store for illumination. Just then, Marshall could make out some movement at the front of the store—a shadowy figure so low to the ground she could not photograph it. The figure turned out to be Stephens' wife. Marshall learned later that when the gunman allowed his wife to go to the bathroom, she slipped out of the store.

Within a few minutes, Stephens, holding a gun to his head, walked out of the store. He told police he would shoot himself at the count of thirty.

Marshall thought to herself, "Surely they will do something about it."

In the silhouette against the store's window she could see that the gun's hammer was pulled back, ready to fire. When he got to thirty, Stephens paused a few seconds. Marshall quickly took a few frames.

Then the gunman fired a bullet into his own head. He slumped to the ground. The crowd rushed in to see what had happened.

"I'm not sure I shot a photo of the body," Marshall says now. "My mind was on getting the film back to the paper."

After racing back to the paper's darkroom and processing the film, Marshall quickly printed the frame of Stephens pointing the gun to his own head.

She found the negative of Stephens holding his wife hostage a difficult one to print because of the sun's flare. Also, because the subjects occupied only a small part of the negative, she had to enlarge the image extensively.

Found after a police officer shot and killed a suspect, this gun was later revealed to be a "throw-down" gun planted by police at the scene of the shooting. The photo provided an important link in a chain of evidence demonstrating a police cover-up.
(Photo by Ken Kobré, for the *Boston Phoenix*.)

The paper's editors felt the suicide picture was too graphic for the front page of the *Fort Worth Star-Telegram* and ran it inside, but they played the hostage photo as the lead picture on page one for the following day.

CRIMES MAKE HEADLINES

Crime, whether it's a hostage situation in Arlington or a riot in Boston, is costly to society. It can be a deep human tragedy for criminals and their families as well as for victims and theirs.

Almost any kind of crime makes a printable story in newsrooms across the country. The cub reporter soon learns that whether it's an atrocious murder or a $100 hold-up of a gas station, the event is considered news in city rooms from coast to coast.

Depending upon the violence of the crime, the amount of money involved, the prominence of the people involved, or the crime's humorous or unusual aspects, the news will receive varying amounts of emphasis.

■ BRINGING THE CRISIS HOME

Crime pictures rivet readers' attention. The success of TV cop shows, dating back to "Highway Patrol" and followed by such shows as "Kojak," "N.Y.P.D. Blue," and "Homicide," proves the solid, unflagging public interest in crime. Actual news photos take viewers from the fantasy of television to actual crisis in the streets. Newspaper crime photos are rare reminders that felonies don't stop at 11 P.M.; they can't be switched to another channel or turned off at bedtime.

The news photo emphasizes the point that crime remains a major local problem.

When readers recognize the street where a man was shot yesterday as the one they work on, when they realize the bank in the holdup is the one where they make deposits, then abstract crime figures—19,120 murders, 404,850 robberies in one year—take on personal meaning.

The public's insatiable curiosity about crime photos accounts also for editors' continued use of such photos. Few readers can

You can predict some crime news. Violence was likely on the first day of busing to achieve integration at South Boston High School. As school opened, mounted police used billy clubs to disperse rock-throwing, anti-busing demonstrators.
(Photo by Ken Kobré, for the *Boston Phoenix*.)

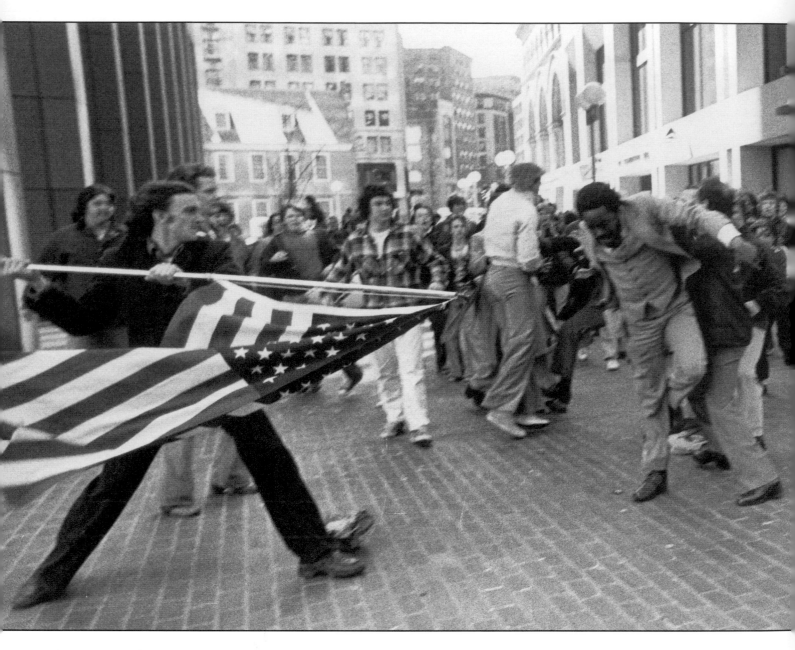

The attacker was part of an anti-busing group that had just given the pledge of allegiance during a demonstration at city hall. The unfortunate African-American man just happened to be walking by. (Photo by Stanley Forman, the *Boston Herald.*)

resist inspecting a picture of a mugging in progress or a grocery store hold-up.

Perhaps readers' curiosity for crime pictures lies in a deep-seated belief that criminals look different from regular people. Although psychologists have disproved the notion of "the criminal face," the reader checks to see if the convict has close-set eyes or a lowered brow—just as the reader suspected. But, to the unending surprise of the newspaper reader, criminals usually appear quite normal. Pictures of murder and mayhem not only excite readers' interest and satisfy their curiosity but also provide information that is hard to visualize from a written description. Photographs of a drug bust show the actual size of ten tons of marijuana. Photos of an ambush explain how near the

sniper actually was to the victims. A portrait shows how frail-looking was the grandmother who murdered five people. A newswriter would have to search long and hard for words that describe a crime scene with the clarity of a simple spot news photo.

■ PHOTOGRAPHING A CRIME IN PROGRESS

Joyce Marshall's photos are rare. Unlike reporters who can reconstruct the details of a mugging from police reports and eye-witness accounts, the photographer must be at the crime scene to get action pictures. Robbers, kidnappers, rapists, and murderers tend to shy away from the harsh glare of public exposure.

A photographer with a good news sense, however, can learn to predict some situations that might erupt into violence. For instance, a group called ROAR, Restore Our Alienated Rights, began organizing opposition to court-ordered busing the summer before South Boston's all-white high school was scheduled for desegregation. The press, tracking the growing size of the protest, evaluated the intensity of the local residents' feelings and predicted chaos, perhaps even violence, on the first day of classes. Photographers and reporters representing both local and national media gathered early in the morning in front of the school. Hundreds of police, assigned to escort the African-American youths from bus to building, stood across the street from taunting white teen-agers and their parents. When buses carrying the African Americans arrived, the crowd broke through the police lines. A full-scale riot started. Mounted police wielding billy clubs scattered the rock-throwing demonstrators. (See page 25.)

During the ensuing violence, the crowd hurled rocks and bottles at newspaper and TV photographers. The police provided no security for the working press; officers even tripped and pushed the photographers. Many demonstrators were arrested. Caught between the police and the demonstrators, the media were hated by both. White residents of South Boston thought the press too liberal in its support of integration; the police believed the press had unfairly criticized them. Fortunately, no photographers were seriously injured.

EVALUATING NEWS APPEAL

Sometimes crime photos take on an importance beyond the news value of the story they report. Because photographers rarely record a crime in progress or an actual arrest, editors usually play these rare photos on the front page regardless of the incident's significance. The photo's value depends not only on the importance of the crime but on the immediacy and freshness of the pictures.

Besides action, the photo editor evaluates a crime picture on the basis of the incident's severity. Were people injured or killed? Few papers failed to run pictures of the bombed federal building in Oklahoma City. Color photos appeared on the covers of both *Time* and *Newsweek*. An editor also evaluates a crime photo based on the size of the property involved. Was a large amount of money stolen? A $2.8 million Brinks robbery produced banner headlines across the front pages of American newspapers.

■ WORKING WITH UNCOOPERATIVE SUBJECTS

George Reidy, a photographer for the old *Boston Herald*, once said, "The true test of a news photographer is getting pictures of criminals entering or leaving police headquarters. The prisoner is moving quickly and trying to hide his face. The photographer has to follow the prisoner, sometimes moving backwards, focusing all the way and always trying to get a shot of the prisoner's face. If the cameraman succeeds at this we can call him a news photographer." To avoid taking the time to refocus, the photographer can walk backwards, keeping a constant distance between the camera and the subject. (See the section on zone focusing in Chapter 6, "Sports.")

As Reidy points out, "It's hard enough to take a picture of a suspect if you know who he is, but how about the situation where you've never seen the suspect before?"

When AP's Walter Green would photograph an unfamiliar suspect at a trial, he would peer into the courtroom and carefully identify what the defendant was wearing. "You want to see how the person is dressed and figure out what door he might come out of," Green says. By asking the sheriff which exit door will be used, the photographer can be positioned there ahead of time.

If defendants don't want to be photographed, they may hide their faces. Green recalls the time that Raymond Patriarca, reputed Mafia boss of New England, was on trial. Speaking to Patriarca's lawyer after the first day of the trial, Green said, "We have great stuff of your client going into the courthouse. With his hands covering his face, your client looks like a real hard-bitten criminal. Why don't you do him a favor and bring him downstairs, pose him outside? Then the photographers will leave him alone."

Patriarca's lawyer consented and persuaded his client to hold still for a picture. "Sure, Patriarca looked more like a criminal in my first set of pictures, but I made the second set because I thought the public wanted to see the Mafia boss's face," recalls Green. "I also knew that a picture of him covering up his face would not make the wires anyhow."

Sometimes photographers take surveillance pictures at night. Using Kodak's P3200 film, you can push the film with extended development to at least 6400. (See Chapter 10, "Cameras and Film.") You get good detail in flat lighting situations. And you can record at least some of the scene even in high-contrast lighting common at night when there is a great difference between brightly lit and dark, shadowed areas.

Producing grainy but recognizable pictures, you can shoot the action of the sleaziest underworld character handing over the payoff money or receiving the dope—even at night under poor lighting conditions.

■ WHY SHOOT FIRES?

Reporting fires is an important job of the photojournalist. Each year more than 500,000 homes catch fire. Fires also destroy apartment houses, stores, office buildings, and factories. Fires sweep through schools where children are having classes. Autos and trucks burn up, and fires devastate forests in all parts of the country.

Altogether, 2 million fires are reported annually, costing more than $12 billion in property damage, according to the National Board of Fire Underwriters. Still more serious than monetary loss, thousands of people die in fires each year.

A photo can show not only the emotion of the participants but also the size of the fire better than words can describe it. If a fire breaks out on the twenty-third story of a building from which an occupant might jump, a photo can indicate just how high twenty-three stories really is. The reader can quickly grasp the danger of jumping. If a wooden warehouse catches fire, requiring four companies to halt the spread of the flames, a photo can give the reader an idea about the vastness of the blaze.

After the fire has been extinguished, a photo of the charred remains carries impact beyond a mere statistical description of the loss. A photo of a house burning or an office worker trapped in a building initiates an empathetic reaction in the viewer, who thinks, "that could be my house . . . that could be me in that building."

■ COVERING A FIRE

Scanner radios are standard gear for spot news photographers. These portable devices, no bigger than transistor radios, fit easily into pockets and can have at least four crystal channels tuned to the fire emergency frequency. The beeper going off on a scanner indicates that someone has pulled the alarm on a fire box. Every fire box in a city has a code so that firefighters know its location. As soon as the alarm sounds, firefighters in the nearest station drop whatever they are doing and head for the pole. They slide down, jump into their boots, and roar off in their trucks in the direction of the fire box. The trucks usually arrive within one to two minutes after the alarm begins to ring. The firefighters first determine whether there is a fire or a false alarm. If they discover a fire in progress, they immediately radio back the size and extent of the hazard.

Get There on Time

This first on-scene report is critical for new photographers. Is the fire big enough and therefore long-lasting enough to get there in time? Most fires would be out by the time the photographer arrives. If the radio report indicates a false alarm or one alarm, pass it up. A scanner report of "working fire," however, indicates a substantial blaze—rated as one-half the intensity of a two-alarm fire. A working fire means the fire is literally working its way through a building—usually giving a photographer plenty of time to arrive.

With two alarms, additional fire companies, with their added trucks, ladders, pumps, and hoses, arrive and spread out down the street. A two-alarm fire ties up several companies for some time. Five alarms mean a major conflagration is under way.

The key to outstanding photographic fire coverage is getting to the fire on time. "If you can't arrive at a fire within a few minutes of the time the first alarm sounds, you might as well stay home," cautions George Rizer, *Boston Globe* photographer.

Plan for Traffic

Check your map to determine the best short-cut route. To avoid the possibility of colliding with fire trucks, shut off your radio, open your windows, and listen for fire engine sirens. When you arrive, find a parking spot that doesn't block fire hydrants—and plan for your escape. "You might be ready to get your film back to the office before the

Don't let your light meter be thrown off by the bright flames at a night fire. While the flames engulfing the house will come out in the final picture, a longer exposure is needed to bring out the building and surrounding areas.
(Photo by Michael Meinhardt, the *Chicago Tribune*.)

Because of the speed at which the rescue team arrives, getting pictures of their life-saving efforts is difficult. But ultimately, these are the best pictures possible from a fire or accident scene.
(Photo by Randy Trabold, *North Adams* (Mass.) *Transcript*.)

Leap for Life: A Fire in Boston

Stanley Forman, three-time Pulitzer Prize-winning photographer, knows his city like the back of his hand. In this instance, he was cruising when he actually smelled smoke and pulled up to the burning house along with police. Trapped on the roof, the man in the pictures first handed down the child. When the woman froze, the man pushed her off before he jumped. The woman suffered minor injuries, but everyone else was okay. Forman approached the fire as if shooting a picture story. He takes the reader through the danger to the trapped residents on the roof, follows up with pictures of the rescue, and comes in tight to end with a close-up of the officer holding the child.

firemen are prepared to leave," explains the *Globe*'s Rizer. "If they're parked in back of you, you'll be stuck until the fire is over and all the men have packed up their equipment. You'll miss your deadline."

Overall Shot Sets the Scene

When you first see a fire, you should take a record shot since you don't know if the fire will flare up or die down. Later, to establish the size of the blaze, the location of the trucks, and the type of building that is burning, you might look for a high vantage point from which you can shoot an overall photo.

Watch for the Human Side

Once you have your overall shot, look for the human side of the tragedy. Are people trapped in the building? Will the firefighter bring up ladders to rescue the occupants or have they already escaped? Do the firefighters have to administer mouth-to-mouth resuscitation or other kinds of first aid?

Meanwhile, don't overlook the efforts of the firefighters to put out the blaze. Without interfering with their work, shoot the ladder and pump companies as they spray water on the flames. Keep an eye out for people overcome by smoke or exhaustion.

Fires inevitably attract people. Whether in a big city or a rural town, a fire brings out an audience—whether neighbors or just passers-by. The crowd stares with wide eyes and open mouths, seemingly transfixed. Try to capture on film this psychological attraction.

Look for the Economic Angle

Show the dimensions of the incident so that the reader learns whether the fire was a minor one or a major conflagration. Take a picture that indicates the kind of structure burned—single-family home, apartment house, business, or factory. Show how near the burned building was to other threatened structures in the neighborhood.

As the fire subsides, seek out a location where you can shoot a summary photo showing the extent of the damage. If you can accompany the fire inspector into a building, you might be able to photograph the actual cause of the blaze. When the fire marshal suspects arson, detectives will be called in to investigate. Investigators at work supply additional photo opportunities.

A photographer can return to the scene of the fire the following day to photograph the remains of the charred building. Often, residents return to salvage their property. The next day's photo of the woman carrying out her water-soaked coat might communicate more pathos than the pictures of flames and smoke of the night before. You also can follow up a fire story by checking to see whether there has been a series of fires in the same area over the past year. If you find that certain blocks of houses or stores tend to have an unusually large number of fires, suggest that the editor run a group of fire pictures on one page, demonstrating the persistency of the fire hazard in that neighborhood.

Features Highlight the Sidelights
Besides spot news, a photographer can find good material for feature photos at fires. A picture story about the Red Cross worker who attends every fire might provide a sensitive sidebar story. A small town may have an all-volunteer company, including a dentist who drills teeth and a mechanic who repairs cars when not battling flames. Capturing this split life in pictures offers a unique photo feature story to your readers.

Get the Facts
Always try to get factual data such as the firefighters' names and companies. Interview both the fire and police chiefs for cutline information: the exact location of the fire, the number of alarms sounded, the companies that responded, an estimate about the extent of the damage, and the names of the injured and what hospitals they were taken to.

■ JUDGING A FIRE'S NEWS VALUE
Every newspaper reports local fires, but their relative significance depends not only on the size of the fire but also on the size of the newspaper. On a small-town paper, a photographer covers almost every fire because residents know their neighbors and are interested in their welfare. A metropolitan newspaper limits its fire coverage to a major conflagration of disastrous proportion, except when people are involved and extensive property damage results. National magazines and newspapers report fires only if they are extensive, engulfing a skyscraper or a whole city.

In addition to the size and the number of people involved in the fire, picture newsworthiness depends on the nature of the burned building. If an airplane erupts into flames on the airport's runway, local residents want to

Five people were injured in this accident. All lived. As the rescue team removed the passengers, the mother asked for her baby. Using a low angle, the photographer created a powerful composition. (Photo by Dan Poush, the *Statesman-Journal,* Salem, Oreg.)

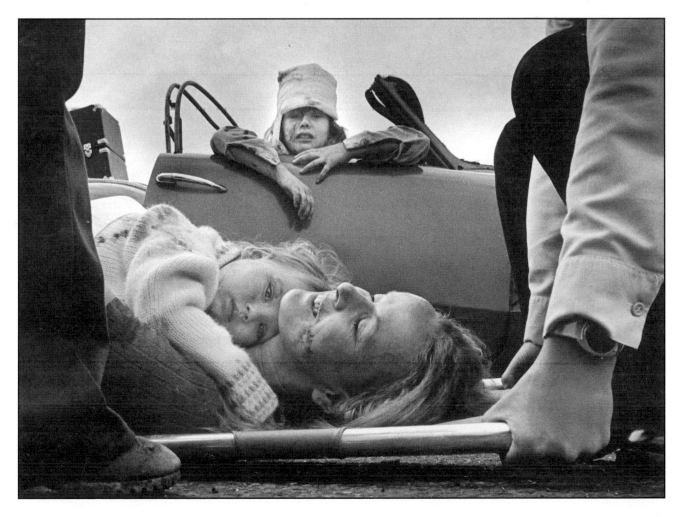

know how it happened. When a factory that employs two thousand of the city's residents goes up in flames, the public wants to learn every detail, even if no one died.

Sometimes a fire that carries little news value as a written story can result in an excellent photo story. For instance, a picture of a tough-looking fireman administering oxygen to a tiny dog tugs at the reader's heartstrings, even if the fire was minor and caused no damage.

■ NIGHT FIRES ARE DIFFICULT

Night fires tend to sneak up between midnight and 6 A.M.—a time when people are sleeping,

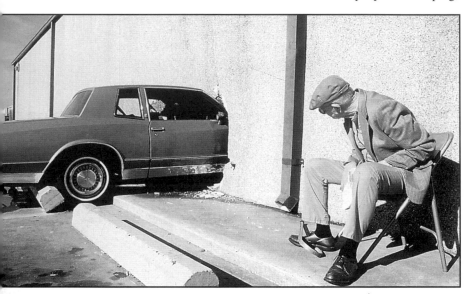

The news value of this accident was relatively minor, but the body language of the driver and the bizarre nature of the mishap give the picture its impact.
(Photo by Stephen Reed, *Alexandria* (La.) *Daily Town Talk*.)

and smoke goes unnoticed. Arsonists choose the nighttime for this reason. Because fires are not reported quickly at night, they tend to be larger and more frequent.

Photographically, night fires pose difficulties. The *Globe*'s Rizer, for example, does not take a light-meter reading at nighttime fires. "Why bother?" he asks. "A meter reading will be misled by the light from the flames and will not give an accurate indication of the amount of light reflected off the sides of the building." For night fires, Rizer uses a slow shutter speed and flash. At a faster shutter speed, the flames would still appear in the image, but the building would go black. Within fifty feet, the flash also helps to light up the building. But with the slow shutter speed, the photographer must avoid even slight camera movement during the exposure.

Rizer recommends resting the camera on a car, a fire hydrant, or holding the camera tightly and leaning against a lamppost to cut down camera movement. And he puts away the strobe when flames start shooting out of every window in the building.

"If it looks like a Christmas tree," he says, "you can shoot in available light, and you'll get great, action-packed fire pictures."

ACCIDENT AND DISASTER: GRIM BUT NECESSARY

■ 100,000 DIE IN ACCIDENTS EACH YEAR

(Dateline Baltimore) One Dead, 21 Hurt in Bethlehem Steel Blast
(Dateline Houston) Fatal Accident on Southwest Freeway Kills Six

So read the daily headlines, as accidents take their toll of more than one hundred thousand lives and ten million injuries each year, according to the National Safety Council. Almost half the accidents in the United States involve motor vehicles. But people also die from falls, burns, drownings, gunshot wounds, poisonings, and work-related accidents.

Accidents make news. If one million Los Angeles residents drive home on the freeway safely on Friday night, that's not news. But if two people die in an auto crash at the Hollywood Boulevard on-ramp, then newspaper buyers want to read a story and see a picture of the accident.

■ ACCIDENT PICTURES SHOCK READERS INTO CAUTION

Why shoot accident pictures?

First, accidents and disasters occur. Mines collapse. Hurricanes strike. Cars collide. Accidents happen. Accidents are facts of life. To record what goes on in a city and to keep readers informed about what's happening constitute two of the major roles of the press.

Second, readers are curious about accidents. Note how many people slow down and look as they pass a collision on the highway. Listen to what people talk about when they get home. Few people will fail to mention a major accident on the turnpike.

Third, people want to see what they read about. A thousand dollars worth of damage means little until the reader sees some visual evidence. Though a story may say that a car was totally wrecked, believability is established when readers see a picture of a Volkswagen mashed into the shape of a discarded tin can.

Fourth, accident pictures grab readers' emotions. Accidents can happen to anyone. A mangled body, lifted from a wrecked car, reminds readers that, but for chance, they might have been in that car. The photo may shock readers into avoiding similar accidents.

If cutlines indicate where an accident happened, readers may be more careful when approaching that intersection.

■ NOT ALL ACCIDENTS MERIT COVERAGE

"Two car pile-up at Larkin and Broadway, ambulance on the way," crackles a scanner radio in the photographer's car. The photojournalist must make a news judgment: Is the accident important enough to cover? Will a picture of a multiple-car crash get play in the next day's paper?

Some factors that influence a decision about the newsworthiness of an accident might include:

• Were people rescued, hurt, or killed? If the driver died and the attending physician puts a passenger on the critical list, the accident will probably get coverage.

• Was the damage excessive? When an oil refinery blows up, putting people out of work for months, the economic impact of the accident merits strong play in the paper.

• Was the accident large? The size of the accident, even if no one was hurt, gives the incident importance, especially if the mishap involves buses, trains, or planes.

• Was a public official or celebrity involved? If the mayor accidentally shoots himself with a gun, the story gains interest beyond a routine firearm accident.

• Was the mishap unique in any way? Did one of the cars, for instance, land in a swimming pool or imbed itself in a wall? Did a husband in one car and his wife in another run into one another?

An accident picture's news value can depend on factors other than the nature of the collision. For example, a small-town paper might feature an accident photo that would not even run in a major metro paper. Fender-benders happen so often in a big city that some dailies don't even bother to cover them.

Television's electronic news-gathering (ENG) equipment also has cut down on the

Just a month before a tornado ripped the roof from this home, it had been featured in an architectural magazine. Using the magazine spread in the photograph helps tell the before as well as the after of this disaster.
(Photo by Robert Cohen, the *Memphis* (Tenn.) *Commercial Appeal.*

Attempting to flee
police, who tried to
stop her from
speeding, the driver
was killed when her
car hurled off an
interstate overpass.
By photographing
from a high angle, the
photographer caught
the drama of the
night search as well
as the location
of the accident.
(Photo by Lannis Waters,
The Palm Beach (Fla.)
Post.)

amount of accident coverage in the newspaper. A major collision on the freeway at 5 P.M. rush hour can roll on the 6 P.M. local news broadcast. Coverage of the same accident in the next day's newspaper seems dated.

Policy at individual newspapers can also determine the play of an accident picture. Some editors think that because auto accidents happen every day they are no longer new, and therefore do not qualify as news.

By comparison, other editors view the alarming rate of injuries and deaths by motor vehicles as a trend—a trend their readers are talking about. These editors feature accident pictures to bring home the horror of reckless driving and perhaps to frighten their readers into better driving habits. (See Chapter 14, "Photo Ethics.")

■ PHOTO POSSIBILITIES: FROM TRAGIC TO BIZARRE

If 100 accidents take place daily in a typical city, no two will be identical. However, all accidents have certain points in common for the photographer.

- **Check Human Tragedy First.** Concentrate on the human element of any tragedy. Readers relate to people pictures. (See page 33.)
- **Make a Record**. Make a straightforward record of exactly what happened at the scene. The viewer, who doesn't know how the two cars hit or where they landed on the street, wants to see the cars' relationship to one another and to the highway.
- **Symbolic Pictures Imply Rather than Tell.** In some situations, the accident story is better told with a symbolic rather than a literal picture. A bent wagon lying in the street carries its own silent message. There is no need to show the body of the dead child.
- **Photograph the Cause.** In many news events such as riots or murders, there is no way of capturing on film the cause of the disturbance. At an accident, however, you can sometimes show clearly what caused the collision. For instance, if a car failed to stop on a slippery street, you might show the wet pavement in the foreground and the damaged vehicle in the background.

    On a dry day, you might photograph the skid marks left by the car as it screeched to a halt. Perhaps the accident was caused by the poor visibility of street signs. In that situation, a picture that showed the confusing array of flashing lights and day-glo billboards that distracted the driver would be effective.

- **Show the Impact.** Accidents affect more than the drivers of the involved vehicles. For example, look in both directions for long lines of blocked traffic and drivers slowing down to gaze as they pass the site.
- **Follow-up.** If accidents keep occurring at one particular site, you might follow up to see if the highway department does anything to correct the hazard. A time exposure of an intersection at night, showing the traffic congestion, might help to spur the highway department into action.
- **Feature One Aspect.** Notice how people adapt to their misfortune. Record the kinds of items people save from their wrecked vehicles. Note whether they act angry, sad, or frustrated. Catch the sorrow on the face of an owner of a new Corvette as she views for the first time her crumpled fender. See if an owner of a thirteen-year-old Toyota reacts the same way when he sees the damage inflicted on his clunker.

    Don't become hardened, however, to accidents. No matter what the size of the mishap, the accident usually is still a major tragedy, or at least a traumatic experience, to the people involved.

■ THE BIGGEST PROBLEM MAY BE GETTING THERE

Taking pictures at the scene of a spot-news event requires a photographer with a cool head, someone who can work under pressure and adverse conditions. You need no unusual equipment or techniques—just nerves of steel and an unruffled disposition. However, before you arrive at the accident scene, you must be prepared. Load your camera and charge up your electronic flash so you will be ready to start clicking the minute you get out of the car.

In fact, getting to the accident in time is often the biggest challenge for the spot-news photographer. If you're stuck on the North Loop and two cars crash on the South Loop, you might find only a few glass shards from a broken windshield by the time you get to the scene. The ambulance has come and gone. Removed by the wrecker, even the smashed vehicles are already on their way to the garage.

Consequently, a spot-news photographer's two most important pieces of equipment—after camera gear, of course—are a scanner radio and a city map. The radio provides the first report of the accident and the detailed map shows the quickest way to get to the scene of the collision. Stanley Forman, three-time Pulitzer Prize winner, attributes his success to the fact that he knows his city like the back of his hand. (See Forman's dramatic

The oil tanker Argo Merchant went aground and broke up off the coast of Nantucket. Thousands of gallons of heavy fuel oil soiled the water. The Coast Guard provided journalists transportation by helicopter to the wreck site.
(Photo by Ken Kobré, for the *Boston Phoenix*.)

fire coverage on pages 30 and 31 and on page 313.)

A spot-news photographer finds that the hardest to cover is the story in which all forms of transportation are down. During a flood, hurricane, tornado, or blizzard, you often can't drive a car or ride public transportation.

Faced with a major natural disaster, you can sometimes get assistance from one of the public agencies such as the police department, fire department, Red Cross, civil defense headquarters, or the National Guard. In case of disasters at sea, you can telephone the Coast Guard. Each of these agencies has a public information officer who handles problems and requests from the media. When a major disaster occurs, many of these agencies provide not only

facts and figures but transportation, as well, for the photojournalist.

When the oil tanker Argo Merchant ran aground, cracked in half, sank off Nantucket Island, and leaked thousands of barrels of oil into the sea, I contacted the U.S. Coast Guard on Cape Cod in Massachusetts. The Coast Guard arranged for me to fly in one of its planes over the site to take pictures. (See above.)

In another instance, when all of New England was buried under four-foot snow drifts during a major blizzard, I contacted the National Guard, which provided me with a four-wheeled-drive vehicle and a driver so I could shoot outlying areas hit by the storm.

As UPI's former New England photo bureau chief, Dave Wurzel, once said, "When a big storm breaks and everyone else heads for home, that's when the spot-news photographer goes to work."

WHEN THE POLICE SAY NO TO PICTURES

The police cite a number of reasons for pushing the media away from crime, accident, or disaster scenes. They sometimes feel (mistakenly) that they have a duty to protect the privacy of citizens from the press, says Donald Middlebrooks and his co-authors of an article titled "Access." The writers point out that sometimes the police claim to be pushing the media away to prevent interference with rescue efforts or to avoid some pre-trial problem that will prevent them from successfully prosecuting their case.

These fears are extremely exaggerated. Too often, these reasons are an easy dodge for getting reporters and photographers out of law enforcement's hair at a time when the police are excited and sometimes overwhelmed by a disaster or crime scene at which they are working. But that doesn't mean you can ignore the police when they don't want you around.

Many police agencies today are using the two-perimeter system in dealing with the media, says Sgt. Carl Yates of the Louisville (Kentucky) police department. The outer perimeter is established first and is intended as a barrier for the general public. An inner perimeter is established for the news media after the scene has been secured.

Yates suggests that photographers look for an officer (preferably a commanding officer), identify themselves, and then ask, "Could you direct me to where you want the news media?" If this fails, ask if there is anyone on the scene in charge of public information.

The sergeant cautions not to violate the inner perimeter once you have obtained clearance to enter it. You actually have no more legal right of access than the general public. What you do have, and what you hope the police will recognize, is a more significant reason to be there than the general public does. (See Chapter 13, "The Law.")

Yates also suggests that you be judicious when using flash at night. "Never underestimate the potential impact of a sudden flash of bright light at a night scene. It can anger officers; in some cases, escalate the incident; or worse, light up officers and others, making them potential targets."

The policeman recommends that, unless an immediate photo is necessary, take time to talk to officers before you start shooting. Try to get a feel for the mood of the scene. Police are particularly on edge when a fellow officer has been injured or killed and may overreact to your presence. "These are times to ask first and shoot later," Yates points out. "Express regrets and ease into the situation."

Finally, Yates observes, don't argue with a police officer. "You can argue until you're blue in the face," he says, "and all you will usually be left with is a blue face." ∎

Police arrest *Times Union* **(Albany, N.Y.) staff photographer Steve Jacobs. Jacobs was backing away from the arrest scene, photographing the officers as they led away a captured gunman who had held an entire university class hostage. The police claimed Jacobs was obstructing their actions.** (Photo by Tim Roske, Associated Press.)

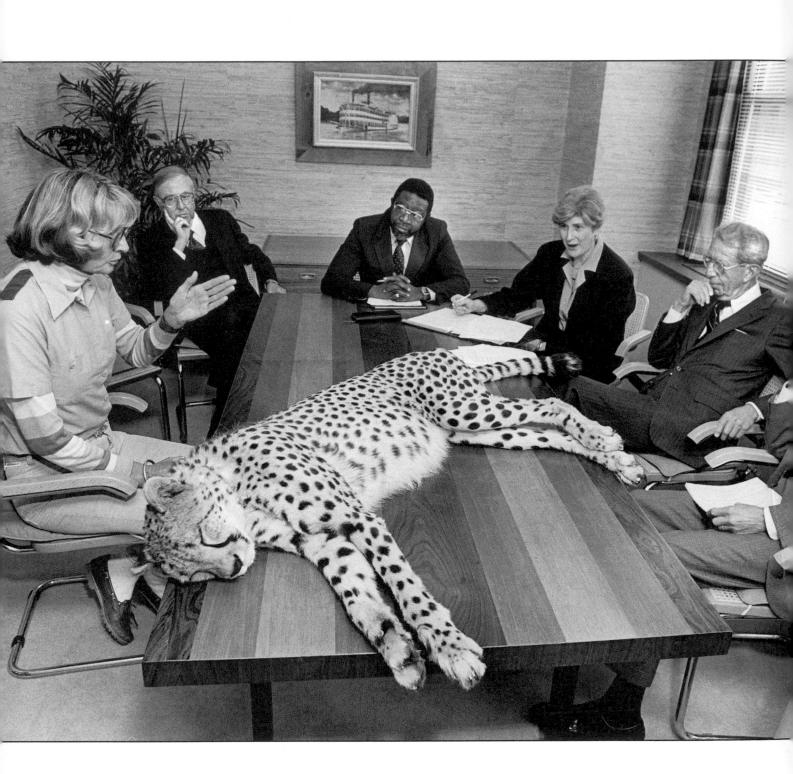

General News

Governmental and organizational news, including

meetings, elections, and awards, accounts for almost

80 percent of the national news sections of *Time* and

Newsweek, according to **Deciding What's News**, by Herbert Gans.

The president alone receives 20 percent of all national affairs cover-

age in these magazines. Local media outlets also devote enormous

space to appointed and elected officials, campaigns, and meetings.

You will find it hard to take a picture that communicates as well as this photo of a fund-raising meeting for the Cincinnati Zoo—complete with cat-napping cheetah. (Photo by Patrick Reddy, the *Cincinnati Enquirer*.)

Therefore, developing visually interesting tech-

niques for reporting these kinds of stories becomes

mandatory for the professional photojournalist.

Jim Atherton faced the problems of shooting revealing political meeting pictures for more than thirty-five years, first for Acme News Pictures, then for United Press International (UPI) and, most recently for the *Washington Post*. Headquartered in Washington during his years in the picture business, he covered some of the most momentous as well as some of the most trivial political moments in the country's recent history. Retired today, he worked Capitol Hill on his beat as the *Post*'s chief political photographer.

Says Atherton, "A committee meeting is like a shooting gallery at the fair. You're there to shoot famous heads. You do not have to hunt down the lions of politics; they are captive on stage in front of you. You take careful aim and shoot with your camera."

■ MEETINGS GENERATE NEWS

Similarly, in other large cities and small towns, photographers and reporters cover the news of governmental meetings because the results of those meetings are important to readers. Meetings possess the same news value as do fires and accidents. Often, the results of a governmental meeting—those

involving changes in the tax rate, for instance—directly bear on the reader's life even more than yesterday's fender-bender.

At each level of power, every governmental body—from city council and zoning board to state legislature to the U.S. House of Representatives and the Senate—forms public policy and takes action at meetings. The city council votes to improve handicapped access. The state legislature puts a ceiling on the mortgage rate. The Senate committee reviews a bill on national health insurance. All these meetings receive extensive coverage in newspapers and magazines, with written stories as well as with accompanying pictures.

Not only governmental bodies plan, decide, or announce decisions at meetings and awards banquets. The United Fund presents a plaque to the person donating the largest gift to the organization's funding drive. The Committee for the Handicapped meets to review the Transit Authority's new transportation facilities. The Chamber of Commerce announces an advertising campaign to bring business to the city. Editors routinely assign photographers to cover these meetings, awards, and press conferences.

The photographer was able to summarize the city council debate about access for the disabled by photographing this man waiting outside council chambers, where the discussion was taking place.
(Photo by Hal Wells, *Long Beach Press-Telegram*.)

Spot news challenges the photographer to get to the breaking story in time. To cover planned news events, the photographer has the advantage of knowing the time and place of the action.

But meetings and press conferences carry a different challenge. They test the photographer's creativity. Unfortunately, a critical meeting of the Senate Armed Services Committee looks very much like an ordinary meeting of the local zoning board. If the pictures remained uncaptioned, readers could easily be confused. Press conferences as well as awards ceremonies all tend to look identical after a while.

A photographer's job, then, is to portray each planned news event in a way that features the event's uniqueness. The picture must be related to the news—a difficult assignment, because planned news often takes place in evenly lit rooms, produces little action, and the participants display few props that would add clarity to the picture. Infrequently, a panelist holds up a sign that tells the viewer clearly what the meeting is about. Few senators carry placards that read "I think we should reduce farm supports." Sometimes, however, you can catch a city council member yawning, or a participant from the audience yelling, thereby summarizing the tone of the meeting.

Also, through the creative application of framing techniques, catching the moment, and using long lenses and light, the photographer can help portray for the reader the excitement, the tension, the opposition, and the resolution of the meeting.

■ FACE AND HANDS REVEAL EMOTION

When Jim Atherton raised his 80–200mm zoom lens at a committee hearing or press conference, he would look for expressive faces. A wrinkled brow, a grin, or a curled lip can add life to a routine meeting picture. Hands, too, reveal a speaker's emotion, says Atherton. Readers understand the meaning of a clenched fist or a jabbing finger.

The *Washington Post*'s political photographer watched both faces and hands when he was assigned to cover Senator Sam Ervin's Senate Select Committee investigating the Watergate break-in. In session for several weeks, the Committee was receiving top play in the nation's papers. The outcome of the Committee's investigation could lead to the first impeachment of a president. The daily sessions turned into a running nightmare for the assigned photographers.

"There was nothing worse than to cover the same damn speakers, with the same panel of senators, sitting in front of the same

green, felt-covered table, day after day," Atherton recalls.

Excitement, however, peaked when John Dean, ex-counsel to President Richard Nixon, took the witness stand. Dean accused the president of the United States of breaking the law to cover up his involvement in Watergate. During the first day of his testimony, Dean read the lengthy text of his speech. The *Post*'s photographer needed a unique approach to dramatize the speaker. "I had to make something with a little pizzazz," recalls Atherton. On that first day, Atherton tried overall shots and close-up head shots, but on the second day of Dean's testimony, the photojournalist concentrated on Dean's hands. Atherton produced a series of close-ups showing the ex-counsel's hands raised as he was sworn in, spread out as he listened to questions, drumming on the table as he read his text, and fidgeting with his pencil as he waited during a recess. Sometimes Atherton would miss shooting a characteristic mannerism the first time it occurred. But, he notes, "I had patience; I knew Dean would repeat the quirk again; I just kept watching."

Isolating one revealing element, Dean's hands, helped tell the bigger story of a young man seemingly cool, but actually nervous underneath, who accused the president of the United States of lying. The poignant pictures were played on the front page in the next morning's *Washington Post*.

Revealing versus Accidental Photos

Atherton warns, however, that a speaker's facial expressions and hand gestures can be accidental and misleading. They might have nothing to do with the personality of the individual or the thrust of the message. Suppose that during a luncheon the governor is discussing closing the border to illegal immigrants. You take 100 to 200 frames. You might catch a shot while he is eating—showing him with his mouth screwed into a knot. This picture, although an actual moment, reflects nothing about the nature of the topic or even the speaker's character. The misleading picture, in fact, tends to distort the news rather than reveal it.

■ PERSONALITIES MAKE NEWS

For Atherton, news meant politicians. He describes political photographers as headhunters on "the Hill." They shoot the faces of the famous. Whatever a Washington politician does is news. Atherton notes, "Washington is the only place in the country where you can take a simple snapshot of an elected official today and have it appear on the front page of every newspaper in the country

The hands of Massachusetts' former Secretary of Human Services, Jerald Stevens, reveal the pressures, the pleasure, the tension and relaxation of this powerful state official. (Photos by Bill Collins.)

Without the woman's sign in the picture, few readers would guess that this meeting focused on free dental care for the aged.
(Photo by Tom Strongman, *Kansas City Times.*)

tomorrow." Translated into local coverage, this means that meetings, speeches, or press conferences in a town take on news value based on the personalities involved and on the importance of the subject debated.

The photographer must know or be able to recognize the players in the game without a score card. If you are not familiar with the participants in a meeting, ask someone for information about the speakers. What are their names? Which are elected officials? Who is best-known? With this information, you can zero in on the most newsworthy individuals.

Props Add Meaning

Props can add meaning to a routine meeting photo. If the speaker or audience member holds up a prop, the reader will have an easier time understanding the point of the photo. If the speaker who denounces the lack of gun control laws brings to the meeting a few Saturday Night Specials, the photographer can photograph the person examining or displaying the guns. A photo of an elderly woman, missing her dentures and holding aloft a poster of a toothy smile, helped summarize a meeting on free dental care for the aged.

■ LIGHTING IS IMPORTANT
Let the Sunshine In

Besides props and facial expressions, the quality of light and the choice of lens can also add impact to a simple meeting picture. When you walk into a meeting room, notice the quantity and quality of light in that room. Is the light sufficient? Is the room lit by natural light from the windows or fluorescent light from the ceiling? Check to see whether the light comes from the front or from behind the speaker's table. Note whether television lights will be turned on during the hearing. If, after "casing" the room, you find the level of light too low, you might ask if you can open the window shades. If there is enough natural light streaming through the windows, you could ask to turn off the overhead lights.

Fluorescent Light is Bland

If natural light is a photographer's best friend, then fluorescent light is the shooter's most dastardly enemy. Fluorescent light is efficient, economical, cool, and saves energy. But for a photographer, fluorescent light is about as exciting as white bread. Fluorescent bulbs emit light in all directions. The light bounces off ceiling and walls and even the floor. With enough fixtures, the light can illuminate every nook and cranny, leaving only dull highlights and faint shadows.

Some photographers, working in a room

evenly lit by fluorescent light, will manipulate exposure and development or select a high-contrast film or developer to increase contrast.

Television lights not only brighten the room but, if used correctly, can also add contrast to the picture. The secret of using television light to add depth lies in not shooting from the same position as the TV camera. If the main spotlight is located to the left of the TV camera, the still photographer benefits from cross-lighting by moving to the right of the TV equipment. The farther you move around the subject, and the greater the angle from the TV camera, the more the light crosses the subject's face. The side of the face nearest the lens is in the shadow. The contrast between the highlight on the far side and the shadow on the near side of the face brings out the texture of the subject's skin and adds roundness, which gives the whole picture an added sense of drama.

Separate the Subject from the Background

A photographer must be conscious of not only ambient room light but also of the relationship between the tonal values of the subject and the background. How will the subject look on film? A dark-suited senator can appear to fade into an oak-paneled wall when photographed with black-and-white film.

The contrast between the tone of the subject and the tone of the background takes on added importance if the picture is reproduced in a newspaper. Newsprint grays out the blacks and muddies the whites. If the original difference in contrast between the congressional representative and the wall were slight, the tonal separation would be completely lost when the picture was reproduced on newsprint.

If you had to take a picture of a dark-suited city council member speaking at a meeting, you might circle the official, and watch the background. You might look for a light-colored wall or door that could offset the subject.

Burning and dodging—whether conventionally or digitally—can help separate the subject from the background, but the technique can produce a light halo around the subject's head if the photographer is not careful. Few politicians deserve a halo.

■ BLOW-UP OR COMPRESSION?

When Jim Atherton would cover an important committee meeting on Capitol Hill for the *Washington Post,* he would carry three camera bodies: two Leicas, one with a 50mm and the other with a 35mm lens, and a Nikon with either a 24mm wide-angle or

Shooting perpendicular to the line of speakers results in a picture with large blank spaces between each person, and each face appears quite small.
(Photo by Jan Ragland.)

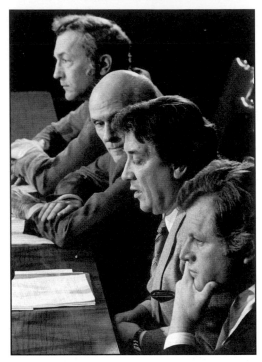

Shooting these dignitaries from the side eliminated dead space between subjects. Photographing with a telephoto lens appears to bring the subjects closer together.
(Photo by James K.W. Atherton, *Washington Post*.)

80–200mm zoom. He would bayonet the 24mm on the Nikon for "overalls" of the conference room but save the zoom for close-up portraits. The close-up, he notes, brings the viewer and the subject nearer than they normally would meet in public.

Says Atherton, "A zoom is difficult to use because everything moves—the focus, the focal length, and the f/stops. Also, the telephoto magnifies my hand movements. I'll lean on any sturdy object available—tabletop, chair, or doorpost—to steady my aim." Atherton recommends hand-holding the zoom lens for maximum flexibility and mobility. Set the shutter speed fairly slow (about 1/60 sec.) in order to use a smaller aperture and get more depth of field. Atherton estimates that hand-holding the lens and shooting at a slow shutter speed resulted in his losing 60 percent to 70 percent of his frames because of image blur. But, Atherton notes, 30 to 40 percent come out sharp. These more rare but striking pictures represent some of the photos that distinguished Atherton from the rest of the photo corps for so many years.

To avoid camera movement and to increase the percentage of sharp pictures,

some photographers use extremely fast lenses and high speed film, or they "push" process their film. Combining lenses with large f/stops, usually f/2.8 or better, and high-speed (ISO 1600 or 3200) or push-processed film allows the photographer to shoot without strobe in most meeting situations. (See Chapter 10, "Cameras & Film," for more about film and developing.)

Besides creating close-up portraits, the telephoto lens offers another advantage when you cover a meeting or press conference. Often, the important figures at a conference stretch out in a line down one side of a table or sit on a platform at the edge of a stage.

If you stand in front of the panelists to take a picture, each participant's head will appear quite small on the final print. Gaping holes of unnecessary space will lie between each speaker. If you move to one side or the other and shoot down the line of dignitaries, the panelists will appear in the picture to be quite close together, with little space between them. (See above left.)

The compression effect becomes more noticeable as you move farther from the subjects and use longer telephoto lenses. However, depth of field decreases as the lens length increases, so you may find it almost impossible to keep a long line of panelists in sharp focus when you shoot with an extreme telephoto.

To achieve maximum depth of field, focus one-third the way down the row of dignitaries. You can put the camera on a monopod or, even better, a tripod if you find you can't hand-hold the telephoto at slow speeds.

With the aperture on a relatively small f/stop, all the subjects will appear sharp. Also, the panelists will look like they are sitting shoulder to shoulder without any dead space between them.

POLITICIANS AND ELECTIONS

Politicians seek interviews and photographs. Press aides dream up news events and organize news conferences to attract coverage. Astute politicians know that re-election depends on good media coverage. The monetary worth of a page-one photo is inestimable—most newspapers will not even sell front-page space for advertising.

A politician plans media events that attract the camera, even if the events themselves have little news value. Called "photo opportunities," these nonevents have been designed for the camera journalist. One such event was held at the White House and reported by Anthony Lewis for the *New York Times*: "11 A.M. Photo Opportunity White House Tree House. At 10:55 that morning 34 reporters and photographers lined up at the door of the White House press room. Then, led by . . . the press secretary, the group trooped across the broad green sweep of the south lawn toward a gigantic atlas cedar tree and the White House Tree House nestled in its lower branches. Squatting in the White House Tree House (WHTH) was the president's . . . daughter . . . and grandson. The cameras clicked, the mini-cams whirled and reporters fired questions at the two children huddled on the platform."

Ed Bradley, CBS correspondent, ruminated, "The White House grinds it out, and we eat it up." Don't assume that recent presidents invented the photo opportunity. John F. Kennedy rarely missed a chance for full coverage. He knew that if he brought John-John, his young son, with him, the press was sure to be close behind.

Ted Dully, a photographer who worked for the *Boston Globe*, points out that if the president puts on a stupid hat for a photo, an editor can't resist using the picture. As Dully says, "Politicians manipulate photographers and photographers manipulate politicians, both to their mutual benefit. Politicians look for free publicity and photographers want

Often the side show is more interesting visually than the main event—particularly when the main event is a press conference or photo op. Here, an entrepreneur packs up at the end of the Clinton inauguration in Washington, D.C. (Photo by Robert Cohen, the *Memphis* (Tenn.) *Commercial Appeal*.)

visual events. Editors think readers want to see politicians in costume."

"The picture of the yarmulke-wearing senator is not wrong," he adds, "it's just not good journalism."

■ THE CAMPAIGN TRAIL

Politicians come alive at election time. The old "pal" leaves the desk in his plush office and starts pressing the flesh at ward meetings, ethnic parades, and organizations for the elderly. The young challenger, by contrast, walks the streets of the ghetto with her suit jacket thrown over her shoulder. Both candidates plaster stickers on cars, erect billboards, appear in "I Promise" TV ads, and attend massive rallies. A photographer can take two sets of campaign pictures: one shows the candidate's public life—shaking hands, giving speeches, and greeting party workers. The other shows the candidate's private life— grabbing a few minutes alone with the family, planning strategy behind closed doors, raising money, pepping up the staff, and collapsing at the end of a fourteen-hour day.

All too often, newspapers present their readers with a one-sided visual portrait of the candidate—the public side, planned and orchestrated by the candidate's campaign directors. The papers print only upbeat, never downbeat, pictures; only happy, never sad, moments. Photographers continue to churn out photos of the candidate shaking hands and smiling—photos that reveal little about the person who is going to run the city, state, or federal government.

Go Behind the Scenes

Political scientists claim that the American public votes for a candidate based on personality. If that is so, the responsibility of the photo editor should be to present a complete picture of the candidate.

The in-depth portrait must include the private as well as the public side. The public might vote its politician in or out of office on the basis of a pleasant smile, but, in the long run, progress in America depends on issues, not personalities. What has the incumbent mayor accomplished in office?

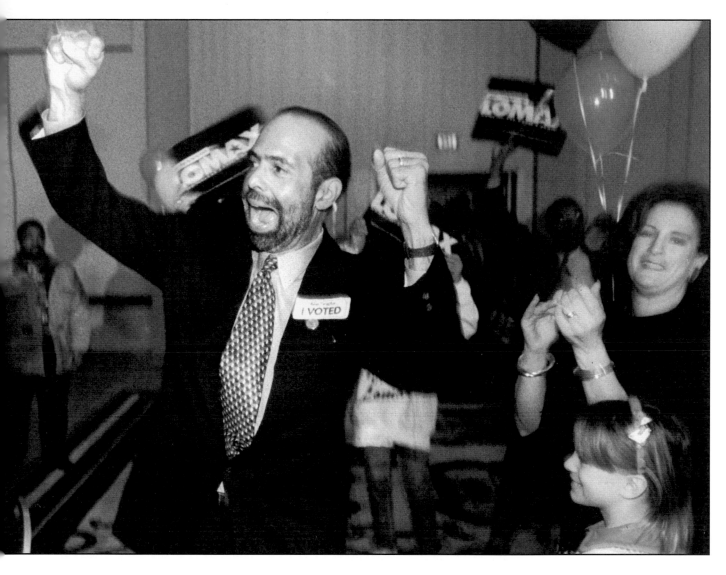

Photograph the Issues

Almost all of a campaign's political issues can be translated into pictures. If the mayoral candidate says city education is poor and should be improved, the photographer must search for supporting evidence of the claim. Are schools overcrowded? Do students hang around in the halls with nothing to do after class? If racial tension exists between black and white students, can the journalist photograph the hostility? A set of realistic photos will transform the rhetoric of a campaign into observable issues. Photographers spend too much time shooting political mug shots and too little time digging up visuals that either confirm or deny the claims of these politicians.

When covering a campaign, election, or any other contested issue, the photographer has the same responsibilities to objectivity as does the reporter. Like a reporter, a photographer can directly distort a scene. A super-wide-angle lens can make a small room look

large. Strong lighting and harsh shadows can transform, in Jekyll-and-Hyde fashion, a mild-mannered speaker into a tyrannical orator. Even more damaging, the photographer, like the writer, can report one side of an issue and, intentionally or not, leave the other side uncovered. Because papers often run only one or two pictures, such biased photo reporting creeps into the paper easily. The honest photographer, however, tries to select the lens, light, and camera angle as well as a representative moment or scene to present a fair view of a complicated topic.

Unfortunately, few staff photographers receive adequate time for investigative political photography. An editor finds it easy to send a staffer to cover a press conference. The editor knows the time and place of the gathering and can guarantee that some usable "art" will result. But readers don't want to see another "mayor talking" picture. They already know what the mayor looks like. They want to determine if the mayor is

Atlanta mayoral candidate Michael Lomax pumps up his supporters after learning the race was forced into a run-off, which he ultimately lost.
(Jonathan Newton, *Atlanta Journal-Constitution.*)

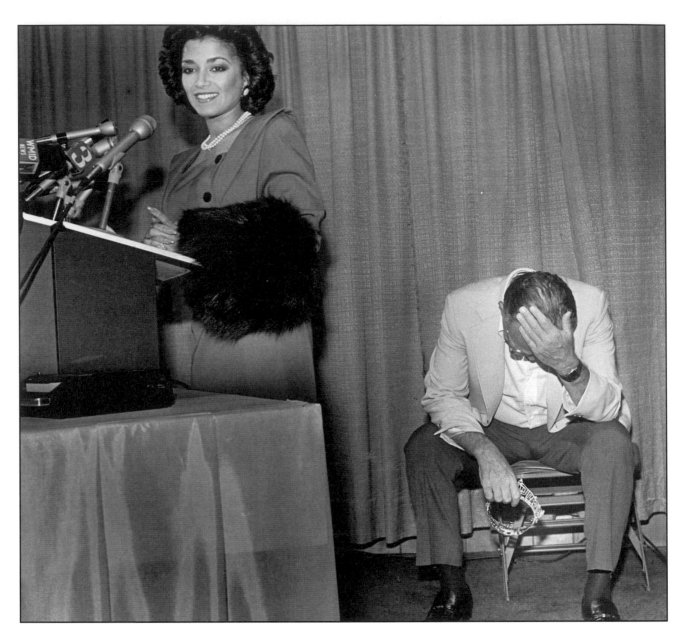

Sometimes a press conference produces a revealing picture. Vanessa Williams was forced to step down as Miss America after nude photos of her appeared in *Penthouse* magazine. Here, the beleaguered Miss America Pageant chairman holds the crown while waiting for the replacement, Suzette Charles, to finish the news conference at which she would be crowned. (Photo by Michael Mercanti, *Philadelphia Daily News*.)

telling the truth about the school system. Pictures can supply part of the evidence for the mayor's assertions or negate his allegations.

Steer Clear of the Pack

Even if you're out conducting photographic political investigations, your editor in all likelihood will continue to assign you to rallies, speeches, and "photo opportunities." Cover these events if you must, but resist the PR-packaged photos politicians hope to see in tomorrow's paper. At the most, look where the packaging has peeled away—but don't be surprised if you can't find it. At the least, turn your camera toward the crowd to find unusual political boosters. And, photographically, struggle to avoid the cliché of simply recording the routine picture—the stock shot.

Without doubt, all political rallies start to

look alike. But, by angling for a new view, like the one of clapping hands and Lloyd Bentsen (see page 48), perhaps you can at least bring back a photo you and your readers haven't seen thousands of times before.

AWARDS: AVOIDING THE GRIP AND GRIN

After politicians' press conferences and meetings, the awards ceremony ranks as the most common planned news event.

"I would like to present this check for $5,000 to your organization," says the president of the local bank as he passes a check to the head of a service organization. Cameras click. Strobes flash. These awards pictures, all identical, give the reader no new insight into the individuals involved in the ceremony. Who are they? Why did the group give the money? Who will benefit? The "grip-and-grin" photo, as it's commonly known, doesn't answer these questions. The picture simply records that two people held a trophy or a check, or just shook hands.

Ted Dully, formerly of the *Boston Globe*, said that awards pictures simply should not run. "They pander to the desires of people to feel important, and they perform no newsworthy function." Many news outlets, however, especially in smaller communities, continue to publish such photos, perhaps for public relations reasons.

If you polled professional photojournalists, they would probably share Dully's sentiments by voting overwhelmingly to eliminate awards pictures. Some news outlets, in fact, have policies forbidding awards photos except for special circumstances. The *Boston Globe*, for example, prints just one awards picture a year—of the winner of the *Globe* Santa Contest, which the newspaper sponsors.

Most editors, nevertheless, continue to assign hand-shaking, check-passing pictures. Sometimes the events deserve coverage. When a small-town citizen wins a million-dollar lottery, that is clearly worth a picture. Sometimes the event is so close to home that a photographer had better not miss it: when your publisher wins the community person-of-the-year award, you will probably take several shots of his receiving the plaque.

The Story Behind the Award

As with meeting pictures and political pictures, the real secret to an awards photo lies in searching out the reason for the ceremony and bringing out this fact in the picture. Sometimes the photographer only has to add a prop to the picture to point out the meaning of the event. If a man wins an award for best marksman, his gun included in the picture cues the reader to the nature of the award.

At other times, the photographer must arrange a portrait to clarify the point of the award. If an employee gets a bonus for stitching more shirts than anyone else in the shirt factory, then the photographer needs to find a time to photograph the worker standing next to her tall stack of finished clothing.

In some cases, an award might even be a peg for a picture story. For example, the ceremony at which Annemarie Madison received an award for her work with people dying from AIDS was, as most of these stiff ceremonies are, a visual zero. However, her dedication and compassion became the subject of a moving photo story that was part of a photo project that won awards of its own—"Helpers in the War on AIDS." (See "Developing a Feature Beat" in Chapter 4, "Features.")

■ **PHOTOGRAPH THE SUBJECT OF THE TALK, NOT THE TALKER**

Even with the best lens technique and a keen sensitivity to light, photographers still have trouble distinguishing for readers the difference between a city council meeting called to increase taxes and a meeting convened to decrease the number of district schools. The

Members of the San Francisco Planning Commission discuss transforming a U.S. Army base into a national park. In addition to photographing the routine-looking meeting (TOP), the photographer captured the base's ceremonial gun salute (BELOW), an activity that will disappear when the base is decommissioned.
(Photo by Michael Staub.)

difference between these meetings lies in what the council members said verbally, not what they did visually. The photojournalist must translate speakers' words into pictures that portray the underlying controversy.

Arthur Perfal, a former associate editor of *Newsday*, gave his view of the problem at a conference of editors conducted by Chuck Scott, then-director of the Visual Communications program at Ohio State University.

"Remember that people talking often supply material for good stories," Perfal said, "but they seldom supply material for good pictures. Particularly when the same officials or the same chairmen are doing the talking. Let the photographer go where the action is—shoot what they're talking about."

You might say photographer Michael Staub took that advice literally. The Presidio, a military base inside the city of San Francisco, is a corner of land fronting the Pacific Ocean, San Francisco Bay, and the Golden Gate Bridge. The U.S. government was decommissioning the base and turning it into a park. In addition to photographing the meeting at which plans for the land's use were being debated, Staub also photographed the ceremonial firing of the base's canon. When the last troops pull out, this daily ceremony will end, which makes it a fitting symbol for the discussions about the base's future—not to mention a more interesting photo than one of more talking heads at yet another meeting. (See page 51.)

■ NURSING HOMES: A CASE STUDY
Translating Numbers into People
In California, investigators determined that, over a three-year period, poor care in state nursing homes was a factor in 126 deaths. The *San Jose Mercury News* decided to investigate the findings.

Mercury News reporters discovered that "An aide shook a 74-year-old man in Long Beach so violently, an investigator said, that his brain was slammed against his skull 'like a clapper in a bell.'" Nurses diligently charted the progression of bedsores on an 81-year-old woman in Los Gatos until there was "black stuff oozing from her body"—but failed to save her life.

Photographing Statistics
The paper's graphics editor assigned Judy Griesedieck to illustrate the series.

Problem one: the subjects of the story, the abused elderly, were dead and buried.

The solution: photograph current treatment of the elderly in nursing homes.

Problem two: aware of stories the paper already had written, nursing home owners and managers did not want a *San Jose Mercury News* photographer anywhere near their nursing homes.

The solution: Griesedieck started the assignment by calling twenty nursing homes. Only two said she could come in and look around. Then Griesedieck talked to the paper's lawyer, Ed Davis, who pointed out that while nursing homes were private property, Griesedieck could enter and photograph if she was invited into the home by one of the residents. She could photograph the person who invited her without being evicted by the management of the nursing home.

Gaining Access
To meet people in the homes, Griesedieck attended meetings of Bay Area Advocates of Nursing Home Reform. Relatives of people in nursing homes, the group members were happy to introduce the *Mercury News* photographer to their mothers, fathers, wives, and husbands who were living with inadequate nursing home care. With an invitation from nursing home patients she met through the advocates organization, Griesedieck began to shoot the story.

In one home, a daughter brought Griesedieck in to see her mother. The older woman had bedsores because of neglect. In another home, a patient would be in bed at 9 A.M. and still lie there—undressed, unattended, and with no outside stimulation—when the photographer left at 5 P.M.

Besides neglect, Griesedieck also found evidence of love and compassion at the nursing homes. The *Mercury News* photographer watched a man who visited his wife daily, bringing his spouse a rose on each visit. The man spoon-fed his wife lunch each day. The husband said to Griesedieck, "I don't think she knows who I am." He started crying.

Griesedieck also obtained entrance to the nursing homes by accompanying a doctor who treated Alzheimer's disease, which makes people forgetful. Here again, she had to get permission ahead of time from every patient or guardian.

The photographer also made arrangements with the California Department of Health Services, which carries out unannounced inspections of nursing homes. The inspectors called Griesedieck the morning of the surprise nursing home visit and, when possible, she followed the health service employees on their investigative raids.

Results
The four-part series in the *Mercury News* ran with Griesedieck's powerful pictures illustrating each day's stories. Under the headline

"A requiem of neglect," reporters described the lack of care that caused each of the 126 deaths that had occurred over the previous three years. The series caused the state commission to relaunch an investigation of California's nursing homes and its system for policing them. The series was a runner-up for the Pictures of the Year Canon Photo Essayist Award.

Griesedieck, however, continued to have nightmares about what she saw. Until leaving California, she continued to visit the old people in several of the homes. "What I saw made me sad," she says. "I might be here some day. People in these homes had great careers—doctors, models—and now. . . ."

And now, at least, people do know about the situation in these homes and can take action because of solid investigative reporting and photography by Griesedieck and her fellow staff members.

■ INGREDIENTS FOR IN-DEPTH COVERAGE

Important Issues

Griesedieck started with an important issue. Her paper had published a number of spot-news stories about deaths due to neglect in nursing homes and about official investigations. The paper had given each of the stories only inside play. In seeing the pattern generated by the numbers—noting the repetition of deaths due to neglect—the paper went beyond the individual news story. The pictures and story attempted not only to document the phenomenon of needless death but also to show the cause of the problem—neglect.

Over the year-long project, Griesedieck tried to bring the statistics—126 deaths in state nursing homes caused by neglect—to light. She zeroed in on individual stories that provided examples of the larger trend. She showed Carrie Chelucci being checked for bedsores. She showed Lucille Dennison, who has Alzheimer's disease, asleep in her wheelchair in the hall of a locked wing in the home.

Just as important, Griesedieck balanced these hard-hitting pictures with those showing love and care by some attendants and doctors.

Time

Like most investigative stories, Griesedieck's took time. The paper made a commitment of resources—a commitment of one photographer's time. Of course, she did not spend full time shooting this story.

But the paper gave her sufficient time from her daily shift to research the issue, make contacts, telephone possible subjects, and wait for their responses. Many newspapers think nothing of assigning a reporter for weeks or even months on an investigative story. Unfortunately, most papers fail to provide sufficient time for good visual reportage.

Display

Obviously, the photographer needed to make powerful images for the article, and Griesedieck's pictures were superb. Equally important, however, the images needed a showcase. The *Mercury News* featured a large lead picture on page one each day the series ran. Its editors also used photos extensively inside.

■ BACKGROUNDING THE NEWS

"No Place to Die: California's Nursing Homes" is an outstanding example of backgrounding the news, a term Sidney Kobré, my father, coined in a book by that name written in 1939. Backgrounding means explaining the cause of a news story. Backgrounding means applying psychology, sociology, and economics to a news event to put it into perspective. While photography is an excellent medium for recording the immediate—the fire, the accident—you can also use photos to explain. In the future, with television's instant reportage of breaking news, still photography will find an increasingly important role in providing in-depth coverage that identifies patterns and explains causes. ■

A San Jose nursing home resident watches as the world goes by.

(FAR LEFT)
H.A. Himmelsbach visits
his wife, Miriam, daily to
feed her lunch.

(LEFT) Awilda Olmoa, a
nurse's aide, combs the
hair of 100-year-old
Gregoria Santos.

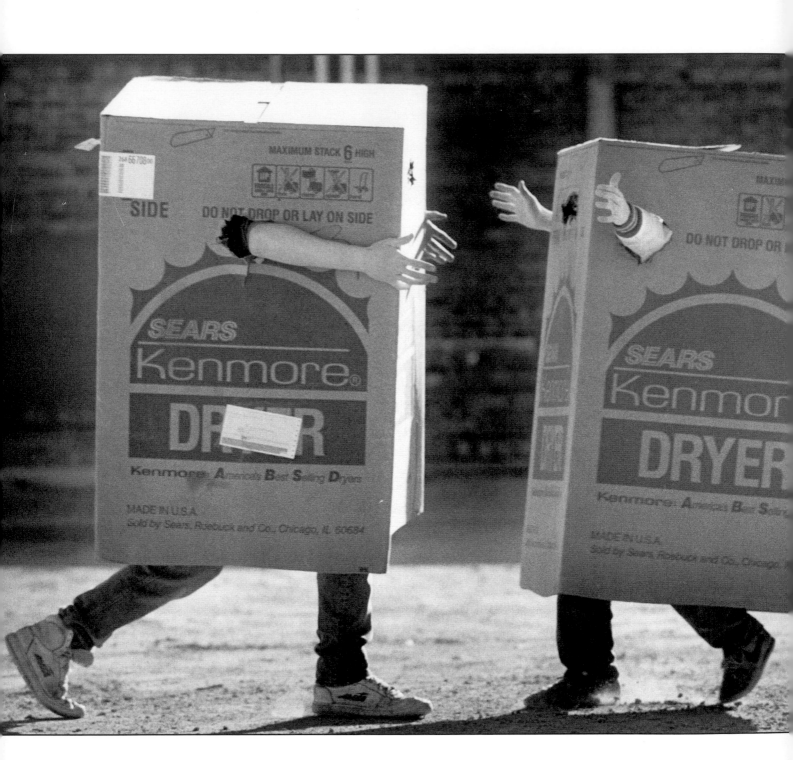

Features

CHAPTER 4

Feature photos provide a visual dessert to subscribers who digest a daily diet of accident, fire, political, and economic news. Many editors argue that, since readers receive so much depressing news in the paper's gray columns of type, subscribers deserve a break when they look at pictures. For some papers, feature pictures not only help to break up the news but have become the mainstay of the front page. Consistently, reader surveys show that subscribers respond favorably to feature pictures.

(See Chapter, 9, "Editing," for more on research about reader preferences.)

Feature pictures provide a visual break from routine news.
(Photo by Jim Evans, Jackson, Wyoming.)

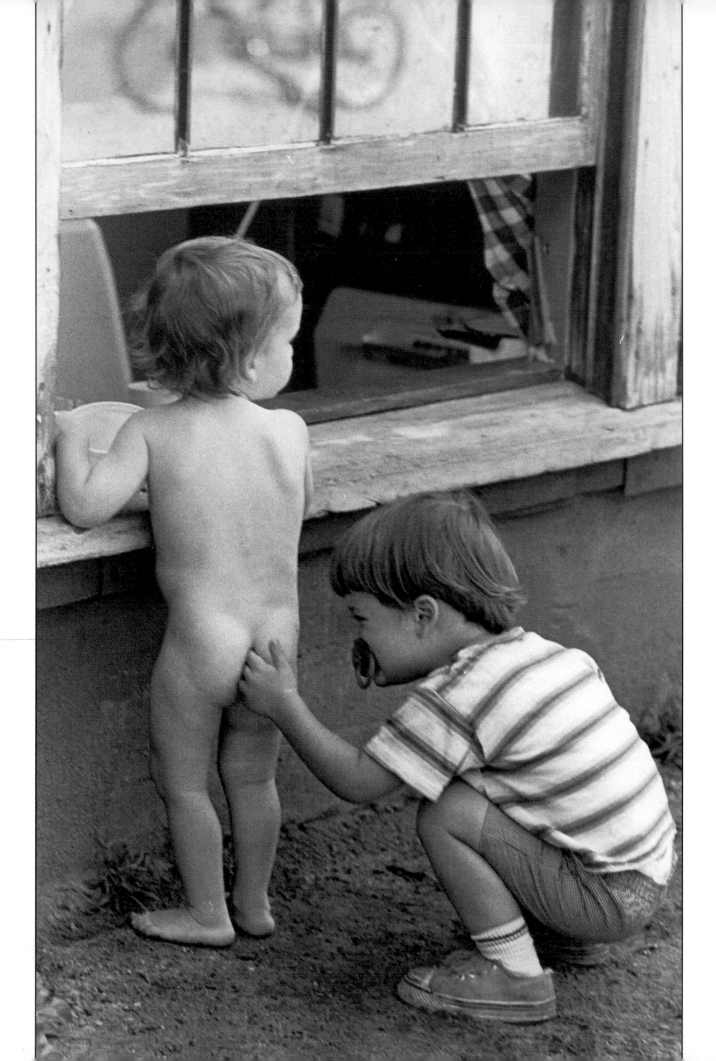

Features also allow newspapers to play up average citizens in circumstances other than accidents and other tragedies.

■ HOW FEATURES AND NEWS DIFFER
Timelessness
Feature photos differ from news photos in several respects. A news picture portrays something new. Because news is timely, news pictures get stale quickly. Many feature pictures, on the other hand, are timeless. Feature pictures don't improve with time, as good wine does, but neither do they turn sour. Some newspapers, in fact, refer to features as evergreens. Like evergreen trees, feature photos never turn brown. Wire service photos showing Carter giving his inaugural speech carry little interest today. Yet pictures like that below will long retain their holding power. Gordon Converse, who worked for the *Christian Science Monitor* for more than twenty years, described feature photography as the "search for moments in time that are worth preserving forever."

Slice of Life
A news picture accrues value when (1) its subject is famous, (2) the event is of large magnitude, or (3)

◄ **A feature picture records the commonplace, an everyday happening, or a slice of life. Children like those at the Harvard day-care center are natural feature subjects.**
(Photo by Ken Kobré, for the *Boston Phoenix*.)

the outcome is tragic. A feature picture, by contrast, records the commonplace, the everyday, the slice of life. The feature photograph tells an old story in a new way, with a new slant. Two children playing games at a day-care center will not change the state of world politics, but the photo might provide the basis for a funny feature picture.

With hard news, the event controls the photographer. Photojournalists jump into action when their editor assigns them to cover a plane crash or a train wreck. When they reach the scene, they limit their involvement to recording the tragedy.

As a feature photographer, on the other hand, you often can generate your own feature assignments. In fact, many newspapers call features "enterprise pictures." You might arrange to spend the day shooting photos of a man who makes artificial arms and legs. Or you might head for the city park, looking for a child playing ball with her parents.

Featurizing the News
News does not stop with fires and accidents—features don't begin with parks and kids. The division between these two types of pictures is not that clear-cut. The sensitive photographer, for instance, could uncover features even at a major catastrophe. This is called "featurizing the news." The main story might describe a fire's damage to an apartment house, and give a list of the injured and

▼ **The contrast between the attention of the cleaning crew and the grace of the dancers gives this picture its appeal.**
(Photo by Michael Macor, the *San Francisco Chronicle*.)

dead. The news photo might show the fire-fighter rescuing the victims with the building burning in the background. For a news feature, the photographer might take a photo of a firefighter being kind to a dog. This picture, along with a caption about the canine rescue, might be printed as a sidebar alongside the main story and photos, which would concentrate on the residents' injuries and the general damage to the building. Likewise, a picture of a driving student behind the wheel of a wrecked car straddles the line between news and feature.

Universal Emotions

Great feature pictures, and there are few, evoke a reaction in the viewer. When viewers look at a powerful feature photo they might laugh, cry, stand back in amazement, or peer more closely for another inspection. The photo has succeeded.

Some features are even universal in their appeal. They will get a response in no matter what country they are shown. When individuals in Russia, China, an African nation, or the United States respond to the same photo, then the photographer has tapped into the univer-

sally understood language of feature pictures.

The term feature picture tends to serve as a catch-all category. In fact, some writers define features as "anything that's not news." Yet many pictures fit into neither the news nor the feature category. Snapshots from a family album, for example, don't really belong in either pigeon hole. How can you learn to recognize a scene with good feature potential? By looking at feature pictures in newspapers, magazines, and books, you will begin to notice a consistent attribute that all features possess.

GOOD FEATURE SUBJECTS

A few years back, each time a new photographer was hired by Florida's *St. Petersburg Times and Independent*, a veteran staffer would draw the newcomer aside to explain the secret ingredients of the feature picture. "Friend," he said, "if you need a feature picture for today's edition, you can't go wrong by taking photos of kids, animals, or nuns wearing habits." These were not bad words of advice because a large percentage of published feature pictures includes kids, animals, and sometimes even nuns.

Few fender benders merit photographic coverage—except when the driver is a trainee at the "Easy Method Driving School." While serious to the student driver, this minor accident takes on the properties of a funny feature photo.
(Photo by J.M. Eddins, Jr., Patuxent (Md.) Publishing Co.)

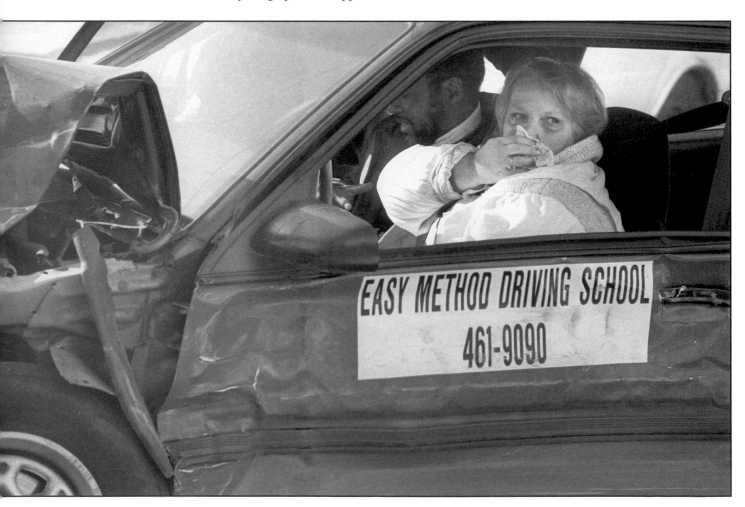

■ KIDS IMITATING ADULTS

Photographers find children to be relatively easy and willing subjects because they act in natural ways, play spontaneously, and look cute. Without any encouragement, children do silly things. To grown-ups, children seem particularly funny when they imitate adult behavior. The child often acts as a mirror, showing the adult how grown-up behavior appears to the younger generation.

A specialist in photographing children when she worked for the *Boston Globe*, Ulrike Welsch always asked permission of parents before photographing youngsters. "That way the parent does not become suspicious and does not interrupt the shooting," Welsch explains. If the parent is not around, Welsch asked the child to lead the way to the adult, giving Welsch the opportunity to secure the permission. Although asking permission interrupts the child's activity, Welsch notes that, as soon as the parent gives the go-ahead, the child always quickly resumes his or her natural play.

■ ANIMALS ACTING LIKE PEOPLE

People commonly attribute human traits to animals. People respond to pictures in which pigs seem to smile or chimps look bored. Pet lovers often believe their animals exhibit human emotions, and treat their animals as if they were little human beings. Dog fanciers feed their pooches at the dinner table, dress them in sweaters for walks, and at night tuck them in velvet beds. One owner even taught her pet bird how to smoke; another fed her turtle ice cream. Such idiosyncrasies supply the material for good features.

■ THE INCONGRUOUS

A photo of nuns holding guns looks odd because nuns and guns don't seem to go together. A revolutionary soldier carrying a 35mm SLR camera would appear equally mismatched. And a woman sunbathing in a graveyard (see page 64) is certainly incongruous, as well. Such photos provide eye-catching features.

■ PEOPLE LIKE PEOPLE

Clearly, the feature does not restrict the photographer to picturing only kids, animals, and nuns, although whenever you can include these elements in a picture, the photo has a

A firefighter comforts a dog while the pooch's house burns. Obviously, people love animals, so animal pictures almost always make poignant features.
(Janet Worne, Lexington, Ky.)

A nun with a gun seems incongruous and therefore provides the subject for a good feature. The guns were actually donated to the camp the sisters administered. (Wide World Photos.)

When children imitate adults, the youngsters prove to be appealing feature subjects. (Photo by Ted Ancher, *Boston Herald.*)

People like people. And who can help but like these two grandmotherly women as they play a grown-up version of dress up? (Photo by Chas Metivier, for *The Gilroy* (Calif.) *Dispatch.*)

greater chance for publication. People of any age prove fascinating when they labor or learn, play or pray. Bob Kerns, a professor of photojournalism at the University of South Florida and a seasoned feature photographer, estimates that 90 percent of the feature pictures in papers across the country center on people.

DISCOVERING FEATURES

I asked several well-known feature photographers where they look for people features.

Ted Dully, who worked for the *Boston Globe*, says that when he had time he would head for the park or the zoo. "If you go where people collect, where things are happening, you have the deck loaded in your favor," he says.

Author of *The World I Love to See*, a book of feature photos, Ulrike Welsch explains that her best human interest pictures are shot outdoors. "Taking features outside is easier," she says, "than my having to go into a shop, introduce myself, and obtain permission from the owner."

■ KEEP A FRESH EYE

To keep a fresh eye for features, Welsch gets in her car and drives to an area she's never seen before. The experience is similar to traveling to a new country, even though the place might be only a few miles away. Whenever you live for a stretch of time in the same place and see the same things daily, you grow accustomed to your surroundings. Psychologists call this phenomenon "habituation." Feature photographers face this same problem. They come to accept as commonplace the unique aspects of the area they cover.

"Whenever I go to a new place, even if it's just a little way down the road, everything is novel," Welsch points out. She notices and photographs the differences between the new environment and her familiar territory. When she first arrives, her eye is sharpest. Those first impressions usually lead to her best photos. "I take pictures I might have overlooked if the subjects were in my back yard," she says.

When the *Christian Science Monitor*'s Gordon Converse looked for feature photo possibilities, he shunned the car altogether. Even if he was on his way to an assignment, he preferred to walk if he had the time. "If you are in a car whizzing through a neigh-

The photographer saw these boxes stacked on the sidewalk and anticipated that the mover would try to transport all of them at once, so he waited until the man returned and got this dramatic shot. The boxes, filled with styrofoam hats, were actually quite light. (Photo by Paul Miller, San Francisco.)

► Taking a camera underwater can provide readers an unusual view of an otherwise familiar swimming pool.
(Photo by John Zich, freelance.)

ᵧ For feature photos, look for the incongruous—like this sunbather in a cemetery on Block Island.
(Photo by Chip Gamertsfelder, *Kettering/Oakwood* (Ohio) *Times.*)

borhood, you miss seeing how the residents respond to one another. This interchange provides the basis for good features."

■ TAKE A CANDID

Constantine Manos, an outstanding freelance feature photographer for Magnum picture agency, looked for candid features during the year he spent shooting 500 rolls of black-and-white and color for a forty-projector slide show called "Where's Boston?" He says that he never posed or arranged any of the pictures contained in the show. Manos says he explored each area of the city on foot, introducing himself to the residents. "If you sneak up on people," he explains, "they have a right to resent you. Instead, if you say 'Hello,' and talk a bit about what you are doing, people will let you continue with your work. All my subjects are aware of me."

Yet Manos caught remarkably candid, uninhibited moments in these people's lives. One of his photos shows the bassoon player in a small chamber quintet leading the group

with complete abandon. Another shows a janitor nonchalantly erasing a blackboard containing a word so long and obscure that few Harvard professors would understand it.

Manos points out that photographers have the responsibility not to offend by their presence. "That is why appropriate clothing is important, and it is also the reason I seldom work with more than one camera at a time. It is especially bad when the second camera body has a big, impressive, fierce-looking telephoto lens." While out shooting, Manos once saw an old woman fleeing from a bearded youth with a big telephoto lens on a menacing SLR. "Why shouldn't she have felt intimidated?" Manos asks.

■ MAKE A PICTURE

Gordon Converse of the *Monitor* says that, while he is happiest when he can capture a candid, doing so is not always possible. "Sometimes you can just take a picture but other times you have to make a picture," he said.

"When there is nothing happening, I will create a situation to make something happen. For instance, while sitting in the office one slow day, I decided to do a story about the window washer at the all-glass John Hancock skyscraper. After I obtained permission, I crawled out on the window washer's platform sixty stories above the city. . . . I gingerly stood on top of the protective scaffolding. A security guard held onto my legs for my protection. As I put my camera to my eye, I could see the window washer in one corner of the frame with the beautiful reflecting surface of the skyscraper sweeping down below. This was the picture I wanted."

Going underwater at a local swimming pool is another way to "make" a picture. Here, the photographer went with a camera where few of his readers go—and in the process captured on film the unusual shot of divers plunging through the water.

Think of a Word

Rob Goebel's funny photo of a burly biker holding his tiny infant son could be either a portrait or a feature. This striking photograph did not originate from an assignment desk, nor was it associated with any writer's story. Instead, the photographer had given himself a set of self-assignments: illustrate different words photographically. Looking for ways to photograph the word "contrast," the photographer arranged a formal portrait of a biker and his young son, Harley. While it could accompany a story about the biker quite well, the picture stands on its own as a feature picture "made" by the photographer.

"Firsts"

Do you remember the first time you tried to play a new sport or learn a new skill or perform in public? From a child's first day of kindergarten to a teen-ager's first date to a parent's first child, firsts hold a special meaning. Someone trying to dance or ice skate for the first time is a potential subject for a good feature. First-timers are, by definition, inexperienced and often nervous. Things can go wrong—balls are dropped, toes get stepped on—all wonderfully human moments that make great feature pictures.

Sequences

Sometimes a single picture carries no humor, but a sequence, like a cartoon panel, can tell a more complete story. With a picture sequence, readers can see how things change over time, can compare before and after.

Pictorials and Weather

From Ansel Adams' shot of Half Dome in Yosemite Park to the standard strolling couple at sunset, pictorials run the gamut from dramatic to saccharin. Whether the shot shows sun glinting off a cityscape or the moon over a pastoral scene, however, readers love pictorials. After all, *National Geographic*, which is filled with beautiful scenics, publishes millions of copies a month.

While pictorials don't carry overriding news value, they do provide relief from the weightier elements of the news diet and sometimes confirm for readers why they choose to live in a particular place.

Dramatic light, usually found early in the morning or late in the afternoon, adds drama to most scenic pictures. Don't overlook, however, snow-frosted trees or fog-shrouded cliffs. In fact, thunder, lightning, and even rain can add picture-possible elements to an otherwise ordinary scene.

Likewise, people's responses to weather conditions—like the cross country skier below—can provide the ingredients for good features.

How people deal with adverse weather—like this cross country skier gliding by a lingerie store after a blizzard—makes for good feature pictures.
(Photo by Rich Riggins, The Patuxent (Md.) Publishing Co.)

The father-son portrait of "Bones" Kah and his young offspring "Harley Davidson" resulted from a series of self-assignments created by the photographer. This personal assignment was to illustrate the word "contrast." (Photo by Rob Goebel, *Indianapolis Star.*)

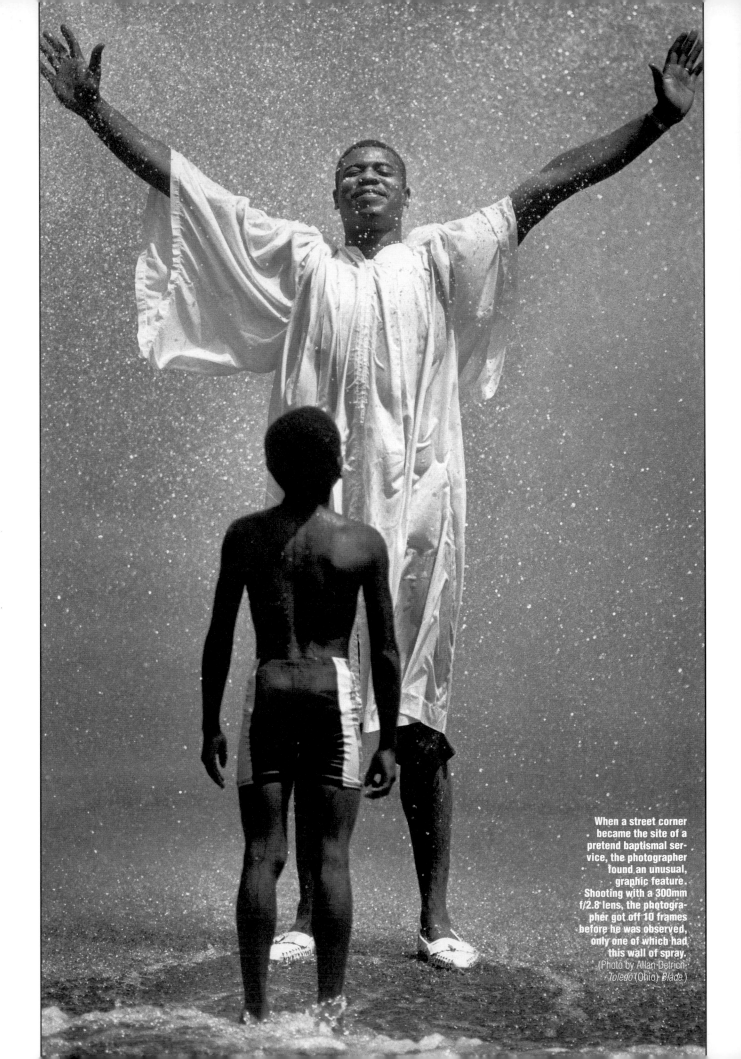

When a street corner became the site of a pretend baptismal service, the photographer found an unusual, graphic feature. Shooting with a 300mm f/2.8 lens, the photographer got off 10 frames before he was observed, only one of which had this wall of spray. (Photo by Allan Detrich, *Toledo* (Ohio) *Blade.*)

Unusual Occupations

Today, more and more people sit behind computers all day. With safe and predictable lives, seeing a rodeo rider atop a bull or even a window washer dangling from the 40th floor can provide many a reader a vicarious thrill.

Think of the character Walter Mitty, who daydreamed of an exciting life. With the camera, you can translate daydreams into real pictures. Danger. Excitement. Challenge. In his book, *The Great Picture Hunt,* Dave Labelle says to look for jobs that involve these elements. Avoid, obviously, the less energetic jobs like accounting and law. Test pilot, high-wire walker, steelworker. These are the jobs few of us will ever do but most of us would like to know about. Use the camera as a ticket into these adrenaline-filled occupations, and you will produce memorable feature pictures.

■ SPECIAL DAYS

Newspapers use special days to provide a hook for stories. Father's Day provides an excuse to write and photograph a story about the new dad, the single dad, the absentee dad, or multiple dads. Keying your feature pictures to a special day provides the news element of timeliness for your picture story. Besides designated days ranging from Secretaries" Day to Martin Luther King Day, you also can be assured that your publication will need pictures for Christmas, New Year's, and the Fourth of July. A common calendar that lists the upcoming holidays will provide an easy stimulus for feature ideas. The challenge for you is to come up with new images about holidays that have been photographed almost from the time the camera was invented.

■ AVOID THE TRITE

The bread-and-butter feature in today's newspaper is still the pretty child playing in the park or the chimp clowning at the zoo. Photographers take pictures of kids and animals so often that these topics have become trite.

Robert Garvin, writing in *Journalism Quarterly*, explains the genesis of the unsubstantial feature picture. "I have known picture editors (including myself up until ten years ago) who, on a dull afternoon, assign a photographer to walk around town and photograph anything he sees. What does he see? On an August day, he sees a small boy in the spray of a fire hydrant, or a group of tenement dwellers sitting on a fire escape. These are so obvious that every passer-by has seen them in the newspaper for the last forty

years. If there is no thought and preparation, one cannot expect striking pictures with more lasting merit."

When Arthur Goldsmith, an editor for *Popular Photography* magazine, judged the Pictures of the Year Contest, he concluded that pictures in the feature category tended to be hackneyed. He wrote, "Feature pictures often mean space fillers for a slow news day. Here are the visual puns, the cornball, the humorous, the sentimental, the offbeat. (Greased pigs and belly dancers were especially big during this year's competition.)"

Goldsmith said editors divide the photo world into two camps. "Either an event is hard news, which usually means violence, death, horror, confrontation, etc., or the event is a 'feature,' meaning something that appeals to our warm, furry sentimentality. But between the two extremes, the agony of the spot-news disaster and the ecstasy of the feature picture, lies that great amorphous zone that is most of our life."

DEVELOPING A FEATURE BEAT

How can the photographer tackle that great amorphous zone outlined by Goldsmith? If photographers hope to produce meaningful features, the answer lies in developing their own specialty area—their own beat.

For years writers have pried loose news by covering a beat. Typical beats include police, hospital, and courts. Reporters on police beats check the precinct headquarters each day to see what is going on. They look over the police blotter and talk to the sergeant to find out if anyone reported a major or unusual crime during the night. Getting the inside track on current investigations, reporters find out about possible suspects. They know when the police plan to carry out a gambling raid or drug bust. They also get to know the personalities in the department—the seasoned police officer as well as the new rookie fresh from the police academy. From these contacts and observations, beat reporters don't just react to the news; instead they can interpret and predict it. If the police go on strike, they can explain why. If a cop dies in the line of duty, they can write a story based on personal knowledge of the officer.

Feature photographers can also cover a beat, but rather than choosing the police, hospital, or courts, they might select education, science, medicine, or religion.

■ GETTING THE IDEA

Sometimes a beat can grow out of one story. While walking in the Castro section of San Francisco, I noticed that people were sewing large, colorful quilts inside a storefront. I

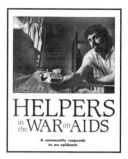

HELPERS
in the WAR on AIDS

A community responds to an epidemic

walked in and asked what was going on. The scene looked like a cross between an old-time sewing bee and a sweatshop factory. One of the volunteers explained that each quilt contained the name of someone who had died from AIDS. Volunteers were sewing quilts to remember famous people like Liberace and Rock Hudson, as well as personal friends, lovers, and relatives who had died from this dread disease. My guide said that eventually the volunteers would assemble all the individual quilts together, forming a massive mosaic that would be displayed in Washington, D.C. The quilts would provide a memorial to those who had died from AIDS. The final piece, which eventually measured more than two football fields in size, would bring home the enormity of the epidemic that some have called a modern-day plague.

According to my volunteer guide, neither the individual quilts nor the mosaic had ever been exhibited at that time. Nor had stories appeared in the national press about this effort called "The Names Project." I called M.C. Marden, the photo editor at *People* magazine, to see if she would be interested in a story. Eventually I received an assignment to photograph Cleve Jones, the founder of the project, as well as to photograph several of the individual memorial quilts.

After the quilt story appeared in *People*, the magazine assigned me to another "AIDS story." Rita Rockett, as she is known in San Francisco, throws a fancy catered brunch every other Sunday for AIDS patients on Ward 5A of San Francisco General Hospital. She brings a breath of sophistication and fun into the hospital's AIDS Ward every other weekend.

The Names Project and Rita Rockett sparked my interest in the San Francisco community that had developed to support people with AIDS. In the face of no known cure for AIDS, this diverse set of groups had sprung up to help the growing number of people afflicted with the deadly disease.

Past Stories on the Topic

Over the previous few years, I had seen several excellent stories about AIDS. The earliest I remembered was by Steve Ringman for the *San Francisco Chronicle*. I also had seen memorable stories photographed by Cheryl Nuss for the *San Jose Mercury News* and Alon Reininger for Contact Press Images. All these stories were moving. All concentrated on the patients, showing their battles against the agonizing deaths they were facing.

I was interested in developing a new angle on the story—a series of vignettes about people who help people with AIDS.

When a group of photo-journalists collaborated on a beat focusing on helpers in the war on AIDS, a host of stories unfurled, including one about volunteers who bring food to people too sick to cook.
(Photo by Mary Calvert, *Oakland* (Calif.) *Tribune*.)

The focus would be on the outpouring of support that had cropped up in the Bay Area to provide emotional, physical, and economic help to people with the incurable disease. The project was eventually called "Helpers in the War on AIDS."

While the original identification and later unraveling of the cause of AIDS provided the basis of important news stories, approaching the issue from the viewpoint of the helpers gave the story a new twist. Readers will look at only so many stories on a topic about dying and death, but they will look at and read stories of people who are willing to put themselves on the line to help others. By emphasizing the life-affirming angle and by giving the story a feature slant rather than a news slant, I hoped readers would be drawn into a story that could otherwise be very depressing.

Organization

One photographer could photograph the AIDS beat. However, in this instance, "Helpers in the War on AIDS" became a group project at the journalism department of San Francisco State University. Each photographer researched, developed, and photographed three stories over a fourteen-week

period. In addition to taking pictures, all group members either worked with writers or provided the text for the story themselves.

Research

Before photography began on the project, the group brought in a number of experts in order to get story leads. Specialists ranged from the city's health department AIDS expert to journalists who had tracked the story over a long period of time. In addition, group members read Randy Shilts' book, ***And the Band Played On***, which analyzes the government's delayed and inadequate response to the growing epidemic. Other leads came from the classified listings in local gay newspapers. Chris Adams, a writer in the group, who has since died from the virus, provided a key link to the gay community.

Having a beat gives a focus to research. Research, in turn, allows you to go beyond the surface facets of an issue to investigate causes of a problem, solutions, and, usually, stories that other journalists have not already photographed or written about extensively.

■ INITIAL STORIES

To get a handle on such a large subject, the

Knowing how much people love their pets, volunteers for PAWS (Pets Are Wonderful Support) care for pets when their owners are in the hospital and then help find new homes if necessary when the owners die.
(Photo by Mary Calvert, *Oakland* (Calif.) *Tribune*.)

photographers divided the topic into sections including medicine, religion, alternative healing approaches, minorities, physical support, emotional support, and so forth. Once the photographers selected subject areas, they began making telephone calls—and telephone calls—and telephone calls. Then the photojournalists arranged for meetings with the subjects. Often these meetings involved no photography at all. In fact, for one story, photographer Anne Wells started by volunteering at the first private nursing home for AIDS patients on the West Coast.

Another of Wells' stories was called "The Godfather," about a man who raised money and then made wishes come true for hospital-bound AIDS patients. If a patient needed a TV, The Godfather would provide it. If a patient needed a bathrobe, The Godfather would bring one. Another photographer, Kim Gerbich, worked on a story eventually called "Mamacita of the AIDS World," which centered on a female social worker who cared for homeless AIDS patients living in a run-down, inner-city transient's hotel. A third member of the team, Mary Calvert, photographed a woman who cared for the pets of people with AIDS. Her organization, called PAWS (Pets Are Wonderful Support) supplied food for pets of people with AIDS and took the animals to visit the sick people in the hospital. Calvert also followed the work of volunteers for "Project Open Hand," an organization that provides meals for shut-in people with AIDS. (See previous spread.)

In the AIDS Ward itself, a nurse allowed herself to be the subject of a story. Photographer Yvonne Soy tried to depict how a nurse works with people day after day knowing they will not live much longer. The project's story list included a makeup artist who helped camouflage the ugly purple scars of Kaposi's sarcoma that sometimes afflict people with AIDS. The list also included a story about a faith healer and her work with the sick.

The story list grew as the photographers dug into the subject. Everyone knew someone who was helping out in the AIDS community. Soon the photographers started to uncover stories about people who helped prisoners with AIDS and workers who helped teen-age prostitutes avoid AIDS.

Start-up Problems

After the photographers uncovered the initial

One story focused on a nurse who volunteered to work in the AIDS Ward of San Franoisoo General Hospital.
(Photo by Yvonne Soy.)

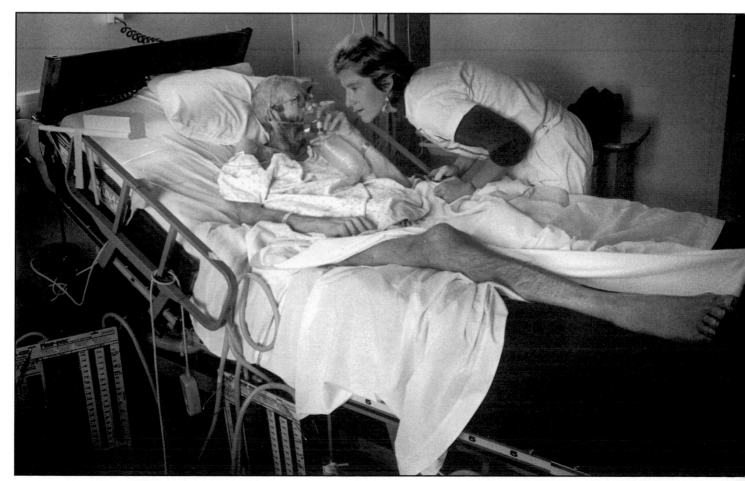

leads for their stories, problems started to crop up. While many of the helpers were happy to have their pictures taken, sometimes their friends with AIDS did not want photos of themselves published. Some didn't want out-of-town friends to see them scarred by Kaposi's sarcoma. Others didn't want people to know they were gay. Sometimes, the photographer would start on a topic, begin photographing the relationship between a helper and a patient, and then suddenly the patient would die. The story would end before it began. In addition, hospitals worried about lawsuits if the photos were published—even though the photographers got photo release forms from every subject. Altogether, "Helpers in the War on AIDS" was a difficult story to photograph.

One Story Leads to Another

For good beat coverage, besides reading daily papers like the *San Francisco Chronicle* and *Examiner* and the special-interest gay papers like the *Bay Area Reporter* and the *Sentinel*, the photographers returned to their primary sources week after week for new leads. Sources such as research experts, specialized doctors, hotline workers, counselors, and friends with AIDS supplied suggestions for new stories.

Sometimes when working on a beat, photographers may find that the first story doesn't pan out. But it may lead to another, even better opportunity—an opportunity a photographer might not have had without developing contacts in the field.

For example, while researching one story for the project, photographer Sibylla Herbrich spoke at length with Ernie, who had AIDS. She asked him if he knew anyone doing extraordinary work with people who had the disease. He told the photographer that she must meet Annemarie.

After getting to know the photographer, Annemarie Madison, a striking woman with long silver hair and a Mother Teresa smile, took the photographer with her as she went day after day to see her "boys." Annemarie's boys were men who, a few months earlier, had been in the prime of their lives. Now they were near death. As a volunteer with the San Francisco Home and Health Care Hospice, Annemarie changed the men's beds, listened to their complaints and fears, and wiped saliva from their mouths. Whatever they needed, she provided. She was both a substitute mother and a father confessor. She was there to ease their pain and to provide dignity to their deaths.

No pictures at first. In the beginning, Herbrich came to know Annemarie and her "boys" before she brought out her camera. Then the photographer obtained permission from each person. Soon Herbrich was photographing everything.

One Monday, the photographer accompanied Annemarie to the hospital to see Ernie, the man who had told Herbrich about Annemarie in the first place. On Wednesday, when Herbrich returned with the hospice worker, Ernie looked much worse. His friends were in the hospital room. Herbrich later wrote about that day:

"On the afternoon of June 9, for the first time I saw someone die. Ernie Smith died of AIDS at the age of 56. I photographed the hours of his dying and for two days I could not process the film. I stared at the one little roll that contained him in life and also in death. He died in the moment of the 'black space' between two frames. . . . I didn't sleep for a long time."

Herbrich's story, along with others in the project were published as a 76-page magazine named *Helpers in the War on AIDS*. The project won the Sigma Delta Chi award for feature photography and tied for first place in the college division of the Robert F. Kennedy Awards for Coverage of the Disadvantaged.

INFORMATIVE FEATURES REQUIRE EXTENSIVE RESEARCH

For more informative features, such as those taken by group members of the "Helpers Project," you will need to perfect your skills as a reporter: (1) pick an area of specialization; (2) make contacts with experts in the field; and (3) become familiar with the issues and new trends on the subject. Once you hear about a story that sounds interesting, make arrangements to photograph it. Often you will need to return several times to secure complete coverage. After shooting the pictures, you can write the captions and submit the feature series. You might suggest to your editor that a more detailed story by a reporter would amplify your series of pictures. To assure more stories on the subject in the future, stay in touch with your sources of information. These contacts will tell you when something new happens that might make striking pictures.

Few newspapers will release photographers to work full time on their beats. Therefore, the photographer must fit his or her special beat around routine assignments. Developing a feature area rarely produces great pictures on the first day. The photographer needs time for research. In the long run, though, a photographer's beat will generate meaningful feature pictures that will remain permanently in the viewer's memory. ■

She's There When Men Die

Annemarie, a volunteer hospice worker, comforts Ernie during his dying moments. After his last breath, Annemarie provides emotional support for his friends and relatives. These pictures are part of a story that was the product of a photographer's beat.
(Photos by Sibylla Herbrich, San Francisco.)

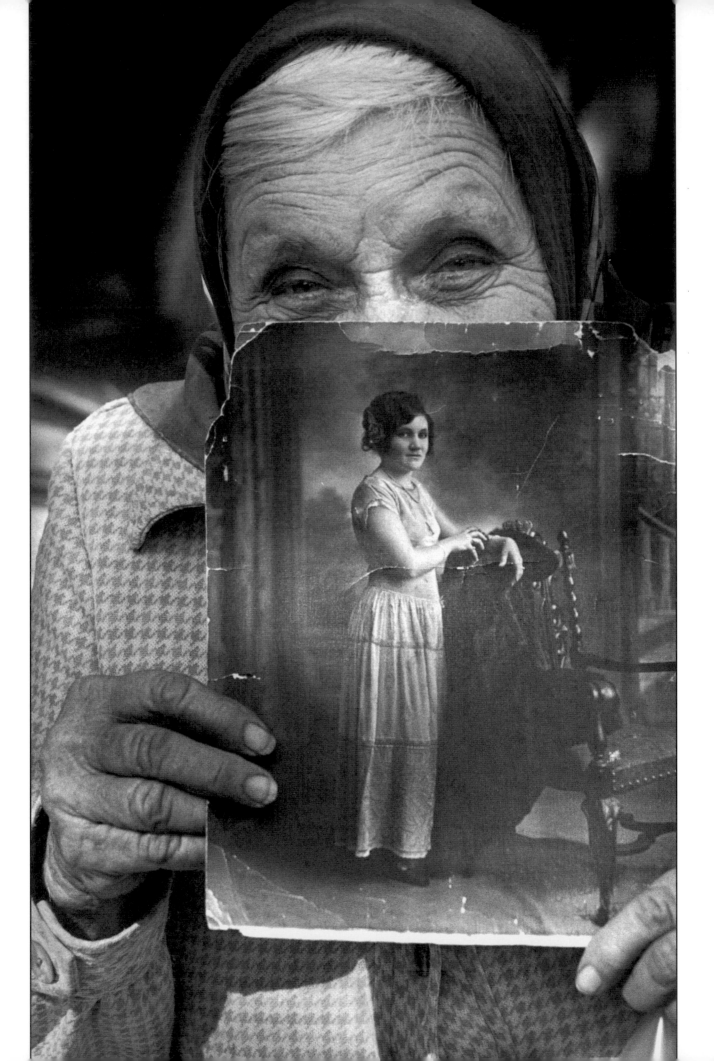

Portraits

CHAPTER 5

EVEN A MUG SHOT REVEALS CHARACTER

In the trade, journalists call a single picture of a person's face "a mug shot" or "a head shot" or "a head-and-shoulders." The casual, slightly derogatory terms indicate that the photo usually runs only about two inches square—one-column wide—in a newspaper or magazine. The photo is not meant to be a revealing study but merely to identify the subject. You might ask why editors print these little postage-stamp sized pictures. The editors respond that their readers want to see what people in the news look like. Whereas a one-column photo won't stand alone in the paper, with a caption the

Even a "mug shot" can take on character when the photographer watches for the best moment. Here, the photographer waited for this 80-year-old retired police officer to take a puff on his cigar.
(Photo by Michael Maher, *Lowell* (Mass.) *Sun.*)

By getting to know the woman through conversation, the photographer put her at ease. As part of the conversation, the woman showed a picture of herself taken many years ago.
(Photo by Timothy Bullard, *Grant's Pass Daily Courier.*)

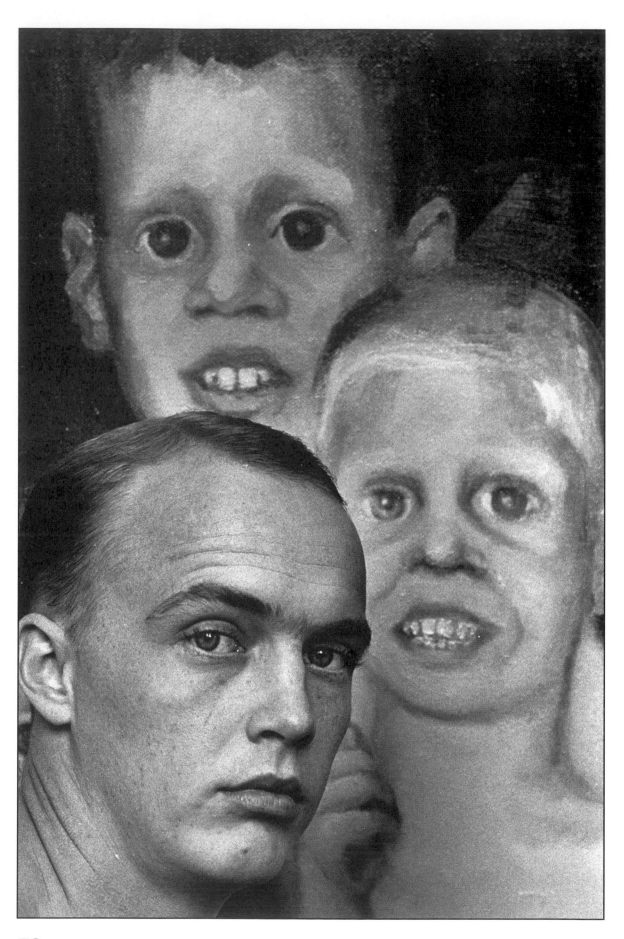

◀ **Eyes looking straight at the camera establish a strong bond between the reader and the artist in this picture. Also, this direct eye contact tells the reader that the picture is a portrait, not a candid.**
(Photo by Ken Kobré for the *Boston Phoenix*.)

photo will tell the reader about the subject's sex, age, and race. The mug shot also gives the reader an idea of the subject's personal characteristics, such as hair style, physical build, and general appearance.

And, finally, research consistently confirms that photographs accompanying stories cause people to read those stories.

When shooting the mug shot, the photographer runs into the danger of sloppy technique and composition. The photographer takes a few quick shots, figuring that the photo will be small and mistakes won't be noticed. Too often, however, the head shot assignment winds up being played as large as a half page

because no other picture is available. So, keep in mind that the mug shot of today might appear on a newspaper's front page tomorrow or become next week's magazine cover.

Tight and Simple

The purpose of the often-used mug shot is to provide a clear, well-lit record of a subject's face. Photographers find this type of portrait easy to take. With a 105mm lens on a 35mm camera, the photographer needs to get only about four or five feet away to fill the camera's viewfinder with the subject's face. A 200mm telephoto lens proves handy if the photographer's movements are restricted, and the photojournalist is relatively far from the subject as often happens at a speech or press conference. Most photographers avoid wide-angle lenses for mug shots, unless they want to exaggerate purposely a person's nose or forehead.

▼ **The director of the Ethnic Dance program was stiff and formal in her office. Once in the rehearsal hall, with the music playing in the background, she started to move to the music's beat.**
(Photo by Ken Kobré for the San Francisco State University Annual Report.)

In black-and-white, the subject will appear to blend or pop out, depending on which background the photographer chooses.

Variety

George Tames, a long-time Washington-based photographer for the *New York Times*, would shoot his subjects looking both left and right. "You never know on which side of the newspaper page the editor will place the head shot, and editors like to have the subject facing into the page."

In addition to a left and right shot, Tames provided his editors with a selection of photos showing different facial expressions. If the news story runs several days, such as in a murder trial, the editor will want to print for each issue slightly different head shots of the persons involved.

Of course, if the outcome of the event is tragic, the picture editor will not want a smiling mug shot to go with the final day's story.

PORTRAIT ELEMENTS

By means of pictures, the photojournalist tells a story about a subject. The portrait of a scientist shouldn't look like that of a steel-worker. An aggressive personality deserves a different portrait from a shy and retiring type.

Three elements add to the story-telling nature of a portrait. First, a subject's face, hands, and body position reflect the sitter's psychological state. Is the subject smiling or looking grim? Are his hands pulling at his beard or resting at his side? Is he standing awkwardly or comfortably?

Second, the location of the picture and props held by the subject tell the viewer something about the subject's profession, hobbies, and interests. A portrait taken in a dark factory, with the worker holding a wrench, says something different about the sitter than a portrait taken in a pristine office with the subject seated at a computer.

Third, an equally powerful message carried by the photo depends on the light and composition of the picture. A heavily shadowed portrait, for instance, might look foreboding. An off-balanced composition could add tension to the picture.

■ CLUES TO THE "INNER PERSON"
Face

Of all the elements in a photo, the face still carries a disproportionate amount of psychological weight. Studies show that children, almost from birth, recognize the basic elements of a face, including the eyes, nose, and mouth. Most people assume they can read something about a person's personality from his or her face. How often have you thought, "That man looks sneaky, I wouldn't trust him"? Or, "That person looks friendly, I'd like to meet her"—all reactions based on a glance at the person's face.

Whether true or not, people assume that the face is the "mirror of the soul." If the face is the soul's reflection, then the soul is multi-dimensional. Even the most sedate face reflects a surprising number of variations. Take a thirty-six-exposure roll of film of one person's face as she talks about her favorite topic. Note the number of distinctly different expressions the person exhibits. Is one frame of those thirty-six pictures true to the nature of the person? Have the others missed the essence of the underlying character of the subject? Arnold Newman says in his book *One Mind's Eye*, "I'm convinced that any photographic attempt to show the complete man is nonsense. We can only show what the man reveals."

The photojournalist usually selects an image of the subject talking, laughing, or frowning, an action coinciding with the thrust of the news story. When a recently appointed city manager expressed fear about his new job, the photo showed him with his hand massaging his wrinkled brow. A year later, a story in which the city manager talks about his accomplishments might show him talking and smiling. The photojournalist's portrait doesn't reveal a person's "true inner nature" as much as it reflects the subject's immediate response to his or her present success or predicament.

Eyes

Where should the subject look? Early journalism portraits taken around the turn of the century showed the sitter staring into the camera's lens during the prolonged time exposures. During the Depression, Farm Security Administration subjects seemed always to stare off into space. Portraits taken during the 1960s and 1970s often showed the subjects looking as if they were in action, never noticing the camera's presence.

Through the 1980s, portraits tended to return to the turn-of-the-century stare. Photographers felt that the viewer would be most involved with the subject of a portrait when the two made eye contact. Besides, photographers argued, when the subject looks straight into the camera's lens, the reader knows that the subject was aware of the photographer—that the photograph was not a candid moment. Eye contact helps the reader differentiate between an arranged portrait and a candid photo.

This convention—subject looking directly into the lens—is in the process of yielding to another. Face to face with so many subjects staring into the lens, some photographers in the 1990s are returning to the Depression-era approach in which the subject looks away from the camera into the distance. Like other stylistic variables that contribute to this kind of picture, this new convention is likely to change, as well.

Hands

Hands help tell the news in a nonverbal way. A news photographer covering a speech won't even bother to click the shutter until the lecturer raises a hand to make a point. When shooting a portrait, watch the individual's hands as she toys with her hair, holds her chin, or pushes up her cheek. A person chewing her fingernails reveals a certain amount of tension about the situation in which she finds herself.

Body Language

Desmond Morris wrote an excellent book, *Manwatching, A Field Guide to Human Behavior*, for those interested in improving their observational skills. Morris documented various types of gestures and signals that people use to express inner feelings. The way an individual stands, whether as straight as a West Point cadet or as bow-legged as a cowboy, might clue the reader about the subject's upbringing. Studying ways people communicate nonverbally can sensitize the photographer to good picture possibilities. (See page 79.) When body language speaks clearly, the photographer grabs the shot.

■ COMPOSITIONAL ELEMENTS ADD IMPACT
Background & Props

As with the selection of props, choice of background can transform an ordinary snapshot into a revealing portrait. Sometimes the subject knows just the right spot for a portrait. Other times the photographer must scout out the location. George Tames of the *New York Times* recalls using his reading of the day's news and the particular assignment to enter the senator's or representative's office with a "battle plan." By knowing his subject ahead of time, he said, "I can take control of the situation." Alfred Eisenstaedt, one of the original *Life* photographers, wrote, "By now I've learned that the most important thing to do when you photograph somebody in a room or outside is not look at the subject but at the background."

Tames and Eisenstaedt would concentrate on the background behind the subject for two reasons. One, the background details help report the story. The run-down shack of the sharecropper tells us about the farmer's problems. The plush office of a new corporate executive indicates one of the job's advantages. Two, the background affects the "readability" of a photo. Readability means that

Creative lighting often makes a portrait special. To achieve this portrait of the captain of a high school chess club, the photographer masked the soft box with a checkered pattern that reflects in the player's glasses and looks like a chess board.
(Rich Riggins, Patuxent Publishing Co., Columbia, Md.)

the subject must not get lost in the details of the environment. In a black-and-white photo, a dark subject can blend into a dark background, never to be seen again. You are about to photograph a white-haired man standing in front of a light wall. When you shoot the picture, the man's hair seems to disappear into the wall. To avoid this problem, place the man in front of a dark wall, and his hair will not disappear.

Because the world is colorful, the photographer might not remember that a red-shirted Santa Claus standing in front of a green Christmas tree background might blend together when photographed with black-and-white film. The reason for this is that red and green are different hues but can be of equal brightness; therefore, the film records them as nearly matching shades of gray. Santa Claus might look as if he were growing out of the tree in the black-and-white print. The photographer can improve readability by choosing a background setting with a tone that contrasts with the subject. You could place Santa Claus in front of a light-toned wall, for instance.

Light as well as background tone helps define the subject. If the person you are shooting has dark hair, the light hitting the back of the subject's head will create a highlight, thereby helping the subject stand out. If you could direct some light toward the back of Santa's head, the resulting hair light will help to separate Santa from the background.

A busy, multi-toned background can clutter up any picture, distracting the viewer's attention from the main event. Keep in mind that a further complicating factor is that the subject-background tonal difference decreases when the photo is reproduced on coarse newsprint.

On the other hand, symbolic props help tell stories. For a portrait of a person who is a photographer, teacher, and writer, portraitists used a range of props including cameras, tripods, loupes, light tables, film boxes, and cable releases to let readers know aspects of the sitter's life and profession.

Lighting

Light can set the mood of a picture. When photographers shoot a picture that is lit brightly but has only a few shadows, the photo is called "high-key." In pictures of brides, photographers often employ high-key lighting because they want to give an upbeat mood to the photo.

When a somber effect is desired, however, the photographer chooses lighting that will leave large areas of the picture in shadow. The photo's dominant tones are dark gray and black. At night, a tough police chief involved in a crime clean-up story might be photographed with the available light of a street corner. The lighting's moody character coincides with the story's thrust.

To add depth to a subject's face, arrange the person so that the main light, whether it is flood, flash, or window, falls toward the side of his or her face. Side light, as compared with direct frontal light, adds a roundness and three-dimensional quality to the mini-portrait. Side light also emphasizes the textural details of the face—a technique especially suited for bringing out the character lines in a person's features.

Alternatively, Hollywood photographers light starlets with a large flat light located near the camera's lens to eliminate any shadows. Shadowless light, sometimes called "butterfly" lighting, tends to eliminate wrinkles, giving a youthful look to the subject in the photo.

Rich Riggins of the Patuxent Publishing Company combined both lighting and props in his portrait of a young chess player. Riggins masked a softbox with taped squares and used it as the main light source. In the resulting picture, the young man's glasses appear to reflect the chess board. (See more on lighting in Chapter 11, "Strobe.")

Composition

Suppose your editor assigns you to photograph a banker. You size up the situation and decide to show the banker as a stable person in the community. You might want to position the person in the middle of the frame, lending balance and therefore dignity to the picture. You have used composition to help tell your picture story, conveying to the reader the point you wish to make about the banker.

Suppose, on another day, you are assigned to photograph the director of the Little Theater, an off-beat dramatic group. You want your picture of the director to be as exciting and tension-producing as a good Hitchcock thriller. By placing the director of the theater on the edge of your viewfinder and leaving the remaining area black, you can produce an off-balanced picture that gives added visual suspense to a photo.

The effect of the final picture changes, depending on whether the photographer fills the frame with the sitter's face or stands back for a full-length portrait. An extreme close-up, for instance, appears to bring the subject so near that the viewer gets the feeling of unusual intimacy with the sitter.

When I was shooting a portrait of an artist in his studio, I noticed the similarity between his face and those of the young boys he was painting. By carefully locating the artist in front of one of his portraits, I was able to integrate the painter's head with the faces of the young boys on the canvas (see page 78). The photograph's composition, which flattens the space between the subject and the background, toys with the notion of which elements are real and which are painted.

ENVIRONMENTAL DETAILS TELL A STORY

From a mug shot or a studio portrait or even from a photograph of an individual animatedly engaged in conversation, the viewer can't tell a banker from a bandit, a president from a prisoner. The wrinkles of a brow or the set of the eyes reveal little about a subject's past, profession, or newsworthiness. An environmental portrait, however, supplies enough details with props and choice of background to let the reader know something about the lifestyle of the sitter. In an environmental portrait, the subject is photographed at home, at the office, or on location, whichever place best reflects the story's theme. As in a traditional studio portrait, the environmental photo generally has the subject look directly into the camera. But rather than sitting the subject before a plain seamless paper background, as in a studio portrait, an environmental portrait positions the person amid the everyday objects of his or her life.

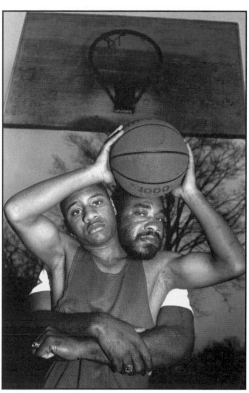

To illustrate how a group of teenagers saw their futures, the photographer posed them in revealing parts of their own environments.
(Photos by Robert Cohen, *Memphis* (Tenn.) *Commercial Appeal.*)

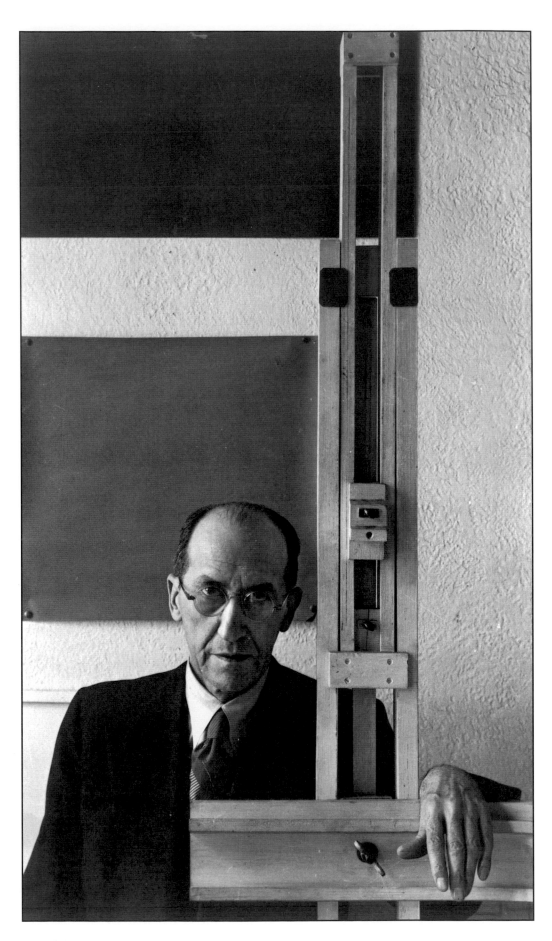

▲ This piece by Piet Mondrian, "Composition," shows the distinctive lines and rectangular blocks the painter used to compose his paintings. (The Museum of Modern Art, New York. The Sidney and Harriet Janis Collection.)

► In this portrait of Piet Mondrian, the photographer used sheets of paper and a painter's easel to reflect the artist's painting style. A comparison of the artist's work (ABOVE) shows the inspiration for the photographic portrait. (© Arnold Newman.)

For Black History Month, editors assigned Robert Cohen of the *Memphis* (Tenn.) *Commercial Appeal* to take pictures to accompany a series of articles about how African-American teenagers and their families view the future. (See page 83.) Cohen shot environmental portraits rather than documentary candids so that a visual consistency would hold the series together as each story ran.

For each portrait, Cohen tried to convey something about the subject's present life and future hopes. For example, one young man viewed joining ROTC as a way to escape his impoverished surroundings. Dressed in his sharp new uniform, the young man salutes amid the squalor of his housing project. Few viewers would miss the contrast. Another young man saw his father, with whom he regularly played basketball, as the key to his future. Cohen posed the two on the neighborhood courts. A mirror provided the device for a third picture, in which a family, bathed in light, is reflected in the mirror with the dark housing project in the background—their future was out of the housing project.

■ ARNOLD NEWMAN: SYMBOLS REINFORCE THEME

Arnold Newman, a master of the environmental portrait who has taken the official photographs of U.S. presidents, famous artists, and corporate executives, often arranges his portraits so the background dominates. The subject in the foreground is relatively small. One famous portrait of Professor Walter Rosenblith of the Massachusetts Institute of Technology shows him wearing headphones with an oscilloscope in the foreground and a maze-like baffle system in the background. The professor's face occupies only a small part of the picture while the lines of the experimental chamber dominate the picture.

Newman says that the image of the subject is important, "but alone it is not enough. We must also show the subject's relationship to the world." Newman goes on to say that "twentieth-century man must be thought of in terms of the houses he lives in, and places he works, in terms of the kind of light the windows in these places let through and by which we see him every day."

The power of Newman's photos lies in his choice of symbolic environmental details that not only show the sitter's profession but also the style of his or her work. For example, Newman photographed the modern artist Piet Mondrian, known for his exploration of pure shape and color, at his easel. (See opposite page.) By creating a composition with the vertical bar of the easel juxtaposed against rectangular shapes on the wall, Newman's portrait of Mondrian suggested the artist's own style.

In the daring and stylistically original portrait of the Beatles' John Lennon and his wife Yoko Ono, the photographer explored the couple's intense psychological relationship.
(Photo by Annie Leibovitz, *Rolling Stone*.)

Portraits don't always have to be an individual picture. In this case, this person's transformation from man to woman provides a more telling psychological portrait than any single picture could.
(Photos by Sibylla Herbrich, San Francisco.)

For a portrait of Dr. Kurt Gödel of the Institute for Advanced Study, Newman arranged the sitter in front of an empty blackboard. The blackboard says to the reader, "Gödel—the academician"; the empty board says, "Gödel—the high-level thinker."

Although Newman might not think of himself as a photojournalist, his approach to the portrait is reportorial. He goes beyond the lines in the subject's face to tell his audience something about the person's work and life.

Technically, the environmental portrait does not differ from any other portrait. The photographer can use a normal or, if necessary, a wide-angle lens. Because the photographer wants to record the environmental background sharply, maximum depth of field is needed. You can increase the depth of field by stopping down the aperture to a smaller opening. This, however, requires a longer shutter speed. The camera on a tripod gives the photographer freedom to use longer exposures—if the subject can hold still.

■ ANNIE LEIBOVITZ: BUILDING A PORTRAIT

For portraits of personalities like Mick Jagger or Paul Newman, the viewer has a frame of reference—the viewer knows the face, has seen the personality on television, in the movies, and on magazine covers. By the time Annie Leibovitz, who has shot many covers for *Rolling Stone* and *Vanity Fair*, photographs the celebrity, the viewer probably has read about the person in gossip columns or heard interviews on talk shows.

Leibovitz tries to go past a topographic map of the face. Her pictures ask the questions: What makes this person famous? What is the psychological factor that separates this individual from others in the field?

Leibovitz is not interested in showing the viewer details of the subject's life or lifestyle. She does not depend on found items in a celebrity's house or office on which to build the picture à la Arnold Newman. She is not waiting and watching for a candid moment in the style of Cartier-Bresson. Rather, she imagines what the picture ought to look like. Then she creates that look.

For example, Leibovitz photographed Dennis Connor, captain of the winning America's Cup racing team, wearing a red, white, and blue shirt, wading in a pond, and sailing a toy boat. Although the America's Cup challenge represents millions of dollars in investments and winnings, the picture caught Connor's little-boy spirit. Leibovitz did not happen upon Connor wading one afternoon in the pond. She and her stylist

FIVE PHOTOGRAPHERS WHO MAKE SUBJECTS UNCOMFORTABLE

THE SHERMAN TANK

"My idea or nothing," this photographer implies. A control freak by nature, this photographer won't take a hint, even when the subject explains that the photographer's idea is off-base and does not reflect the reason the subject is in the news.

Your subject should be your collaborator in the portrait. If you're experiencing resistance to your ideas, back off—and listen. Involving your subject from the start will avoid this kind of problem.

LOST AT SEA

"Why am I here?" the photographer's actions suggest. This photographer has no idea about why the subject is in the news, has not scouted the environment, nor found story-telling props. "What should I shoot?" hardly gives a subject much confidence. "Look happy" rarely elicits a natural-looking expression.

Do your homework ahead of time. You'll not only preserve your subject's time and patience, but you'll demonstrate that you're a real news professional.

ALL THUMBS

"Hold it a little longer," says this photographer. Meanwhile, the camera droops forward on the insufficiently tightened tripod as the light stand and strobe waver precariously off to the side.

"Control your equipment before it controls you"

should be the photographer's motto. Obviously, become familiar with your equipment—especially the tripod—before starting a shooting session.

ALL BUSINESS

With cameras blazing, the session starts. No time wasted. Click, click.

Hold on. Get to know your subject. Why not spend a few minutes forming a human bond? You might learn a revealing detail that will make the portrait special. Plus, most people are nervous about having their picture taken. Even a small comment like "Nice jacket" can help some people feel more relaxed. By straightening a tie or smoothing a collar, you'll show your subjects that you're not out to visually destroy them.

MOTOR DRIVE MANIAC

"Click whoosh, click whoosh, click whoosh." The photographer hits the camera's motor drive, shoots off a burst of frames, and barely looks at the subject. Without watching the subject's eyes, hands, lips, or general body language, this shooter is likely to miss genuine impromptu moments by not paying attention to the subject's gestures or expressions.

Leave your motor drive to sports or news events. For portraits, put the camera on a tripod, focus, and then look over the top of the camera body to maintain eye contact during the session. Refocus and reframe only when the subject moves.

Photographers can find an infinite number of ways to photograph anyone. The only limitations are the photographer's creativity and the subject's time and patience. Props in these pictures help tell that this subject is a photojournalist, a teacher, and a writer.

(FROM LEFT TO RIGHT, PHOTOS BY:
FIRST ROW: Joan M. Williams, Astrid Riecken, Eric Slomanson, Sarah Prall. SECOND ROW: Eli Bishop, Kaia Means, Herman Segovia, J. Michael Staub. THIRD ROW: Stephanie Martin, Angela Hayes, Nelson Carrrera, Bob Farley.
FOURTH ROW: Naomi Malig, unknown, Cindy Russell, Gary Nougues. FIFTH ROW: LuAnne Cadd, unknown, Joan Williams.

bought the props, dictated the clothes, and located the perfect pond.

Leibovitz builds rather than takes a picture. In conjunction with her subject, she dreams up a visually startling way to portray that individual. Leibovitz, for example, photographed actress Whoopi Goldberg in a white bathtub filled with milk. The *Vanity Fair* photographer has a remarkable ability to coax celebrities to cooperate. She persuaded John Lennon to lie, nude, curled in a fetal position around his wife, Yoko Ono (see page 85). She cajoled Meryl Streep, the multifaceted actress, to wear white face paint while pulling out the skin of her cheek as if it were a rubber mask.

Leibovitz's pictures lie somewhere between psychological portraits and photo illustrations. Her mannered, stylized approach has influenced many other magazine and newspaper photographers.

PUTTING YOUR SUBJECT AT EASE

If a subject doesn't feel comfortable, the best photojournalistic techniques in the world won't produce a revealing portrait. When a photographer disappears behind the camera, even if it is a relatively small 35mm, the photographer loses eye contact with the subject.

The subject is left alone to respond to a piece of coated glass and a black mechanical box, items not conducive to stimulating conversation. To loosen up and relax the subject, each photographer has developed a personal technique. Keep in mind that an approach that works for one photographer might not work for you. Here are some choices to consider.

■ STIMULATING A REACTION

Chip Maury, director of photography at the *Indianapolis Star,* used to work for the wire services and had little time to wait around for photos. He used the shock approach. When taking a head shot of a staid individual, he would ask the person to share a favorite four-letter word. The effect certainly works better than asking the person to say "cheese." For another approach, I ask the person to say the "ABCs" in a conversational tone. No subject thus far has reached "Z" without laughing.

■ CREATIVE BOREDOM

When you have time, the boredom technique works well; if you hang around long enough, often the subject gets tired of posing, and you can shoot natural-looking photos that result in casual, relaxed portraits.

The photographer took command of this situation by having a person dress up in the gorilla suit and pose between the owners of the costume shop.
(Photo by Sandy Shriver.)

For a creative group portrait of San Jose State's *Spartan Daily* photo staff, everyone jumped into the university's long-awaited new pool for an underwater picture. After many tries, the photographer was able to get a photo of the whole staff at the same time. (Photo by Michael Burke, *Redding* (Calif.) *Record Searchlight.*)

Arthur Grace, who has been a staffer for both *Time* and *Newsweek* and the photographer for the book **The Comedians**, says "once you put people in a location, you just wait and they will get lost in their own thoughts." Grace just sits there. "Maybe I'll take one frame to make them think that I've started, but I haven't." Eventually, the subjects get so bored they forget they are having their picture taken and they relax. That's when Grace goes to work.

■ CONVERSATION

One of the most enjoyable aspects of photojournalism is meeting different kinds of people. Conversations with subjects often loosen them up. During a shooting session, the talk usually turns to why the person is in the news. When they become engrossed in explaining their involvement, they forget about the camera.

Sometimes photographers should research their subject. To photograph President Carter upon his arrival in Washington, D.C., Tames of the *New York Times* read Carter's book, **Why Not the Best**. Tames tried to know enough about his subject for a preconceived notion of "what I was going to get before I got there." Tames would calm his subjects down with "strokes." He massaged their egos—who can resist that? Tames would put subjects at ease because they would sense he was their friend. "I have never deliberately made a bad picture of anyone," he once said. His media-conscious subjects knew Tames' reputation for honesty. Tames also never shot

a roll to the end because he found that as soon as he put his camera down, the conversation would liven up. He used those last frames to catch the subject—uninhibited and animated.

■ TAKE COMMAND

The difference between the veteran Tames and a shy young photographer is that the *New York Times'* cameraman took command of the situation rather than holding back. "You have to learn to influence politicians in a way that they will do what you want them to do," he explains. He was frank with them. He would tell a senator, "Look, this is only going to run one column, I need you to stand by the window and smoke your pipe."

The senator responded because Tames exuded professionalism. Tames says, "Anytime I could control the situation I did. I shot candids only when I had to." But Tames also knew when not to push his subjects too far. "I could tell immediately when enough is enough," he says.

■ USE A TRIPOD

Alfred Eisenstaedt emphasizes the psychological side of the portraitist. "You have to be able to sense very quickly when you meet someone whether you can back-slap him and call him by his first name right away, or whether you must be reserved and formal on your first meeting." Sensitive to his subject, Eisenstaedt avoids the disruption of picking up and putting down the camera by using the tripod and cable release technique. He puts his camera on a tripod and focuses, which frees him to talk directly and keep eye contact with his subject while snapping pictures. "For me," he says, "this method often gives the most relaxed pictures."

John Loengard, who was a staff photographer for the old *Life* and later its director of photography, now shoots regularly for the monthly version. He takes all his indoor portraits with his camera atop a tripod. In fact, he carries along no strobes or other lighting equipment when he goes on assignment. He feels artificial lighting looks artificial.

Loengard places his subjects near a window or some other source of interesting light and uses the tripod to take slow, deliberate pictures. The tripod allows him control over the depth-of-field so that he can manipulate the sharpness of the background. He says that, as long as the subject doesn't move, he can make an interesting portrait with a minimum of equipment and time. In fact, subjects can remain still for long periods. Mathew Brady took sharp pictures of Abraham Lincoln using well over a minute-long exposure.

GROUP PORTRAITS
■ SHOW ALL THE FACES

A prime requirement of a formal group picture is that it shows, as clearly as possible, each person's face. This takes careful planning. Arranging people shoulder to shoulder might work, but if the group grows to more than a few people, the line will be too long, and each person's face will appear small in the final image. Instead, you could arrange the people in one row behind the other. Typically, you want to have short people in front and the taller ones in back. With a large group like a band or a football team, you have little choice but to arrange the members, military style, at different levels but in a fixed formation.

■ SOFT LIGHT IS BEST

For group portraits, soft light that creates the minimum of shadows is usually the most effective. If you can, avoid lighting that creates strong, well-defined shadows typical of a bright, sunny day. When you must take a large group portrait on a perfectly clear day, look for the open shade of a tree or large building to provide even lighting.

■ ADD ZEST TO SMALL-GROUP PORTRAITS
- **Try Different Levels.** When the group is limited to between three and eight members, creativity is possible. Try to keep each person's head on a different level. By having them kneel, sit, and stand, you usually can arrange an attractive juxtaposition of heads so that each is spatially located

on a different elevation. The closeness of the bodies holds the picture together; the staggered arrangement adds visual interest.
- **Dress Alike.** A group of clowns in costume could lighten up a graduation picture at the Ringling Brothers Clown School.
- **Hand 'em Props.** A cooking class holding spatulas and saucepans would serve up an interesting picture of their activities.
- **Watch the Background.** Women welders in front of the foundry where they work would reinforce the viewer's understanding of this group's profession.
- **Pose Carries Information.** A group of teen-agers slouching in front of a low-slung car tells a different story than the same group posed sitting in classroom chairs.

"JUST ONE MORE"
Finally, knowing the location of the door is just as important as knowing where the shutter is. With a few frames left at the end of the roll (just in case) you should pack your gear before you wear out your welcome. Photographers have a bad reputation for asking for just one more picture. Leave in good standing because you never know when your subject will be in the news again and you will need to make a new portrait. ■

In a group portrait, try to stagger the placement of heads to allow each to occupy a different level. This arrangement maximizes the size of each face. (Photo by Vincent S. D'Addario, Springfield (Mass.) Newspapers.)

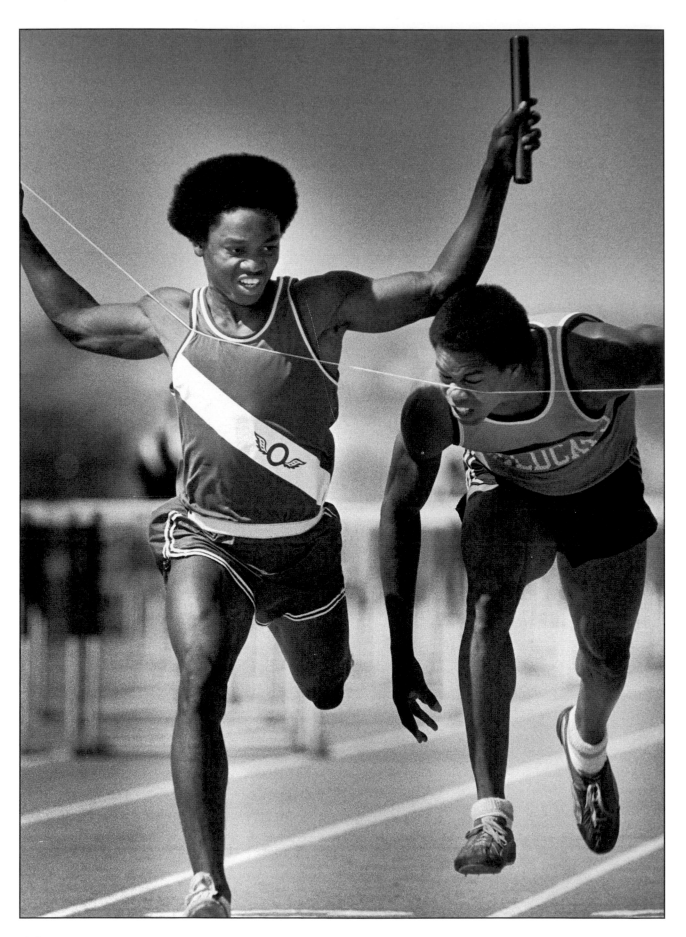

Sports

Sports photographers are like athletes. They must have the aim of a football quarterback, the reflexes of a basketball guard, and the concentration of a tennis player.

Sports photographers talk about getting in slumps just as baseball players who are having trouble at the plate get into ruts.

"At the beginning of the season I'm rusty," says Brad Mangin, a sports freelancer whose clients include *Sports Illustrated*

By zone-focusing on the finish line, you are guaranteed a sharp photo of the winning runner. A check of your depth-of-field scale will tell you how far the range of sharpness in the picture extends. (Photo by Patrick Downs, *Los Angeles Times*.)

and the National Basketball Associated Photos.

"After a few games I get into the groove.

Some newspapers rotate their staffs on sports

assignments, so it's hard for them to find a groove."

Just as players on the field cannot afford to lose their concentration, so photographers on the sidelines must be aware of every subtle movement in the game. Mangin tries to avoid talking to other photographers on the sidelines but sometimes slips up. "I was socializing with Kim Komenich from the *Examiner*," he confides, "and we both missed a key play at last week's home opener." Pam Schuyler, who photographed for the Associated Press and produced a book about the Celtics basketball team, says that she won't even sit next to other photographers when she is shooting basketball pictures because the other photographers distract her too much.

■ TIMELY PHOTOS PARAMOUNT

Sports photographers strive to create an image on film that captures in a unique way the fast-paced action and drama of competition. A good sports photo and a well-written news story have similar characteristics: both are timely and both have high reader interest.

Timeliness in a sports picture is essential. Nobody cares about a week-old game score, but millions of viewers stay up to see scores on the eleven o'clock newscast. Interest is so high in sports that millions of people watch the World Series on television, and even more see the summer and winter Olympics.

Sports is big business, and the financial side of football or baseball rates as much attention as any other business story. Players are bought, sold, and traded for millions of dollars: clubs approach the bidding block, ready to spend millions for promising superstars. Readers want to see pictures of these superstars sinking a basket, knocking a home run, or winning a marathon. Editors are aware of this star-gazing. During my interview with George Riley, who shoots for UPI, he commented that "a paper is more likely to run a picture of a top star hitting a home run than a lesser player doing the same thing, even if the pictures are equally good."

So sports photographers have to become sports fans; they must read regularly the sports section of the paper to learn who the top stars are, and what newsy things have happened to them lately. Frank O'Brien, who shot for the *Boston Globe* for many years, would comb the sports pages every day to pick up information on a player he might have to cover. He looked for stories about injured players and major trades, about fights and feuds among players and between players and coaches, about impending records,

and about disputes over money. O'Brien also would study the paper to see if a player was having a hot streak that week. This news angle adds an extra dimension to a sports photo. If a player has made news on the sidelines, readers will want to see what that player will do on the court or the field.

When Hank Aaron hit his 715th home run to break Babe Ruth's career record, every camera in the stands clicked because the event was big news. A broken record is history in the making. As sportswriter George Sullivan told me, "One job of the newspaper is to record history." In baseball, especially, there seems to be an almost endless array of records to break. Surely, the record book has listed the left-hander who had the most hits during an out-of-town night game pitched by a southpaw.

Photographers can't memorize the record book, so they should check with the statistician before every game to see if any new records are likely to be broken. A record-breaking homerun or free-throw might be the most newsworthy moment of the game, and an editor will want to see a picture of the event.

■ SUMMARIZING THE GAME IN ONE PHOTO

A sports story's lead usually contains the names of both teams or players and the outcome of the game. It also describes the game's highlights—the turning point or winning goal, the star of the game, and injuries to important players. Knowledgeable sports photographers follow the game closely enough that their pictures complement the story's lead.

"I always try to develop the lead picture that will parallel the thrust of our wire story," explains Riley. "The wire service will often play up the top scorer in the game, so I will need a picture of him in action." If a particular play changes the course of the game, the photographer should have a shot of this play on film.

A good sports photographer watches all the action but doesn't stop when the final gun goes off. Sometimes the expressions on the athletes' faces after a tense meet tells the story better than an "action" shot.

Sports shooter Mangin says that at the end of a game, he looks for the crowd's elation or anything else that

Thinking he had won, the biker on the left raised his hands just before the finish line. The biker on the right passed him at that moment. This sports news photo leaves no doubt in the viewer's mind which cyclist won the race.
(Photo by Scott R. Linnett, *San Diego Union-Tribune*.)

will characterize the game's emotional flavor. "If you are working for the hometown paper, you need to photograph the jubilation or dejection at the end of the game," Mangin says.

These pictures will often tell more about the outcome of the game than the peak action. With the action picture, you don't know who won unless you have the key play, Mangin points out.

■ CATCHING REACTIONS ON AND OFF THE FIELD

The sports photographer looks for the interesting, the unusual, the emotional, the unexpected, both on and off the field. What's happening on the bench can be as interesting as what's happening on the field. Watch the field and the sidelines simultaneously. You might lose some action plays sometimes, but you will get great emotional, story-telling pictures this way.

Coaches are under tremendous pressure because their jobs are on the line every time

the team takes the field. A picture of a coach pacing the sidelines, yelling at the referees, or jamming his finger at other coaches can reveal his underlying tension. Players feel that same pressure. The clenched jaw of a player sitting on the sidelines or the wince of an athlete wearing a cast could also tell the evening's story.

■ CAPTIONS NEEDED

Whether the picture shows critical action on the field or reactions off, the photographer must have complete caption information. The caption, as it is called in a magazine, or cutline, as it is known in a newspaper, is the explanatory line of type usually below the printed photograph.

If it is not obvious from the picture, a caption should answer the five Ws plus the H: Who? What? When? Where? Why? and How? Readers will know that the photo depicts a basketball game if a basketball is in the picture. But they might not know whether the picture was taken in the first or last

Good sports photographers keep on eye on the bench as well as on the action.
(Photo by Lui Kit Wong, *Virginian-Pilot.*)

quarter of the game, or the identity of the players, or the significance of the play.

A photographer's nightmare is to bring back 200 shots of a game, develop the negatives, select one frame with excellent action, and then not know the names of the players, what happened, or when the action took place. Fortunately, players wear large numbers on their uniforms. If the numbers are visible in the print, the player can be identified by matching the number against the roster list in the program. To determine when the play occurred, one trick is to take a picture of the scoreboard after each major play or at the end of each quarter. By working backwards on the roll from the scoreboard frame, the photographer can determine when each shot was taken and which play led to which scores.

Play-by-play statistics sheets, available from officials after the game, also help photographers write accurate captions. Besides shooting frames of the scoreboard, sophisticated sports photographers usually take notes during the game. In baseball, there is time to record each play if you use a shorthand notation (for example FB = first base, HR = home run). In football, jot down a short description after each play. Riley comments, "Keeping track of the plays can get tricky at times. This is where newcomers usually have the most trouble in sports photography." (See Chapter 9, "Photo Editing," for more on caption writing.)

SPORTS AS FEATURES

Sports might be as timely and may command as much reader interest as any story in the newspaper. But sports events aren't hard news—they're entertainment. A football game, no matter who wins or loses, is still a game. You might have a side bet resting on the World Series, but the outcome of the game will not affect your life beyond giving a moment's elation or depression (unless, of course, you've staked your savings on your favorite team).

When looking for features, draw your lens away from the field action to view the fans in the stands. Diehard fans go to great lengths to show their support for the hometown team. From funny signs to outrageous outfits, fans come prepared to root or rout the players of their choice.

Players themselves can also provide grist for funny pictures. For many athletes, the pleasure of playing has never been lost. During the game, keep your eye on the dugout or the bench.

Rich Riggins of the Patuxent Publishing Co. found a funny feature by watching the

referee at a swim meet. The ref was just talking to a swimmer but held the starting gun as if he were holding up the athlete.

Try to get into the locker room after the contest is over.

The news approach to sports usually involves getting sharp, freeze-frame action shots of players hanging suspended in midair, grasping for the ball. Sometimes this literal approach robs the sports photo of its most vital element—the illusion of motion. A more impressionistic feature approach can add drama and reinforce motion in a still photograph. Certain camera techniques can heighten the effect. A sports photographer might pan a cyclist's action by setting the camera on a slow shutter speed and following the subject with the lens, intentionally blurring the background while keeping the subject sharp. (See page 99.) Such a picture can have more impact than would a traditional news photo of the winner of the bicycle race, in razor-sharp detail, crossing the finish line.

In a sports feature photo, the photographer ignores the critical winning moment in favor of capturing the atmosphere of the event. Impressionistic pictures of this kind transcend the actual event and become a universal statement about the sport. A bone-crushing tackle made by a football player may resemble a delicate pirouette when captured by a skilled photographer. In **Man and Sports**, a photo exhibit and catalogue produced by the Baltimore Art Museum, the outstanding sports photographer Horst Baumann said that there is an increasing appreciation for the impressionistic, nonfactual but visually elegant portrayal of sports.

TECHNIQUES OF THE SPORTS PHOTOGRAPHER
■ FREEZING ACTION

Sports photography requires specialized technical skills because of the speed at which the athletes move and because of the

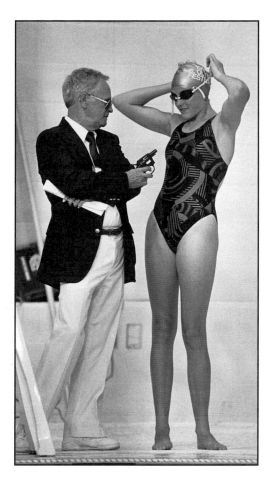

Often, you will find the best sports features on the sidelines, like the one of this swim meet official making a point with the starting gun.
(Rich Riggins, Patuxent Publishing Co., Columbia, Md.)

Shutter Speeds for Action Parallel to the Film Plane				
Type of Motion	**Speed**	**Camera-to-subject distance**		
		25 feet	**50 feet**	**100 feet**
Very fast walker	(5 mph)	1/125	1/60	1/30
Children running	(10 mph)	1/250	1/125	1/60
Good sprinter	(20 mph)	1/500	1/250	1/125
Speeding cars	(50 mph)	1/1000	1/500	1/250
Airplanes		_____	_____	1/500

limitations of position imposed on the photographer. To stop motion in action sports like baseball, football, and basketball, photographers try to shoot with a shutter speed of at least 1/500 sec.

Says Eric Risberg, a top sports shooter for the Associated Press, "The slowest I ever shoot is at 1/500 sec. At a 1/1000 sec., things get a lot sharper."

Four factors affect the apparent speed of a subject and therefore determine the minimum shutter speed to stop motion:
1) the actual speed of the subject;
2) the apparent distance between subject and camera;
3) the focal length of the lens; and
4) the angle of movement relative to the camera's axis.

Speed. You will need a faster shutter speed to stop or freeze the action of a track star running a 100-yard dash than you will to stop the action of a Sunday afternoon jogger. To freeze a sprinter, the shutter must open and close before the image of the runner perceptibly changes position on the film. Therefore, the faster the subject runs, the faster the shutter speed you must use to stop the action and avoid a blur on the film.

Distance. A second factor affecting the image on the film is the camera-to-subject distance. If you stand by the highway watching speeding cars go by, you may observe them zoom rapidly past you; but when you move back from the edge of the highway 100 feet or so, the apparent speed of the cars is considerably less. Speeding cars on the horizon may appear to be almost motionless. Translated into shutter settings, a general guideline for this effect is that the closer the camera is to the moving subject, the faster the shutter setting needed to stop or freeze its movement.

Lens Length. Whether you get the camera closer by physically moving it toward the subject or remaining stationary and attaching a telephoto lens, thereby bringing the subject apparently closer, you must increase your shutter setting to freeze the action. Suppose you are 50 feet away from the track with a 55mm lens. A

Minimum Shutter Speeds Required to Freeze Action				
SPEED OF CAR (MPH)	**SPEED OF CAR** 25 MPH 50 MPH 100 MPH	**DISTANCE TO CAR** 50 MPH 50 MPH 50 MPH	**DIRECTION OF CAR** 50 MPH 50 MPH 50 MPH	**LENS FOCAL LENGTH** 50 MPH 50 MPH 50 MPH
DISTANCE 100' **FROM** **CAR** 50' **TO** **CAMERA** 25'				wide normal tele
SHUTTER SPEED	1/250 1/500 1/1000	1/250 1/500 1/1000	1/250 1/500 1/1000	1/250 1/500 1/1000

shutter speed of 1/500 sec. would be adequate to get a sharp picture of a car speeding at 50 mph. However, if you keep the same lens but move forward to within 25 feet of the railing, you must set the shutter at 1/1000 sec. to freeze the car's movement. If you change from a 55mm to a 105mm lens but still remain at the 50-foot distance, you would still have to use 1/1000 sec. shutter speed (see diagrams on this page). The rule is this: when you halve the apparent camera-to-subject distance, you need to double the shutter speed to get the same representation of motion.

Angle. The angle of the subject's movement relative to the axis of the camera also affects choice of shutter speed. A car moving directly toward you may appear to be nearly stopped because its image moves very little on the film. Yet the same car— moving at the same speed, but this time moving across your line of vision—may appear to be traveling quite rapidly. This phenomenon means that if you position yourself to photograph a car 50 feet away going 50 mph moving directly toward you, you would need only 1/125 sec. shutter speed to stop the action. From the same distance, the same car moving across your line of vision would require 1/500 sec. to stop the motion.

Peak Action

With some movements, it is possible to stop the action at a relatively slow shutter speed by timing the shot to coincide with a momentary pause in the motion of the subject. Athletes come to almost a complete stop at the peak of their movement. Consequently, the photographer can use a relatively slow shutter speed and still get a sharp picture. In track, for example, when a high jumper reaches the apex of his leap directly above the bar, his vertical motion is over. He can't go any higher, and, for a split second, his vertical motion will cease before gravity pulls him back to earth.

A basketball player shooting a jump shot follows the same pattern: he leaps into the air, reaches his peak, hesitates, and then shoots the ball before he begins dropping back to the floor. A pole vaulter's leap is another example of this type of motion. A sports photographer can use a slower shutter speed to stop action at the

► To retain a sense of movement in this still photo of an antique tricycle, the photographer panned the camera and exposed the film for 1/15 sec. as the cyclist pedaled by.
(Photo by Ken Kobré, for the *Boston Phoenix*.)

peak of the vault by anticipating where the peak will occur and wait for the athlete to reach the apex of the arc.

Panning

While a fast shutter speed allows the photographer to catch the action of the play, the resulting frozen figure may not capture the essence of the sport. Freezing a player in mid-air can rob the photo of any illusion of movement. To solve this problem, you can use a technique known as panning: use a slow shutter speed and follow the subject during the exposure. This technique produces a picture with a relatively sharp subject but a blurred and streaked background. A pan shot

▼ With an 85mm lens, the photographer needed a shutter speed of at least 1/500 sec. to stop the sweat flying off these fighters' faces.
(Photo by Jim McNay.)

is dramatic and can make even the proverbial "Old Gray Mare" look like a Triple Crown winner running at breakneck speed.

On sports assignments for *Life* magazine and *Sports Illustrated*, Mark Kauffman has tried the panning technique on several different events. In **Photographing Sports**, a book about his work, Kauffman said, "Panning is something like shooting in the dark. It's practically impossible to predict the final result. Background colors will move and blend together giving shades and tones and creating hues which we cannot predict."

If the photographer doesn't follow the subject smoothly, the image won't be sharp enough. Many photographers can't afford to risk a pan shot because the editor counts on having at least one tack-sharp photo of the principals in the event. Therefore, the photographer never gambles solely on a pan shot for an important news assignment. "When on assignment," Kauffman cautions, "get the picture the editor needs first—then, if you have time, experiment with a pan."

The choice of lens is critical in panning. A long lens allows the photographer to back off from the subject. The farther the camera is from the subject, the slower the photographer can pan—thus achieving more control. The lens, however, must allow a field of view that is wide enough to accommodate the anticipated action.

In panning, use your viewfinder to spot the subject as it moves into view. Pivot your head and shoulders so that you keep the subject in the viewfinder at all times. When your subject is in front of you, release the shutter without interrupting your pivot. Be sure to follow through after you snap the shutter. The trick is to have the camera moving at the same speed and in the same direction as the subject.

■ FOCUSING: HOW TO GET SHARP IMAGES
Manual Focus

Whether you use a slow shutter speed to pan or a fast shutter speed to freeze the action, the subject will not be sharp unless the lens is critically focused. Focusing a lens on a

Because of the inherent delay caused by reaction time, a photographer could have missed a key moment like this without realizing it.
(Photo by John Coley, *Palm Beach Post*.)

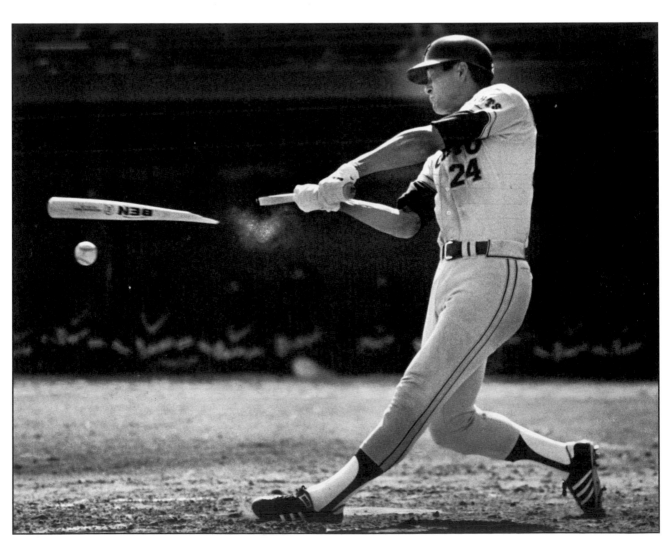

rapidly moving subject takes considerable practice.

Follow-focusing requires eye-hand coordination. As the runner moves down the field, you must move the lens' focusing ring to maintain a sharp image on the ground glass. When the runner is near, you must completely rotate the focus ring to keep the subject sharp. When the runner speeds into the distance, a little twist of the ring suffices to pop the runner in or out of focus.

To follow-focus, use the ground glass on the edges of your viewfinder, not the split image or micro screen in the center. For most shooters, these focusing aids are too slow for the continuous movement of sports action.

The photographer must adapt eye-hand coordination to each lens length and camera brand. Each lens requires a different amount of movement to achieve sharpness. Like a musician playing the same note on a base fiddle, cello, or violin, the photographer must learn different eye-hand motor skills, depending on whether he or she is using a 100mm, 400mm, or 600mm lens. Even more confusing is the difficulty of switching among brands of cameras. Some focus clockwise, others counterclockwise. Whenever possible, try to stick to one camera brand to avoid this confusion.

One veteran shooter always recommended to new photographers that they stand beside the highway to practice follow-focusing on cars. Select a car, he said, and try to keep its license plate in focus as it moves down the road. Track car after car, and soon, without thinking about it, your hand will move the lens barrel the exact amount necessary to hold focus as the speeding car passes in front of you, zooms down the highway, and recedes from view.

Don't be discouraged if every negative of your sports action is not tack sharp. Few sports photographers bring back 36 perfectly focused exposures. However, with practice, the number of razor-sharp frames will increase.

For many assignments, sports photographers shoot with lenses in the 200mm to 600mm range. From the perspective of sharpness, the bad news is that long lenses have narrow depth of field even at small apertures. This means that unless the lenses are exactly focused, the pictures will look blurry.

Shallow depth of field means that the lens is intolerant of imprecise focusing. The good news is that when you site through long lenses, the image pops in and out of focus very cleanly and dramatically on the viewfinder's ground glass. Critically focusing a long lens is actually easier than focusing a wide-angle lens. (See Chapter 10, "Cameras and Film.")

Shooting at 1/1000 sec. from a bouncing flat bed truck with a 400mm lens, the photographer focused on the lead runner but, at f/5.6, still kept the pack clear enough to be readable.
(Photo by Jim Collins, Worcester (Mass.) Telegram & Gazette.)

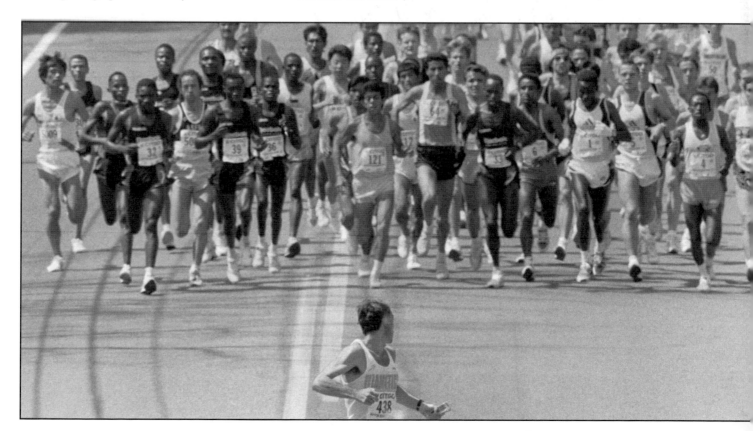

Zone-focusing

In sports like auto racing or track and field, when the photographer can predict exactly where the subject will be—at a finish line or a specific hurdle—photographers use a method called zone-focusing. To zone-focus, manually prefocus the lens for the point at which you expect the action to take place, and let your lens' depth of field do the rest. As the subject crosses the predetermined mark, frame and shoot your picture. Your picture will be sharp not only at the point at which you have focused but for several feet in front of and behind that point—depending on the depth of field of your lens, aperture, and distance from the subject. (See page 92.)

Once you have prefocused and determined your depth of field, you know the zone in which you can shoot without refocusing. When the subject speeds into the framed area, you can take several shots as long as the subject is within that zone. At an equestrian event, for example, the sports photographer can prefocus on the hurdle and wait for the horse and rider to jump.

In baseball, the action occurs in definite places—on the bases and at home plate. Baseball is ideal for zone-focusing, and some baseball photographers even label the base positions on their lenses. First, they sit in a fixed position between home plate and first base. Then, they put a strip of white tape around the lens barrel next to the footage scale. They focus on each base, home plate, the pitcher's mound, and the dugout, and mark on the tape labeling each point. When a runner breaks to steal second, the photographer can quickly rotate the lens to the "2" position, and the lens will be in sharp focus to catch the player sliding into second base.

Only a motor drive would have caught this sequence of Mary Decker tripping during the Olympic games.
(Photos by Bruce Chambers, *Long Beach* (Calif.) *Press-Telegram*.)

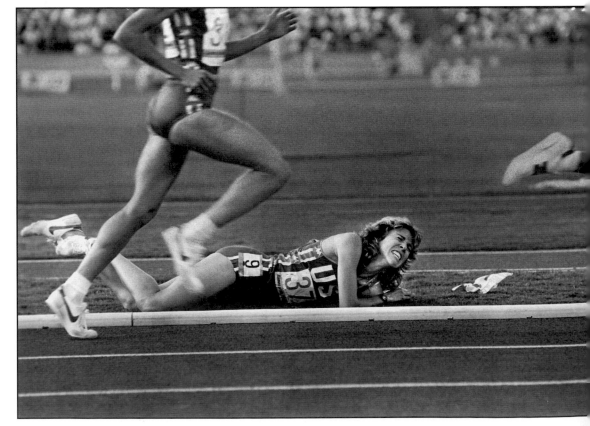

If the action suddenly switches to third base, a short twist of the lens to position "3" and the photographer is ready for the new action. Some long lenses provide adjustable click points for this purpose. With the click stops, the photographer does not have to peer through the lens, spending time to find the optimum focus.

Autofocus

With some of the latest camera lens combinations, the camera's autofocus option can outperform even the most practiced photographer's eyes and hands. With the camera and lens set on autofocus, the photographer frames a runner flying over the hurdles in the viewfinder. The viewfinder has etched into it lines indicating one or more areas through which the photographer can autofocus. Once locked onto the moving target, the photographer can activate the autofocus feature by partially depressing the shutter release. As the runner moves toward the camera, the lens will automatically rotate, keeping the athlete in focus. A good autofocus system will smoothly follow the hurdler without hesitantly searching. As soon as the photographer presses the release, the lens immediately rotates the appropriate amount and thus produces the sharpest possible image. Some of the most advanced autofocus systems have a coreless motor built into the lens that not only turns to the correct point of focus quickly— quicker than a photographer could manually turn it—but comes to a complete halt when the image is sharp without any fine-tuning.

These systems were devised to fire and continuously advance at many frames per second while tracking a fast-moving subject. Manual follow-focusing is easy when you're not firing off many frames. But when you want to shoot a rapid sequence of shots, the mirror is up more than down, which interrupts viewing and makes it difficult to manually follow-focus.

Some autofocus lenses will even work under low light conditions. They can track a runner coming toward or moving away from the photographer at practically any speed in a poorly lit indoor gym. While the autofocus systems do depend on contrast (i.e., a light/dark image in the area of the focusing sensor), almost any situation short of a completely blank wall or perfectly clear sky will provide enough contrast.

With some systems, the photographer must center the athlete in the middle of the viewfinder for autofocus to work.

Those with multiple focusing sensors in the viewfinder allow the primary subject to be off-center while the camera lens stays on track. With these models, the photographer can select the designated off-center areas in the viewfinder for autofocusing. If the photographer wants to automatically follow-focus a runner who is on the left side of the frame, the shooter can do that. To shift to a runner on the right-hand side, the photographer can readjust the autofocus area. Other camera systems advertise a wide-area autofocus sensor that allows for continuous autofocus without any need for sensor selection. Some cameras advertise a "lock-on" feature that assures that the player will stay in focus.

No autofocus system produces sharp pictures every frame, but the new generation of equipment comes closer than ever before. With some autofocus systems, the camera will focus on the closest object in front of the focusing sensor. If you are tracking a halfback running down the field, and a ref gets in the way, the camera will switch focus to the interloper and lose track of the halfback. When the halfback appears again, the lens has to search for the new point of focus. However, with the "lock-on" feature and faster motors in some new systems, the ref's momentary interruption won't cause the focus to shift. Even if the player briefly moves out of the autofocus sensor's area, the system will return to the prime subject.

Many of today's sports shooters have switched from manual to autofocus systems. The *San Francisco Chronicle*, among other newspapers, has sold its entire inventory of pool equipment to invest in the latest autofocusing systems. Photographers report as much as a thirty percent improvement in the number of sharp pictures they can bring back from an event using autofocus compared with manual-focus lenses. Even shooters who cover only sports—and who are accustomed to bringing back sharp images—claim to get even better results using the new autofocus technology.

"In a sequence of eight to ten frames, I get seven or eight that are sharp," says George Tiedemann, a contract photographer with *Sports Illustrated*, in describing his conversion to the new technology. "That's better than the four or five I used to get." John Iacono, a *Sports Illustrated* staffer, is another of the converted. "Before, when I had a sequence of a guy running with the ball, I'd have one or two shots in focus," he testifies. "Now every frame is sharp."

Tiedeman says that the new technology has dramatically increased his odds even when shooting car races. "I was shooting cars coming diagonally across, flying by me at speeds well over 100 mph. I put the 600mm on autofocus and just nailed those guys."

[handwritten margin note: lock on → activate by partially depressing shutter release. probably can't pre-focus because would lock on background?]

While not a necessity, autofocus lenses and cameras seem like the best tools for those who don't want to miss a sharp picture of the critical play. (See also Chapter 10, "Cameras and Film.")

THE SPORTS PHOTOGRAPHER'S BAG OF SOLUTIONS
■ FIXED-FOCAL-LENGTH TELEPHOTOS

A sports photographer can't just run onto the playing field with a wide-angle 20mm lens and snap a picture of the action. To get an image large enough to see clearly, the sports specialist usually must use long telephoto lenses. The telephoto adds drama to the drama, and heightens the impact. With these long lenses, whether manual or autofocus, you magnify what you want to show by eliminating all other distractions. In addition, using these lenses helps to pop the key player out of the pack, leaving a distracting background lost in an out-of-focus blur. In fact, some photographers always use the widest lens aperture to achieve minimum depth of field, therefore knocking out, as much as possible, the distracting background. (See pages 92, 95, and 110.) Long lenses also can be a creative tool because they pull things together in a way the human eye never sees. Because a telephoto lens appears to compress space, objects appear much closer together in depth than they really are. (See page 101.)

Unfortunately, telephoto lenses are not the sports photographer's panacea. The telephoto lens itself has inherent problems. For instance, the longer the lens, the less depth of field; therefore, focusing becomes even more critical. With extreme telephoto lenses like the 500mm f/4, 600mm f/4 and f/5.6, and the 800mm f/5.6, there is no margin of error. The focus must be perfect, or the shot is lost.

Critical focusing is just one challenge when you use a telephoto lens. Another is the exaggerated effect of camera movement on the picture's sharpness. The lens length exaggerates any camera movement and, thus, slight camera-shake can result in a blurred final image. A 200mm telephoto, compared to a normal 50mm lens, magnifies the image four times, but it also magnifies camera-shake by the same amount. With any very long lens, it is sometimes necessary to use a monopod, a one-legged support.

Additionally, if your eye is not perfectly aligned with the optics of the lens, one-half of the split-image focusing circle will tend to go dark when you use a long telephoto lens. If possible, use a focusing screen without a split-image circle on the ground glass.

Even though telephoto lenses are difficult to use, they do put the viewer right in the middle of the action. Many photojournalists carry the 300mm f/2.8 as regular equipment.

■ ZOOM LENSES

Rather than carry a satchel of different lenses, some sports photographers prefer to use zoom lenses. With the zoom, you can continually change the focal length of the lens, so that one lens is doing the work of several. Because you can zoom to any millimeter within the range of the lens, your framing can be exact. Sports photographers also like the zoom because it lets them follow a player running toward the camera while it keeps the player's image size constant in the viewfinder. Another advantage of the zoom is that you can get several shots from a single vantage point without moving. For instance, you can zoom back and catch all the horses at the starting line of a race; then, after the horses leave the gate, you can zoom in to isolate the leader of the pack—all this by just a twist or push of the lens barrel.

But even this versatile lens has some drawbacks. First, a zoom is usually heavier than a single-length telephoto lens. You can balance this increased weight, however, against not having to carry as many lenses to get the same effect.

Second, the zoom lens' widest apertures are sometimes smaller than the maximum aperture on an equally long fixed focal length lens, so the zoom is less useful in low-light situations such as in indoor arenas or at night games. Manufacturers, on the other hand, have introduced mid-range (80–200mm), relatively fast (f/2.8) telephotos, but the lenses are still fairly expensive.

Third, focusing and zooming simultaneously as the subject moves can be difficult to coordinate. You can develop this skill with practice, of course, but it does take time. Also, autofocus cameras help a lot in this situation.

Although zooms aren't a cure-all, the AP's Risberg maintains that they are "one of the best tools for sports photography."

Iacono of *Sports Illustrated* uses both fixed-length and zoom lenses. He uses a fixed-length 300mm, a 400mm, and a 600mm on monopods, with an 80–200mm zoom on his shoulder and a 55mm hanging on his chest. He keeps the 55mm around his neck in case a play develops right in front of him. If it does, he quickly grabs the 55 and gets off a couple of quick one-handed "Hail Mary" shots.

■ THE MOTORIZED CAMERA

Either attached to your camera or built into the body, a motor drive allows you to fire a series of frames without manually advancing the film between each shot. Every sports photographer interviewed for this book used a motor drive, but several mentioned that in some instances a motor drive caused them to miss the peak action of the play.

Sports photographer George Riley says that "motors can throw your timing off, and sometimes the best pictures come between the frames." However, Riley quickly points out that, on a controversial play, the photographer needs the motor drive to fire off a sequence and show how the play developed.

Pressing the motor drive trips the shutter, advances the film, and cocks the shutter again for the next picture faster than you can blink an eye. If you use the motor drive semi-automatically—one frame at a time—you need not remove the camera from your eye to advance the film. Or you can shoot rapid-sequence pictures, depending on the make of the camera, at a rate of two to five frames per second, or even faster with some cameras, without taking your finger off the shutter. This rapid-fire pace increases your chances of capturing peak action.

As in working with all photographic equipment, you must learn the technique of using a motor drive. With the motor drive set on "continuous," you should begin shooting before the action starts and continue holding down the shutter release until after it stops. This will expose a series of frames that encompasses the complete play. From the sequence, you can choose the best frame, one you might have missed had you advanced the film manually. (See pages 102 and 106.)

Because no sane photographer wants to be subjected to a barrage of speeding hockey pucks or powerful slam dunks, a motor-driven camera also can be placed in a remote location such as inside a hockey goal or behind the plastic of a backboard. The camera can be activated either by an electrical wire or by a radio control. Firing the camera remotely can give the photographer a unique vantage point, right in the middle of the melee.

■ DEVELOPING THE FILM FOR DIMLY LIT SPORTS

Outdoor sporting events present few lighting difficulties, but indoor and night sports can be tricky to shoot because of low light. First, poor light means that you must set your lens on its widest aperture. Unfortunately, this narrows the depth of field and reduces the

Combining the action-stopping effect of the strobe with a relatively long available-light exposure (1/4 sec.) leaves ghosting around the riders and imparts a sense of action to this bike race photo.
(Photo by Dave Eulitt, *The Topeka* (Kansas) *Capital Journal.*)

When using a motor drive, start shooting before the action starts and keep shooting until the play is completed.
(Photos by Brad Mangin.)

chances for a sharp picture. You also might have to turn your shutter dial to a slower speed to compensate for the low light conditions, but this, too, may blur the image in the final picture.

Sports photographers shooting in poorly lit gyms, dark hockey arenas, or unevenly lit outdoor stadiums at night, select the fastest film available. The introduction of 1600 ISO color and 3200 ISO black-and-white film has saved the day for many sports shooters.

But sometimes even these fast films are not sensitive enough for shooting high school football, where half the stadium's light bulbs are burned out, or in dungeon-like basketball gyms. In these situations, photographers overrate their film, effectively underexposing it, and then partially compensate for the lack of exposure by increasing development. (See Chapter 10, "Cameras and Film.")

■ DON'T HOCK YOUR STROBE YET!

A few sports situations demand electronic flash, whereas others merely benefit from the use of this lighting source. The electronic flash from a strobe begins and ends so fast that the flash will stop just about any action you might encounter.

Although the lighting effect from a single strobe on camera looks harsh and unnatural, the resulting image will be sharper than a blurred shot taken with available light at a shutter speed too slow to stop motion.

Sometimes, flash even enhances a sports picture. David Eulitt was shooting a bicycle race for the *Indianapolis News* when he combined strobe and available light in one exposure. The strobe stopped the racers' motion and produced a sharp image. The slow shutter speed, which let in the available light, added a ghosting effect that gave the photo a feeling of motion.

Some photographers like to set up strobes for a spectacular multilight photo at indoor and night sports events. Two lights can be synchronized with a connecting wire or photoelectric slave cell that fires both units at the same time.

Some large newspapers, and several major magazines such as *Sports Illustrated,* light entire sports arenas with a battery of huge strobes.

Photographers connected to these systems can shoot with slow, fine-grain color film and still get outstanding results. The elaborate multilight installations require a great deal of money and time but provide the photographer great flexibility and increase the number of quality images. (See Chapter 11, "Strobe.")

ANTICIPATION
■ KNOWING WHERE THE BALL WILL BE BEFORE IT GETS THERE

At one time, photographers were allowed to work on the field of major league baseball games, but this freedom was curtailed because of the antics of photographers like Hy Peskin. An outstanding photographer, Peskin was covering a close game between the Giants and the Dodgers from a spot behind first base when he saw a ball hit into right field. He realized there would be a close play at third base. With the volatile Leo Durocher coaching at third, Peskin knew there would be a scene. As the right-fielder chased down the ball, Peskin took the shortest route to third base—over the pitcher's mound and across the infield. Peskin, the runner, and the ball all arrived at third base at the same moment. Peskin got his pictures, but after similar incidents, photographers were barred from the playing field of major league games.

Had Peskin anticipated third-base action before the play began, he could have positioned himself near that baseline, or he could have focused with a long lens on third.

The key to getting great sports photographs is anticipation. Anticipation means predicting not only what's going to happen but where it's going to happen. You must base these predictions on knowledge of the game, the players, and the coaches.

Anticipation in football, for example, means that you must know the kind of play to expect—run, pass, or kick. Then you must predict who will be involved in the play—quarterback, running back, or pass-receiver. And finally, you must guess where the play will take place—at the line of scrimmage, behind the line, or downfield. Basing your position on these predictions, you would station yourself along the sidelines, usually at the point nearest the expected action. Choose the appropriate lens and follow-focus the player you expect to get the ball. Then, wait—and hope the action will follow the course you have predicted.

■ COUNTERACTING REACTION TIME

Besides anticipating the action of key players, you must also press the shutter before the action reaches its peak. In baseball, for instance, if you hit the trigger of your camera when you hear the crack of the bat against the ball, your final picture will show the ball already headed for left field. You would swear that you squeezed the shutter at the same instant the bat met the ball, yet the picture clearly demonstrates the shutter was delayed. Why?

A lag-time occurred between the moment you heard the crack of the bat and the moment you pressed the shutter. Psychologists have termed this lag period "reaction time," and they are able to measure precisely its duration. The delayed reaction is caused by the amount of time it takes you—first, to recognize that an important play is in progress; second, to decide if a picture should be taken; third, to send a positive signal to the muscle group needed for the movement, in this case the index finger; and, fourth, to contract the muscles in the forefinger and thereby release the camera's shutter.

Even after the shutter trigger is depressed, there's another delay while the camera itself responds. Even the most sensitive shutter still takes time to function. This shutter reaction time is the fifth step. All five steps added together account for the reaction time between seeing the action and taking the picture. You run through these same steps every time you take any picture, but the cumulative length of reaction time becomes critical when the subject is a baseball moving at 90 mph.

■ WAITING 'TIL "ALL HELL BREAKS LOOSE"

The AP's Schuyler describes baseball as a "Zen sport" that requires infinite patience to photograph because the action erupts in spurts, and instant response is needed. "You wait and wait, and nothing happens. Then, all of a sudden, all hell breaks loose," says Schuyler. "I get bored easily at a baseball game and then I lose my concentration. That's when the big action always seems to occur!"

It does appear sometimes that nothing ever happens in baseball. In fact, the perfect game from the standpoint of a baseball aficionado is a "no-hitter." Sports writers still refer to the "great" game in the 1956 World Series when Don Larsen of the Yankees pitched a no-hitter. Not only were there no hits but also no walks and no errors, either. Twenty-seven Dodgers went from the dugout to the plate and back again without reaching first base.

Unfortunately, there was no action for the photographer to shoot in this perfect baseball game. The picture that is remembered shows Larsen pitching his last ball, with a row of Dodger zeroes on the scoreboard in the background.

When you suspect the play is going to take place at home plate, prefocus on this base and wait for the slide. Capturing catcher, runner, and umpire at the base, this photo contains all the needed story-telling elements of a good sports photo.
(Photo by Dale Guldan, *Milwaukee Journal.*)

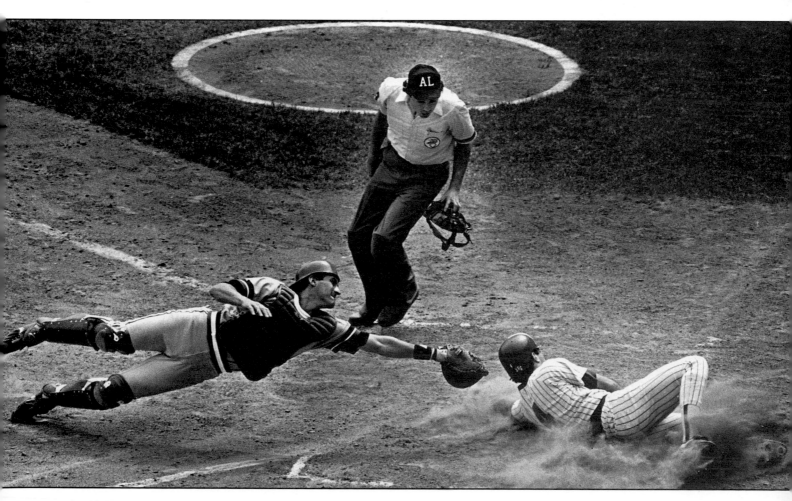

■ SLIDING SECOND

Luckily for the photographer, a no-hitter is rare. Most games have at least some action at the bases, and baseball, like all sports, has its standard action shot. In baseball, the standard photo is the second-base slide.

When the play is going to take place at second base, train your telephoto lens on the base, focus, and wait for the action. With a motor drive, the timing does not have to be so exact because the camera fires several frames per second. If you press the release as the slide begins, and hold it until the umpire makes the call, one frame is likely to coincide with the peak of the action. Often a good series of pictures results. If any of the photos in the series show the intense expressions on the players' faces, these pictures will have added human interest.

■ STEALING BASE

When the key play is a second-base slide, the photographer simply zeroes in on the base and concentrates. A more difficult situation occurs when a notorious base-stealer

ventures into no-man's land between first and second. The pitcher could try to pick off the runner at first if he thinks the runner has too daring a lead-off, or the catcher could peg the runner if he breaks for second. Cover this split action by prefocusing one camera on second base and setting this camera aside; then focus another camera on first base and keep the camera to your eye. You can snap a picture of the pick-off on first, or, if the runner heads for second base, you'll have time to raise your other prefocused camera and catch the slide at second.

When a runner gets to second base and is officially "in scoring position," you should prefocus on home plate. On the next fair play, the runner might try to score.

■ RUNNER VS. THE BALL

One general rule is to follow the runner, not the ball, with your lens. A routine catch in the outfield makes a routine picture. Except with a short fly, when either the infielder has to catch the ball in back of him, or the outfielder has to dive for it, keep your camera focused on the base path runners. AP's Risberg, however, says he has taken exciting pictures of outfield play with an extremely long telephoto lens. He also points out that, during slow games, the shooter should watch the reactions of batters. For games without much action, he says, the dugout provides good picture opportunities.

Photographers position themselves several yards back from the base path between home and first base, or home and third base, or in the press gallery. From these positions, especially when shooting high school, college, and professional baseball, sports photographers prefer a 300mm or 400mm lens to cover the infield and a 600–800mm to cover the outfield.

A sandlot or Little League playing field measures a shorter distance, hence a 135mm lens covers the infield easily.

■ THE UNUSUAL

Baseball is a team sport played by individuals, each with his own strengths and his own repertoire of favorite stunts. One ballplayer might hold the season's record in stolen bases, while a pitcher might lead the league in pick-offs at first. With this combination, the smart photographer has the camera lens focused and aimed squarely at first. One batter might be a consistent bunter; another might consider a bunt below his dignity under any circumstance.

The more you know about the idiosyncrasies of the players, the better your forecasts and your pictures will be.

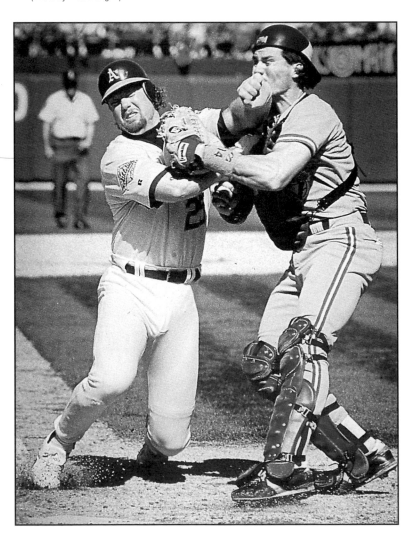

Taken with a remote camera attached to the backstop, the photographer activated a foot switch to catch this clash at home plate. (Photo by Brad Mangin.)

Although the dust-swirling second-base slide is a sports photographer's guaranteed "bread-and-butter" shot, sometimes the shot can be overworked. "You can almost take the slide shot out of the files, the situation starts to look so similar," says one shooter.

When shooting for *Sports Illustrated*, Brad Mangin will position himself in the photographers' box behind first base and shoot with either a 600mm lens or a 400 f/2.8 with a teleconverter.

"This is a basic, good safe angle for shooting second base, home, and the outfield," he says.

For a different shot, he sets up a remote camera before the game. He clamps it on the backstop behind home plate, points it toward third base, and prefocuses a little past home to anticipate the slide at the plate. He connects the remote camera to his box position with a long wire, uses either a foot switch or a button to trip the remote camera, and reloads between innings.

When a play occurs at home, he activates the remote and also shoots with his long telephoto because sometimes the batter in the on-deck circle blocks the camera.

"You can go ten games with no play at the plate," he says, "but when you get the head-on shot, it's got a lot of impact."

The antics of the team manager may provide a rich source of photographic material. When he strides onto the field, you can bet sparks will fly whether he harangues the umpire or yanks out the losing pitcher.

A photographer can shoot baseball without being a Zen master. Just remember that you will never go hungry if you consistently catch your bread-and-butter action picture, the second-base slide. But you are more likely to be eating steak and lobster if you cover all the important action on the field.

FINDING THE FOOTBALL

When you cover a football game, you face some of the same problems as does a 250-pound defensive tackle. Before each down, you and the football player have to predict which way the quarterback will move on the next play.

After the center hikes the ball, you and the tackle must react quickly and make adjustments as the play unfolds. Will the quarterback hand off to a speedster for an end-run or to a powerful halfback for a bruising plunge through the center? Or will the quarterback

Photographs of players making mistakes like this pass interference are often more interesting than plays executed successfully. The photo was taken with a 600mm lens from the press box.
(Photo by George Honeycutt, the *Houston Chronicle*.)

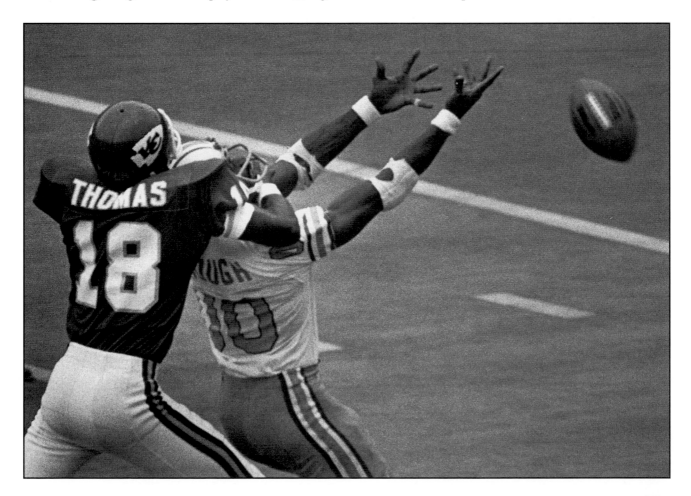

throw a quick spike for short yardage or a long bomb to the end zone?

As the defensive player considers the options, the sports photographer likewise anticipates the call and prepares for the play. You must be in the right place at the right time, with the right equipment, ready and waiting for the action: runs, passes, and punts.

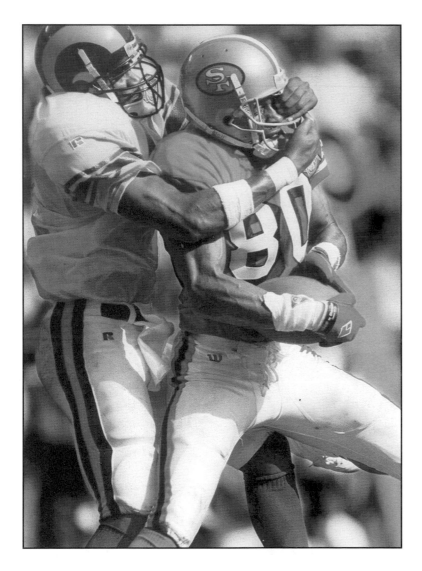

Using a long telephoto at it widest aperture helps to blur the background and separate the 49ers' receiver, Jerry Rice, from distracting elements behind him. (Photo by Matthew J. Lee, *Long Beach* (Calif.) *Press-Telegram.*)

■ WATCHING FOR THE RUN

On a run, track the football as it is snapped by the center and either carried by the quarterback or handed to another backfield player.

Most teams tend to run the ball on the first down because a run is generally considered a safer play than a pass, or, as former Ohio State coach Woody Hayes put it, "Only three things can happen when you pass, and two of them are bad." Therefore, cautious quarterbacks like to keep the ball on the ground on the first down. Caution also dictates the use of a running play on a third down when the

team is just one or two yards shy of a first down. Some teams, particularly the Big Ten power squads, with their strong running backs and blockers, carry the football not only on the first and third down, but are very likely to run on the second down, as well.

■ SHOOTING THE "BOMB"

The photographer can anticipate a pass on the first down instead of a run only if the team is behind on the scoreboard, needs long yardage on the play, or wants to stop the clock. A quarterback might go to the air on the second down if the team is just a few yards short of first down; he knows he still has two more downs to pick up the necessary ground. The photographer can bet with good odds on a third down pass if the team has lost ground or failed to advance the ball on the first two downs.

A photographer can predict the "Big Bomb" by noting the score and watching the body language of the quarterback. If the quarterback drops back far behind the line of scrimmage, firmly plants his feet, pumps the ball a few times, and then cocks his arm way back behind his head, the player is very likely winding up for a long throw.

Once you read these cues and see a "bomb" in the making, you should immediately swing the barrel of your telephoto lens downfield, focus on the expected receiver, and follow his pass pattern.

Do not try to track the ball as it flies through the air; you couldn't focus fast enough to keep the ball sharp. Observe the direction of the quarterback's gaze for a tip off on which downfield receiver will get the ball. Good sports photographers know that even the best quarterback has to look where he's throwing the ball.

■ ADJUSTING YOUR POSITION

At each down, station yourself a few yards ahead of the scrimmage line. Then, when the play begins, wait for a clear, unobstructed view of the ball carrier before you press the shutter release. At most stadiums, photographers are permitted to roam freely from the end zone to about the 35-yard line on either end of the field. To avoid distracting the coaches and sidelined players, photographers are prohibited from moving in front of the benches at the center of the field.

Photographers must stay behind the sideline boundary strip at all times and never get between the player on the field and the yardage marker poles. If you had to jump back quickly as the thundering pack of players headed toward the sidelines, you could trip on the marking chain and get trampled—a high price, even for the most dramatic action shot.

All 50,000 pairs of eyes in the stadium are searching for the pigskin. The ball itself is the center of interest because everyone wants to know who has the ball and what's happening to it. Therefore, you have an obligation to get the brown leather ball in your picture as often as you can. The players, however, trained by their coaches to protect the ball at all times, will make your task difficult.

But not every picture must involve the ball carrier. After all, when one 250-pounder, with an indestructible frame and shoulder pads, meets another human impasse capped by an impact-resistant helmet, something has to give. The confrontation scene might be spectacular—even if it occurs ten yards away from the ball.

A 400mm lens will cover the action. If you try to cover midfield action with a shorter lens, the image size on the negative will be too small for a high-quality enlargement. With a versatile 80–200mm zoom, you can photograph from the end zone when the team is on the ten-yard line and goal to go. In addition to the 200mm and 400mm lenses, some photographers carry an extra body with a 50 mm or 35mm wide-angle attached for moments when the play runs toward them. Also, the wide-angle comes in handy when, at the end of the game, the team carries the coach on their shoulders or slumps off in defeat.

■ AVOIDING THE "STANDARD STUFF"

When Pam Schuyler covered football for the AP, she looked for dramatic catches, fumbles, collisions, and flagrant penalties such as face-masking or illegal holdings. She is always searching for the unusual football picture. "You get only a half-dozen super pictures a year if you are lucky," she says. "The remainder is standard stuff."

DON'T BE FAKED OUT IN BASKETBALL

The ball travels so lightning-fast in basketball that following the ball is like keeping your eye on the pea in the old shell game. Unlike football with its discreet downs, and baseball with its clearly defined plays, the basketball game rolls on at full speed until a point has been scored, a foul called, or the ball goes out of bounds. The basketball might be bigger than a baseball or a football, but keeping track of it can be just as tough.

The AP's Risberg says that he concentrates on watching the ball and the players' arms. They tip him off when he is trying to anticipate action.

Pam Schuyler, who spent two intensive

years covering the world-champion Boston Celtics for a picture book she photographed and wrote called *Through The Hoop: A Season With the Celtics*, formed some valuable theories about anticipating basketball action. Schuyler says that the key problem in photographing basketball is learning to read the "fake," the quick twisting and jerking movements that players use to "fake out"

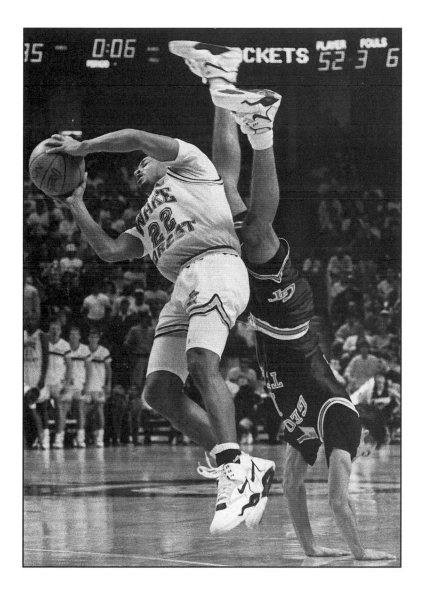

their opponents and get a clear shot at the basket. As Schuyler says, "They often fake out the photographer, as well."

Schuyler points out that a pro basketball player can fake not only with his hands and arms, but also with his legs and feet. Therefore, Schuyler has discovered that watching the player's stomach muscles provides the best clue to the timing and direction of the player's movement. "A player cannot fake with his stomach, so where the stomach of the player goes, his arms, legs, and head will soon follow," Schuyler says. Basketball players wear tight, thin jerseys that cling to their ribs like surgeon's gloves. "You can easily see a basketball player's stomach muscles contract through his jersey, just before he breaks for the hoop."

Schuyler points out, however, that you can't constantly stare at the abdomens of all the players during the game because you have to spend most of your time and attention tracking the path of the basketball.

■ SIDELINE POSITIONS
Many basketball photographers sit on small stools or kneel on the floor behind and a little to either side of the basket. Then they shoot with their 50mm or 85mm lens about 10 to 15 feet into the court and wait. Schuyler, however, prefers to gamble on more unusual shots. She follow-focuses the ball as it is tossed around the court. She rotates the lens barrel as fast as she can, trying to keep the ball in sharp focus as it flies from one player to another. Follow-focusing the ball is tough. "You get more bad, out-of-focus shots when you follow-focus, but your good shots are usually worth it," Schuyler says.

After the first few minutes of the game, Schuyler identifies the key players and notes where they execute most of their plays: under

While you might not use a photo like this from every game, shooting from the rafters of the gymnasium offers a refreshing angle on the sport. (Photo by Michael Murphy, the *Houston Chronicle*.)

the backboard, to the right of the foul line, and so on. She then positions herself as near as possible to this focal spot. If the action spot changes as the game progresses, she shifts her sideline position.

With her two favorite basketball lenses, the 85mm and the 180mm, Schuyler covers the entire court. From a vantage point under the basket, she shoots with the 85mm; from mid-court, she works with the 180mm. She always sets the shutter speed at 1/500 sec. to freeze movement. "At slower speeds, I've found the players' hands move so fast they tend to blur." Many photographers include the 300 f/2.8 in their regular arsenal. This lens allows the shooter to cover the action at the far end of the court.

■ THE "ARMPIT" SHOT

The standard bread-and-butter basketball photo, nicknamed the "armpit" shot, shows the lanky basketball player jumping off the floor with arms extended over his head, pumping the ball toward the basket. Pro players use the jump shot so often that the conscientious photographer actually has to work hard to avoid taking this standard photo.

■ SKIPPING THE CLICHÉ

Photographers who cover basketball regularly try to find alternatives for the armpit shot, figuring that readers will consider the shot a boring photographic cliché.

For unique basketball pictures, Schuyler is always on the lookout for loose basketballs on the court. "You can bet when a ball's free, there will be a scramble for it and then a fight to gain possession of it," notes Schuyler. "Players fouling one another always look funny on film and these seem to be the pictures people remember longest. When a ball bounces loose on the court or a foul is committed, the rhythm of the game is broken. A mistake was made. The game gets interesting, and so do the pictures."

When you can't attend the practice sessions of a team, or when you don't have time to learn the team's basic patterns, concentrate your coverage on the player with the star reputation. Stars tend to score the most points and snag the majority of rebounds. Also, stars don't just sink baskets like regular folk; they exhibit individual styles and almost choreographed moves. Michael Jordan, for example, seems to counteract gravity as he floats through the air, passes the basket, and, as if it were an afterthought, changes direction in mid-flight to sink a hoop. A good sports photographer tries to capture on film the style of the star. ■

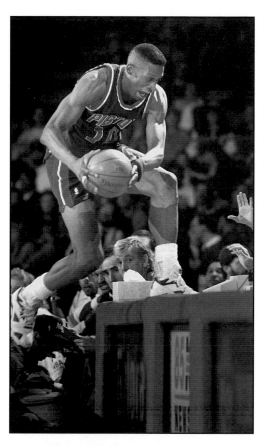

The photographer followed the action right off the court to catch this surprising shot of a player retrieving a loose ball off the media table. (Photo by Glenn Asakawa, the *Rocky Mountain News*, Denver.)

Watch for fouls committed during the game, like this one between the Seattle Supersonics and the L.A. Lakers. This moment reveals the intensity of the game. (Photo by Larry Steagall, the *Bremerton* (Wash.) *Sun.*)

Photo Story

With the advent of high-speed presses that could quickly dry the ink on glossy coated paper, Henry Luce published the first issue of *Life* in 1936. Soon after *Life* began publication, other large picture-dominated magazines with names like *Look*, *Click*, *Scoop*, *Peek*, *Pix*, and *Picture* hit the stands. These magazines also ran pages of pictures on a single topic. Though some stories in these competing magazines were candid, most were heavily scripted. Even after World War II, magazines continued to produce highly scripted picture

The young man in the back seat is not happy about his mother's new marriage. The picture is from a photo story about what happens when divorced parents marry new partners. (Photo by April Saul, *Philadelphia Inquirer.*)

Police officer Alan Keith was writing a traffic ticket near the Blue Hills Reservation in Milton, Mass., when a speeding car clipped Keith's horse, Tivoli. The impact threw the policeman and fatally injured his four-legged companion of three years. Keith embraced this injured friend, then was helped away by fellow officers as Tivoli was put down.

Within the space of a few minutes, an entire drama unfolded in front of Jim Mahoney's camera. In this sequence of pictures, Mahoney concentrated on telling the story of the policeman and his reactions to the loss of his equine partner.

The original edit that appeared in the *Boston Herald* overlooked the photo of the officer with his arm around the horse. The photo was later run in *Life* magazine. The newspaper also omitted the photo of the veterinarian putting down the horse. Editors considered the photo too graphic.

These pictures show the emotional side of a police officer, a sight rarely revealed on film. Mahoney notes that most officers are seen as "John Wayne" types, never expressing fear or sadness. He says that perhaps the unusual combination of the tragedy for this animal, combined with the clear grief of the officer, accounts for the reason the pictures not only received good play in the paper and on both AP and UPI wire services but also generated so many sympathetic letters and phone calls.

(Photos by Jim Mahoney, *Boston Herald*.)

▲ Officer Alan Keith tries to calm and comfort his horse, Tivoli, after the horse's leg was broken by a passing drunk driver. A fireman places an icepack on the officer's head.

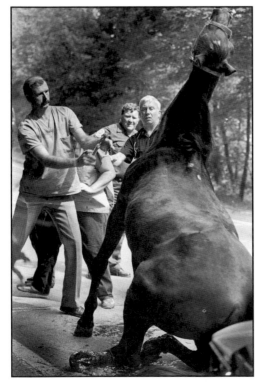

▲ A veterinarian readies a shot that will quickly and painlessly kill the horse, whose leg was severely broken.

▲ Officer Keith is led away as the veterinarian administers the shot to Tivoli. The officer returned to the mounted police force soon after the accident.

stories. *Look* magazine, for example, published in its January 8, 1946 issue, a story on quick-frozen, precooked, ready-to-serve meals (today known as TV dinners). The opening picture featured a "family" in their living room casually reading and playing records. The caption read: "2:00 P.M. 'How about dinner?' asks Mother." The following overly lit pictures show a woman taking frozen meals from the refrigerator, putting them in the oven, and then taking the food out after fifteen minutes. The final shot shows "family members" in their Sunday best, seated around the table, prepared to eat the new frozen cuisine. The photographer's shooting script, which specified opening and closing shots as well as a record of the preparatory steps in between, obviously left no room for real people or candid moments to interfere with the slick look of the pictures. The photos look like stills from an ad.

■ FOLLOWING THE FLOW

Toward the end of the 1940s, photographers began experimenting with a freer form of picture story development. W. Eugene Smith, working for *Life* magazine, broke with the typical prescripted story line. Smith's pictures of country doctor Ernest Ceriani of Kremmling, Colo. (pop. 1,000), actually documented the rural physician's life—without a New York editor predetermining the story's look and point of view (*Life*, September 20, 1948). By staying with the doctor long enough, six weeks in all, and by recording the doctor's everyday activities as well as the emergencies and traumas he handled, Smith built a realistic story about this dedicated health worker. While the story still had cohesion, it was based on Smith's observations, not the preconceived ideas of a New York editor who demanded an overall and a close-up for the script. By staying close to his subject long enough and by observing carefully enough, Smith fashioned a revealing story that explained the life of this rural doctor. (See also "Nurse Midwife," pages 118–129.)

In the tradition of Smith, photographers today continue to photograph long-term projects. While Smith spent six weeks photographing the Colorado doctor for *Life*, few of today's magazines or newspapers will fund a project of this length. Consequently, many photographers shoot extended stories on their own time, or they turn to agencies outside the publishing industry for grants or foundation support to underwrite their projects. Whether personally financed, grant-supported or underwritten by a newspaper or magazine, the picture story provides the one

place in photojournalism where the photographer can explore a topic in depth, present a point of view, or show with pictures the many sides of an issue.

DEVELOPING IDEAS

Talking with other people alerts you to good picture story ideas. Someone's description of the effects of crack on children exposed to the drug in the womb, or a tip about a women's motorcycle gang called the "Fantastic Foxes," might provide the catalyst for a story. Perhaps an issue addressed in a topical book or movie might stimulate your interest to investigate the subject with your camera. The conversation might turn to a national trend like elder care. This trend story can be localized for your area with a picture investigation of a nursing home in your town such as the one photographed by Judy Griesedieck for the *San Jose Mercury News*. (See pages 54–55.)

Like any good journalist, the photo reporter must rely on basic journalistic research skills, a highly sensitized nose for news, and a trained sense of whether what smells like news can be reported visually, as well.

■ VIEWERS RELATE TO PEOPLE STORIES

Maitland Edey, an editor on the staff of the old *Life* magazine, concluded, "Great photo essays have to do with people: with human dilemmas, with human challenges, with human suffering." People's lives, even if they are not in crisis situations, still provide the basis for most of the best photo stories.

Photo stories about people usually break down into three categories: the well-known, the little-known but interesting, and the little-known who serve as an example of a trend.

WAITING, the young mother leans forlornly against the window, ignoring sympathy and looking for Maude's car.

FRIGHTENED AND SICK, the nervous mother is helped by Phoebe Gadsden, the first midwife she called. Mrs. Gadsden, a practicing midwife who attended Maude's classes (*pp. 144, 145*), has helped at several deliveries but felt that this one needed special attention and so decided to ask Maude to come and supervise.

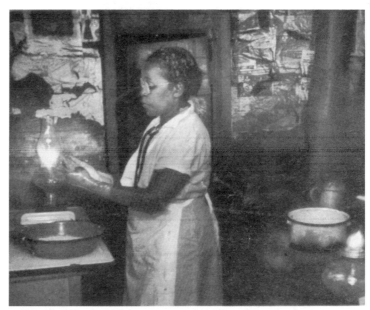

MAUDE GETS READY in the kitchen by lamplight. In addition to the stethoscope and gloves, her equipment consists of about $5 worth of such items as clean cloths, bits of cotton, scissors, cord ties, Lysol, surgical gown and mask and a blood-pressure gauge. Her deliveries are always made under aseptic conditions.

IN DEEP PAIN, the 17-year-old mother writhes, mumbling prayers while Mrs. Gadsden holds her hand. She could do little to relieve pain because she is not permitted to administer any drugs. The mother was worn out and weak even at the beginning of her ordeal, having previously gone through a period of false labor.

Nurse Midwife

MAUDE CALLEN EASES PAIN OF BIRTH, LIFE AND DEATH

PHOTOGRAPHED FOR LIFE BY W. EUGENE SMITH

[So]me weeks ago in the South Carolina village of Pineville, in Berkeley [co]unty on the edge of Hell Hole Swamp, the time arrived for Alice Cooper [to] have a baby and she sent for the midwife. At first it seemed that every-[thi]ng was all right, but soon the midwife noticed signs of trouble. Hastily [she] sent for a woman named Maude Callen to come and take over.

[A]fter Maude Callen arrived at 6 p.m., Alice Cooper's labor grew more [seve]re. It lasted through the night until dawn. But at the end (*next page*) [she] was safely delivered of a healthy son. The new midwife had succeeded [in a] situation where the fast-disappearing "granny" midwife of the South, [arm]ed with superstition and a pair of rusty scissors, might have killed [bot]h mother and child.

[Maude Callen is a member of a unique group, the nurse midwife. Al-[tho]ugh there are perhaps 20,000 common midwives practicing, trained [nur]se midwives are rare. There are only nine in South Carolina, 300 in [the] nation. Their education includes the full course required of all regis-[ter]ed nurses, training in public health and at least six months' classes in [obs]tetrics. As professionals they are far ahead of the common midwife, [an]d as far removed from the granny as aureomycin is from asafetida.

[Maude Callen has delivered countless babies in her career, but obstet-[ric]s is only part of her work. To 10,000 people in a thickly populated rural [are]a of some 400 square miles veined with muddy roads, she must try to [be] "doctor," dietician, psychologist, bail-goer and friend (*pp. 140, 141*). [To] those who think that a middle-aged Negro without a medical degree [ha]s no business meddling in affairs such as these, Dr. William Fishburne, [dir]ector of the Berkeley County health department, has a ready answer. [W]hen he was asked whether he thought Maude Callen could be spared to [do] some teaching for the state board of health, he replied, "If you have to [tak]e her, I can only ask you to join me in prayer for the people left here."

[W]EARY BUT WATCHFUL, MAUDE SITS BY AS MOTHER DOZES

4 A.M. As hard labor begins, the face of Alice Cooper seems to sum up all the suffering of every woman who has ever borne a child.

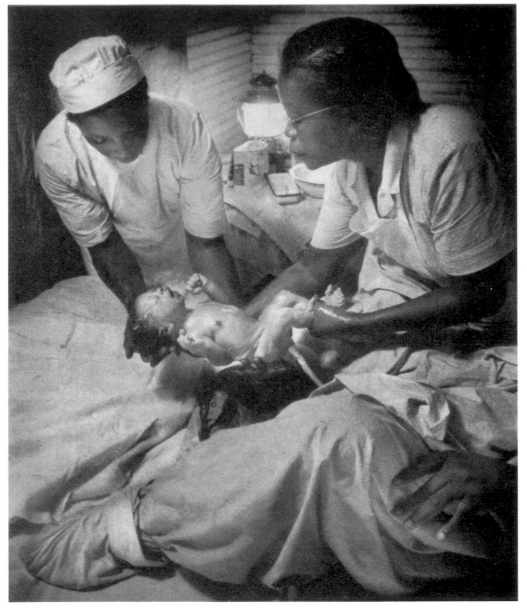

5:30 A.M. A few seconds after the normal delivery, Maude Callen holds the healthy child as he fills his lungs and begins to cry.

5:45 A.M. The mother's aunt, Catherine Prileau, tries to soothe her so that she will go to sleep and begin to forget her misery.

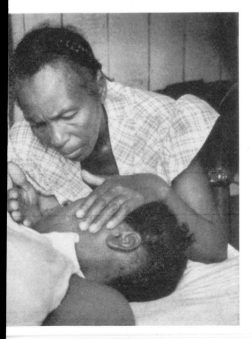

5:40A.M. The long suffering over, the mother first sees her son. She had no name for him, but a week later she chose Harris Lee.

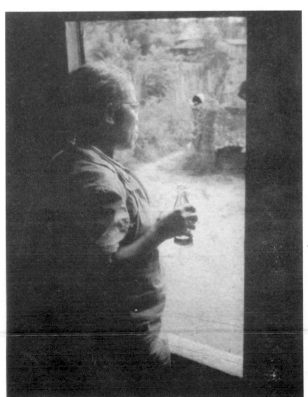

6:20 A.M. Her work over at last, Nurse Midwife Callen quietly takes the first nourishment that she has had for more than 27 hours.

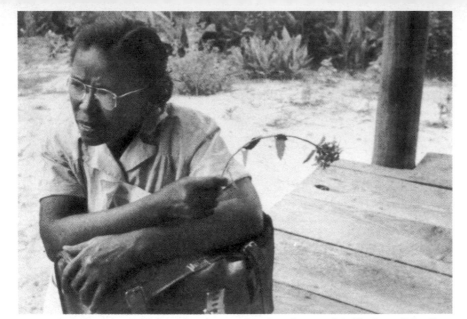

MAUDE AT 51 has a thoughtful, weary face that reflects the fury of her life. Orphaned at 7, she was brought up by an uncle in Florida, studied at Georgia Infirmary in Savannah, became a nurse at 21.

HEALTHY TWINS, who were delivered a day apart last year by Maude, get a quick once-over when she stops in to see them and to pump herself a drink of water. Only about 2% of her patients are white.

MAUDE'S 16-HOUR DAY

Maude's duties as midwife are no more important than those as nurse. On her daily rounds she sees dozens of patients suffering from countless diseases and injuries. She visits the nine schools in her district to check vaccinations, eyes and teeth. She tries to keep birth records straight, patiently coping with parents who say, "We name him John Herbert but we gonna call him Louie." She tries to keep diseases isolated and when she locates a case of contagious illness like tuberculosis she must comb through her territory like a detective, tracking down all the people with whom the patient may have been in contact. She arranges for seriously ill men like Leon Snipe (right) to go to state hospitals, and she keeps an eye on currently healthy

babies to see that they remain that way. Whenever she is home—she is childless and her husband, a retired custom-house employe, sees her only at odd hours—she throws open a clinic in her house to take care of anyone who wanders in. And sometimes patients like Annabelle McCray Fuller (below, right) will travel all the way from Charleston, 50 miles away.

Maude drives 36,000 miles within the county each year, is reimbursed for part of this by the state and must buy her own cars, which last her 18 months. Her work day is often as long as 16 hours, her salary $225 a month. She has taken only two vacations and has now become so vital to the people of the community that it is almost impossible for her to take another.

TUBERCULOSIS CASE, 33-year-old Leon Snipe, sits morosely on bed while Maude arranges with his sister for him to go to state sanatorium. Maude had met him on road, noticed he was thin, wan and sickly.

AFTER ANOTHER DELIVERY Maude departs at 4:30 a.m., leaving the case in charge of another midwife. Since she is already up, she is likely not to go to bed but to continue through rest of morning.

ACCIDENT CASE is brought to Maude's door one night. Annabelle Fuller was seriously cut in an auto accident and Maude had given her first aid. Now the girl returns to have her dressings changed.

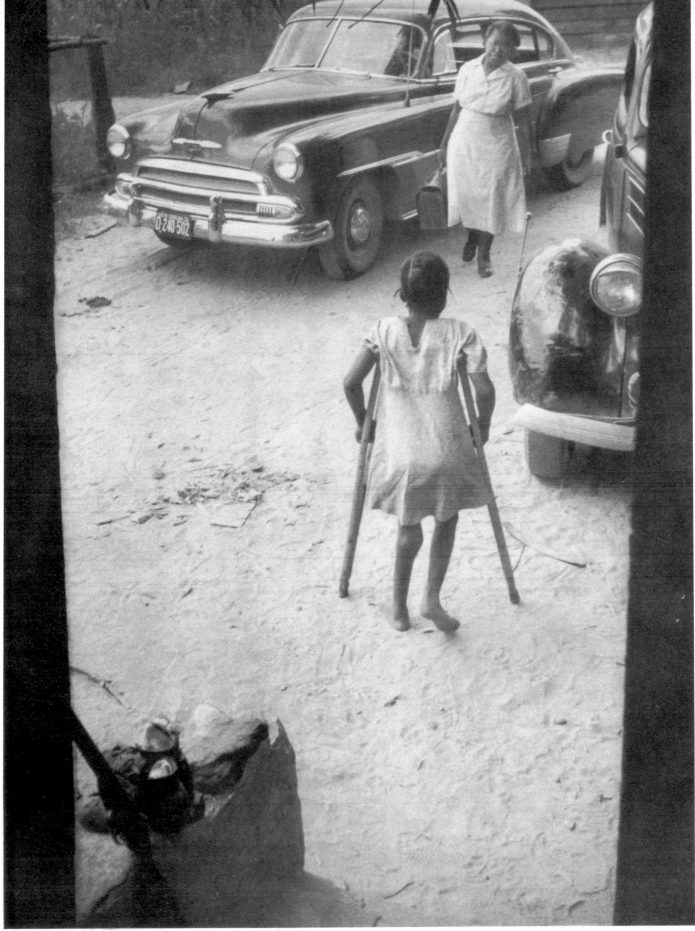

CRIPPLED GIRL greets Maude at her door. Last summer Maude arranged for her to go to a state camp for crippled children which had strict entrance requirements —each child had to have two dresses and one pair of pajamas. The girl could not meet these, but after Maude got her one dress and one pair of pajamas, she could.

NEW DRESSES for 9-year-old Carrie (*right*) and 8-year-old Mary Jane Covington were dropped off by Maude on her way to a patient. Occasionally, as in this case, she gets clothing from friends or charitable organizations and distributes it where she thinks it is most needed. But sometimes she buys the clothes herself.

SIMPLE KINDNESS overwhelms an old man. Frank McCray had a headache one day in 1927, soon was paralyzed, and has been in this chair ever since. He broke down and wept when Maude stopped in.

EXTRA DUTY assumed by Maude includes cashing of relief checks and dealing with storekeepers for several people who are mentally incompetent or, like this man, blind. She paid his bills for him and counted out change so he could buy some tobacco.

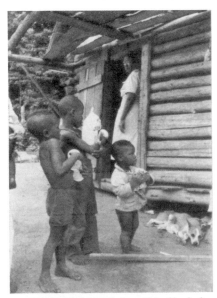

STORE-BOUGHT FOOD donated by Maude fascinates youngsters outside log cabin. She frequently finds families with only two or three items on their diet, recently found this one living entirely on corn.

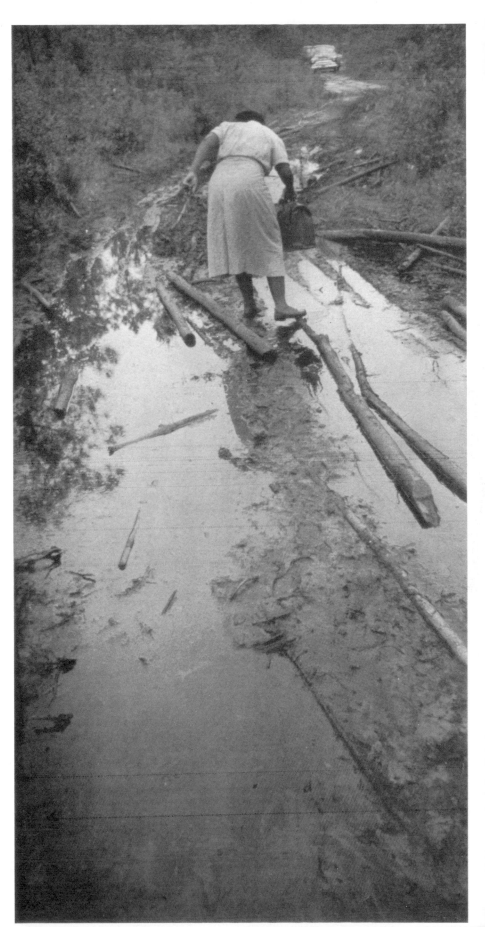

AFTER A CALL she wades back to her car. Roads like this are not unusual. At the end of some of them in the '20s, she "found people who did not know the use of forks and spoons."

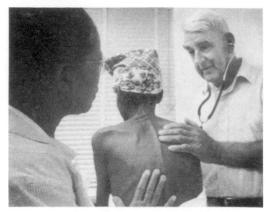

DR. W. K. FISHBURNE, head of the Berkeley County health department, examines a patient brought to hospital by Maude.

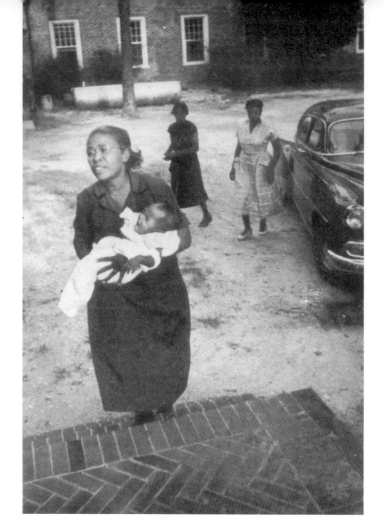

MAUDE AND M.D.

When she is not visiting her patients in their homes, Maude holds clinics in churches, school buildings and backwoods shanties throughout her district. Some are for a single purpose—inoculations, classes for midwives or expectant mothers, examinations for venereal disease. Others are open to all comers with all ills. All are part of the activities of the South Carolina State Board of Health, Maude's ultimate employer, which has perhaps the best state midwife-education program in the U.S., although a recent budget cut seriously threatens it.

At her clinics Maude does not compete with doctors. There are not enough M.D.s in any case to cover the territory, and whenever her patients are in need of treatment that Maude is incompetent or unauthorized to give, she takes them to the health department clinic or the county hospital. There she works under the direction of Dr. William K. Fishburne (*above*), from whose shoulders she has taken an enormous amount of work.

DYING BABY who is suffering from acute enteritis is rushed to hospital. Mother brought her to Maude, who took her temperature (105°) and raced 27 miles in hope of saving her life.

TRANSFUSION was almost impossible because fever's dehydration had affected arm veins and doctor had to try one in neck. Baby died before he could get blood flowing.

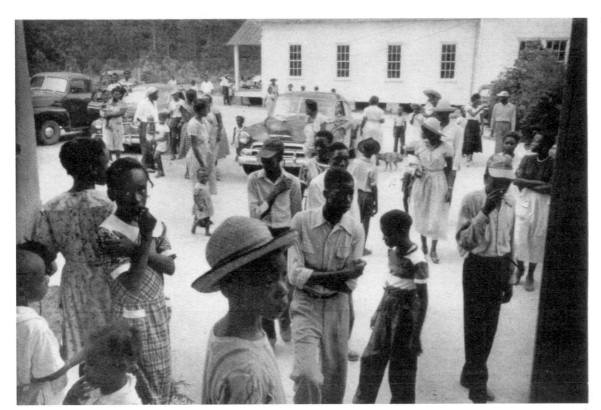

OUTSIDE A CLINIC held in school, crowd waits to see Maude. On one afternoon, with one assistant, she gave 810 typhoid shots, later went out and delivered another baby.

INSIDE A CHURCH, Maude inspects a patient behind a bedsheet screen. She dreams of having a well-supplied clinic but has small hope of getting the $7,000 it might cost.

MAKING A DELIVERY PAD in patient's home according to classroom method, Maude crimps together the edges of several pieces of newspaper. Her materials must be makeshift; even paper is scarce.

INCUBATOR is made of box and whisky bottles full of warm water. The bottles are placed at foot and sides of box, then covered with layers of cloth. This will sometimes work for as long as two or three hours.

CRIB is made of an old fruit crate propped near a cold stove. Maude must demonstrate even this simple idea—she has seen newborn babies thrown into bed with older children where they might suffocate.

TEACHING A MIDWIFE CLASS, Maude shows how to examine a baby for abnormalities. She conducts some 84 classes, helps coach about 12 new midwives each year. These midwives, who are already practicing, return to Maude for monthly refresher courses which open and close with a hymn. Few have more than fourth-grade education but are trained for two weeks at the state midwife institute and are very proud of their calling. Unlike Maude, they get fees for deliveries, set at $25 but often paid in produce.

SEEING SOUND

Each picture individually shows one way of depicting sound. Together, the photos take on an added dimension. An essay is usually produced by a single photographer, but it can also comprise the work of several photojournalists. Here, the essay emphasizes camera technique as a way of turning a non-visual subject into something you can see on the printed page.

◄ The saxophonist, Anthony Braxton, swayed during a long exposure, creating this blur effect. Notice the microphone is still sharp.

(Photo by Michael Grecco.)

▲ A straightforward photo of a child listening to music through earphones.

(Photo by Greg Schneider, San Bernardino (Calif.) Sun Telegram.)

▲ For this photo of a folk singer, the photographer held the camera steady for 1/2 sec. and then moved the camera in an arc before closing the shutter.

(Photo by Ken Kobré for Photo Associates, Denver.)

◄ Double exposure of Bruce Wilkerson, bass player of the "Atlantics."

(Photo by Pamela E. Chipman.)

the little-known but interesting, and the little-known who serve as an example of a trend.

The Well-known

Photo stories about well-known personalities provide the primary content for several larger circulation magazines. The best-read section of *Time* magazine, called "People," gave Time, Inc., editors the idea for a picture magazine featuring personalities as the sole subject. Naturally, the editors called the magazine *People.* This popular weekly publishes a steady diet of photos showing the lives of the famous and the infamous. Not only *People* but an assortment of other magazines, from *Vanity Fair* to *Esquire,* publish an endless variety of stories about movie stars, T.V. personalities, media moguls, and politicians. Today, in fact, celebrity stories dominate the contents of most mass circulation magazines.

The Little-known but Interesting

In addition to the famous, *People* magazine prints photo stories about little-known people who either do something interesting or exhibit eccentric characteristics.

Hero or not, the person must do something to fascinate readers. George Willis, who climbed the outside of the World Trade Center, or the champion stacker of bowling balls (see page 238) are examples of people with unusual accomplishments. The story about Rudi Gomez, fourteen-year-old child prostitute, surely qualifies as an example of someone living an unusual lifestyle (see pages 134–139). Maude, the nurse midwife whose story was told by W. Eugene Smith, (see pages 117–129) also fills this bill.

The Little-known who Represent a Trend

Another type of personality story investigates the life of a little-known person who is an example of a new trend or developing style. For example, almost seven million children in America are living with a stepparent. April Saul, of the *Philadelphia Inquirer,* explored this trend on film in her story "Remarried. . . with children." (See pages 148–149.)

At times, the photographer wants to explore an abstract topic. Personifying a topic helps readers relate. Zeroing-in on one person affected by atomic radiation or focusing on one person living on the streets dramatizes the general problems of nuclear power or homelessness. Readers identify with the woes of a little-known individual much more than with the problems of a political group or a sociological class. For photographers, converting a topic into human terms provides a visual clothesline on which to hang the individual points of the picture story.

Both Tom Gralish's story about homelessness (see page 21) and my story about the effects of crack exposure on children (pages 142–145) help to translate disturbing social trends into individual photographic examples.

■ SPOTTING TRENDS

Whereas a news story has a specific time peg, a trend story identifies a gradual but demonstrably real change that might include changes in the public's buying preferences, lifestyles, or a technological shift in an industry. For example, a news story might read, "The First National Bank went bankrupt yesterday." By comparison, a trend story might say, "The number of two-income families increased dramatically during the past ten years." A trend doesn't start one day; it happens gradually over time.

Surprisingly enough, the *Wall Street Journal* is an excellent source for picture story ideas. Although the international business newspaper reproduces no photographs itself, the *Journal* does report on interesting trends in the business world: trends that the photographer can translate into highly visual photo stories. Not only are the *Journal* stories often first to spot a trend, but the stories are usually well researched. For major trend stories, which appear on the left, middle, and right-hand columns of the front page, *Journal* staffers spend months researching and gathering data before they begin to write.

After reading the *Wall Street Journal*'s story, the photographer should find visual verification of the trend. The camera reporter must transform the economic charts and abstract statistics from the *Journal*'s article into subject matter for eye-catching pictures.

■ TEST YOUR THEME WITH A HEADLINE

How does a picture story differ from a collection of pictures on a topic? A story has a theme. Not only are the individual pictures in the story about one subject, but they also help to support one central point. Here are some headlines for stories without a theme:
• "All you ever want to know about . . . "
• "A day in the life of . . ."
• "Aspects of . . ."
• "Scenes from . . ."
Stories with these headlines might contain beautiful or even powerful pictures, but the pictures don't add up to a story. They remain the photographer's observations without a story line or central message.

On the other hand, a theme story such as crack cocaine's lasting effect on children (see pages 142–145) tries to visually identify only the specific behavioral reactions that the drug has on children who were exposed to crack in their mother's womb. This set of pictures does not tell the reader everything about crack or how to take care of newborns. Rather, the story tries to show the special behaviors crack-addicted infants exhibit—such as constant crying, painful expressions, and the need for soothing motion.

Once you have decided on a story and started to shoot it, try writing a headline for it. Easily nailing down a headline indicates you have a clear focus for the story. Make sure your headline is specific to the story and differentiates your point of view from other stories on the same topic.

Headline completed, see if you can include or reject pictures on the basis of whether the photos fit the story's headline. If the headline is so encompassing that all the photos fit, your theme is probably too broad.

You can devise many themes from a single situation. Even after you have finished shooting, you might find that by re-editing your pictures, you can produce a different story line. Each theme demands a different edit not only for the opening spread but also for all the pictures that follow. Just for fun, try changing the titles on any of the stories in this book, and see how you might change the edit.

■ FIND A NEWSPEG

Whether you are an employee or a freelancer, an editor is more likely to use your picture story if it has a newspeg. A newspeg tells the reader why the story is being seen now instead of six months ago or six months in the future. If you can tie your picture story into a front-page news item, then your story will take on more immediacy.

Suppose your story revolves around the life of a family doctor. You might peg your pictures on a recent study showing that the number of general practitioners is decreasing nationally. Or suppose your story concerns your town's emergency medical squad. If a squad member died last month while trying to save a child's life, your timeless story about the unit's general operations can be pegged to this recent news event.

Some magazines commission picture stories that the editors hold until a related news event breaks. The news sections of the daily newspaper, therefore, provide excellent sources for story ideas because the news leads are timely.

Thousands of illegal immigrants cross the southern borders of the United States daily, but the story has news value if the governor of a state makes a campaign promise to stop the flow of immigrants. Hal Wells' story documenting an illegal border crossing (see page 133) was tied to the signing of an immigra-

tion bill. Taken a month before or after, the pictures would have been less newsworthy.

■ VISUAL CONSISTENCY

Regardless of their subject matter, pictures take on an additional quality when they appear on a printed page. In a successful layout, the photos interact with one another and form an eye-catching, compelling picture-story. When the layout is unsuccessful, the pictures remain separate units simply co-existing on the page.

What clues the reader that a group of pictures interacts as a story rather than functions independently as individual images, such as the ones you see on a gallery wall?

To link pictures together visually, photographers use pictorial devices. With a visually unified essay, the viewer sees in almost every picture either the same (1) person, (2) object, (3) mood, (4) theme, (5) perspective, or (6) camera technique.

Same Person

The easiest way to tie pictures together into a photo story is to concentrate on one person. Restricting the scope to one individual helps to define the focus of the series. The person's identity, repeated in each photo, threads the story together and gives the layout continuity. (See "Nurse Midwife," pages 118–129; "Rodney's Crime, pages 152–156; "Julie: Lifestyle of a Punk," pages 230–231; "Living with Horrific Headaches," page 160.)

With a picture story, the camera, like a microscope, magnifies the subject's daily routine. The results of the visual probe depend on the subject's accessibility and cooperation. The photographer shadows the subject as long as the person doesn't object, and as long as the paper or magazine will finance the effort. In the heyday of the big glossy picture magazines and their lavish photo budgets, photographers were given considerably longer time to shoot personality stories than they are today. When John Dominis was on the staff of *Life* magazine, he worked on his story about Frank Sinatra for four months before the story was finished. Later, as picture editor of *People* magazine, with its much smaller photo budget, Dominis assigned photographers to personality profiles and expected the job done in a half day.

For a story about Julie, a midwestern punk who still lives at home, photographer Donna Terek wanted to go beyond a series of pictures of weird-looking kids who sport outrageous hairdos. The photojournalist tried to explain one young person's way of rebelling against her middle-class upbringing. The story shows Julie wearing a ring in her nose

CROSSING THE TEXAS BORDER

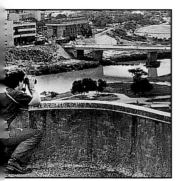

Some stories take a year or more to shoot (see pages 152–157). Others can be shot in a day or less. Hal Wells set out to photograph migrant Mexican laborers illegally entering the United States over the Texas border. He started by contacting the border patrol, whom he

◄ A border patrol agent uses the Laredo Hilton rooftop as an observation point for spotting illegal aliens.

photographed in the morning on their stakeout. Later in the day, he waited for a group of Mexicans to cross the Rio Grande carrying their dry clothes. At first, the immigrants were wary of the photographer, suspecting that he was part of the patrol. After awhile, they trusted him and waded into the water. Wells completed the mini-story with pictures of the border patrol

stopping, arresting, and handcuffing some of the immigrants. In one day, Wells was able to summarize the hundreds of border crossings and arrests that constantly take place. The pictures tell a clear story of how many immigrants try to cross and what happens to some of them.

(Photos by Hall Wells, *Long Beach* (Calif.) *Press-Telegram.*)

◄ Illegally crossing the Rio Grande, which separates Mexico from the United States, the immigrants try to keep their clothing dry.

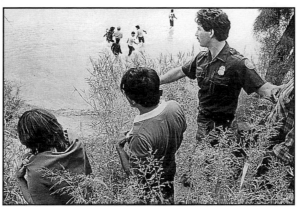

► Monitoring the river bank alone, an agent manages to capture some members of the group trying to cross.

▲ Border patrol stations report that apprehensions of illegal immigrants have declined since the signing of the immigration bill.

RUDI GOMEZ: CHILD PROSTITUTE

Rudi Gomez, 14, hustles. He doesn't steal or deal drugs. He sells his body to older men.

Stephen Shames' story reveals the life of this child who uses prostitution as a way to survive in an adult world. For the story about child prostitution, Shames could have taken pictures of young boys hanging out in Times Square, where Rudi makes his meager living.

However, this story goes far beyond simple surface images. Zeroing-in on one boy who prowls the area, the story digs deep into the life of Rudi Gomez. The photos help the reader understand the life of the child from the South Bronx. A drunk, unemployed, and abusive father. Parents and eight siblings all living on $308 a month from welfare.

The story shows the child's entertainment as he does gymnastics on a subway car's strap hangers and as he badmouths people at the pinball parlor. Then the story discloses how Rudi makes a living. The pictures show an older man picking up Rudi. The story's crucial and unforgettable final photo takes the reader inside a barren room. Here Rudi, in his underwear, lies on a mattress, awaiting an older man wearing a sleeveless T-shirt, who looms over the youngster.

This story does not just give a slice-of-life of this street hustler. Rather, it carries the reader through the child's life and tries to explain how a 14-year-old could wind up in this condition.

(Photos by Stephen Shames, Visions.)

ON THE STREETS OF NEW YORK

◄ A policeman and a security guard lecture Rudi after he's been thrown out of a pinball arcade for bad-mouthing and other poor behavior.

◄ Rudi can't take being at home too long. He returns only to shower or change clothes. His real life is on the street. He sleeps in subway cars, bus depots, and trucks, under staircases in houses and, in the summer, in parks.

◄ Rudi does gymnastics on the strap handles as he rides the subway from the South Bronx to hustle on Times Square. Fifteen or twenty other boys from his block make the same trip for the same purpose every day.

In a moment of anger,
Rudi picks up a broom and
strikes his brother.

▼ Rudi Gomez lives in a run-down, burned-out, boarded-up section of the South Bronx in New York.

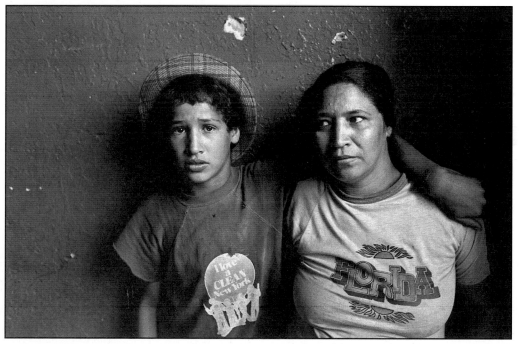

▲ Rudi is one of Efigenia Gomez's nine children. She speaks English poorly and does not exactly know how Rudi makes his living when he goes to Times Square. His father, unemployed, remains constantly drunk and beats up his son.

HUSTLING

▲ Rudi calls one of his
customers on the phone.

Rudi feigns a smile at a man just before being picked up by him in the subway's pinball arcade.

The man with Rudi keeps this apartment near Times Square for the purpose of bringing boys to it for sex. The man, in his 60s, lives with his mother. Rudi does not consider himself a prostitute or a homosexual. He simply sells what he has. His body.

and a tattoo on the side of her shaved head. Other pictures catch Julie working, partying, kidding around with her boyfriend, and sitting stiffly on a couch next to her straight-looking younger sister and mother. To drive home the contrast between her old and new lifestyles, a final photo shows the orange-haired punk carrying her boombox and sporting a black leather jacket and spiked boots as she returns home to her parent's run-of-the-mill suburban house. With this final picture, the reader has a surprisingly rounded picture of this young woman's life. (Part of this story is reproduced on pages 230–231.)

As a freelance photographer in New York, Stephen Shames spent a year and a half photographing a 14-year-old boy who sells his body on the streets near Times Square. Like onion layers, each photo in the story comes closer to the core of this child's life.

The photos (see pages 134–138), published in the German magazine *Stern*, first reveal Rudi Gomez's home life in the Bronx—his mother, alcoholic father, and nine bothers and sisters living on $308 a month from welfare. Other pictures explore his street life—hustling in Manhattan, stealing, and picking up older men and having sex with them. The photos try to explain how this young child survives in an adult world. Their power lies in the photographer's ability to take us someplace we have never gone—to visually verify the life of one child's misspent youth.

Shocking but fascinating, the story draws us into the life of this young street hustler. The pictures put the child's life into perspective by showing his home environment. Finally, they do not hold back in showing what this child actually goes though to make a living. Few readers will be able to ignore the problem of child prostitution or forget 14-year-old Rudi Gomez.

Same Object or Place
Sometimes the same object appears in all the pictures. In a story about rats, photographed by James Stanfield of the *National Geographic* (July 1977), for example, each photo featured a rat of some kind—a trained rat, rats as objects of worship, rats as lunch. These kinds of stories tend to document the most amazing or most photographic aspects of a subject. The story is not about the life of one rat. It does not detail a day in one rat's life. Nor does it show the impact of rats on one family or town. Rather, it tries to portray interesting aspects of rats around the world.

Place stories often fall into this category. A travelogue that shows the most interesting stops on a visit to Paris would be held together by the visual consistency of the city

even if no other connecting device were used. The images in Chris Larsen's picture package on the Gilman Street punk club (see pages 198–199) are cohesive because the same graffiti-covered walls appear in the background of every picture.

Same Theme/Editorial Point of View
Some photographers tackle social issues with their pictures. Such photo essays try to lay out society's problems. Stephen Shames' essay on child poverty in America, which won numerous awards, is a collection of pictures depicting the toll of poverty on American children. All the pictures in the essay, coming from a common point of view, attempt to elicit a similar reaction in the viewer.

Other essays attempt to show how people are trying to change or solve a problem. *Helpers in the War on AIDS*, by students at San Francisco State University, was a project to document how a group of dedicated professionals and volunteers attempt to ease the lives of people with AIDS (see pages 70–75).

In both essays, individual subjects were selected and final pictures chosen that reinforced the basic theme—*poverty* in the first set of pictures and *helping* in the second.

Sometimes a group of pictures attempts to compare and contrast an aspect of life. André Kertez compiled an entire book showing all the ways people read. He showed people reading on benches, lying down, and standing up. The pictures documented people reading in the library, in the park, and on rooftops. Each picture added an element to the central theme.

Similarly, the essay on "Seeing Sound" (see page 130), turns an auditory subject into a visual delight through a number of different photographic techniques.

Pictures alone might be interesting, but, published together, photos allow the reader to compare two or more different approaches to the same problem. Compare-and-contrast photo essays have ranged from how people wait in line to how they cut their hair or wear the latest fashion statement.

Consistent Technique, Perspective, or Common Visual Mood
A uniform camera perspective also can add a coherent atmosphere to a picture story. If, for example, the photojournalist takes all the pictures from the air, the reader sees the world from a consistent vantage point. Doug Kapustin, of the Patuxent Publishing Co., rented a fixed-wing airplane for an afternoon and flew over suburban Maryland to produce a cohesive and unique look at ordinary

scenes, like parking lots and highway interchanges, that most people take for granted. (See pages 158–159.)

To capture a child's view of the world, a photographer might shoot the pictures from two feet above the ground. Again, the same perspective in each picture interlocks the images.

W. Eugene Smith once took an extended series of pictures from the window of his downtown New York loft. The pictures of the street below were connected not just by the fact that they were all taken in the same place, but also by the restricted view of the camera.

Holding a topic together by shooting a series of portraits also provides a consistent perspective, whether the people are the royalty of Europe or the homeless of America. Sometimes, the photographer uses a consistent background—perhaps just seamless paper or a portable piece of painted canvas. At other times, the photographer shoots each subject in his or her environment. Even with the environmental portrait, however, the photographer needs to use a consistent approach to lighting and subject placement for the photographs to provide a unified look on the printed page. Robert Cohen's portraits for Black History month (see page 83) demonstrate this approach to consistency.

THE NARRATIVE

Without structure, words alone don't form a sentence. Regardless of how beautiful or powerful each word is, taken as a group, they don't add up to a coherent thought without the underlying structure of grammar.

Pictures, likewise, remain individual images unless they are integrated into a cohesive narrative story.

All short stories share a common structure, argues Pulitzer Prize-winning author Jon Franklin, in his book **Writing for Story**.

Franklin, who twice won the prestigious award for feature writing, says that stories revolve around a complication. He defines a complication as any problem a person encounters. Being threatened by a bully is a complication. Having a car stolen or being diagnosed with cancer is a complication.

Complications are not all bad, Franklin says. Falling in love is a complication because you may not know whether the other person is in love with you. Winning the lottery means you have to figure out how to spend the money—and pay the taxes.

Complications that lend themselves to journalism must tap into a problem basic enough and significant enough that most people can relate to it. When a mosquito bites you, you have a complication, but one that

reflects neither a basic human dilemma nor a significant problem. Discovering you have cancer and might die, on the other hand, is a basic problem significant to most readers.

The second part of a good story involves a resolution, which, Franklin says, "is any change in the character or situation that resolves the complication."

Whether you are cured of cancer or die from the disease, the complication is resolved. Franklin points out that most daily problems don't have resolutions and therefore don't lend themselves to good stories.

Journalists often cover a story's resolution without ever showing the complication. "Endings without beginnings attached," Franklin calls these kinds of articles.

Applying Franklin's analysis of story development to photojournalism reveals that photographers shoot racial confrontations or political victories without putting the situations into context. Here, photographers are shooting the story's resolution without showing the problem or complication.

Alternatively, photojournalists sometimes concentrate on the complication but never present a resolution. While they document a social ill like poverty or drug addiction, their documentaries don't turn into narrative stories. These photographers legitimately document the complication of having no money or of the craving for narcotics or alcohol, but the photos don't show how someone finally earns money to survive or kicks the habit—how someone resolves the problem.

While complications often don't have resolutions, resolutions almost always have complications. When John Doe wins the Olympic high jump award, you know that he faced many hurdles to get there. The story comes to life only when you show both the challenges on the way to the top (the *complication*) as well as the final victory (the *resolution*).

A compelling photo story requires action. The complication must be visual and not just internal. The subject must try to resolve the complication by doing something.

A woman sitting in a wheelchair presents a *complication*. The reader can see that the woman is faced with a problem. However, her sitting there alone doesn't provide the subject matter for a story. If the wheelchair-bound woman wants to walk, then the photographer has a potential narrative photo story. Showing the woman struggling to get out of the chair and finally learning to stand and walk would provide a possible *resolution* to the story. After many attempts, photos of her walking alone would complete the story. The story is not a description of a handicap but a tale of her efforts to overcome her

Exposed to crack cocaine in the womb and born addicted to the drug, this newborn experiences severe withdrawal symptoms. Conservative estimates suggest that at least 11 percent of all newborns in the United States today were exposed in the womb to one or more illicit drugs.

◄ Bathing is one of the few ways nurses have found to comfort drug-exposed newborns. Soap and warm water soothe the frantic babies. The bath also removes the sweat that envelopes them as they go through withdrawal.

Text & Photos by Ken Kobré

The first few "crack" babies — infants *exposed to cocaine in utero by their crack-smoking mothers — were born nearly 15 years ago. Today, a wave of children with what has come to be known as Crack Syndrome are entering the nation's public schools. Increasing numbers of these drug-exposed children are now in kindergarten, first, and second grade — and America's schools are unprepared. In fact, society in general has provided inadequate support for handling these often difficult-to-handle youngsters.*

Annually, between 375,000 and 700,000 "crack" babies are born in the United States, but neither the Department of Education nor the Department of Health and Human Services has yet set up a comprehensive preschool intervention program. Only five states define drug-exposed children as eligible for special education, says Patricia O'Keefe, director of communications for the National Association for Perinatal Addiction Research and Education (NAPARE).

Until recently, a prenatally drug-exposed child's prognosis was grim. Born prematurely to crack-addicted mothers, these children were thought by researchers to be living time-bombs — damaged mentally and physically and perhaps even a threat to society once they are grown. This group of children has even been called the "lost generation." Media reports, from Rolling Stone *to* Time *magazine, have described some of the intellectual delays and extreme aggressive behavior associated with these children. Recent research, however, shows that, with intervention, some of the prenatally drug-exposed babies can grow up healthy—emotionally, physically, and mentally.*

But where will the intervention take place, and who will pay for it?

▲ The San Francisco police department makes 10,000 drug arrests a year. The majority involve cocaine in rock form—crack. When a pregnant woman takes a hit of crack cocaine, the fetus loses sufficient blood and air— and suffocates briefly. For the mother, the drug's euphoric effect lasts only about 20 minutes. For the growing fetus, the cocaine stays in its system for more than two weeks. In the womb, in fact, the child is often re-exposed because the cocaine does not pass through the placenta to the mother but remains in the amniotic fluid surrounding the baby.

► Reducing extraneous noise and light also helps prevent overstimulation. When held, these "at-risk" babies tend to arch their backs, pull away, and cry until they exhaust themselves. Experts note that these behaviors interfere with child-parent bonding.

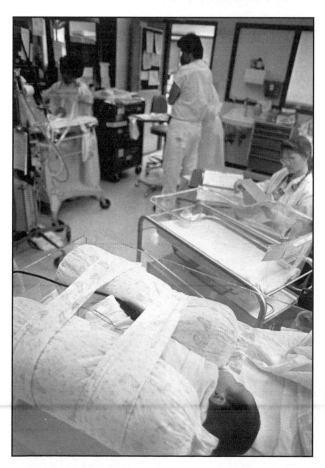

◄ The infants are wrapped tightly in blankets so that when they cry their arms won't flail about and cause the babies to re-stimulate themselves. Short-staffed, nurses place the babies on mechanical rocking beds. The large cylinders on either side of the baby assure that it won't slide as the bed tilts back and forth.

(Continued on following page.)

SCHOOLS FACE THE PROBLEM

► At the Parent Child Intervention Program preschool, one youngster gives another a swift kick for no apparent reason. Thirty-four percent of at-risk children exhibit "extreme emotional and behavioral tendencies along with a low tolerance for frustration," according to a recent study. In one-on-one situations, most of the children are able to focus their attention. The behavioral problems occur during less structured times.

(Continued from previous page.)

A colleague who teaches special education at the university told me about the growing problem teachers were reporting as "crack babies" started to show up in classrooms. He noted that these children were hard to control, and that teachers often sent them to special education classes. Even there, the children continued to disrupt the classroom, fight, and throw temper tantrums. The special education teachers were equipped to work with retarded children, not students with behavior problems.

I located articles about the disruptive nature of these youngsters but could not find that anyone had ever photographed the class disruptions, the kicking, and the inability to concentrate. After some research to establish the extent of the problem and its possible consequences, I applied to the Gannett Foundation, now called the Freedom Forum, for a grant to photograph the problem and its consequences.

Access proved extremely difficult. School officials did not want to admit that they had a hard-to-handle behavior problem that they could not

cope with. Mothers were hesitant to identify their children as crack-exposed.

Finally, the local city hospital gave me permission because, overwhelmed with crack babies in the neonatal ward, they were expending enormous resources. Drug-addicted newborns require a staff of specially trained, round-the-clock nurses. Next, I found a researcher who was using IQ and behavioral tests to follow up with crack-exposed children and scientifically determine the nature and extent of their problems. Finally, after many telephone calls and visits, I located a school principal in East Palo Alto who had set up a special early intervention project for crack-exposed children. She gave me access to the classroom.

Since I did not have time to shoot one child from birth through first grade, I photographed different children in each age group—from two-day-old newborns through first-graders. Like the layers of rock that represent geologic time periods, the pictures show the effects of the drug on children in different age groups as they develop.

▲ For some at-risk children, the slightest disruption will set off a temper tantrum. Children of this type exhibit extreme mood swings. Because they cannot use adults for solace, they become withdrawn. Researchers have learned that early intervention focusing on interaction with other children, individual work on children's problem areas, and parent counseling can help at-risk children improve significantly.

▲ To calm some of the at-risk children at nap time, a teacher stretches her legs across one child, holding the youngster down while massaging the back of another student. The first group of students in the early intervention program now being "mainstreamed" into classes with average children are showing signs of keeping up.

physical limitations. Rather than being "a story about someone who is disabled," the story's outline might read:

At first, after the accident, the subject **is confined** to her wheelchair.

Then she **exercises and swims** for therapy. Next, she **steps** haltingly.

Finally, the subject **walks** alone.

Jim Mahoney, of the *Boston Herald,* photographed a narrative story about a mounted police officer whose horse was injured by a passing car (see page 116). The officer faced the *complication* of dealing with his injured horse, which was in extreme pain. The short story was *resolved* when the veterinarian put the horse out of its misery. The drama lasted only a few minutes, but the sequence of pictures showed the reader what the officer had to go through and how the problem was resolved.

Sarah Prall's story documenting her husband's battle with Horton's Syndrome, which causes incurable blinding headaches, includes both the *complication*, the headache, with at least a partial *resolution*—massage therapy and meditation that are helping relieve the man's eight-year torture.

Stanley Forman, three-time Pulitzer Prize winner, produced a complete story with a *complication* and *resolution* built in when he covered a fire in the Boston neighborhood of Dorchester. (See pages 30–31.)

Forman was cruising the city with his scanner radio turned on, looking for spot news, when he actually smelled smoke. He pulled up next to a house as flames were billowing out of the first floor.

As Forman arrived, police cars came screeching to a halt with their sirens blasting and lights rotating.

Stranded on the roof of a burning porch, a man and a woman clutching a baby looked desperately for help.

Flames curled up from the porch below. The family was trapped *(complication)*. Firefighters had not arrived with a ladder. The father bent over the edge of the roof and delicately dropped his child into the arms of a waiting policeman, who safely caught the child.

Then the mother panicked. Afraid to jump, she froze. The man literally pushed her off the roof to save her life. She fell to the ground, slightly injuring her leg. Then the man himself leaped to safety.

To complete the narrative news story, Forman photographed the medics carrying the mother away on a stretcher as the building blazed in the background and also caught a picture of the policeman hugging the child he had saved *(resolution)*.

■ A NARRATIVE STORY IN THREE ACTS

Sometimes a story involves several complications and resolutions. Each complication/resolution is like an act in a play requiring one or more two-page spreads to tell an aspect of the plot. You could treat as a three-act play, for example, the classic *Life* essay "Nurse Midwife," by W. Eugene Smith, reproduced on pages 118–129.

Jim Hughes, one of Smith's biographers, says in his book ***W. Eugene Smith: Shadow and Substance***, "Gene began to approach his story about Maude Callen as he thought a playwright might." Smith himself said, "I think this (analogy to drama) comes closer to being what a picture story is, . . . "

In the first act, Maude, the nurse midwife, has been brought in to oversee a difficult birth *(complication)*. In the photo, Maude sits watchfully by as the expectant mother rests. The *resolution* for the first act is found in the following spread, when Maude delivers a healthy baby.

The second act, called "Maude's 16-hour day," leads with a picture showing a child on crutches walking toward Maude. The caption explains that last summer Maude arranged for the girl to attend a camp for special children. The camp had strict entrance requirements—each child had to have two dresses and one pair of pajamas. Maude supplied the clothes so the child could go to camp. While the picture sets up the *complication* (girl on crutches approaches Maude), the caption suggests the *resolution*—Maude had provided the clothes for camp. The real visual resolution for the second act, however, does not come until the following page. This page shows a different little girl showing off a new dress provided by Maude.

Life called the final act in the layout "Maude and M.D." The *complication* shows Maude bringing a dying child to the doctor. While the layout's next picture shows the child, just before death, in the doctor's care, the third act's (in fact, the whole story's) real *resolution* is contained in the last picture. In the drama's final photo, Maude teaches a class in midwifery. She holds up a healthy baby while lecturing to a roomful of eager students. Maude passes on her knowledge of modern medicine's life-saving techniques, which will save the lives of mothers and babies in the future *(resolution)*.

Smith's story, by the way, did not just include pictures showing the story's *complications* and *resolutions*. The narrative contained photos used by Smith to make a particular point or to flesh out aspects of a character not captured in the leading pictures. In the opening spread, for example, Smith included a picture of Maude washing her hands. He was making the point that she performed her deliveries under antiseptic conditions. In the third spread, a quiet portrait of Maude holding a flower portrays yet another side of the woman's personality.

While "point pictures" provide development and explanation to a story, used alone they don't move along the narrative. Point pictures provide expository breaks to fill in the story's gaps. Those that show the *complication* and *resolution* are the ones that thrust the story forward.

■ YOU DON'T HAVE A LIFETIME TO SHOOT THE NARRATIVE STORY?

Writers can reconstruct past events just by interviewing someone. For the photographer, the biggest problem with shooting narrative stories is that many complications faced by potential subjects simply don't take place in the relatively short time span allotted for most assignments. Sometimes, months or even years go by before a person resolves a complication. Editors allot today's photojournalists only a few days to work on most stories. Here are a few ways you might compress time in a narrative story.

Resolution Near at Hand

Pick a story in which the resolution is near at hand. If you want to shoot a story about a political newcomer running for mayor, zero in on the subject a few weeks before the primaries or before the actual election. At this time, you will be able to show how the candidate grapples with the complication of getting into office: glad-handing, strategizing, chain-smoking, meeting late at night, preparing for television interviews. The narrative story will resolve itself on election eve or perhaps the mayor's first day in office. Starting too early or too late, however, means you may miss the complication or resolution.

In February, Ron Bingham set out to shoot a story on open adoption, an arrangement in which a pregnant woman planning to give up her newborn selects the parents who will adopt the child. Bingham did not want to take pictures of couples playing with their recently adopted child or shoot a series of portraits of mothers who had given up their children at birth. He wanted to shoot a narrative story in which he was present at all the important emotional moments that a birth mother and adoptive parents go through.

To show the relationship developing between the biological mother and the adoptive parents and to pull off the story by his deadline—mid-May—he knew he had to pick a woman who was near term.

Life Formula for Visual Variety in the Photo Essay

For a typical assignment at the old *Life* magazine, the editors expected the photographer on location to shoot at least eight basic types of photos to ensure complete coverage of the situation and to guarantee enough good pictures for a layout.

1. **INTRODUCTORY OR OVERALL:** Usually a wide-angle or aerial shot that establishes the scene.

2. **MEDIUM:** Focuses on one activity or one group.

3. **CLOSE-UP:** Zeroes in on one element, like a person's hands or an intricate detail of a building.

4. **PORTRAIT:** Usually either a dramatic, tight head shot or a person in his or her environmental setting.

5. **INTERACTION:** People conversing or in action.

6. **SIGNATURE:** Summarizes the situation with all the key story-telling elements in one photo—often called the decisive moment.

7. **SEQUENCE:** A how-to, before and after, or a series with a beginning, middle, and end (the sequence gives the essay a sense of action).

8. **CLINCHER:** A closer that would end the story.

Life photographers who took all eight types of photos for a story had a high probability of bringing back to the office a set of pictures worth publishing. Because the formula helped to assure visual variety, the designer had many layout options. Like a good writer provides variety in sentence length and structure as well as in the selection of nouns and verbs and adjectives, the photojournalist needs to provide different kinds of images to give a story visual interest.

Keep in mind that following the *Life* formula does not necessarily produce a newsworthy or narrative story. Instead, the formula helps assure that all the pictures a photographer takes won't just be portraits or medium shots. As word choice and sentence structure alone do not make a written story, the *Life* formula does not guide the photographer in the content or the structure of the story.

Life editors didn't use all the photos from an assignment. But they knew that, with the formula, whether the photographers were shooting in Hollywood or Haifa, they would bring back a viable array of pictures that could be formed into a *Life* essay. (See W. Eugene Smith's "Nurse Midwife" essay, pages 118–129.)

Few newspaper photographers have the time to shoot the entire list of combinations described above. Most would evaluate the time they can spend on the assignment against other stories they have to cover. Photographers working for dailies often have to shoot more than one assignment a day. Magazine photographers usually can take more time on a story than their newspaper counterparts. But even the photographers hired by the national glossy magazines must limit the time they spend on an assignment. Only on major stories of vital interest will some progressive newspapers and a few large magazines, such as the *National Geographic*, release a photographer for long periods to produce in-depth picture coverage.

Unlike prescribed Hollywood stories, real-life stories don't always end as you might expect. After following the relationship between the mother and prospective adoptive parents for three months, a dramatic change occurred. Following labor and delivery, the adoptive parents first held the child. Then the birth mother held her . . . and did

► Mari-Lynn and Alan Walkowitz got married—
she to Frank Hryskanich (FAR RIGHT),
he to Diana Banfield (RIGHT).
In both cases,
Mari-Lynn and Alan's children—
Nicole, Keith, and Craig (FROM LEFT) attended.

▼ At his FATHER'S wedding,
Keith declined ring-bearing
duties despite the entreaties of
(FROM LEFT) his brother, his
soon-to-be stepbrother, his
sister, his soon-to-be stepsister,
and his soon-to-be stepmother.

At his MOTHER'S wedding, Keith did serve as ring-bearer but threw a tantrum when he couldn't get a drink of water.

Despite Keith's tantrum, and tears from Nicole, they, like brother Craig, danced at their MOTHER'S wedding reception.

Almost seven million children are living with a stepparent, according to the Census Bureau. There are almost 4.5 million step-families in the United States, and the Step-family Association of America estimates that 1,300 new ones are being formed every day.

Any photographer would find these statistics hard to explain in pictures. April Saul, of the *Philadelphia Inquirer*, found a solution. She set out to photograph one divorced couple in which both partners were getting remarried.

Usually, unless the subjects are famous, weddings, funerals, bar mitzvah, and christenings remain private affairs uncovered by the media. But Saul realized that the two separate weddings of a divorced couple would provide the perfect setting in which to play out the problems blended families face.

Keith Walkowitz is 5 years old, and he has one brother, one sister. He also has two mothers and two fathers. Sometimes, he even has another brother and another sister. Keith belongs to two stepfami-lies. Keith and his two sets of parents turned out to be the perfect sub-jects to show the compli-cations of these new familial arrangements. Keith's objections when he was supposed to be the ringbearer in his father's wedding and his tantrum after his moth-er's ceremony helped show, in a compelling way, the painfully diffi-cult transition children experience when their parents remarry.

After their MOTHER'S wedding, there was a bit of trouble. The kids left their clothes 20 miles away, complicating the honey-mooners' getaway.

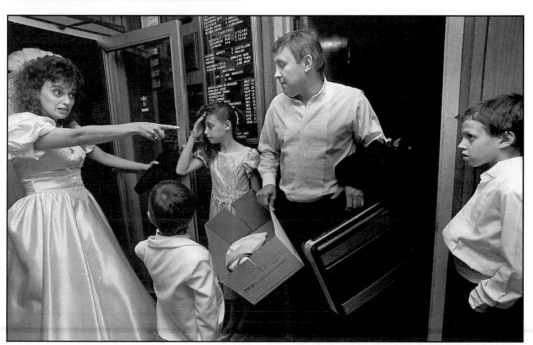

not want to let her go. The adoptive parents left the hospital empty-handed.

Small Resolution Will Do

Within a story, you might zero in on a small resolution rather than the ultimate resolution to the complication. You might follow a person with cancer through a bone marrow transplant and photograph some of his or her recovery. You might end the story with dismissal from the hospital even though this juncture might be only the first step in an eventual cure. Although your camera has not recorded the ultimate victory over death, you have told a unified story.

John Kaplan followed murder suspect Rodney Woodson for more than a year (see pages 152–157). He started when the young man led police to a wooded area in the east end of town where Rodney had hidden the gun used in a shooting (*complication*). During the search, Kaplan met Woodson for the first time and continued to follow the case over the course of a year.

Was Rodney guilty? Innocent?

Would he get a jail term (*resolution*)?

Like a true narrative story, the reader does not know the outcome. By following the events in Rodney's life, including trips to his lawyer's office, his time out on bail, and, finally, his trial, Kaplan recorded the progress of an unfolding tale.

Hal Wells' story about illegal aliens crossing the Texas border also has the *complication* and *resolution* built into a short period of time. The immigrants he followed tried to cross the Rio Grande (*complication*) and were arrested (*resolution*) all within one day. (See page 133.)

Existing Pictures

Investigate photo albums or archives to show what your subject or location used to look like. If your story is about a successful banker who has overcome a poverty-stricken past, can you show the *complication* with photos of the person as a youngster living in a cold-water flat or a run-down shack?

Without these pictures, the banker's success (*resolution*) would seem unearned. If your story is about a neighborhood, can you find old pictures from the historical society or your paper's morgue that would indicate whether the neighborhood used to be wealthy or poor, or perhaps even farm land or forests?

Separate Paths

For some narrative stories, you might find two people who have taken separate roads in life. Suppose you want to tell the story of an escapee from the ghetto. To document the

story in real time would take years, following someone from childhood through adolescence to success or degradation as an adult. Rather than document one person's entire life, you might find brothers or sisters raised in the same conditions. One took to the streets and now sells drugs. The other stayed in school and now teaches at a university.

A picture story of the drug-selling sibling would show the *complication* but not the *resolution*. A story of the scholar would reveal a resolution but miss the problem. Photographing both lives, perhaps, could lead to an imaginative narrative story.

Different Developmental Stages

Likewise, photographing the long-term impact of crack cocaine on newborns does not require following one child from birth through pre-school. To address the impact at different critical stages, I photographed the infants suffering withdrawal at San Francisco General Hospital, (*complication*) toddlers in a testing program (*partial resolution*), and then crack-affected youngsters in an early intervention program in an East Palo Alto school (*partial resolution*.) Part of the story is reproduced on pages 142–145.

■ NATURAL NARRATIVES

Some stories lend themselves to the narrative approach. Consider those about an athlete preparing for the big match. Here the *complication* is the athlete's desire to win. The story follows the athlete through the rugged, sweaty, training regime. Finally, the athlete wins or loses the big contest (*resolution*).

Many adventure stories have a built-in *complication* as well as a *resolution*. Bob Gilka, director of photography at the *National Geographic* at the time, assigned Keith Philpott to photograph an exploratory raft trip down Africa's Omo River. (See page 161.)

Starting in the Omo's headwaters, near Ethiopia's capital city of Addis Ababa, the trip ended 600 miles later at the river's destination, Lake Turkana. The built-in *complication* involved overcoming the river's perils, including fighting off hippos. The rafters also experienced adventures along the way and witnessed the primitive lives of natives living near the river. The story's natural *resolution* showed placid Lake Turkana.

■ THE INHERENT APPEAL OF A NARRATIVE STORY

Shooting narrative stories takes research, scheduling, and time. Narrative stories often require the patience of Job and the planning of an air traffic controller. Sometimes the end is not predictable when you start. However, all the difficulties are worth it. Rather than presenting an interesting collection of pictures that holds readers for a few minutes, the narrative story sucks the viewer into the subject's predicament.

With a narrative story, readers start to care about the subject and want to know how the person is going to solve the dilemma. What is going to happen? When picture stories are done well, readers remain on the edge of their chairs, waiting to see the last picture that reveals the story's outcome.

The story has a plot line—not an invented, preplanned script typical of the magazines of the 1930s and 1940s—but a real story line in which people face problems and overcome them in some way.

Most important, the reader comes to care about the story's protagonist. Whether you are telling a story about Maude, the nurse midwife, or Rodney, the young man accused of murder, the subject is not shown just once, but is repeated in picture after picture. The reader gets involved in the subject's life. Will Maude deliver the baby following her patient's difficult pregnancy? Will a jury find Rodney guilty of murder? And, perhaps, if the story has merit and is well photographed, the reader won't just give a passing glance to the pictures and move on but will remember the story, repeat it, and, perhaps, show it to others.

COMPARING THE DOCUMENTARY AND PHOTO ESSAY TO THE NARRATIVE STORY

The great photographers of the Farm Security Administration (FSA) set out to document the severe poverty resulting from the 1929 depression and dust bowl. These photographers also documented government aid in the form of work programs and housing provided by Franklin Delano Roosevelt's Works Progress Administration (WPA). While the landmark photo project set out to show both complications and resolutions, its organizer, Roy Stryker, never intended to tell a narrative story. FSA photographers did not follow one family or even a set of families through their trials and tribulations on the way to economic self-sufficiency. Rather, Stryker's photographic corps provided not a story but an important historical record (document) of the times.

Similarly, when the *National Geographic* assigns a "place story"—a story on Kansas, for example—the magazine makes no attempt to produce a narrative. The opening picture of wheat fields does not set up tension that will be resolved by the following images of dairy farms and women baking pies. There is no need for relief in the concluding spread that shows a rural school

teacher waving good-bye to her students. Even "point pictures" that show a modern city skyline and pulsing factories don't form a narrative. While each individual picture might be strong, no story line holds the images together. The viewer can stop anywhere in the section without losing the flow of the layouts. Instead, each picture makes a point that the editors hope will document and explain to the reader some aspect of the area.

The photo essay also differs from the narrative photo story. A story has a fixed line that proceeds from one moment in time to another. With a photo story, like a spoken or written story, you don't know the end when you start. Therefore, the story line determines the sequencing of the pictures in the layout.

For example, consider John Kaplan's story about Rodney Woodson. The story opens with Rodney leading police to the gun he used in the shooting—and ends with Rodney in jail. The story's natural flow dictates the layout. The story moves from picture to picture— Rodney in the police car, Rodney's mother in the lawyer's office, followed by Rodney on bail visiting his son. Relentlessly, the story moves toward its unhappy conclusion.

An essay, on the other hand, tries to present a consistent point of view. But it does not require a definitive order. With no story line, the layout does not have to present the pictures in a particular sequence.

The essay on sound (see page 130) could start with the little boy listening to music or the time exposure blurred shot of the folk singer playing his guitar. Each picture tries to show a different aspect of a non-visual experience, but the group of images has no timeline. The essay on Maryland from the air (see pages 158–159) also has a consistent point of view but no story line. The same analysis applies to Chris Larsen's punk club picture package (see pages 198–199). The pictures, which reflect punks' anti-establishment attitude—from slam dancing to giving "the finger" to the photographer—constitute an essay but don't tell a narrative story. Nothing happens to anyone. No one faces a conflict and overcomes it. The pictures simply provide a cohesive portrait of this club.

Some stories lend themselves to the narrative story form—others to the essay approach with a point of view. Each is difficult in its own right.

To see great photo stories, consider subscribing to *Outtakes*, P.O. Box 1582, Litchfield, CT, 06759, and to *Reportage*, P.O. Box 1584, Birmingham, AL, 35201–1584. Both magazines are solely devoted to publishing stories told in pictures. ■

CONFESSION
TO A KILLING

After the death of John Bolder, Rodney Woodson turned himself in and later made a deal. As a condition of bail, he would lead police to the weapon. Woodson had never been in trouble but now faced a legal system about which he knew nothing.

As the suspect, in the foreground, stands by at a housing project, a police detective reaches into a hole to retrieve the gun.

◄ As Woodson sat locked in the back of a detective's car while police continued to look for bullets, the suspect knew that his life would never again be the same.

STORY & PHOTOS BY JOHN KAPLAN

first met Mrs. Woodson on a blustery October night nearly a year earlier when Rodney turned himself in. Two men had tussled in a Hill District alley and one—John Bolden, 34, was dead.

The story of their fatal argument had gotten barely a mention on the tube and a paragraph in the papers. After the Pittsburgh Press received a call from Woodson's attorney, James Ecker, I decided to accompany our police reporter as Woodson turned himself in.

Woodson, who had never before been arrested, was teary-eyed and scared. I had pictured him in my mind as a faceless, evil manifestation of murder, but all I saw was the fear in his eyes of a legal system he knew nothing about. None of the anguish or subtleties of the previous night's events were portrayed in our news story the next day. Still, I was intrigued because I felt that this young suspect was more than just a statistic.

In general, newspapers and television rarely humanize crime stories that aren't "big

news," and this case certainly didn't involve famous or influential people.

Woodson made a deal. As a condition of bail, he would tell police where he had hidden the gun that killed Bolden. The 22 caliber pistol was right where Woodson had said he hid it.

Cassandra Woodson and her husband eventually raised bail, and Rodney was back on the street, splitting time among his mother, son DeAndre, 2, and friends from his housing project.

Woodson arrived at the courthouse for his trial. After huddling in the hallway with his lawyer, the defendant walked to the men's room, and I wondered whether I dared follow. Woodson stood tensely at the sink, head bowed, staring at the porcelain. I clicked off two frames and left the room.

The prosecution began its opening argument by notifying jurors that Bolden had been shot three times, once in the back of

the head. Bolden was robbing and choking Woodson when the defendant fired, argued his defense lawyer.

When Woodson took the stand, he seemed calm but anxious, like a schoolboy about to give his first oral report.

While awaiting the verdict, I wished Woodson luck. Mrs. Woodson cradled her son's cheeks while reminding him to be strong. Rodney, in turn, wiped her tears.

As the jury foreman rose and announced the defendant guilty of voluntary manslaughter, Woodson pursed his lips, and his mother started to cry.

After nearly a year, my story was almost finished. I wanted to know how Woodson felt

about the verdict. It took two months of letter writing, phone calls, and gentle persuasion before I was finally granted access to obtain the ending shot.

Woodson's hands covered his face as he spoke. Woodson said, "I don't want (my son) to follow in my footsteps."

For over a year, John Kaplan had the tenacity to follow this story through its ups and downs—never knowing how it would end. The pictures and text constitute a true narrative tale. They tell a cohesive story rather than presenting only the beginning of an event or its conclusion. Most crime reporting shows the victims of a murder at the crime scene or the accused being led away to a police car. Kaplan's story is different.

From the beginning, the reader gets to

Continued on following page.

→ Standing on his head increases the blood flow to Brown's face and provides some relief from the headache's attack.

▼ Only one in ten thousand people suffers from the condition called Horton's Syndrome, which produces headaches that feel "like a red hot poker is driven up the base of my skull and coming though the top of my head," says Michael Brown, who has suffered from the disease for eight years.

Horton's Syndrome, doctors say, causes the most intense pain a human being can endure. It results in the highest suicide rate of any pain-related illness. For eight years, Michael Brown has tried every traditional and non-traditional cure from beta blockers to witch doctors to combat the pain. Brown's wife, photojournalist Sarah Prall, at first tried to ignore her husband's screams at the onset of his attacks. She finally decided to photograph his ordeal instead. Photographers often shoot illustrations for stories about headaches because there usually is nothing to see when people have one. Prall's unique access provides an intimate and rare look at pain.
(Photos by Sarah Prall.)

▲ Resting his head against the cool bathroom tile provides Brown temporary relief from a Horton's attack.

→ Message therapy and two hours a day of meditation have helped reduce the headaches' severity and frequency.

DOWN ETHIOPIA'S OMO RIVER

↑ Starting out at the headwaters of the Omo near Ethiopia's capital city of Addis Ababa, the explorers see the river in the distance.

A group of explorers and naturalists paddled down Ethiopia's Omo River on inflatable rafts. The adventurers faced heat, unsanitary water, friendly and unfriendly natives, and hostile hippos along the way. Alive and well at the end, they finally reached the mouth of the river as it fed into Lake Turkana.

Trip stories, like this one that Keith Philpott shot for *National Geographic*, have a nat- ural narrative with complication (overcoming the problems of getting down the river) and resolution (arriving at the destination) built in. (Photos by Keith Philpott for *National Geographic*.)

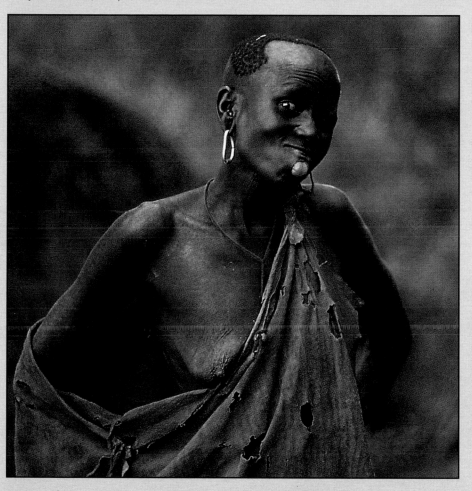

↑ To impress the outsiders, this villager sticks her tongue through a hole in her chin.

↑ Traveling in inflatable rafts, the group carries enough food for half the trip. They restock midway, where the river intersects a road.

↑ Hippos consider the explorers' rafts a tasty snack.

↑ Visitors share the travelers' campfire.

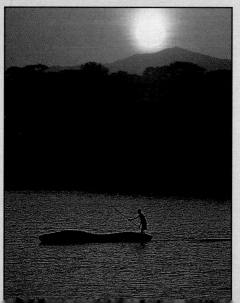

◄ After 600 grueling miles, the adventurers successfully reach the end of their journey at Lake Turkana.

TOO
MUCH
TV?

Illustrations

CHAPTER 8

Today's photojournalists are borrowing the techniques of the advertising photographer to illustrate stories based on issues and abstract ideas. This blend of advertising technique and photojournalism—the editorial photo illustration—came about as newspapers and magazines shifted from the "simple account of what happened yesterday" to analysis of what happened over a period of time and to evaluations of what may happen in the future. This change in journalistic emphasis from immediate reaction to longer-term interpretation of the news has led to stories about more abstract

A product illustration, like the top picture below, is often an attractive still life that simply shows what an object looks like. An editorial illustration, like the lower picture, depicts a concept. Here, the concept is how to protect yourself against the vapors of the odoriferous onion. (Photo illustrations by Joseph Rodriquez, *Greensboro* (N.C.) *News & Record.*)

In this visual metaphor, a TV set becomes the head—and brains—of a television addict. (Photo illustration by Peter Haley.)

always possible, says Jay Koelzer, who specialized in photo illustrations for the *Rocky Mountain News*. "The photographer needs to take the reader somewhere outside the bounds of reality and the printed page," says Koelzer. "The photo illustration is the chance for the photographer to make people think."

According to a survey conducted by Betsy Brill for a master's thesis, more than three-fourths of the newspapers in the United States use photo illustrations. Almost every magazine, particularly *Time, Newsweek,* and *U.S. News and World Report*, uses editorial photo illustrations, especially on their covers. In fact, the rise of the issue-oriented photo illustration may be the most significant change in the history of photojournalism since the 35mm camera introduced the era of candid photography more than a half century ago. Today's photojournalists are creating pictures from whole cloth. Subjects are actors, backgrounds are sets, the lighting is artificial. Only the film is real. Yet these pictures run on the same newsprint and often on the same page as documentary photographs, in which the photographer has traditionally remained only an observer, not a participant.

■ DIFFERENT KINDS OF PHOTO ILLUSTRATIONS
Product Photos

The product photo is a photograph of a real object, usually involving food or fashion. For example, the food editor might assign a photo to accompany a story about the lowly onion. To show how onions differ, the photographer might artfully arrange a number of different onions, ranging from white to red.

Illustration fashion photos, too, are product photos that simply record what an outfit looks like. Some newspapers and magazines run fashion photographs of average people on the street—candids that accompany a story about new trends in hemlines or the new look in pleats. These types of photos are not illustrations. Instead, they are like other candid features a photographer might take. While the setting of a fashion show is staged, the photos document a real event.

A fashion illustration, on the other hand, might show off a new clothing line. Almost all pictures in fashion magazines result from photographers working with models to create idealized photographs of new clothing trends.

The setting might be a seamless background or an empty beach, but the pictures never look real. Stylists prop the pictures in such a way that the situations look better than real life. The photographer is not trying to illustrate an abstract editorial concept or imitate reality.

—and non-visual—issues, such as those dealing with economy, psychology, and science. Stories might include causes for a bull or bear stock market, cures for manic-depression, or potential results of gene splicing.

To satisfy an increasingly visually literate readership, editors who understand photography's appeal often assign illustration photos rather than pen-and-ink drawings to accompany these difficult-to-visualize stories.

Photo illustrations work best when used to communicate concepts, feelings, and the intangibles for which a literal picture is not

Whether the photograph is of an onion in soup or a swimsuit on a woman, the photographer tries to accurately and attractively record the object. The photographer is not trying to create a concept nor dupe the reader into thinking the picture is really a candid.

Editorial Concept Illustrations

As the visualization of an idea, the editorial concept illustration may employ actors or models to create the photographic image, but the total effect is that the viewer instantly recognizes fantasy, not reality. By using subjects out of proportion with other props, backgrounds apparently reaching into infinity, and other trompe l'oeil, the concept photo, also called the issue photo illustration, lures the reader, like Alice, into a surreal Wonderland of ideas. No reader would mistake Wonderland for reality. Carl Fischer's startling photo illustration of aging, for example, combines photographs to create an image of a woman's face—half-young, half-old. (See opposite page). Fischer, who developed the modern photo illustration for magazines through his covers for *Esquire,* also used the concept illustration approach for a story about Andy Warhol, the pop artist famous for transforming everyday objects into paintings. One of Warhol's most famous images showed row after row of Campbell's red-and-white soup cans. Fischer created a picture that gave the impression that Warhol was drowning in a huge can of tomato soup. (See opposite page.)

To illustrate a story about latchkey children (youngsters who come home to an empty house while their parents work), Jeff Breland created a collage for the *Columbia Missourian* that conveyed the concept of children—perhaps perilously—alone. In Breland's cut-and-paste image, a little boy dangles from a huge key ring in the lock to a gigantic door. (See page 177.)

The subject of an editorial photo illustration might be about aging, latchkey children, or it might involve politics or food. But if you create a concept photo about onions, you won't produce a photo of the onion itself. Rather you may try to show how people defend themselves against the vegetable's vapors. A photo of a chef wearing a gas mask while cutting onions would illustrate the concept of protection against the odoriferous onion. (See page 163.)

Docudrama

The docudrama photo illustration, by contrast, actually appears to be real. Here, the photo looks just like a candid but is really a complete creation or re-creation. Rather than abstracting or idealizing, like the product photo or the concept illustration, the docudrama photo imitates reality; intentionally or not, it fools the reader.

To illustrate the problem of population growth in Colorado, the photographer shot an overall of downtown Denver with the mountains in the background. In the studio, keeping the light from the same direction as the overall, he photographed two models holding umbrellas. With the computer, he cloned the models, obliterating their faces so that they would become generalized figures representing all newcomers. Finally, he melded all the elements together into one image.
(Photo by Jay Koelzer, for the *Rocky Mountain News.*)

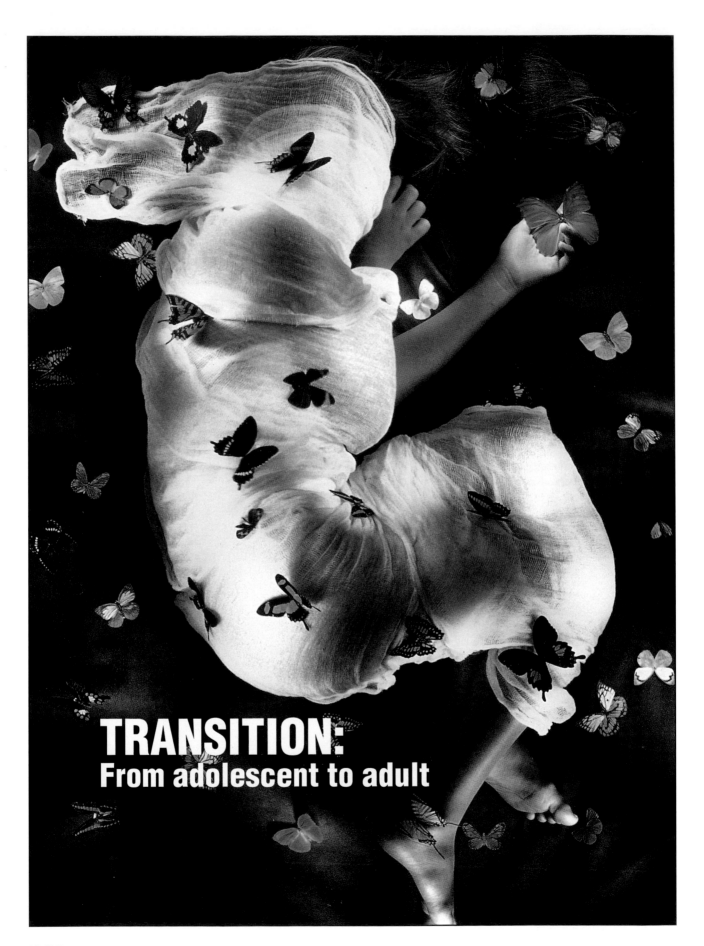

TRANSITION:
From adolescent to adult

◄ To illustrate a story about changing from adolescence to adulthood, the photographer used the metaphor of a caterpillar in its cocoon transforming itself into a butterfly. To achieve the visual effect, the photographer painted with light—individually exposing each element of the picture, including every butterfly, to a narrow incandescent beam during a long exposure. (Photo by Jay Koelzer, *Rocky Mountain News*.)

Avoid this approach at all costs. The docudrama approach is a tempting one to photographers with little time to establish contacts for a documentary story or to conceive and prop a concept photo. To set up a real-looking photograph may not seem so far from what an artist does to "illustrate" a story, but such photographs threaten to undermine a publication's credibility.

Breland's picture of a latchkey child dangling from a key chain, mentioned earlier, is clearly unreal. When another newspaper ran a story about latchkey children, the accompanying "photo illustration" showed a lonely-looking child sitting on a doorstep. While this young model surely was not really alone or lonely, the reader's only clue to the deception was the tiny tag line "photo illustration." The reader had no way of knowing from the the picture that the image was a fake.

And, equally important, do latchkey children really look lonely? The one thing we know is that they do in the imagination of this docudrama photographer. (See page 177.)

PRODUCING EDITORIAL ILLUSTRATIONS

Often, after a photo illustration appears, you can hear the following conversation in the newsroom.

The writer whines, "This headline doesn't go with the gist of my insightful story."

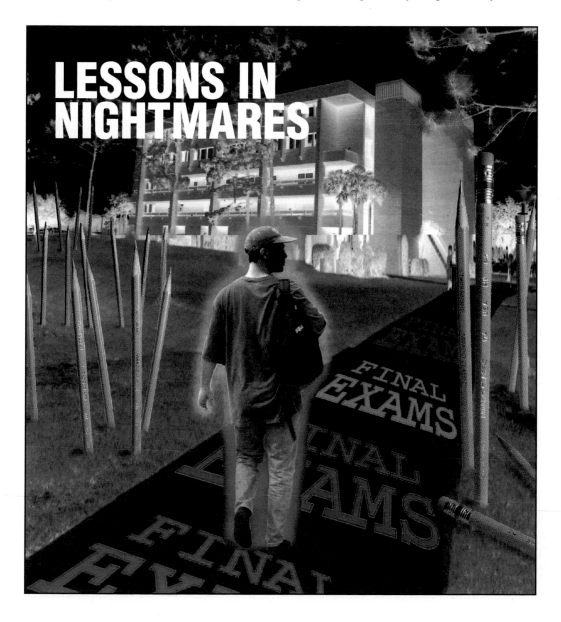

LESSONS IN NIGHTMARES

◄ Few readers would mistake this depiction of a student's fear of final examinations for a documentary photograph. The stake-like, oversized pencils sticking out of the ground, played off against the spooky building with its reversed color, gives this photo its unreal, nightmarish quality. (Photo by Tom Burton, *Orlando Sentinel*.)

The copy editor replies, "When I wrote that head, the story wasn't ready, and I never saw the picture."

From the photo department: "The ugly headline type runs across the model's face. How can I create great art surrounded by insensitive people?"

And, from the page designer's corner of the room: "The inept photographer didn't leave room for type on the picture. And anyhow, the vertical picture didn't fit into the horizontal hole on the page left me by the copy desk."

Avoid this scenario.

When producing an editorial photo illustration, get all the players together from the beginning. The advertising world calls a group like this a creative team. Japanese business calls it a quality circle. Regardless what you call it, get everyone together who will participate in the creation and execution of the photo illustration. By communicating, not only will all team members perform their own creative tasks better, but knowing what others are doing will also help dissolve territorial battles.

This complicated-to-produce but striking illustration was for a story about cryonics, freezing dead people in hopes of a future cure of the disease that felled them.
(Photo by Susan Gardner, *Ft. Lauderdale* (Fla.) *Sun-Sentinel*.)

■ BRAINSTORM THE CONCEPTS

Alex Osborn, a partner in Batten, Barton, Durstine & Osborn (BBD&O), a large New York advertising firm, formulated one method for bringing workable, productive ideas to the surface. He called his method brainstorming. He recommends getting a group of people in a small room where everyone can voice his or her ideas, no matter how foolish-sounding the suggestions. Each suggestion stimulates and generates the birth of another suggestion. A brainstorming session can produce more than a thousand ideas, Osborn claims. Brainstorming works even if you just talk over your ideas with another person.

In his book *Halsman on the Creation of Photographic Ideas*, Philippe Halsman, who produced more than one hundred *Life* covers, explains why he uses the brainstorming technique. "You are not alone, you face someone who serves you as a sounding board, who prods you and who expects you to answer. . . . Your system is stimulated by the challenge of the discussion. There is more adrenaline in your blood, more blood flows through your

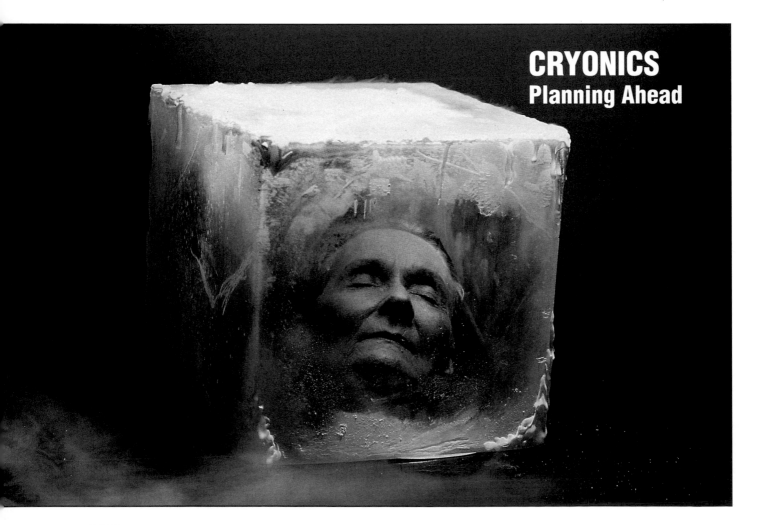

CRYONICS
Planning Ahead

brain and, like an engine that gets more gas, your brain becomes more productive."

One cardinal rule prevails when working in a brainstorming session: never put down anyone else's ideas. Like turning on the lights at a high school dance, a negative comment will be inhibiting. By the end of the brainstorming session, surprisingly, good ideas will float to the surface and poor suggestions will sink out of sight from their own weight.

■ WRITE A HEADLINE

After each member of the group has read the story or heard a presentation of the central theme, everyone should try to write a headline. Compared with writing headlines for a news story and documentary picture, writing headlines for a photo illustration requires the writer to take a different approach.

In a traditional news headline, the desk editor tries to summarize the story in a few words. The headline usually includes an active verb: "The president proposed new legislation today."

A photo illustration headline might have no verb. In fact, the headline might consist of only a phrase or sentence fragment. The headline might be a play on words like a pun, or it might work off a movie play or song title. Or the words might raise a question.
- "Is there a hare in your soup?" for a story about rabbit stew.
- "M-M-M Mail order" for a story about buying food through the mail.
- "Making the first move" for a story about women asking men on dates.

Once all group members have read the story, the group must try to write several headlines. Don't stop to analyze each one. Never reject any idea at this stage of the process. Let your thoughts flow. Then read over each one to see if the idea lends itself to a photo. Almost always, the best idea pops out.

■ TRANSLATE WORDS INTO IMAGES
Symbols

Once you have the headline you must translate the words into pictures. When you translate to picture language, you speak with symbols, analogies, and metaphors. You are trying to find visual ways to express amorphous, sometimes theoretical ideas and concepts.

For photography, however, concepts must become something concrete.

For example, how do you say America or American without words? You might use a

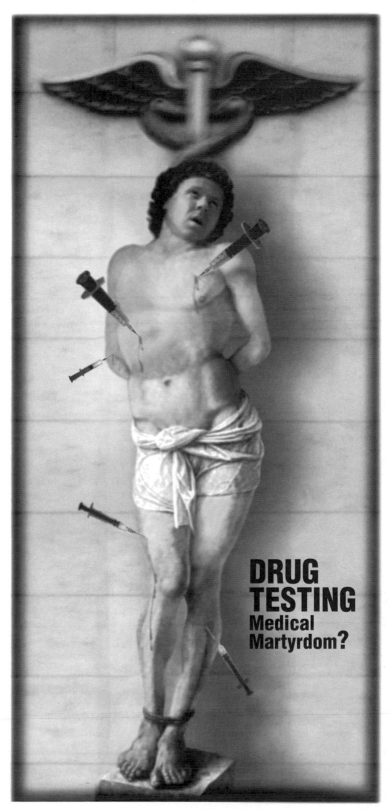

With St. Sebastian, who died from arrows shot into his body, symbolizing martyrdom, the photographer illustrated a story about college students who volunteer for money to test new drugs. With the help of the computer and an out-of-copyright painting of the martyred saint, the photographer replaced the arrows with syringes and used the traditional symbol of the medical profession for a background above the figure. (Photo by William Duke for *Spy* magazine.)

DRUG TESTING
Medical Martyrdom?

generally accepted visual representation of an idea—a symbol like the Stars and Stripes. You could use an actual flag or turn something else into a flag. You might decorate a cake in red, white, and blue to symbolize America's birthday. The Statue of Liberty also serves as a symbol of the United States, as does the "Uncle Sam Wants You" recruiting poster from World War I. Grant Woods' painting, "American Gothic," which shows a farmer and his wife staring stoically out at you, also has become a U.S. symbol.

Photographs themselves can become symbols. Joe Rosenthal's photograph of the

WHERE'S THE CURE?

The metaphor of finding your way through a maze helped illustrate this story about patients trying to locate drugs not yet approved by the Federal Drug Administration (FDA). The mortar and pestle at the end of the maze is a commonly recognized symbol of medicine.
(Photo by William Duke for *U.S. News and World Report.*)

flag-raising at Iwo Jima has been reproduced and transformed so many times it has become a symbol of American patriotism.

If you were trying to illustrate a story about France, you might use an Eiffel Tower, a baguette, or a bottle of wine.

Balanced scales suggest justice; a dove represents peace; a gun symbolizes war. A lightbulb often stands in for abstract concepts like thinking or ideas.

Carl Fischer, who produced many famous *Esquire* magazine covers, says that some symbols exist in our subconscious, like those described by the psychoanalyst Jung with his

archetypes. These are images that seem to occur in every culture. The multiarmed Indian god, Shiva, appears over and over as a symbol for handling multiple tasks.

Literature, too, can provide visual symbols. The nose of Pinocchio, which grew longer with each lie he told, turns the act of lying into a concrete object. William Duke, in an illustration for *Spy*, a humor magazine, played off the image of St. Sebastian, who has come to symbolize martyrdom. The story concerns college students who, to earn money, sell their bodies to test new compounds for drug companies (see page 169). The same photographer used the image of a man with a cap, holding a gun and carrying a bag over his shoulder, to symbolize a thief in an illustration about computer crime.

Symbols can be reinterpreted or newly invented. As pointed out by Steven Heller and Seymour Chwast in the *Sourcebook of Visual Ideas*, smokestacks were used at one time to symbolize progress. Today, they represent pollution. Still, the skull and crossbones, an ancient symbol for poison, continues to evoke the message "hazardous to your health."

Metaphor
When you use a metaphor or simile, you replace one image with another to suggest a likeness of some characteristic. For instance, you might substitute an hourglass for an old person to suggest aging. In this situation, the hourglass becomes the passing of time. The sand at the bottom of the hourglass represents age. Sand can also become power. Sand sifting through hands could become a metaphor for disappearing power.

In a photo illustration for *U.S. News and World Report*, William Duke used a maze as a metaphor for finding your way through the medical bureaucracy in a story about patients trying to obtain potentially life-saving drugs before they were approved by the Federal Drug Administration (FDA).

Similarly, the word "love" often is replaced visually with something heart-shaped or with, perhaps, a rose.

The metamorphosis from caterpillar to butterfly could represent the change from childhood to adolescence as in the photograph created by Jay Koelzer for the *Rocky Mountain News*.

A TV screen becomes the head of a television addict. A woman swings at a golf ball with a giant feather for a story about light golf clubs.

■ SELECT THE MOST WORKABLE IDEA
Simplicity and practicality come into play when you are pondering a list of headlines to

illustrate. Sometimes, the least number of props, models, backgrounds, and special effects give the best chance of producing a successful photo illustration. For instance, suppose you have selected the following headline: "The nuclear family crumbles." You could illustrate this idea by breaking apart clay figures in the form of a family.

Great idea, but . . . You don't know how to work in clay, so you call a sculptor friend.

She says, "Great idea, but . . . I'll need five days and $500."

Your editor says, "Great idea, but . . . I need the illustration in three days, and we have a $20 prop limit."

It's time either to rethink the visual for the headline or to continue down the list to find a different headline that can be illustrated more easily. Remember, the nuclear family can unravel just as easily as it can crumble, and knitting a family portrait just might be easier than sculpting it.

■ PRODUCE THE PICTURE

Once you have a headline to accompany a visual and have drawn a sketch, you need to plan the location, props, and models. On a big-budget ad shoot, you might hire a stylist to find the props, call a casting director to locate models, and ask a location specialist to scout the best backgrounds. On a low-budget shoot, you probably will play all the roles.

Props

Remember that precise propping can perfect the picture, whereas inappropriate props can destroy the desired illusion. For example, a photographer was assigned to illustrate a story about an English butler serving tea. The sketch called for the butler to wear a bowler hat. The photographer returned from the local theatrical prop shop with a hat that was black like a bowler but round on top like a hat worn by the Amish. No self-respecting English butler would be seen serving tea (or much else) in such a piece of headgear. While viewers of the picture might not spot the exact error, they would sense something was wrong about the high-tea scene.

On a low budget? Here are some ways to find props for a limited outlay of cash: you can find period props in antique and second-hand stores. Stores with guaranteed return policies will come in handy at times like this. High schools and colleges maintain costumes for their theater departments. They, too, will often lend out period clothing for photo shoots.

When William Duke needed a maze for his illustration on locating potentially life-saving drugs, he created the maze out of balsa wood and added a real mortar and pestle. He photographed the setup using a wide-angle lens with the light positioned from behind sweeping forward. Next, against white seamless paper, his assistant photographed Williams himself, wearing a hospital gown, from behind. The photographer set up the shot with the light at the same angle as in the original maze picture. Then Duke printed the negatives, one at a time, onto the same sheet of paper. On top of the photographic paper, Duke had placed a piece of dry mount tissue, which helped to soften the images and allowed them to blend more

COMPUTER CRIME

To symbolize crime, the photographer used an old-fashioned image of a burglar with a gun. To depict the computer, the photographer added a circuit board as the background.
(Photo by William Duke for *Newsweek*.)

easily together. The tissue also added to the image's abstract effect.

Models

You don't need a trained Shakespearean actor to model in your photo illustration. Most illustrations don't depend on facial expressions or acting. They do, however, depend on stereotypes. You need a person who fits the part. For an editorial photo illustration about runners hitting "the wall" at fifteen miles, you may not need a world-class marathon runner, but don't pick a couch potato, either.

Save your couch potato friend for the story on the dangers of being sedentary.

William Duke often uses himself as a low-cost model in his illustrations. In addition to putting himself into his medical maze (page 170), the photographer constructed his illustration of St. Sebastian from an out-of-copyright painting of the martyr's body topped with Duke's own face (page 169). The photographer even played the thief in his illustration about computer crime (page 171).

Backgrounds

A background is a photograph's most important layer when you are creating the mood of a photo illustration. To avoid the confusion between true and manufactured pictures, photographers have shot a great many successful photo illustrations against seamless paper backgrounds. The seamless paper adds an abstract quality to a photo since almost nothing in the natural world is ever seen against the purity of simple black or white.

Award-winning photographer Jay Koelzer, however, says that photographers can "look at the background not as something to make disappear but rather as something to add to the image so that it will carry a stronger statement." Koelzer frequently combines realistic backgrounds shot on location with subjects photographed in the studio to produce eye-catching, intellectually challenging images. For example, he photographed Denver's skyline for an illustration about population growth in Colorado. In the studio, he photographed two models holding umbrellas. Using the computer to assemble the final image, he replicated the photos of his models, erased their faces, varied their sizes, and positioned them on the background. Like images from a René Magritte painting, the faceless characters appear to be gently rising and falling over Denver's cityscape with the Rocky Mountains in the background. Although the background is real, no one would mistake the final picture for a documentary photo. (See page 165.)

The bottom line with all photo illustration, including use of the background, is that the reader should instantly know that the image is created, not recorded. Don't confuse the reader. Here is one place you can slip over the line from editorial illustration to docudrama.

Time

Allow time—lots of time—to conceptualize, prop, and photograph an editorial photo illustration. Editors are accustomed to

Theater distributors were bringing back the movie *101 Dalmatians*. For an illustration, the photographer propped an entire movie theater with dogs from a local kennel club. The well-trained dogs in the front row sit unattended, but the less well-behaved animals in succeeding rows are firmly held in place by their owners, who are hiding under the seats.
(Photo by Melanie Rook D'Anna.)

101 DALMATIANS
Play it Again, Spot

asking someone from the photo department to run down to Castro and 14th streets to take a quick shot before the 5 P.M. deadline. Unfortunately, editors frequently maintain the same mind-set when they request editorial photo illustrations.

Most photo illustrations, however, require much longer than two hours. Photo illustrations can take hours that stretch into days. Dreaming up concepts takes time. Rarely do the first headline and visual that come to mind result in the final photo. Propping takes shopping. Without the right props, the picture will look amateurish. Finding the perfect model can be as difficult as finding the perfect spouse. Then comes shooting. With the patience of Job, the meticulousness of a watchmaker, and the flair of a set designer, you will build the picture. The clock ticks by as you move the main prop from left to right. Each change requires an adjustment of the lights. After you've taken many Polaroids to check each detail, the time finally arrives to expose the film. The moment is almost anti-climactic.

When the editor at the *Sun-Sentinel* in Fort Lauderdale, Florida, assigned Susan Gardner to illustrate an article on cryonics, the photographer knew to allow time for the whole production. First, Gardner commissioned a fake block of ice from Plexiglass. She sprayed this with fake snow, lit it with blue gels, and created a mist with dry ice. A hole in the bottom of a table allowed the model to slip her head inside the cube.

The first model, however, took one look at the set and backed out, saying it would be "detrimental" to her career. Her replacement, an elderly woman, was touched up with some white and blue makeup. One month elapsed from the original concept to the final exposed 2¼ chrome on Fujichrome 50D.

Melanie Rook D'Anna, shooting for the *Mesa* (Ariz.) *Tribune*, wanted to illustrate the return of the movie *101 Dalmatians*. She contacted the local Dalmatian kennel club and persuaded the members to bring their dogs to a movie theater—all at the same time. She positioned several highly trained dogs on the front row. These dogs followed the commands of their owners to stay.

The rest of the dogs were not so well-behaved, so their owners hid under the seat cushions with their dogs resting comfortably above. The photographer filled the theater with more than eighty-one Dalmatians, all sitting in their seats at the same time.

The addition of popcorn, colas, and careful lighting gave this picture its striking look.

ELECTRONIC CUT AND PASTE

To create a surreal effect, you might want the picture's subjects to appear completely out of proportion. Perhaps you want the mayor of New York towering over the Empire State Building, or a sailor carrying the QE II under his arm.

To do so, you might need to photograph each element separately and then combine them. If you can't photograph all the subjects and props at the same time in the same location, remember to keep the light consistent for each image you plan on combining later on.

For example, if the light appears to be diffused and coming from the upper left side of the scene, keep the same effect on all subsequent photos. Then, when you put all the elements together, the final picture will look natural, since the light will appear to be coming from only one source.

Computers have come along to make life simpler for the photo illustration photographer. In today's high-tech age, you can scan in old images or new ones. Rather than physically cutting and pasting images, you can electronically alter them to your satisfaction.

Once you've scanned the pieces, you can easily change the size, color, and left-right orientation of each separate image. You might place the subject into another setting (see pages 165, 167, 171, 173, 267) or take the head off one subject and put it on another (see page 169). In fact, just about any effect you can imagine can be accomplished with the computer. (See Chapter 12, "Digital Images.")

For a story called "Cable Surfing," about the trend of television viewers quickly sampling many channels, Tom Burton separately photographed a real surfer, a T.V. remote control device, and a group of images representing various television programs.

He used the computer to combine all the images. By angling the remote control device just right and adjusting the size of the surfer, the remote control in the final picture appears to have become a surfboard.

The computer usually speeds up the mechanics of creating a photo illustration. Having shot or gathered the individual pieces for the illustration and scanned them into the computer, you can manipulate and combine all the parts seamlessly.

To illustrate the trend of viewers quickly sampling a wide variety of cable television channels, a behavior nicknamed "channel surfing," the photographer combined a photo of a real surfer with an image of a remote control device and a series of pictures representing various T.V. channel options.
(Photo by Tom Burton, *Orlando* (Fla.) *Sentinel.*)

Beware, however, that combining pictures with the computer can absorb much more time than originally planned. Even powerfully fast computers can take a long time to process complex images.

Don't Infringe Copyrights

Another word of caution. Copyright protection extends to "found" images in magazines, newspapers, and on the World Wide Web.

Unless the image is one you have shot or one that you have express permission to use, don't be tempted by the ease of scanning it into a computer to use someone else's photograph or work of art to enhance your photo illustration. Doing so is illegal—regardless of how much you "change" the original.

SOME WORK, SOME DON'T

Some editorial photo illustrations cause the reader to say, "Dear, you have to see this. It's just too funny." Others don't stop the reader at all, or, even worse, they cause the reader to ponder the strange picture, wondering why anyone would go to the trouble to publish it. Why do some photo illustrations hit the reader like a sledgehammer and others leave no mark at all?

■ WEAK PHOTOS

Sometimes the photo is weak. Every day, readers see slick ads produced by high-priced ad agencies. Consequently, readers are accustomed to illustrations that appear flawless.

Poorly planned editorial photo illustrations look unprofessional. If the models look like they were grabbed right out of the newsroom, if the set looks like it was a corner of the darkroom, and if the whole production looks like it was thrown together between assignments, then the final photo will probably look amateurish.

For an illustration titled "Sitters can be a pet's best friend," the photographer had a subject pretend she was reading comics to two German shepherds. The scene, however, took place on a beat-up old couch. The rundown setting distracted from the concept.

Why DON'T These Illustrations Work?

A good image in this example was matched with a weak headline. A better head might read "Picture Perfect Pears."

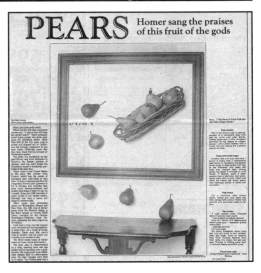

This headline and this picture leave the reader wondering just what the central theme of the story is. The headline, not the subhead, should tie the picture and the words together. A nicely executed photo loses its impact with a weak headline.

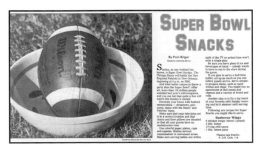

This illustration combines an unimaginative headline, "Super Bowl Snacks," with a picture that is too literal. Try thinking of some alternatives for both words and pictures.

One newspaper ran a photo illustration showing a man's hand writing on a chalkboard with the words "American education stumbles." The foreground contained a few books sitting vertically on a desk. The strong headline in this instance was not supported by an imaginative visual. The photographer failed to find a symbol for American education or to play off the idea of stumbling.

■ POOR HEADLINES

While editorial illustrations often fail because of poor photography, they also fail because of poor headlines. Rather than leaving 'em laughing, an unclear or confusing headline leaves readers scratching their heads.

Sometimes, even clear headlines are not enough—if the headline is clear but dull. Beware of headlines that start out "Everything you ever wanted know about pizza" or "The entire history of bicycles."

Sometimes the writer has provided a label headline like "Potatoes." A headline like this probably came from a story that had no theme or focus. When the headline and story lack a clear focus, the photographer winds up taking a generic picture of a potato rather than illustrating a concept about the potato. Suppose the story had focused on the role of the potato in the Irish famine or had described the many nutrients contained in potatoes. Either article would lend itself to a possible editorial photo illustration. If the story has no focus, however, the photographer is left to photograph the potato itself, a vegetable all too familiar to most readers.

Sometimes headlines are too news-oriented. Photo illustrations work best with ideas, not events. Avoid headlines like "Stock Market Drops for Third Straight Day."

■ HEADLINE AND PICTURE DON'T MESH

Still, the headline might be great. The photo might be eye-popping. But if the two do not mesh, then the final package looks like an afterthought. Sometimes the reader gets the impression that the headline was written without the editor seeing the photo. Or the page looks like the photographer never saw the headline or story before snapping the shutter.

One copy editor wrote this catchy headline: "When marriage seems like war." The photographer produced a strong photo showing a couple having a highly stylized argument. The man's tie is blowing out behind him. Both models look like they are talking with their hands. The problem: they don't look like they are at war. The couple appears to be arguing in the wind, not battling. The words and pictures, like the married pair depicted in the picture, don't communicate.

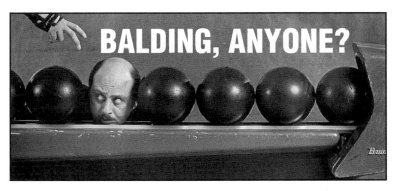

THINKING CREATIVELY: A STRUCTURE

John Newcomb's *The Book of Graphic Problem-Solving: How to Get Visual Ideas When You Need Them* is based on the premise that visual problem-solving starts with words. He suggests that the starting point is the editor's working title for the story.

Take a story about men who are losing their hair. The editor's working title: "Are you worried about balding?" Start by analyzing the nature of the subject.

■ LIST THE FACTS

What is balding? How would you describe balding to someone from another planet? What words might you use? Round, smooth, hairless. List some of the characteristics of the subject, including:

Source

What is the source of the problem or item you are illustrating? In this example, where does balding come from? What causes it?

After you come up with a good headline like this one, try drawing a rough sketch of the final layout. (Photo illustration by Marilyn Glaser; sketches by Ben Barbante.)

RAPE

Victim of the system
that provides justice

By BARBARA KUENY
Pentagraph staff

She talks about the attack in a calm, detached voice, as though it happened to someone else. But her bitterness is unmistakable.

A crime is an act of violence. But for many victims, the crime itself is only the beginning of a chain of events that continue to trouble their lives.

Susan O'Neal wound up feeling victimized by the very justice system she hoped would vindicate her.

Susan was raped by two men in 1980. She was then 21. One of the men served a two-year prison term for violating his bail bond. The rape charge against him was dropped.

The rape charge against the other man was reduced to battery in exchange for his testimony against his friend before the grand jury.

Some time had to elapse before Susan could talk.

Interview with a man convicted of rape on page D6.

about what happened. But she is still angry at the way her case was handled. She believes the justice system failed her.

Susan met the two men who would eventually rape her at a neighborhood bar. The men were sitting at a table with some of her friends. She invited her friends to a party her roommate was giving that night, and the men also appeared.

They made sexual advances toward Susan all night and she kept telling them she was not interested in having sex with them, and expected them to take her at her word.

Later that night, Susan decided she wanted to go to her bedroom to sleep. One of the men followed her

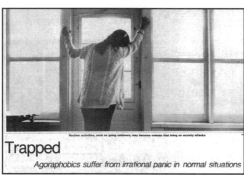

Trapped

Agoraphobics suffer from irrational panic in normal situations

Routine activities, such as going outdoors, may become ordeals that bring on anxiety attacks

Pictures like these docudramas are too real-looking to be effective photo illustrations. Unintentionally or not, they can mislead the reader. Of these published pieces, only the photo to the left carried the tag line "photo illustration."

Balding in men is a hereditary trait that comes from their mothers, grandmothers, and greatgrandmothers.

Delivery

If the topic is about a service or object, describe how it is delivered. If the story is about a new cure for balding, how would the patient get the cure? By pill, by surgery, or by a new diet?

Size

How large is the object or problem—both physically and emotionally? In the balding assignment, is the hair loss partial or complete? Does balding make men feel like jocks or like jackasses?

Weight

Is the subject of the assignment physically or emotionally heavy or light? Is it a crushing burden, or is it a minor irritant? Do those with only a few wisps of hair left on their heads feel dragged down or light-headed?

Winners/Losers

Who gains and who loses with balding? Most stories requiring illustration have a winner and loser, a survivor, and a victim in the plot. At first, you might not think anyone gains from balding. But charlatans with patent cures gain, as do pharmaceutical companies that develop cures for balding. Doctors who perform transplants gain. Wigmakers gain. Psychiatrists gain. Who loses? When hair falls out, not only do bald men lose hair, but sometimes they lose their wives or girlfriends, too.

■ FACTS BECOME PHRASES

As you have just seen, Newcomb's method requires you to identify the facts about your topic. Write each answer down without worrying about being creative. Just start listing information.

Next, try sayings, phrases, proverbs, or any other bits of traditional wisdom. In the list of facts, we noted that the source of

balding is genes inherited from the mother—not the father. Try the headline "Balding—Not Dad's Fault." To illustrate this idea, you could photograph a bald man holding a hairless baby.

In the fact list under weight, we noted that some bald men feel like jocks and others feel like jackasses. Think about twisting the emphasis. To express the idea that bald men are not burdened by their hair loss, twist the line "Blondes have more fun" to "Bald men have more fun." Now illustrate this line with a photo of a Telly Savalas-like character, bald and proud of it, sitting in a bar surrounded by women.

■ PLAY WORD GAMES

Now take the key words from each of the facts above and play word games with them. For instance, in describing the nature of a bald man's head, we listed the word "smooth." Smooth as a balloon, as a billiard ball, as a bowling ball. Imagine a bowling ball looking like a bald man's head. The phrase "Balding, anyone?" could evolve into a photo of a bald man with his head in a rack of bowling balls.

From the editor's original working title, "Are you worried about being bald?" came first a set of facts about baldness. The facts led to plays on words and phrases. These sayings, puns, and double entendres produced many visual ideas that could easily illustrate the story.

The final photograph, by the way, of the man's head lined up next to bowling balls, has since been shown to hundreds of editors, photographers, and others. The photo has never failed to bring the house down with appreciative laughter.

WORDS OF CAUTION
■ DOCUDRAMA CONFUSION

Like editorial photo illustrations, docudramas are created situations. However, as we've seen, docudramas look natural rather than surreal. By mimicking reality, docudramas cause confusion in readers' minds.

Look at the tearsheets on this page. Isn't it conceivable that a photographer could have happened upon this attack and photographed it on the spot? Some poor woman might well be standing at her door, afraid to leave her home—but not this one.

Even with the words "photo illustration" published beneath the picture—which not all carry, by the way—photographers should avoid docudramas. Docudramas detract from a paper's credibility. The reader should never have to ask, "Did that picture really happen that way?"

The job of the photojournalist is to show the world as it is, not as the photographer imagines it is.

Editorial photo illustrations, by contrast, add to the reader's understanding and fun. A picture should either be real or so outrageous that no reader is fooled. Don't leave the reader in the twilight zone of the docudrama.

■ PROBLEMS IN PLACEMENT AND IDENTIFICATION

While most editorial photo illustrations are likely to appear on the lifestyle, food, and fashion pages of newspapers, the Brill survey found that a sizeable majority (nearly 67 percent) do occasionally run on the front page. According to the survey, in fact, only about 23 percent of the responding newspapers "never" run editorial photo illustrations on page one.

Furthermore, nearly 78 percent of newspapers use editorial photo illustrations on the same pages as documentary-style photos—leading to possible confusion among readers as to what is real and what is not.

Further leading to a possible credibility gap, the survey found that almost half the newspapers failed to identify editorial (excluding food and fashion) photo illustrations as created images.

They did not even label the pictures with a special phrase like "Photo illustration by . . . "

Imagine for a moment a newspaper that sprinkles its editorials and analysis—unidentified—throughout its pages, including the front page. How would a reader, accustomed to the straight news on page one, know where fact ends and interpretation begins?

Failing to identify created photographs is every bit as serious as failing to properly identify written editorial comment—and playing editorial photo illustrations on the front page or alongside documentary photographs is as questionable as mingling editorials with unbiased news stories.

While newspapers prior to the Civil War did not hesitate to mix fact and opinion on the front page, most modern newspapers shy away from this practice and carefully limit opinions to a well-marked editorial page or clearly designated opinion column. The same stringent rules should be applied to editorial photo illustrations. Regardless of how unreal they may appear, they, too, should be labeled and segregated from straight photo reporting.

■ PRACTICAL AND ETHICAL GUIDELINES

The following are practical and ethical guidelines for using photo illustrations:

- Eliminate the docudrama. Never set up a photograph to mimic reality, even if it is

Docudrama vs. Concept Photo

LATCH-KEY KIDS

For more and more families, after-school child care has become a serious dilemma

labeled a photo illustration.
- Create only abstractions with photo illustration. Studio techniques, for example, can help to make situations abstract—the use of a seamless or abstract backdrop, photo montage, or exaggerated lighting. Contrast in size and content, juxtaposition of headline and photo—all can give the reader visual clues that what appears on the page is obviously not the real thing.
- Always clearly label photo illustrations as such—regardless of how obvious you may think they are.
- Never play photo illustrations on news pages. Restrict them to feature pages or to section fronts. Display them in a way that is obviously distinct from straight news or feature pictures.
- If you haven't the time to do a photo illustration right, don't do it. Suggest another solution. ■

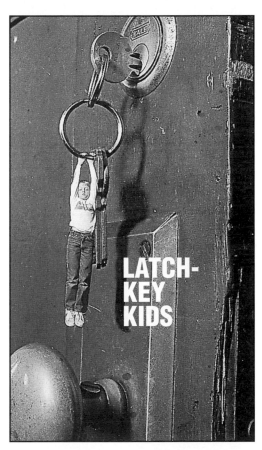

Avoid docudramas such as the one above. They fool the reader. Instead, create a concept photo like the one below it, which is so abstract that no one will mistake it for real.
(Photo illustration at bottom by B. Jeff Breland.)

Photo Editing

Photo editing takes strong eyes, a sharp grease pencil (if not a sharp computer monitor), and the psychological strength to reject thousands of pictures while seeking the one frame or part of a frame that tells the story and has visual impact. Technically poor negatives that are out of focus, under-exposed, or overexposed are easily rejected. And, having viewed

thousands upon thousands of images, the experienced editor only glances at static, routine, outdated, duplicate, or clichéd photos. But, when a unique image catches an editor's

Much detail would be lost if this photo were run small. Here, a church member faints at the peak of a faith healer's sermon.
(Photo by Sandra Shriver.)

eye, the picture is like a red traffic light signaling "STOP."

■ START WITH IMAGINATIVE ASSIGNMENTS

Striking pictures result from sound assignments. The picture editor runs down the list of news stories on the day's log, to determine which lend themselves to pictorial reporting, which need an inked illustration or computer graphic, and which need no accompanying artwork at all. With limited staff and resources—and most newspapers and magazines fall into this category—the editor must choose to cover stories with a certain amount of intrinsic visual interest.

Bruce Baumann, who was assistant managing editor/graphics for the *Pittsburgh Press*, warns that a photo department should not become a "service station." He points out that a photographer's job is not just to provide the service of illustrating a writer's story.

The enlightened photo editor, therefore, not only assigns the listed news stories of the day, but also generates pictorial story ideas as well. The photo editor might ask a photographer to cover the background or sidelights of a news story in addition to the breaking event itself.

For example, a news conference is called to announce a $4 million grant for retirement homes. Although a picture of the press conference may be necessary, it has little chance of producing exciting photos and less opportunity for providing readers with valuable information about aging or the crisis in care for the elderly. The story is concerned basically with statistics—the percentage increase in care costs—and with the number of dollars spent on nursing home facilities.

The photo editor might try to interpret these statistics visually by instructing the photographer to spend several days in a nursing home. These kinds of photos would help translate the dull, itemized costs of research into more human terms. The reader would see the conditions of the facility and the regressive effects of aging on the home's clientele. A photo showing an aging patient alone in a hallway can bring the dollars-and-cents issue home to the reader. (See pages 54–55.)

■ SELECT THE PHOTOGRAPHER

The sensitive, perceptive photo editor realizes the strengths and weaknesses of the available staff and freelance photographers. Not all photographers like sports; only a few take funny pictures. Some photographers notice subtle shadings of light and shade, whereas others have an eye for action. Matching the correct photographer with the appropriate assignment can be a complex task for the photo editor. In fact, the primary way a magazine editor controls the look of

the publication is through the selection of photographers with different styles, says Peter Howe, editor and publisher of *Outtakes*. Howe was photo editor of the *New York Times Magazine* and director of photography at *Life* magazine.

The photo editor should provide the photographer with all the available information on an upcoming story. The more a photographer knows about an assignment, the better he or she will cover it. The editor should give the photojournalist clips of previous and related stories to fill in the background and put the story in context. The editor should suggest possible contacts who can provide further information. And, of course, if the story is expected to run with a photo layout rather than a single picture, then the editor should forewarn the photographer about the number of pictures that will be needed.

The photographer borrowed a ladder from a nearby store to get this bird's eye view of children drawing self-portraits. Some photographers have a special knack for features.
(Photo by Nick Carlson, the (Fargo, N.D.) *Forum.*)

The child had been removed from her parents and placed in this orphanage because her mother was a crack addict. Through the courts, the father is trying to win custody of the child. In this scene, the child prepares to leave for a visit with her father. Which frame would you have selected from this take? (Photos by Jeff Vendsel, from The Struggle for Life Project.)

Ideally, after the film has been shot and processed, the photo editor reviews the contacts with the photographer, selecting the frames that best fit the story.

■ FIGHT FOR SPACE

Next begins the behind-the-scenes job for the photo editor, who battles for adequate space for the photographer's pictures. The city editor, wire editor, feature editor, and sports editor each try to hoard sections of the paper for their stories; consequently, the photo editor must be just as aggressive as the other editors in fighting for picture space. Great pictures never seen by the readers are as worthless as great pictures never assigned or taken.

■ CAMERA SKILLS NOT REQUIRED

Surprisingly, one skill that is not necessary to be an outstanding photo editor is the ability to take pictures. Many of the best-known photo editors never learned to use a camera; others, although they know the basic techniques, never practiced photojournalism.

Robert Wahls, a photo editor for the

New York Daily News, says he was better off not knowing about the mechanics of a camera: "It just bogs you down," he says. "What you need to edit pictures is in you—not the camera."

John Durniak, formerly of *Time*, *Look*, and the *New York Times*, and Tom Smith, who was *National Geographic*'s illustrations editor, both spent most of their lives handling pictures, not lenses. Bob Gilka, long-time director of photography for the *National Geographic*, was never a shooter. Roy Stryker of the Depression-era Farm Security Administration, who produced probably the most complete and lasting still-photo documentary of any era, never took pictures himself. The most famous example, however, is Wilson Hicks, an executive editor of *Life* magazine. He sent photographers to every point on the globe; he hired and fired the best photojournalists and set the direction of the field for years to come. Yet he never took a picture that was published in his own magazine. No one has proved that shooters don't make good photo editors, but camera knowledge is not a prerequisite for becoming a successful picture desk executive.

■ THE HAZARDS AND SATISFACTIONS OF DO-IT-YOURSELF PICTURE EDITING

Should photographers edit their own work? In the past, the old *Life* and *Look* magazines represented diametrically opposed positions in this controversy. *Life*'s Hicks said that photographers are too emotionally involved when taking pictures to evaluate the pictures objectively during editing. Former *Look* art director Will Hopkins argued the opposite philosophy. At *Look*, the photographer and photo editor, as well as the writer and art director, operated as a closely knit group, each contributing to the final story, without letting job titles limit each participant's input.

Life staffers received assignments, covered the story, turned in the film, and waited until the magazine appeared, to see which of their pictures had been selected and how they had been played. *Life* photographers had almost no control over stories after shooting them.

Specialists in picture research, picture editing, caption writing, text block writing, and layout took the photographer's raw material and produced a finished photo essay.

By comparison, each photojournalist at *Look* magazine stayed with the story from conception through shooting to editing and paste-up. Tim Cohane, *Look*'s sports editor for twenty-one years, recalled that, in the initial stages of each assignment, he sounded out the ideas of photographers and layout people. "If you can use their enthusiasm and combine your ideas with theirs, you will come up with imaginative picture stories," said Cohane. "The photographer voiced his opinions at each stage of the story's development."

Over at the Time-Life building, Hicks used to argue that photographers evaluated their own pictures on a different basis from their editors. The photographer, who might have dangled from the top of a mountain in subzero weather to get a particularly evocative picture, attached more significance to

Studies show that readers prefer feature pictures—like this accidental slip of the skirt during a rehearsal— over sports and news pictures.
(Photo by Scott Eklund, *Bellevue* (Wash.) *Journal American*.)

the resulting image than did the editor, who evaluated the picture's merits impartially, without considering the trials and tribulations under which the photo was taken. The photographer's familiarity with the difficulties of the assignment might affect personal objectivity.

On many small newspapers, a photojournalist shoots an assignment, develops the film, chooses the frames, scans the negatives or prints the pictures, and delivers the completed images to the editor's desk or computer; no one else inspects the original negatives. What this system gains in efficiency, it loses in objectivity. The editor or managing editor does not have to view the negatives; the photographer, however, should find someone who was not present at the news scene to offer an impartial opinion.

Photographers should try to avoid the "shoot-and-ship system," so often practiced at national magazines, in which the photojournalist shoots the pictures and ships them to the newspaper or magazine, along with a few sketchy cutline notes, never even catching a glimpse of the negatives before the pictures are published. The photographer, like the reporter, participated in the news event and therefore has a better idea of what

actually occurred than does an editor in an executive office. Photojournalists should be involved, if possible, in the picture-editing process at all stages.

STRATEGIES FOR PICTURE SELECTION
■ THEORIES OF PICTURE SELECTION

Laura Vitray, John Millis, Jr., and Roscoe Ellard, in *Pictorial Journalism*, a 1939 book on news photography, tried to develop a mathematical formula for determining reader interest in pictures. The researchers assigned points for the degree of news value of the event, the notoriety of the subject, and the amount of action in the picture. But many newspaper editors did not adopt the formula because it did not define the word news, neither did it provide a yardstick for measuring the subject's notoriety, nor a system to quantify the degree of action in the picture. Also, editors felt limited when required to judge all pictures on only three scales.

Stanley Kalish and Clifton Edom, in their book *Picture Editing*, added several new factors to consider when selecting pictures. They advised editors to look for pictures that not only had news, notoriety, and action, but also eye-stopping appeal. By "eye-stoppers," the authors meant pictures that contained interesting patterns, had strong contrasts in tonal value, or could be uniquely cropped (like extra-wide horizontals or slim verticals). Then, after the readers' attention was engaged, the pictures should also hold interest. What galvanized readers' attention, they said, depended on the subject matter. A picture about love or war was more likely to maintain attention than was a photograph about farming or economics. Some topics, the researchers concluded, are intrinsically more interesting than others, regardless of the quality of the photo.

■ RESEARCH INDICATES READERS' PREFERENCES
Fires, Disasters, and Human Interest

Researchers over the intervening years have conducted several surveys to determine subjects that have intrinsic interest for readers. The first study of any size was conducted by the Advertising Research Foundation, which surveyed readership of 130 daily newspapers varying in size, circulation, and locality. The Continuing Study of Newspaper Reading, completed eleven years later, was statistically analyzed by Charles Swanson to determine what categories of pictures were the most read. From the 3,353 photos in the study, Swanson reported in *Journalism Quarterly* that fire, disaster, and human interest were among the top-viewed categories. Least-viewed picture categories included sports, fine arts, and the family.

Researchers Malcolm S. MacLean and Anne Li-An Kao studied the responses of 32 subjects to a variety of photos. As reported in *Journalism Quarterly*, they determined that test subjects generally liked "celebrities, children, happy old ladies, roses, and animals." What they disliked were "Mussolini and his mistress hanging by their feet, dead American soldiers, and dead bodies in general."

Liking photos and being interested in them are not synonymous, however. Because the respondents did not like what was in the photographs doesn't mean that they weren't interested in the subject matter. The photographs at the extreme ends of the scale also tended to be the ones that respondents indicated aroused the most emotion.

In general, readers say they don't like to look at dead bodies. In a clever study, James Roche altered cutlines of photographs to observe how readers would react if they thought the person in a photograph was dead versus whether they thought the person was alive. His survey found most respondents appeared more accepting of the "victim-lived" than of the "victim-died" photograph.

For her master's thesis, Gretchen Farsai asked whether newspaper editors, as compared with the general public, would run controversial pictures. She showed to both editors and non-editors in the Los Angeles area controversial photos, including the Kent State shooting of a student by a National Guardsman, crowd-filled stands collapsing at the Indianapolis Speedway, a Buddhist monk burning himself in Vietnam (see page 292), Vietnamese children fleeing napalm, and an execution in the streets of Saigon (see page 316). Not surprisingly, the twenty-two editors were more willing to publish the shocking pictures than were the non-editors. Women, interestingly, viewed the highly charged photographs more negatively than men, yet were more willing to see them published.

Features Preferred

Joseph Ungaro, chairman of the Associated Press Managing Editors (APME) photo committee, with the assistance of Hal Buell, AP's assistant general manager for news photos at the time, polled 500 readers to find out what types of pictures they liked. The AP survey reported that readers liked human interest and feature pictures most. Readers found general news and sports least interesting. Out of the many photos presented in the AP picture survey, readers selected as their favorite a photo of a big fluffy Saint Bernard kissing a little child.

An innovative research technique called Eye-Trac Research systems, run by the Gallup Applied Science Partnership, Princeton, New Jersey, further supports the AP survey that readers prefer features to news. The Eye-Trac research uses two tiny television cameras mounted on the subject's head to record where, how long, and in which order a subject looks at photos in a newspaper or magazine. Whereas older studies asked readers what they liked or remembered about pictures, this equipment actually records the amount of time a subject stares at a given photo.

Qualifying her statement by restricting her conclusions to "some newspapers and audiences," Sharon H. Polansky, vice president of the research organization, says that the majority of subjects reading newspapers gravitate more to feature than to news photos. She says feature photos have a slightly higher "attention" factor.

Women More Picture-minded

Surveys indicate that all readers do not have the same taste in pictures. Based on the data of the Continuing Study of Newspaper Reading, Swanson found that women are more picture-minded than men. He concluded that women have a greater interest in a larger number of picture categories than men do, and they also differed from men in their preference of specific categories. In a survey published in *Search* magazine, Randall Harrison found that men tend to prefer photographs of events, whereas women prefer pictures of people. Both sexes looked more at pictures of women than at pictures of men.

Forty years ago, researchers Malcolm MacLean and William Hazard found that women rated "blood-and-violence" pictures lower than their male counterparts—a finding supported by Roche's more recent study, which showed that women more often than men tended to reject photographs containing dead bodies.

The new Eye-Trac research, however, which actually measures how long people's eyes remain on images, did not find gender differences when the testers presented news and feature pictures.

One category in which men and women do differ is their reaction to sports pictures. Although the overall statistics of the picture surveys indicate that sports is a low-preference category, this finding results from the fact that women look at baseball, basketball, and football pictures only half as much as men, according to Swanson's analysis.

Other recent Eye-Trac research demonstrates that males look at black-and-white

Gallup's Eye-Trac Research involves the placement of two miniature video cameras on a subject's head. One camera focuses on the eyes, the other on the printed page of whatever material the subject is holding. The equipment creates a videotape showing precisely where and how long the subject looks at a page. (From *presstime* ©.)

sports photos more often than females do. Surprisingly, however, the Eye-Trac researchers also found that, when the sports photos were in color, men and women paid equal attention to sports photos—an important finding if editors realize that color on the sports pages—more so than in any other section of the paper—may help attract wider readership to that section.

Conclusions

With so few studies available, and the studies themselves differing in sampling and survey techniques, generalizations have to be limited. Several conclusions, however, do seem justified. Human interest pictures received high ratings from readers. Not surprisingly, the public liked to look at pictures of people engaged in funny or unusual activities. Sports, on the other hand, appeared at the bottom of the surveys. In fact, a Lou Harris survey found that newspaper editors overestimated the public's interest in sports stories.

Sports pictures should not, however, be eliminated from the newspaper. A newspaper's inherent advantage over its nearest competitor, television, is that newspapers can display an array of items simultaneously, letting individual readers pick the news articles they are interested in pursuing and disregard those that do not pique their curiosity. Women can look at people pictures while men can review sports photos. Television, by contrast, is linear. It can display only one item at a time. Therefore, it presents only items that have mass viewer appeal. Television selects its subjects based on what the station managers think will have the broadest common pulling power for all sexes and ages. Newspapers do not have to be edited this way. A newspaper can present a variety of items, each of which will appeal to a select group of interested readers.

■ CAN PROFESSIONAL EDITORS PREDICT READERS' PREFERENCES?

Who knows what kinds of pictures people like? Logically, you might assume that photo editors know their audiences, but another study by MacLean and Kao, published in *Journalism Quarterly*, suggested that editors are just guessing when they predict reader response to pictures. The researchers asked average newspaper readers to sort through pictures and to arrange them in order—from most favorite to least favorite photos. Then the researchers asked a group of experienced photo editors and a group of untrained students to sort through the same photos. The editors and students arranged the photos in the order they thought the readers had

organized the photos. The editors and students based their predictions on statistical information they had about the readers. MacLean and Kao hypothesized that, the more information such as age, sex, and occupation the editors and students had, the more accurately they could predict the likes and dislikes of readers.

Surprisingly, the researchers' hypothesis was wrong. Professional photo editors performed little better than even chance when given minimal or even detailed information about their readers. Furthermore, photo editors did no better at predicting than did the students. However, once the professionals had seen how their readers sorted one set of photos, the editors could anticipate how readers would sort a second set. These predictions were even better if the editors knew more about the reader, including the person's age, hobbies, and lifestyle.

Until the editors had seen readers' selections, however, they could not predict an individual reader's preferences. Clearly, more editors should find out what pictures their readers are actually looking at, rather than base editorial decisions on their own biases.

The Bus Survey

Robert Gilka, former director of photography for the *National Geographic*, tells a story about Charlie Haun, a picture editor in Detroit who used to make his own surveys: "Every couple of days, Haun would ride the bus in Detroit and look over the shoulders of bus riders who were reading the paper. He would note which picture their eyes stopped at, how long they dwelt on each photo, and see if they read captions." Gilka points out that although Haun's method was primitive, "Charlie probably knows more about pictures than most of us today." Haun, from his bus rides, came to the same conclusion that MacLean and Kao did from their research. Identifying what pictures people have picked in the past is the best determinant of what pictures they will choose in the future.

■ DO READERS AND EDITORS AGREE?

To discover if editors and readers agree on what constitutes interesting and newsworthy photos, the Associated Press Managing Editors photo survey mentioned earlier was designed to determine which kinds of pictures readers liked, as well as which type editors preferred, and whether readers and editors shared the same taste. The results indicated a surprisingly close agreement between readers and editors. Both selected the same photos in the sports, general news, and feature categories. Editors' and readers' opinions, however, differed radically on the use of dramatic news pictures. By a two-to-one margin over readers, editors chose action-packed, often violent, and sometimes gruesome news pictures. A majority of the readers not only disliked such pictures, but also thought that violent pictures should never be published. As the pictures became successively more gruesome, fewer readers voted for photos in this category.

As MacLean and Kao discovered, editors cannot predict an individual's photo preferences. Yet, as the AP survey indicated, except for spot news, editors' and readers' tastes are generally similar.

When it came to picking a favorite picture, however, editors and readers diverged. Readers chose the Saint Bernard-kissing-child picture. Editors chose as most interesting the photo of the lifeless body of a hanged Bangkok student being beaten by a right-wing opponent. (See page 184.)

When I interviewed AP's Hal Buell, he tried to draw some conclusions from his picture survey: newspapers have to be all things to a lot of different people. Editors must print what people want and also what the editors think is significant. A news outlet, in the end, must print some of both in order to present a complete picture of the world: pictures of dogs kissing kids as well as pictures of political violence.

■ WHAT READERS DON'T SEE

Pictures in the media should reflect our society. Sounds good.

Unfortunately, editors tend to ignore, deliberately or through benign neglect, whole population segments, including African Americans, gays and lesbians, Hispanics, Asians, and women of all races. Researchers Paul Lester and Ron Smith found that in 1942, only 1.1 percent of the pictures in *Life*, *Newsweek*, and *Time* included African Americans. Today, while these magazines run more images of African Americans (8.8 percent), this number does not match the 12.3 percent of the American population this group constitutes. Michael Singletary came to the same general conclusions when he looked at how often African Americans are portrayed in newspapers.

In a 1974 study of the *Los Angeles Times* and the *Washington Post*, Susan Miller found that pictures of men outnumbered pictures of women in both papers. In 1980, Roy Blackwood replicated Miller's study and found that the imbalance had actually worsened over the intervening years. Men clearly dominated page one, inside news pages, business pages, and the sports section. Ratios of photos of men to photos of women ranged from more than 20:1 for sports, to about 2:1 for entertainment. Overall, pictures of men outnumbered pictures of women nearly 4 to 1 in the *Post* and nearly 3 to 1 in the *Times*. Barbara Luebke came to the same conclusion when she studied four Connecticut newspapers fifteen years later, in 1989. She found that men are shown not only more often but also usually as professionals and sports figures, whereas women are portrayed as spouses—despite the fact that 50 percent of the work force is composed of women and 23.8 percent of professional athletes in the United States are female.

Besides women and African Americans—and other ethnic groups, for that matter—newspapers tend to ignore gays and lesbians. When Gail Fisher shot a photo story about two lesbian women in the late 1970s, her newspaper at the time, the *San Bernardino* (Calif.) *Sun* thought the topic too dicey to run. As recently as 1992, Joseph Bernt and Marilyn Greenwald found that 25 percent of the senior editors at daily newspapers would not run pictures of two people of the same sex kissing. A series about teen gays titled "Growing Up Gay: A Crisis in Hiding," shot by Rita Reed and published in a 14-page, ad-free section of the *Minneapolis Star Tribune*, is a notable exception.

Readers rarely think about pictures they don't see. Out of sight, out of mind. Editors should be especially aware of the pictures they are not assigning or are simply omitting. Readers depend on the news media for a balanced picture of the world. Leaving out whole segments of the population presents a notably biased view.

Besides not publishing photos of minority groups, editors tend to censor pictures that they think their readers simply won't like. (See "Ethics, Chapter 14," for a full discussion of this issue.)

CROPPING: CUTTING OUT THE FAT

Regardless of how good the original is, if a photo is butchered on the cropping table or reduced to the size of a postage stamp, no one will see the picture. Newspapers do this every day. Says Roy Paul Nelson, author of ***Publication Design***, "The typical daily or weekly newspaper is not designed, really; its parts are merely fitted together to fill all the available space, sort of like a jigsaw puzzle." To save their photographs, more and more camera journalists are getting involved in layout. These photographers want a say in how their pictures are cropped and sized.

■ PERFECT FRAMING IS RARE

When you take a picture, you must decide what to include in the viewfinder and what to leave out. The impact of a picture often depends on this decision. By including too much in a picture, you run the risk of distracting the viewer from the main subject. By framing too tightly, on the other hand, you might leave out important story-telling elements. Photographers carry a variety of lenses to enable them to zoom in or draw back to include only the important pictorial elements.

Every photo cannot be perfectly framed in the camera, however. To save the shot, the photographer must enlarge the negative in the darkroom and crop the print with the adjustable borders of a printing easel—or make the crop in the computer (see Chapter 12, "Digital Images").

If, however, the photographer does not crop the picture in the darkroom or if a publication is not using the digital darkroom, the layout editor provides a second line of

Cropping this picture into a slim horizontal and running it across two pages gives it added impact.
(Photo by Jim Clark, *Springfield* (Oreg.) *News.*)

defense. Looking at the 8"×10" print, with all its distractions, the layout editor can cut out the extraneous by putting crop marks on the photograph's white border. These marginal marks indicate to the printer the area that should be left in the final reproduced halftone. The editor can cut out as much of the picture as necessary from the top, sides, or bottom of the print by merely drawing a short line with a grease pencil where the new border of the picture should be.

Even if tight framing in the camera eliminates distracting elements, not every subject fits neatly into the format of a 35mm negative. Neither will all subjects fit naturally into a 2¼"× 2¼" square or a 4"×5" rectangle. Some subjects are low and wide, like a classroom chalkboard; others are tall and skinny, like the Washington Monument. Consequently, no matter how carefully you compose, real world images may not perfectly fit the frame. In these situations, all you can do is shoot and then crop the negative later.

Cropped version.

Editors use arrows to indicate crop marks. Here, the editor cropped off the distracting white jacket on the left of the original for this photo of a streaker at a rugby match.
(Photo by Ian Bradshaw, Syndication International.)

Original version.

Crop the Excess

Like a writer editing copy, the layout person should emphasize the significant elements in the picture by eliminating extraneous material that carries little meaning. If a person's expression gives the picture sparkle, zero in on the face and cut out the peripheral material.

Light, bright areas of the picture, like windows and lights, tend to attract the eye. If these windows and lights are extraneous to the main subject, they may distract the reader. Avoid a competing area that might distract a reader's interest from the photo's primary subject. Crop out these irritating sidelights from the picture.

When Ian Bradshaw photographed a streaker being escorted from a rugby field by waiting policemen, one of whom used his helmet as a "modesty shield," the photographer also caught the distracting white jacket of a bystander. Upon seeing the print, most editors cropped out this irritating element before publication by marking the picture with arrows indicating which part of the image the printer should include.

If the action occurs in one corner of the picture, focus on that area. The layout editor should have a reason for leaving in each area of the picture. No corner of the picture should remain just because it happened to be in the original negative. The rule is: save the meat of the photo by cutting out the fat.

Crop Ruthlessly

"Crop ruthlessly," advises Edmond Arnold, a pioneer of modern newspaper design. "Cut out anything that's not essential to the picture, so that the reader's attention won't be distracted or wasted. Ruthless cropping leads to stronger images."

Research supports the notion that eliminating extraneous details helps a picture. Gallup's Sharon Polansky, recording eye movement as subjects perused print materials, found that the simpler a picture's background, the more attention the photo received.

Preserve the Mood

The editor's red grease pencil can save a picture or destroy it. Cropping can improve a picture by eliminating irritating details. But mindless cropping can ruin the intent of the picture by slicing off areas of the photo that give the image its mood. The sensitive editor

Be careful when you crop not to cut out important elements. The feeling of flight in this photo would be lost with a tight crop.
(Photo by Kent Porter, *Santa Rosa Press Democrat*.)

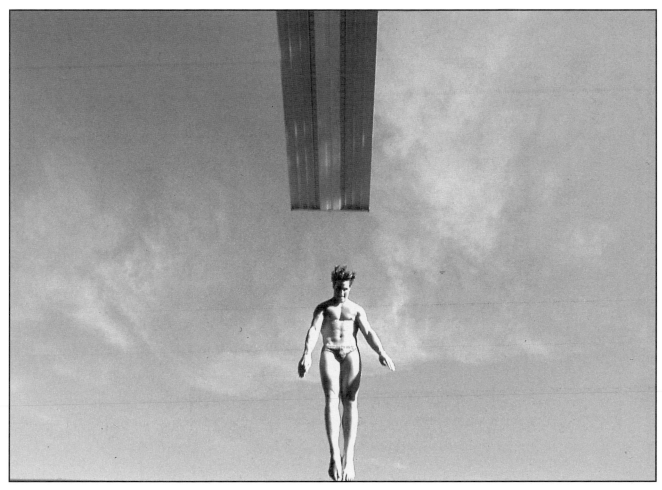

preserves the ingredients that give a picture its arresting look by leaving the brooding gray sky in a scenic or including the messy bookshelves in a college professor's portrait.

Sometimes a blank area in the picture balances the action area. Leaving a little room

The editor's most perceptive skills come into play when cropping a picture containing a person. The editor must be careful to operate, not amputate. Parts of the body can be cropped off, but usually the crop mark should not fall on a joint like an elbow or knee. If the editor divides the head from the neck in a photo, some of the shoulder should be left so that the head will have a platform to sit on. The layout person can crop into the face of a person, but should not leave half an eye or just part of a mouth. Look at the pictures of the dancer and decide which crops seem natural and which crops seem arbitrary and absurd.

Some insensitive designers dream up pages before they even see photos for the spread. When they receive the glossies, they slice and dice them into the preplanned shapes of their layouts, regardless of the photos' content. If these designs call for thin verticals running down the right-hand side of the page, these graphic artists care not if they have to chop up a perfectly composed horizontal shot and leave in only one eye and the tip of a nose—as long as the picture fills the predetermined space. These thoughtless people crop pictures to fit their designs, not to tell stories with photography.

(Photo by Kim Johnson, *Sacramento Bee*.)

on the print in front of a runner helps create the illusion that the athlete is moving across the picture. Similarly, some blank space in front of a profile portrait keeps the subject from looking as if he or she is peering off the edge of the print.

Besides mood, insensitive cropping can rip away parts of the picture that give it context. Sometimes it's important to know that a riot occurred in the ornate foyer of city hall or in a barren, dusty field. An editor's overzealous cropping could eliminate these informational, telling details.

■ REDUCED QUALITY: THE PRICE OF CROPPING

A perceptive editor can improve a photo's impact using thoughtful cropping, but sometimes at a price. Enlarging only a very small portion of the original negative or blowing up just a part of the final glossy magnifies

any defect in the original picture. If the original negative lacked perfect sharpness, then the published picture will look soft and indistinct. Even if the original is sharp, enlarging a portion of the negative expands each grain of the film, thereby decreasing the photo's resolution. The more the image is enlarged, the more the grain is visible. Enlarged grain means the detail of the photo may be obscured to the point where the print takes on the texture of rough sandpaper. The photographer faces a dilemma then. While the technical quality of the picture decreases when a photo is drastically cropped and enlarged, the visual impact of the photo often is improved. Cropping, therefore, involves a tradeoff between poorer quality but better composition. Taking a one-inch square segment of an 8"×10" photo and publishing it as a half-page spread in the newspaper might produce a

The price of extreme enlargement is increased grain and decreased quality. Only for news as unusual as this airplane stowaway falling to his death should poor quality photos be enlarged to this extent. (Photo by John Gilpin, Wide World Photos.)

perfectly composed picture that is too fuzzy for the viewer to appreciate.

Few situations merit an extreme blow-up from such a tiny portion of a picture. Generally, however, a good photo editor will opt for a dramatic image at the expense of some sharpness and grain. The editor reasons that it is better to catch the reader's attention with an exciting photo than lose the reader with a technically sharp but dull image.

SIZING UP FOR IMPACT
■ A BATTLE FOR SPACE

A battle between writers and photographers rages daily on many newspaper and magazine staffs. Its outcome determines the size of the pictures in the next day's paper or next week's magazine. The wordsmith, backed up by the copy and managing editors, fights for small pictures to leave room for plenty of type. Reinforced by the photo editor, the photographer demands that the pictures be printed large enough so that readers will not miss them.

The camera contingent argues that, the larger the picture, the more powerful its impact. And, in fact, ample evidence sup-

ports this claim. According to a study by Burt Woodburn, the average newspaper story is read by only 12 percent of its subscribers. In the same paper, Woodburn found, the average one-column picture attracts 42 percent of its readers.

In "Reader Interest in Newspaper Pictures," published in *Journalism Quarterly*, Woodburn concluded that as the size of a photo increases, the number of readers grows proportionately. The 42 percent, for example, grew to 55 percent when the photo ran across two columns. A four-column-wide picture caught the attention of about 70 percent of the readers. Both Seith Spaulding, in his paper "Research on Pictorial Illustration," and Hyun-Joo Lee Huh, in "The Effect of Newspaper Picture Size on Readers' Attention, Recall and Comprehension of Stories," verified Woodburn's findings.

When all other factors were equal, not surprisingly, Gallup's Sharon Polansky came to the same conclusion using Eye-Trac data. As reported in *Eyes on the News*, she confirmed that increasing size also increases attention to a picture. She found that one reason "mug shots" receive little attention is because edi-

The picture must be displayed large to see the detail in a close-up shot like this one of a woman replacing a contact lens.
(Photo by Ken Kobré, for the *Boston Phoenix*.)

tors play these portraits so small. The research demonstrated that 44 percent of the subjects looked at a one-column mug shot whereas the rate increased to 92 percent when readers viewed the same photo at three columns wide.

Even this axiom—bigger size gets more attention—has exceptions. The axiom's corollary might read: if the subject matter is exceptionally galvanizing, even small pictures will be noticed. Polansky noted during one of her studies that a tiny ad showing a female mud wrestler (with lots of torso showing)—played on the inside of a sports section—got much more attention than its size would have predicted. When it comes to sex, at least, picture size is not the only determinant for reader attention.

In addition to eliciting reader attention, bigger pictures draw readers into stories and also aid them in recalling the stories. A study by William Baxter, Rebecca Quarles, and Hermann Kosak found that, while a small, two-column picture accompanying a story does not help the reader remember the story's details, a large picture, six columns wide, measurably improves readers' recall of details in the accompanying article.

Hyun-Joo Lee Huh replicated those find-ings in a study at Syracuse University but went on to show that, in addition to attracting a reader's attention and aiding in recall, a larger photo also improved readers' compre-hension of a story. When asked about the outcome of a story with no accompanying picture, only 13 percent of the readers gave a correct answer. However, comprehension increased with the addition of photographs, with well over 75 percent of those who read the same story accompanied by a large photograph understanding the text and explaining its significance. The picture's size influenced readers to read the words as well as understand the implications of the article.

According to the Syracuse University study, the presence of a larger picture proba-bly causes readers to read more of the accom-panying story, which then results in greater recall and better comprehension of the article.

What's the message for reporters and edi-tors? Reporters should be begging editors to run large pictures with their stories if they want readers to notice their writing, under-stand its implications, and be able to remem-ber the information later. Large pictures don't just decorate the page. Big pictures attract readers' attention, lure them into an accompanying article, and help them

Good page layout usually involves playing pictures so that one image dominates. Dominance is achieved through size. The dominant picture seems large especially when it is played alongside considerably smaller images. If the dominant and subordinate images are too close in size, they compete for the reader's attention.
(Photos by Jim Gensheimer, *San Jose Mercury News.*)

Running a three-picture sequence tells the story of Bo Jackson breaking a bat over his knee better than any single image in this set. (Photo by Brad Mangin, for *Sports Illustrated*.)

complete the story, remember its facts, and comprehend its meaning.

Reporters, editors, educators, and almost anyone else involved in communications constantly complain that the MTV generation does not read. Even for those more familiar with changing channels than with turning pages, editors have at their disposal a tool that influences reading. Like a magnet, big pictures draw in readers of all ages to the associated story.

Increasing a picture's size gives an editor more "bang for the buck." True, editors will need to sacrifice the number and length of stories on a page to handle larger pictures. However, subscribers will read, remember, and understand the remaining stories rather than overlook those well-crafted, carefully researched words altogether.

The never-ending battle between the word and visual camps continues, but the photographer can gain space if he or she is willing to sacrifice a few weaker pictures so that stronger ones can be printed larger.

Photographers should fight for space when their images are striking. Bad photos, of course, should not appear in the paper, but if they must be printed, play them small. Oversizing a technically poor photo calls attention to its deficiencies. On the other hand, underplaying an exciting, technically sharp photo does a disservice to photographer and reader alike.

■ WHEN SIZE IS NEEDED
Drama
Armed with academic research and Arnold's axioms, the photographer fights for larger photos so that the audience can easily see the textural detail of the original image. A one-column head shot is so small that it communicates almost nothing, and the person is barely recognizable. With a four-column head shot, the reader can examine the two-day-old whiskers on the mayor's face, or the size of a contact lens on a woman's finger (see page 194).

Detail
A long shot, such as an overall of a church interior (see page 178) or an aerial from a plane, also demands space. Compressed into one column, all the details blend together and lose the bits of information that give the picture meaning.

"Exquisite," remarks the reader who sees a larger-than-life, oversized photo. A common object, like a pencil or pen, a contact lens, or even a media-worn face, becomes fresh and exciting when magnified beyond its natural size.

Contrast
Printing some pictures small and others big heightens the contrast between them, adding to the interest of the page. Publishing all pictures in a 3"×5" size produces a deadening effect. No individual picture dominates. It appears that the editor simply could not decide which photos were most important.

Just as a reporter or copy editor emphasizes certain points of an article by putting them in the lead, the layout editor spotlights certain pictures by playing them larger than the other photos on the page. (See page 195.)

PAIRING PICTURES FOR THE THIRD EFFECT
Sometimes one picture can sum up an event. The flag-raising at Iwo Jima, or the explosion of the Hindenburg needed only one photo to tell the story. Other situations require several. Pairing photos, according to Wilson Hicks in his landmark book *Words and Pictures*, causes a third effect. The reader looks at the two pictures separately and then mentally combines them. The effect is different than what any picture alone can produce.

■ PICTURE SEQUENCE/SERIES
Sometimes a little story takes place in a short period of time. Running a series of pictures brings more understanding than printing any single image. For example, Brad Mangin, who freelances for *Sports Illustrated*, was photographing the Oakland A's when Bo Jackson, on the opposing team, got mad, picked up a bat and broke it over his knee. The mini-story needed at least three pictures run together to explain what happened from the time Bo lifted his knee, when the bat came down, and when he was left holding half a bat in each hand. Mangin shot the sequence with a motor drive. (Also see the Mary Decker accident during the Olympics, page 102.)

■ PACKAGING PICTURES
Some situations are multifaceted. One photo just won't explain all the diverse elements.

For example, Chris Larsen wanted to show the activities of an alternative punk club in Berkeley, Calif. The Gilman Street Project is run by teenagers for teenagers. A single overall picture of the club didn't show the spiked mohawk hairstyles or the basketball game kids play between sets. Just a close-up of the slam-dancing mosh pit would miss details like the tatooes ringing the neck of one of the teenagers. The picture package, shown on the following spread, brings together a range of elements that allow viewers to see a more complete view of this club.

A risqué fashion show for women (LEFT) is paired with a photo of a beauty contest (BELOW LEFT). Played together, the pictures deliver a stronger editorial message about the sexes than either could alone. (LEFT: Photo by Curt Johnson, *Long Beach* (Calif.) *Press-Telegram.* BELOW LEFT: Mike Smith, *Detroit Free Press.*)

■ UNRELATED PICTURE PAIRING
Different Pictures—Similar Meanings

In written language, different words can have similar meanings. With pictures, different images can carry similar messages. Language experts call words with related meanings synonyms. A thesaurus is filled with examples of synonyms. Pictures with similar messages could be called visual synonyms.

Pairing pictures that were taken at different times and places but carry the same editorial statement allows the reader to see the common elements in the different images. The reader draws comparisons between the different photos. For example, you could publish side-by-side pictures of a man judging a beauty contest, and women watching husbands and boyfriends stage a risqué fashion show. While the two pictures were photographed at widely different times and places, one in Texas and the other in California, and taken by two photographers, Mike Smith and Curt Johnson, pairing them makes an editorial statement about the sexes. Similar in editorial content and point of view, the two pictures might be considered visual synonyms. They look different, but their underlying meaning is similar.

Visual Homonyms

On the other hand, some words—like "to," "two," and "too"—sound the same but carry completely different meanings. These are called homonyms. Likewise, some pictures look superficially similar but carry dissimilar information. For example, a picture of an Egyptian pyramid and a photo of a pile of oranges might look similar—both are shaped like triangles. Some pairs may be entertaining, but, because the pictures share no editorial relationship, a reader trying to find their common editorial thread may be confused. The pictures have no real journalistic commonality.

Be careful, then, of visual homonyms,

► Up to seven bands a night play the club and split half the club's proceeds (NEAR RIGHT).

► Many of the fans adorn more than the walls with grafitti. Here a young man wears a tattoo "necklace." (FAR RIGHT)

▼ In the mosh pit, the punkers slam dance by throwing their hands or elbows in all directions, kicking their boots upward, banging into each other and pushing anyone or anything in the way. It looks like a violent shove match. "But," one of the participants says, "it's not about violence, it's a way of supporting the band, getting into the music, and just having a good time."

▼ Nope. It's not a bad hair day. The mohawk haircut, a typical punk 'do, stands out against the graffiti-covered wall. Every square inch of the club is covered in graffiti.

The Picture Package

The Gilman Street Project is a Berkeley, Calif., punk rock club run for and by teenagers. No alcohol, no drugs. Just ear splitting music played by live bands.

No single picture describes the place. Grouping a set of pictures together into a picture package reveals a number of the club's facets.

(Photos by Chris Larsen, from the Next Generation Project.)

◄ The punks have an "anti" attitude, which this picture summarizes.

photos unrelated except by looks. Pairing such pictures can lead to editorial abuse. Pairing pictures that are not intrinsically connected editorially can lead to silly or, in even worse situations, offensive results. Some readers would object to pairings that don't relate editorially. Others would vehemently disagree with the pairing.

I once saw a collection of unrelated pictures of overweight people—shot by different photographers for different purposes—published together on a page in a photo book. The editor must have thought it clever to assemble these editorially unrelated pictures together because they shared a common visual element: overweight people. I thought his decision was tasteless and insensitive. What was the message?

THE CAPTION: STEPCHILD OF THE BUSINESS

Some pictures—such as Norman Rockwell's cover illustrations for the *Saturday Evening Post*—need no words. The idea portrayed is so simple or its emotional content so powerful that the illustration tells the story clearly and immediately without any captions.

But most photos do need words. The old Chinese proverb relates that a picture is worth a thousand words, but the corollary to the proverb is that a picture without words is not worth much.

A picture raises as many questions as answers. Look at the pictures on these two pages and ask yourself if you know who is in each picture, what is happening, when the events took place, and why the action occurred.

Pictures usually answer these questions only partially. A picture that can stand completely alone is rare. The point is not whether photographs can survive without words or words without pictures, but whether pictures and words can perform better when they are combined.

Why is this mother crying and her daughter wiping her tears with a stuffed toy? Without a complete caption, readers would not realize that the woman's son had been murdered in Italy, where she and her husband donated the boy's organs so others could benefit. That act of kindness in response to the violence that took the boy's life caused the number of organ donations in Italy to soar.
(Photo by John Burgess, *Santa Rosa* (Calif.) *Press Democrat.*)

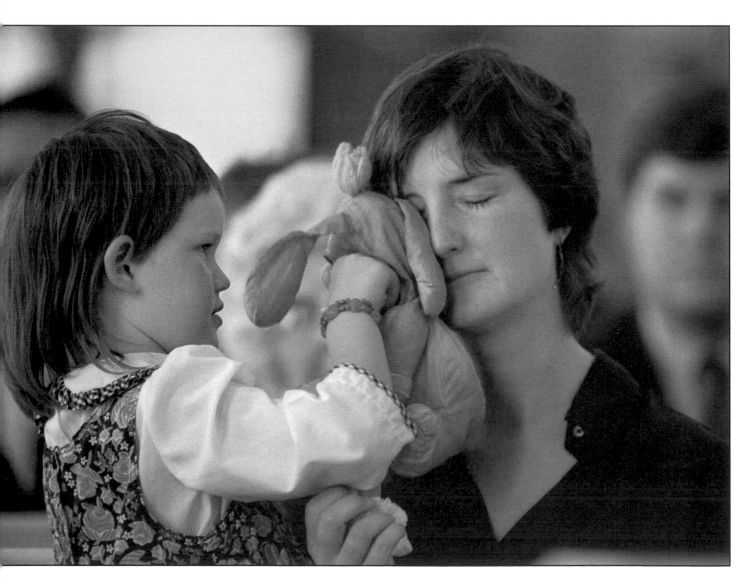

WORDS INFLUENCE PICTURE MEANING

When Jean Kerrick was assistant professor of journalism at the University of California, Berkeley, she conducted research to determine the influence that captions had on readers' interpretations of pictures. Captions, she found, can at least modify and sometimes change the meaning of a picture, especially when the picture itself is ambiguous. A caption can change from one extreme to another the viewer's interpretation of the same picture.

Kerrick presented a profile shot, of a well-dressed man sitting on a park bench, to two groups of subjects. She asked the groups to rate the picture on several subjective scales. The scales ranged from "good to bad," "happy to sad," "pleasant to unpleasant," and so forth. Then, the first group was shown the same picture with this caption: "A quiet minute alone is grabbed by Governor-elect Star. After a landslide victory, there is much work to be done before taking office." The second group was shown the same picture with a different caption: "Exiled communist recently deported by the U.S. broods in the Tuileries Garden alone in Paris on his way back to Yugoslavia." Both groups were again asked to rate the picture on the evaluative scales.

Kerrick found that, after the first group read the positive caption, they rated the picture "happier," "better," and "more pleasant" than they had originally judged it. The second group of viewers, who read the caption about the exiled communist, changed their rating of the picture in the opposite direction—the photo now seemed "sad" and "unpleasant." In this example, the caption completely reversed the impression initially given by the picture alone.

In a similar study, Fred Fedler, Tim Counts, and Paul Hightower used high-impact news photos and varied only one or two words in accompanying captions. They did not find striking changes when they varied just a few words of the captions with this particular set of pictures. Perhaps changing captions influences neutral pictures but not those that tell a clearer and more dramatic story like the ones in their study.

Pictures appear to serve as a primitive means of communication but carry out their task instantly. Words function as a sophisticated means of communication, but lack the impact of the visual message. Pictures transmit the message immediately, but words shape and give focus to that message.

PICTURES DRAW ATTENTION TO WORDS

Pictures need words, but words also need pictures. A picture serves a story as an exclamation point does a sentence. Regardless of its content, the photo says to the audience, "READ THIS STORY. IT'S IMPORTANT!" By adding a picture related to the news, an editor adds significance to the story. Functioning as a banner headline, the picture flags down the readers' attention to a given spot on the newsprint page (see also "Batle for Space," page 194.)

WRITING CLEAR CAPTIONS

The need for clear and concise caption-writing is obvious. Readers often determine whether they are going to read an entire article based on what they gleaned from a picture and caption. If you glance through some newspapers, however, you may get the impression that the first person to walk into the city room wrote the captions in the paper that day. Writers polish their story leads, and photographers polish their lenses, but no one shines up the captions. Writers claim that caption-writing is beneath them, while photographers often seem to find an important blazing fire to cover when the time comes to compose captions. The caption—the stepchild of the newspaper business—is the most read but least carefully written text in the paper.

Poor captions sometimes result when photographers fail to get adequate information at the time they take the pictures or forget to include the information when they write the captions. Howard Chapnick, who ran the Black Star picture agency for many years says, "One cannot err on the side of providing too much caption information. The editor who finds a photographer who understands the importance of detailed captioning will figuratively embrace him bodily and professionally."

Former *People* magazine photo editor John Dominis tells the story of holding up the magazine's production because a photographer did not send in one critical identification. Lights in the New York headquarters burned past midnight as the editors carried out a desperate search by telephone for the forgetful photographer. Editors, writers, layout artists, designers, and production staff all waited hour after hour for the missing caption, costing *People* magazine thousands of dollars in overtime.

PUTTING THE FIVE Ws IN A CAPTION

"A caption is a verbal finger pointing at the picture," wrote John Whiting in his book *Photography Is a Language*. Captions, like fingers, come in many sizes and shapes. The opening words of a caption must capture the reader's attention just as do the lead words of a news story or feature. The caption writer starts off the sentence with the most newsworthy, interesting, or unusual facts. Copy desks have developed several varieties of captions, each emphasizing a different element of the story.

What

The reader wants an explanation of what is happening in the picture; hence, the first words of the cutline should explain the action. Unless the situation in the picture is obvious, the cutline must describe what is going on.

After two years of drought, it rained in the southern part of the state yesterday....

Further down in the cutline, the writer can fill in the other details of the story by giving the remaining four Ws.

Who

The who may be emphasized in the caption when the person in the news is featured. **President Clinton said yesterday that he will spend the weekend at Camp David.**

In this situation, the newsworthy aspect of the picture is the person, President Bill Clinton. The fact that the president was speaking outweighed what he had to say or where he said it.

A person's name should lead the caption only when that person is well-known to the readers of the magazine or newspaper. Do not start the caption, "John Doe said yesterday that the budget should be slashed."

No one knows John Doe, so placing his name prominently in the cutline neither adds to the picture's interest nor explains its news value. However, if John Doe's face is recognizable in the photo, he should be mentioned somewhere in the caption. People's names are always included in the caption even if they are not famous. Someone—spouse, parents, friends—certainly will recognize them. Also, readers can misidentify the person in the photo if the name is left out of the caption. Often you may hear, "That woman in the picture in the paper today looks just like . . . "

Many editors will not run a picture unless the photographer has included in the caption the names of all recognizable people.

The wire services, whose pictures go

around the world, write in the person's first and last name, regardless of the individual's national prominence. If a child is pictured, the photographer should get the name and the age of the youngster. This information often adds additional human interest.

The collie pup would have drowned if the Selleck girls (left to right) Debbie, age 3, Heidi, age 5, and Becky, age 7, had not pulled their dog, Sam, from the stream in time.

Note that readers are given clear directions about which girl is which with the phrase "left to right." Sometimes the words "top row," "wearing the tie," or other identifying features will help readers match the faces in the photo with the names in the cutlines.

When/Where

Photos rarely tell the reader exactly when or where the pictures were taken. If this information helps the reader understand the picture, supply the location and the time. Use the day of the week, not the calendar date.

José Canseco hit the home run yesterday that gave the A's their win over the Giants. (Not "Canseco hit the home run July 6.")

The writer should begin the cutline with time or place only when that fact is significant or unusual.

At 3 A.M., Mayor Ted Stanton finally signed the zoning bill.

Or: Standing in the sewer, the water commissioner, Edna Lee, explained the new drainage system.

Why

Some caption writers claim that explaining why the action occurred in a picture takes away the reason for reading the story and thus causes readers to skip the adjoining article.

Other news photographers and editors argue that extensive captions pique reader interest for the main body of the story.

Because of the transit strike, highways leading into the city were jammed at the early morning rush hour today.

Without answering the "why" of this imaginary photo, the image alone would not make sense.

Without a caption, readers would not know that these two men are lawyers fighting an oil company's pollution. (Photo by Sibylla Herbrich, *San Francisco Law Journal.*)

Sometimes pictures capture great emotion but, without captions, readers may be unable to determine just what emotion they are seeing. Are these women happy or sad? Did they win or lose the event? (Photo by Paul Chinn, *Los Angeles Herald Examiner.*)

■ FILLING OUT THE DETAIL

The caption is the place to tell readers if the subject in the picture was posed. If the photographer took the picture with a special lens, or manipulated the print in the darkroom, this fact should be noted. In fact, anything about the scene in the picture that differs significantly from the actual event and, therefore, might distort the facts, should be explained in the caption.

Small Detail

Casually glancing at a photo, readers might miss an important but small detail. The cutlines can focus attention on various parts of the picture, emphasizing the elements the photographer thinks are important. The cutlines can supply details about the four senses—hearing, tasting, smelling, feeling—that the picture does not convey.

Quote

Sometimes this purpose can be accomplished by including a catchy quote.

"Some days I wish I had never left Kansas," said rock star Dorothy Oz on the eve of her thirty-fourth record-breaking performance.

Taste, Smell, and Touch

How something tastes or feels might explain a subject's reaction in a picture. Without an explanatory phrase in the caption, the picture might not make sense.

David Krathwohl, 10, Jerry Lazar, 9, and Lou Madison, 11, struggle to climb an oil-covered plastic pole. . . .

Color

Even though black-and-white photos record the world in almost infinite detail, one visual element is left out: color. When color is an important aspect of the scene, the cutline must supply this missing dimension.

The Franklin High Majorettes, dressed in bright pink uniforms and matching pink tennis shoes and carrying pink batons, marched and twirled in front of the Franklin County Courthouse yesterday.

Before and After

A camera shutter, open for 1/500 sec., results in a photo that accurately describes what happens in that brief span of time. But the photo does not inform the readers about what happened before or after that split

What had happened before this picture was taken lends great importance to what the reader is seeing now. Years ago, the Cambodian refugee in the car fled the Khmer Rouge and came to the United States. The photographer accompanied the man on his first —and perhaps last— trip back to Cambodia. The people outside the car are his sole surviving relatives, and all realize this may be the last time they see him again. (Photo by Bruce Chambers, *Long Beach* (Calif.) *Press-Telegram*.)

second; the causes of the event and its effect are absent. Cutlines must supply the befores and afters.

Special Camera or Computer Effects

Whenever your picture's overall look is the result of a special photographic effect, your caption should let the reader know how you accomplished this. When Marshall Spurrier was assigned to photograph the farmers who grew a large pumpkin, he placed the vegetable on the ground, attached an ultra-wide lens to the camera and positioned the man and his wife on either side of the frame, several feet back. The resulting picture made the vegetable look as if it were as big as a house. Spurrier used the picture's caption to explain how he achieved the effect.

Besides the distorting effects of the wide-angle lens, sometimes you might need to point out the compression effect of an extra-long telephoto, color shifts produced when shooting in mixed lighting, or elements changed with digital manipulation. (See a full discussion of ethical issues regarding computer-manipulated photos in Chapter 12, "Digital Images.")

■ CAPTION-WRITING STYLES

Write short, declarative sentences with as few words as possible. Avoid complex sentences. Don't put unrelated facts in the same sentence. Keep facts separated with periods, not commas or other punctuation.

The AP's Hal Buell, assistant to the president at Photostream, says, "Skip the adjectives and adverbs in a caption. Let the picture speak for itself."

Two schools of thought differ on the tense of verbs in captions. The first group advises putting everything in present tense because the words in the caption are describing a photo immediately in front of the reader. The present tense also involves the reader more than does the past tense. Says Karen Cater of the *Seattle Times*, "Present-tense captions give a sense of action, immediacy, and life to a photo."

The opposing view advocates using the past tense because all the action in the picture has already taken place.

John Brown tags (tagged) the runner to make the last out in yesterday's game.

Avoid the obvious. Phrases like "firefighter fighting blaze" or "basketball player going for hoop" are unnecessary because readers can see that, in the first picture, the people are firefighters, and, in the second, that the athlete is a basketball player.

Phrases like "pictured above" also add no new information. Captions should avoid telling readers what they can find out for themselves by looking at the picture.

Special effects such as the close placement of the wide-angle lens (28mm) used in this picture should always be explained in a caption. (Photo by Marshall Spurrier, *Chanute* (Kans.) *Tribune*.)

Avoid speculation about what the subject might be thinking. Such guessing can be inaccurate and give a wrong impression.

Claire Katz smiles with happiness as she receives a check from the president.

For all we know, she is putting on an act. She might really think that the check was far too small for her efforts. The photographer has no way of looking into a subject's mind. And, of course, no one can read an animal's mind. Don't fall into this trap:

These pigs seem to be wondering if. . . .

Write simply. The best cutlines are written with no cute or pretentious prose, no clichés, and no painful puns that take the enjoyment out of the photo. Remember, puns are the lowest form of caption writing.

And, finally, please don't forget to identify old photos from the morgue as file photos.

Otherwise the reader might think they were taken yesterday.

■ FINAL ADVICE

Caption writers—both neophytes and pros—must always remember to start with the picture. Looking at the picture will help avoid the mistake one caption writer made. The caption read, "Police seized a quantity of opium." But in the picture, there were no police and there was no opium.

Joseph Kastner, who was the head copy editor and caption writer for *Life* magazine, said that the discipline required for caption writing is of an order that no other kind of journalism requires. "And when this discipline is exerted, he said, "it produces writing that is as taut, as spare, as evocative, and as cogent as any writing in journalism today." ■

A good caption would go beyond the five Ws to include how this boating accident happened and what might prevent another like it in the future. (Photo by Allan Detrich, *Toledo* (Ohio) *Blade.*)

Cameras & Film

A news photographer's bag is like a doctor's bag—both contain the essentials for handling any emergency the professional might face. Each photographer, like each doctor, carries different equipment, depending on personal needs and taste. Some photographers are partial to extra-long lenses, whereas others like wide-angle lenses. But all news photographers pack enough gear to handle any assignment, whether the event they cover takes place in the brilliant light of day or the pitch black of night. A news photographer must have a sturdy camera,

It takes a lot of "glass" to cover some events. This array of heavy-duty cameras and lenses awaits the early-morning launch of a space shuttle.
(Photo by Steven Blake Heiner.)

a variety of lenses, a strobe, and, of course, film—lots of film.

■ THE NEED FOR RUGGED EQUIPMENT

The most expensive piece of equipment you will buy will be your camera system. Purchasing cameras and lenses can cost from hundreds to thousands of dollars. In the past, some cameras, because of their ruggedness, gained popularity among news photographers. In previous years, photojournalists chose the Graflex and, later, the 4"×5" Speed Graphic. The twin-lens reflex Rollieflex and the rangefinder Leica became popular after World War II. During the 1960s, the single-lens reflex Nikon and Canon dominated. Today, with miniaturization and automation, no single camera dominates the industry.

Yet today's photographers face the same problems that the Graflex user did. They want a camera sturdy enough to take the bashes of the business; they need a camera that can be subjected to freezing weather one day and melting temperatures the next. Yet they want that camera to continue to function perfectly, frame after frame.

■ BUILT-IN EXPOSURE METERS ARE STANDARD

When manufacturers first brought out cameras with built-in light meters, many photojournalists discounted the new technology. "Who can trust a built-in light meter?" they asked. "It can't possibly be as accurate as a hand-held meter." Gradually, however, most photographers adapted to the built-in meter.

Next, manufacturers brought out a camera that automatically set the aperture once the

photographer had selected the shutter speed. Camera designers called this option "shutter priority." They also developed a reverse option called "aperture priority," in which the photographer selects the desired aperture setting, and the camera adjusts the shutter speed for the correct exposure. Again, photojournalists were leery. "How could an automatic camera possibly get the exposure right?" they queried.

Then camera companies developed the "programmed" exposure mode that sets both the aperture and shutter speed. Now seasoned photographers were really suspicious. The camera was setting the exposure with no help from the photographer. In fact, some cameras today are so sophisticated that they recognize whether the photographer has attached a wide-angle or telephoto lens and then adjust the shutter speed accordingly—matching longer lenses with faster speeds to prevent problems with camera movement.

"Are all our years of experience and street smarts and seat-of-the-pants guessing going to go down the drain?" some photographers demanded.

Few photojournalists today would leave the newsroom without a light meter built into their camera that can perform a variety of exposure readings. With the advent of extremely sensitive cells and tiny, on-board computers that can evaluate various parts of the scene to determine the ideal exposure, the built-in light meter performs remarkably well. As long as the photographer knows when to override the automatic light meter— sun flaring directly in the lens, for example—photojournalists have found that the in-camera meter works well for shooting both black-and-white and color.

Freelancer Keith Philpott (see page 212) says the automatic light meter allows him to shoot while moving from one light level to another without worrying about exposure— allowing him to concentrate on his subject's reactions, not on the mechanics of the camera.

BEWARE OF EXTREMES

Automatic light meters are generally accurate except when the majority of the picture is either all-white or all-black. Backlighting also presents a challenge to automatic exposure meters.

Joel Draut, of the old *Houston Post,* switched to manual reading when he shot a funny face carved in snow. With an automatic light meter reading, the snow would have turned gray. Draut opened the aperture about two stops above the light meter's reading to compensate. Chris Butler, who shoots for the *Idaho Statesman,* carefully took a reading of

---

Keeping Your Camera Dry

Marty Forscher, a 50-year veteran of the camera repair business, warns photographers "to keep your camera dry." This is particularly important with newer cameras that have electronic circuitry. The electrical contacts can corrode on exposure to moisture, especially salty moisture at the beach. Forscher notes that when David Douglas Duncan, a well-known war photographer, shot pictures in Korea under the worst rain and mud conditions possible, Duncan used a simple underwater camera and got wonderful results.

Today, there are also various "rain hoods" available commercially that fit over photographer and camera and help keep both reasonably dry. These fold up easily for storage in a camera bag.

Forscher suggests that if you're caught in the rain without a raincoat for your camera and have neither an underwater camera nor waterproof housing, wrap your regular lens and camera body in a plastic bag sealed with a rubber band. Cut one hole in the front of the bag to let the lens stick out, and another in the back of the bag to enable you to see through the viewfinder. Put the lens and eye-piece through the holes and secure them with rubber bands. Now you can operate the camera through the bag, but you can shoot and view through a clear area. Remember to keep the front element of the lens dry because drops of water on this element will distort the image on the film.

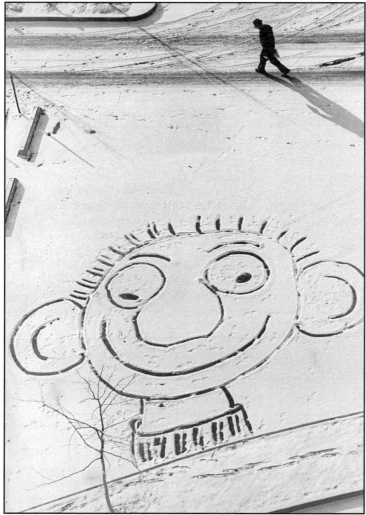

When to override your automatic exposure meter

▲ In a predominantly dark scene like this one, the camera's automatic light meter would be fooled into overexposing the final picture. In a situation like this one, take a meter reading off the subject receiving the light. The photo catching the light is of the man's 11-year-old daughter, who was abducted and murdered. (Photo by Chris Butler, the *Idaho Statesman.*)

◄ A camera's automatic exposure meter would see this predominantly white scene as 18 percent neutral gray and underexpose the final picture. For proper exposure in similar situations, increase your exposure about two stops or take a reading off something in the same light that reflects a neutral gray. (Photo by Joel Draut, *Houston Post.*)

the doorway before reframing his dark and moody portrait of a man whose 11-year-old daughter had been abducted and killed. (See previous page.) With the father in silhouette and the picture of his daughter lit by a stream of light from the open door, the center of the picture was black. On automatic, the camera would have given a false reading, overexposing the whole picture. By taking an in-camera reading of the brightly lit doorway and holding the exposure setting while reframing, Butler produced a correctly exposed negative.

■ AUTOFOCUS CAN HELP

If photojournalists resisted automatic light metering, they were even more skeptical initially about automatic focusing (AF). "How could a mechanical motor replace the eye–hand coordination of a trained shooter with twenty years' experience?" they asked.

At first, autofocus 35mm single-lens reflex (SLR) cameras with interchangeable lenses could focus automatically only in bright light. Then camera designers developed more sensitive light receptors, more sophisticated computer chips, and faster motors to turn the lenses. Today's autofocus cameras can follow-focus and even anticipate the location of the subject as it moves toward or away from the lens.

With some autofocus lenses, the photographer can prefocus on the finish line of a race, and the first runner crossing the finish line will automatically trip the shutter. This is performed by an accessory multifunction back that replaces the standard camera back. Using its focus-priority setting, the camera back allows the photographer to manually set a focus point where the action is to happen—with any lens, including non-autofocus lenses. When the autofocus sensor detects the subject, it automatically fires the camera shutter. This is often referred to as freeze focus or trap focus.

With some cameras—even in extremely low light or total darkness—the photographer can use a dedicated strobe that emits near-infrared light, which allows the camera to

One Pro's Camera Bag

Keith Philpott has been both a newspaper and magazine photographer. Based in Kansas City, Missouri, Philpott has shot assignments for the *National Geographic* and works extensively for *People* magazine. Here he explains the contents of his camera bag and the reasons for his choices.

CAMERA. The Nikon F4 is a highly sophisticated electronic camera, yet it handles much like the mechanical cameras of a few years ago. This old-fashioned user-friendliness, coupled with the new camera's extreme durability, is why it's my choice.

I carry two camera bodies because I often need two different lenses in a situation, a wide-angle and a medium telephoto. Also, if one camera body malfunctions, the other will save the day. Finally, I carry twin cameras because sometimes I shoot black-and-white and color on the same assignment.

LENSES. My favorite lenses are wide-angles, with the 20mm f/3.5 topping the list. I like the 20mm because I

can squeeze a lot of information into the frame. However, this lens can distort severely and should be used carefully.

I covet the 35–70mm AF (autofocus) f/2.8 lens for its speed, sharpness and commonly used focal lengths. And I also frequently use the 80–200 (not shown). The zoom capability is useful when you're confined to one spot and for the occasional "zoom" effect. The 55mm f/2.8 macro is indispensable for close-up work and doubles as a normal lens. My lenses include the 105mm f/2.5, 180mm f/2.8, and 400mm f/3.5. The 105mm and 180mm are used mostly for tight people shots and for details.

I use the 400mm for sports and for special effects like compressing a hilly highway into a dramatic scene. When the Nikkor TC-1.6 tele-converter is added, the 400mm becomes autofocus and a powerful 640mm lens. Despite its weight, size, and hefty purchase price, I always take this lens on the road, where I carry it in a nondescript fanny pack.

ELECTRONIC FLASH AND METER. I carry Nikon's SB-24 strobe because it's perfectly matched to Nikon's F4 camera. Some of the strobe's more esoteric functions include an infra-red beam that allows the F4 camera to focus in total darkness.

I use the precise fill-flash capability made possible with through-the-lens (TTL) metering, which measures the actual light coming through the lens and reflected off the film. I sometimes use an extension sync cord so I can aim the flash in different directions and still keep its automatic features functioning.

Although the flash can be used automatically, I still

focus the lens accurately and automatically. Photojournalists can take pictures at night, in a dark back alley—without ever focusing the camera. Just point, shoot, and get well-exposed, sharp pictures.

Steve Rice, director of photography at the *Miami Herald*, estimates that sports shooters who were getting 60 sharp pictures out of every 100 are returning to the paper with 90 to 95 sharp images when they use the latest autofocus equipment.

Ken Hawkins, who shoots for Sygma picture agency, reports a more conservative 20 percent improvement, especially for photographers who are over forty years old. (See Chapter 6, "Sports," for a description of how to use the autofocus lens.)

Hail, Hail Mary

Photojournalists agree that the autofocus feature offers one clear advantage over manual focus. Sometimes a photographer is caught in a situation when, with nothing in the vicinity to provide height, he or she needs to shoot over the heads of a crowd. For instance, at the end of a football game, everyone on the field crowds around the winning coach. Before autofocus, sports photographers used to prefocus the camera and then hold it high above their heads—pointing at the coach, firing, and praying that the focus was correct. This shot was called a "Hail Mary"—after the prayer many photographers offered when they took a picture in these less-than-ideal circumstances. With autofocus, the photographer can shoot a "Hail Mary" over the top of a crowd and have more assurance of getting a sharply focused picture of the winning coach.

For the photojournalist, selecting and framing the subject and precise timing form the key ingredients of picture taking.

Setting exposure and focusing are mechanical necessities to achieve good pictures. Pressing the shutter just as the mayor grimaces or the boxer throws a punch determines the difference between a routine picture and one that tells a story.

---

carry a Minolta strobe meter to verify exposures when using manual strobes. I also frequently use a LumiQuest diffusing baffle for softening the strobe's light.

FILM. I carry lots of film, both black-and-white and color transparency. My film—sixteen rolls to a container—travels in Tupperware food storage boxes. Stripping away boxes and plastic film cans cuts weight and bulk by about 60 percent. (Plus you have the added benefit of attending a Tupperware party to buy the containers.) With the plastic film carriers removed, your camera bag can go quickly through airport X-ray machines. Hand check your film to avoid repeated exposure to X-rays.

FILTER. I carry ultra-violet (UV) filters, which cut down on haze for scenic shots and provide protection for the front element of my lenses. I also carry a neutral density filter (ND), which functions like gray sunglasses for the camera. On a sunny day, when I want to use a wide aperture, I attach this ND lens, which doesn't change the color of the light, just the quantity.

Finally, I always carry a fluorescent-daylight (FLD) filter for shooting transparencies under fluorescent lighting.

BATTERIES. Always carry extras and buy them WHENEVER you shop.

NOTEBOOK & PENS. Take notes on a napkin if you must, but I recommend a special notebook for the purpose. The longer I'm in this business, the more notes I take. I use a standard reporter's notebook or a large steno pad. Both fit nicely in the back pocket of my camera bag. I also carry caption sheets and shipping envelopes.

I carry two kinds of pens, fine-point Pilot markers for note-taking and indelible markers for labeling film cassettes. Take plenty of pens because they dry out or are lost frequently.

SPECIAL TOOLS. Like many photographers, I fool around with gear a lot—improving and designing my own equipment. One of my own adaptations is a pair of pipe vice-grips connected to a Leitz ballhead. I use this hybrid clamp as a makeshift tripod, light stand, and I even used it once to secure a pair of jumper cables to a frozen rental car in western Nebraska.

Other favorite tools include the Leatherman survival tool, a kind of combination needle-nose pliers and Swiss Army knife. The pliers are the most-used option on this unit.

I even carry a make-up brush for dusting lenses and camera bodies. And I bring along a cable release so that I won't jiggle the camera during long exposures. The mini-mag flashlight in my bag runs on AA batteries and is waterproof to thirty feet. You'd be surprised how often you have to photograph in the dark, and the mini-mag produces enormous amounts of light for its size.

BAG. I needed a sturdy bag that could carry everything except my 400mm lens. I've carried this Tamrac from Darwin to Adelaide shooting a solar car race in Australia. The bag has seen the natives of Tahiti, the mysterious statues of Easter Islands, the plains of Kansas, and it's still going.

The more photojournalists can concentrate on what's in front of the camera and the less they have to fiddle with their equipment, the more telling photos they will produce.

■ ZOOMS REPLACE FIXED FOCAL LENGTH LENSES

Today's engineers have developed an array of fast, sharp zoom lenses that cover the majority of focal lengths most photographers regularly carry in their bags. Unfortunately, fast, wide-aperture zoom lenses also will snare a significant portion of your first paycheck. However, using a single zoom lens does save the cost of owning two or three individual lenses.

Buyer beware, however. First, some zoom lenses change apertures as you zoom through the focal length range. For instance, an 80mm to 210mm zoom lens might have a maximum aperture of f/4 at 80mm, but when you zoom it to 210mm, the maximum aperture has decreased to f/5.6.

In general, for shooting available-light photography indoors, you will find these variable-aperture zooms too slow for practical work. You usually need at least an f/2.8 mm lens for available-light indoor photography.

Second, zoom lenses are internally complicated and therefore more prone to alignment errors when the lenses are knocked around at a football game or in a street riot. Treat zoom lenses with extra care, and check their sharpness a regular intervals.

ONE BLACK-AND-WHITE FILM FOR MOST OCCASIONS
■ STANDARDIZING WITH ONE BLACK-AND-WHITE FILM

Most photojournalists working in black-and-white use one type of film to shoot most of their assignments. With a versatile ISO 400 film, they can handle everything from an outdoor rally at noon to an indoor press conference in a dingy City Hall office. Standardizing on one film minimizes the chance for mistakes when covering multiple assignments and meeting tight deadlines. Also, one film simplifies a camera bag. The photographer doesn't have to pack different emulsions for every event or change of weather. Also, with a relatively fast film, the photographer can move from outdoors to indoors, sunlight to shade, without wasting time rewinding and changing to a different film.

Most cameras today have shutter speeds above 1/1000 sec., and many reach 1/8000 sec. Thus the photographer can even use larger apertures outdoors while continuing to shoot with the same fast film.

■ SHOOTING IN LOW LIGHT
Overrating Film

For low light, many photographers continue to use their standard film but adjust its speed and the film's development time. This combination of overrating the film and adjusting development is often called "pushing" the film—something photographers do for several reasons.

First, low light means that the photographer must set his or her lens at its widest aperture. Unfortunately, this narrows the depth of field and reduces the chances for a sharp picture.

Second, the photographer might have to turn his or her shutter dial to a slower speed to compensate for the low-light conditions—but again, this may blur the image in the final picture, due to either camera or subject movement.

To get sharp pictures under minimal light conditions, such as a gym, you can overrate your film's ISO. This allows you

to use a higher shutter speed and/or a smaller aperture.

For instance, the AP's Eric Risberg was assigned to cover a match between the L.A. Lakers and the Golden State Warriors. He used Kodak Tri-X film, which is rated at ISO 400. At that speed, the exposure in the Oakland Coliseum would have been 1/125 sec. at f/2.8. To capture the moves of L.A.'s center, the AP photographer rated his ISO 400 film at 1600. He set his light meter accordingly and got a new metering of 1/500 sec. shutter speed at the same aperture.

"Push" Processing

Simply giving the overrated film longer development in a standard developer, such as Kodak Developer D-76, is not satisfactory if the film was shot under normal or high-contrast lighting conditions. The overdevelopment will only produce more contrast without a true gain in sensitivity.

Overdevelopment will build up the highlight areas of the negative but will not provide more detail in the film's shadow areas.

True gain in sensitivity depends on an increase in the detail of the picture's darker areas. Overdeveloping the negative in a standard developer only works satisfactorily if the film was taken under flat lighting conditions such as a gray, overcast, or foggy day.

It does not work for most other conditions.

To compensate in the darkroom for over-rating the film on assignment, use high-energy developers. For normal and high-contrast lighting conditions, developers such as Acufine, Diafine, Ethol's UFG, and Edwal's FG-7 with sodium sulfite specifically compensate for shadow detail.

When you increase the normal ISO ratings, thereby underexposing the film, these developers act more on the shadow area of the film than on the highlight, and consequently produce a negative with a fairly complete tonal range.

Every photographer who shoots black-and-white pictures in dingy gyms or poorly lit stadiums has settled on one or another of the high-energy developers. Many have found that an FG-7 and sodium sulfite combination gives excellent results for ISO 400 film rated at 1600.

The manufacturer's directions call for increasing development times to 12 minutes at 70° F to build up shadow detail. You must also eliminate all agitation except at the halfway point to cut down on highlight blockage.

Finally, the sodium sulfite part of the combination helps to keep down the base fog level for the extended development time. (See manufacturer's directions for more details.)

Many photographers prefer Kodak T-Max developer which, Kodak says, works as both a normal and a "push" developer. With T-Max developer and T-Max film, experiment with different development times and temperatures to produce the negatives you like best. But be very careful to control the temperature, agitation pattern, and time.

Regardless of which alchemist you heed, you pay a price when you rate your black-and-white film above normal. That price is enlarged grain. Grain tends to become more pronounced and to clump at higher ratings. Although unattractive for display prints, enlarged grain rarely shows up in newspaper reproduction. But, because of the higher rating, you do get sharper pictures. These inflated ratings enable you to shoot sports or other action pictures—unencumbered by strobes, cords, batteries, and delayed recycle times—and still get sharp, motion-stopping pictures.

"Magic Film"

For times when you need film speed, Kodak T-Max P3200 comes to the rescue. Originally dubbed "Magic Film" by the photographers who tested it, the film can be shot at 1600, 3200, or even 6400 and beyond with excellent results. AP's Risberg shot Dizzy Gillespie at the Monterey Jazz Festival using the film rated at 1600.

Eric Slomanson rated the film at 3200 to capture the expression of a wheelchair-bound father holding his adopted son for the first time. Other photographers are using the film under even more adverse conditions. (See examples on previous spread.)

Ilford also has manufactured a fast black-and-white film with similar capabilities to Kodak T-Max P3200.

With the new films, photographers are shooting basketball games with longer, slower lenses; night football, without strobe, in poorly lit high school stadiums; and drug busts lit by street lamps and police car headlights.

Shot on ISO 400 "pushed" to 1600, this photo of competitive swimmers "shaving down" to increase speed in the water was difficult to shoot because of the steamy and foggy conditions in the shower. (Photo by Kurt Wilson, *The Missoulian*.)

SHOOTING WITH COLOR FILM
■ HOW READERS REACT TO COLOR

Readers prefer color to black-and-white. That's what J. W. Click and G. H. Stempel found in their study of reader reaction to page design. This finding was supported in a follow-up study by the Poynter Institute Color Project, conducted by Drs. Mario Garcia and Robert Bohle.

Readers think color photos are more realistic. That's what an International Newspaper Advertising and Marketing Executives survey concluded. Not surprisingly, the researchers also discovered that readers dislike poor color reproduction.

Readers remember color better. That's what the Newspaper Advertising Bureau discovered in a test of recall as opposed to attention. Color ads were recalled more frequently than black-and-white ads. Readers, however, did remember black-and-white ads in greater detail and for a longer period of time.

According to *Eyes on the News*, by Dr. Mario R. Garcia and Dr. Pegie Stark, readers pay attention to single color and black-and-white photos about equally for feature subjects, but color news and sports photos get more attention than their black-and-white equivalents. In research using an Eye-Trac device developed by the Gallup organization in Princeton, New Jersey, researchers found that

- Black-and-white news pictures got 77 percent attention, which rose to 88 percent when the same picture was shown in color. For sports pictures, the differences were even greater.
- A black-and-white sports picture grabbed the reader's attention 64 percent of the time, whereas the same color photo got 80 percent attention. Further analysis showed that this jump occurred because women pay attention to color photos of athletes but not to black-and-white photos of sports figures.

This photo at the World Cup soccer matches at Pasadena's Rose Bowl was shot on ISO 400 color negative film. *Register* photographers only shoot with color negative film when they are on the road and have to transmit pictures back to the paper.
(Paul E. Rodriguez, *Orange County* (Calif.) *Register*.)

▼ **COLOR NEGATIVE CONTACT: Exposures varied by one stop for each photograph**

▲ **MACHINE-CORRECTED PRINTS FROM ABOVE NEGATIVES**

▲ **COLOR TRANSPARENCY FILM: Exposures varied by one stop for each photograph**

- With features, running color or black-and-white made no difference in terms of getting the reader's attention. Features with or without color nabbed a reader's attention about 78 percent of the time.
- Color does seem to catch the reader's eye when he or she is presented with a package of photos. With a group of photos, the researchers found, subjects paid more attention when the same pictures were reproduced in color. (See Chapter 9, "Photo Editing.")

■ TRANSPARENCIES VERSUS COLOR NEGATIVE FILM

As American newspapers and magazines converted from black-and-white pictures to color during the 1980s and 1990s, a debate raged in photo labs from Seattle, Washington, to Miami, Florida. The debate centered on two options—shooting with transparency film (also called color reversal, chrome, or slide film) or shooting with color negative film.

Chrome supporters prefer what they call the richness of transparencies and point out that you can edit slides as soon as they have been processed—no need for contact sheets and then color prints.

Proponents of negative film respond that, once you get used to looking at color negatives, you can read them as easily as you can a black-and-white negative. However, Sandra Eisert, a former *San Francisco Examiner* director of photography and also a former picture editor at the White House and at the *San Jose Mercury News*, notes that, even after years of reading color negatives, she can rarely evaluate the expression on a person's face without the aid of a contact sheet. Not only are color negatives in reverse, with each tone different from how it will appear in print, but the negatives have an orange mask. The editor's eye and mind must perform a series of complicated transformations to imagine how the image will look when it is finally printed.

F　　　　　G　　　　　H

◄ Transparency film (LEFT) has a narrow acceptable exposure range. In contrasty lighting situations, the film does not handle detail well in both shadows and highlights. Although exposure F has the best overall exposure, its highlights are still a bit "hot." The ideal exposure probably lies between E and F.

▲ When prints are made from color negatives (ABOVE), the film exhibits an impressive tolerance range for under- and overexposures that nonetheless produce acceptable enlargements.

Most magazines today reproduce from transparencies almost exclusively, observe chrome proponents. They argue that you get better reproduction from transparencies. With transparencies, separations are made from actual film that was in the camera. With prints, the separation is made from a second-generation image. The negative represents the first generation; the print, the second.

However, photo expert Peter Krause, in a report to a National Geographic Society seminar that was later published as "The White Paper on Newspaper Color," observed that "while color transparency images show a somewhat better overall color reproduction than color prints, this finding does not hold true with film speeds above 200."

As more and more publications use computers to scan in and separate both original transparencies and color negatives, the truth is that either a transparency or a negative is "first generation"—which means that there will be little technical difference in how

either medium will reproduce. Many publications already prepare photos for the presses without making a color print. (See Chapter 12, "Digital Images.")

Tipping the balance at many news outlets is that negative film does have a wide tolerance for under- and overexposure. Some photographers say that they can expose one to two stops under and up to three stops over the meter reading, depending on the film stock, and still produce an image. If the photographer's exposure is more than a third of a stop off with transparency film, however, the final image will be washed out or muddy. (See above.)

In addition, the different colors of different light sources affect the overall hue of the final pictures.

With transparency film, what you see is what you get. Even with the ability of computers to adjust color balance digitally, most correcting for transparency film still must be done while shooting, whereas color negative

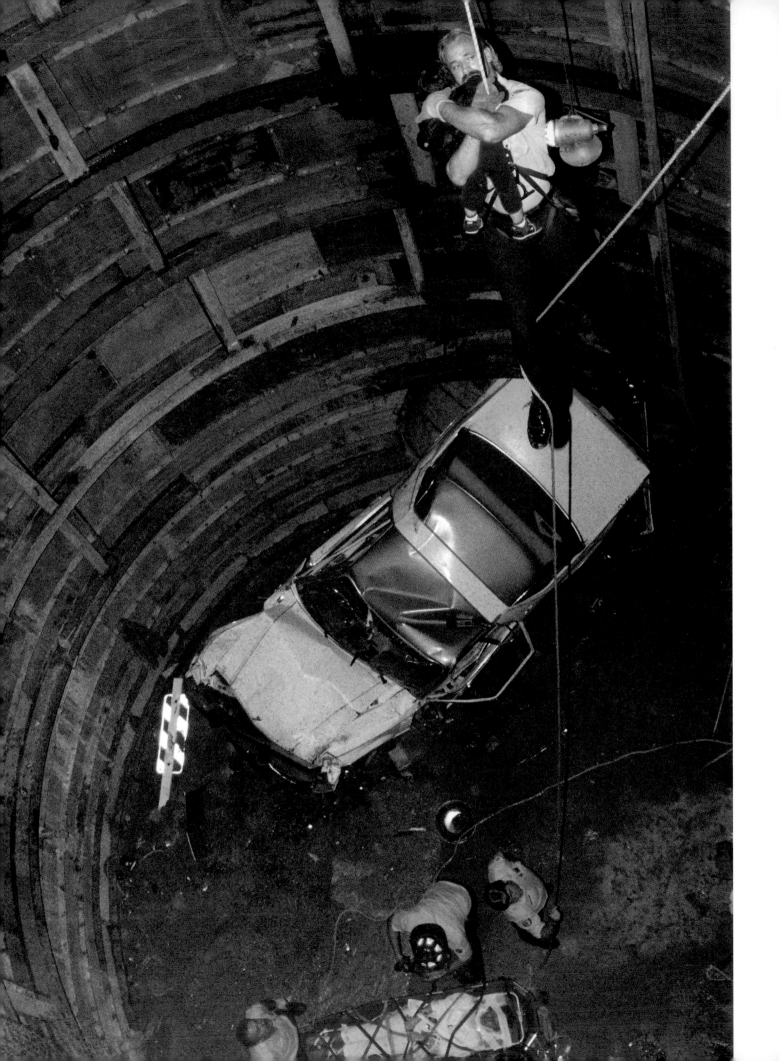

film can be filtered either in the enlarger or in the computer.

Because the transparency has a limited exposure tolerance, correcting after the original exposure can be difficult or impossible, leaving photographers little opportunity to adjust color after the film has been shot. Photographers using transparency film must go to great lengths to match film to light sources, filter out unwanted colors with gels, or shoot aided by strobes to achieve attractive, color-balanced photos. (See pages 223 and 224.)

Color negatives, on the other hand, allow for a lot more variation in exposure. In fast-breaking news situations when photojournalists have trouble producing perfect exposures on every frame, the inherent forgiving latitude of color print film might save the once-in-a-lifetime shot.

Consequently, both sides agree that transparencies have one distinct disadvantage over negative film. This disadvantage, say many photographers, represents its major drawback for news work. Because of transparencies' narrow exposure latitude and problems with color balance, the photojournalist shooting with transparency film can no longer shoot quietly and unobserved from the corner of a room, using only available light and a few rolls of high-speed film. Today, the shooter with chrome in the camera often rolls into a shooting assignment with 100 pounds of lighting gear on a cart. After unpacking the lights, setting up the light stands, plugging in the power pack, putting together the soft box and umbrellas, test-firing the strobe, and exposing a Polaroid, the photographer turns to the subject and says, "Now let's have some candid shots."

Daniel Doughtie studied this phenomenon in his master's thesis, "Have the technical problems associated with color changed the shooting style of news photographers?" Doughtie argues that, because shooting transparency film requires more artificial lighting, photographers who use it are controlling their subjects, and "photojournalism is reverting to the 'Speed Graphic' style of photography." (See Chapter 15, "History.")

So because of the need for correct color balance and adequate lighting, as well as the desire for less intrusive shooting styles, many street shooters prefer color print film. In

◄ **Color negative film, on which the picture to the left was taken, has wide exposure latitude (see pages 218–219), which makes it ideal for spot news, like this freak accident. Remarkably, no one was hurt.** (Photo by Craig Hartley, *the Houston Post.*)

▼ **Most magazines and many newspapers continue to use transparency film because of its rich quality and ease of editing.** (Photo by Hal Wells, *the Long Beach Press-Telegraph.*)

general, they find they can handle it more or less like traditional black-and-white film without all the lighting and filtration hassle associated with transparencies.

With color print film, the photographer can correct color imbalances in the darkroom or in the computer.

Scott Henry, of the *Marin Independent Journal* points out that, at Candlestick Park, home of the San Francisco Giants, night baseball shot on transparency film requires filtration, which effectively reduces the film speed. He finds better results shooting with fast color negative film rather than with transparency film. Toby Massey, assistant bureau chief in Washington, D.C., for the Associated Press, recommends 400 ISO color negative film under most conditions. For low-light situations, photographers are going two routes. Some use ISO 1600 film out of the box. Others prefer to start with ISO 800 and push it to 1600. Under extreme circumstances, photographers have pushed the 1600 film as much as two stops—to 6400.

Today many newspapers that started with transparency film have since converted to color print film. The Associated Press shoots all its assignments on color negative film and, without making prints at all, scans the negatives and transmits images around the world. (See Chapter 12, "Digital Images.")

TRANSPARENCIES: A PRIMER
■ CHOOSING THE RIGHT FILM

For transparency films, many photographers give Kodak's family of Kodachrome films (ISO 25, 64, and 200) the best rating for color and sharpness, but they find that the film is inconvenient to process.

While many magazine photographers shoot exclusively with Kodachrome, few newspaper photographers have this luxury.

To process Kodachrome, the lab must add color dyes at the time of development. This critical process requires expensive equipment ranging upwards of $1 million for the machinery alone.

To maintain the tight tolerances that Kodachrome requires, a lab needs a full-time chemist to monitor the operation. While a few large cities have labs that offer 24-hour turnaround (or less) for Kodachrome processing, most newspapers and magazines need their film even faster.

Use daylight film when lighting an indoor scene with electronic flash. Combining the strobe with a long shutter speed allowed the computer screen to become an integral part of this portrait of the first African-American owner of an IBM dealership.
(Photo by Ken Kobré, for *San Francisco Business*.)

Newspaper photographers, in particular, usually select one of the color transparency films that have color couplers built in.

These include Kodak's family of Ektachrome films and also Fuji's Fujichrome line. These films, which can be developed in less than thirty minutes using the E-6 process, come in a wide range of speeds.

When possible, most photographers prefer to shoot with the slower films because the color looks richer, images look sharper, and grain is less noticeable.

Both Kodak and Fuji have a line of super-saturated color slide films that produce exceedingly vibrant colors. Photographers often choose these films for scenics and travel photography.

For shooting in low-light conditions—like a baseball game in a domed stadium, or night football—some photographers prefer to use fast film right out of the package.

As with photographers working with color negative film, however, many report better results "pushing" slower films—underexposing the film by one or two stops and then overdeveloping the film during the first step in processing.

Remember the old body builder's motto: No pain, no gain. The same holds true when you "push" film.

While you gain film speed, you'll be pained to see lower quality in your pictures. "Pushing" film increases contrast in highlights and middle tones while the density of the blacks gets thinner.

Photo expert Peter Krause observes that when you "push" color film, grain becomes more noticeable, and color balance shifts, as well.

Nevertheless, some photographers report better results when "pushing" slower films than when using higher speed but inherently grainier films.

Fill flash used outdoors helped to bring out detail in these backlit subjects while still preserving the highlights in the picture.
(Photos by Daryl Wong.)

The time of day a subject is photographed—particularly a building—affects the mood of the final picture. The mood shifts from stark at noon (NEAR RIGHT) to rich in late afternoon (FAR RIGHT).
(Photos by Ken Kobré.)

Fluorescent Tubes

Although most office buildings, hallways, classrooms, and other public spaces are lit with fluorescent tubes, no manufacturer makes a color transparency film specifically designed for use under fluorescent lights.

When shot under fluorescent lights with daylight-balanced film, pictures come out with a decidedly green cast.

Shooting under the same conditions with tungsten film washes the pictures with a strong blue tint.

To complicate things further, each type of fluorescent tube, whether warm white or cool white deluxe, emits a slightly different color. The name says white, but the resulting color on your transparency film won't be.

Because most photographers don't want to scale ladders to verify the make of each fluorescent tube before shooting, they use a standard filter or filter pack to subtract unwanted tints. The standard filter or pack adequately subdues the green of fluorescent lights in most locations. Some photographers use an FL-D filter with daylight film. Many, however, have found a 30 magenta color-correcting (CC) filter used with daylight film works well for handling most fluorescent-lit situations. When using tungsten film, an FL-B filter should do the trick.

Flash plus Fluorescent

Sometimes photographers shooting with daylight film need to combine strobe and available

The early evening sky, just after sunset, offers a warm afterglow for a background. To capture both the mime and the view outside her luxury hotel, it was necessary to balance the exposure of the electronic flash with that of the outside available light. (See Chapter 11, "Strobe," for more on balancing strobe and available light.)
(Photo by Ken Kobré, for *San Francisco Business*.)

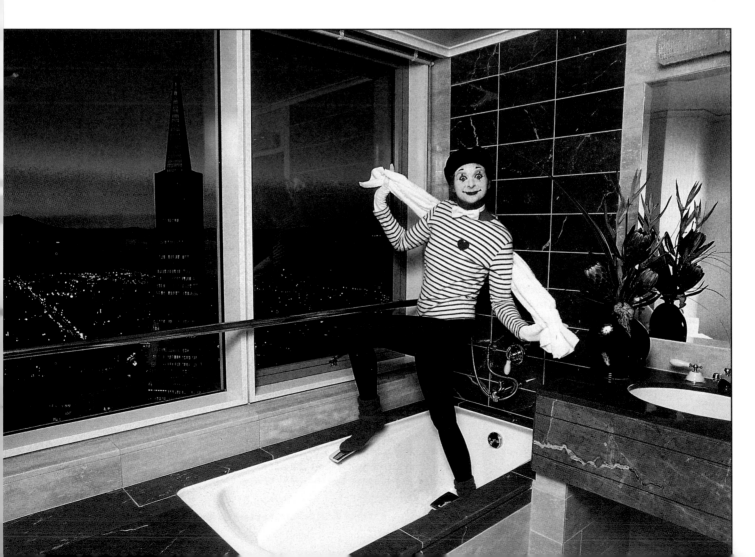

fluorescent light. (See page 225.) By placing a window-green gel over the strobe, both the light from the flash and the available light will have the same tint.

Thus, the addition of a 30-magenta CC filter in front of the camera's lens eliminates the green wavelengths from both the fluorescent lights and the green wavelengths from the filtered strobe, leaving correctly balanced light to reach the film.

The resulting transparency will look perfectly normal.

COLOR CONSIDERATIONS
■ TIME OF DAY IS CRITICAL

Editors unaccustomed to color sometimes disregard the hour of the assignment when they set up a photographer's schedule. They ignore the angle and the color of the light. For an indoor job, timing might be less crucial, but for an outside assignment, timing is everything.

A painter picks oils from a palette to create mauves and maroons. Likewise, a photographer picks the time of day to capture the delicate pinks of morning or the bold reds of late afternoon. By selecting one time of day over another, you can determine the color of light striking your subject when shooting outdoors.

From 5 A.M. to 5 P.M., color changes, intensity changes, and mood changes. A routine shot of a building taken at noon becomes an *Architectural Digest* photo at 6 P.M. A common mug shot photographed at 10 A.M. becomes a gallery portrait taken at sunset. The selection of time to photograph is as important as the choice of lens or film.

Dawn

While you can't control when a peace demonstration or a car wreck will occur, you often can select the time of day for shooting an outdoor portrait or a building exterior. For soft shadows and monochrome colors, shoot at dawn.

Midday

Some photographers try to avoid the harshness of the midday sun. Although colors might appear bright in transparencies or prints, people photographed on a sunny afternoon often have shadows running across their faces. These unflattering shadows can turn eye-sockets into billiard pockets.

When you must shoot portraits on a bright, clear afternoon, try (1) moving your subjects into the shade of a building or tree, or (2) turning your subjects so that their backs face the sun. Here is where you can use fill flash (see Chapter 11, "Strobe") to your advantage.

To show both the landing strip outside and the air controllers inside, the photographer waited until the waning afternoon light matched the exposure of the indoor light. Note also in this series of pictures how the color and quality of light changes as the time of day changes.
(Photos by Ken Kobré, for *San Francisco Business*.)

Late Afternoon

Late afternoon light is the choice of many photojournalists working in color. As the sun falls lower in the sky, its rays travel farther through the atmosphere. Molecules of water in the sky tend to scatter the short, blue wavelengths of light. The long, red wavelengths pass freely toward earth. This is why, as the sun sets, late afternoon light turns redder and redder. Also, shadows stretch as the sun drops. The long, picturesque shadows lend a sculptured look to a scene. Greens and reds seem more saturated under this waning light.

Although the reddish light of late afternoon usually flatters a subject, you will occasionally need a more technically correct picture at this time of day.

To reduce the excessive redness of late afternoon, use tungsten rather than daylight film if you are shooting transparencies. (A #81 filter accomplishes the same results but results in the loss of effective film speed.)

Tungsten film will filter out many of the long wavelengths of light present in the late afternoon. The result: a more normal, color-balanced picture. If you are shooting negative film, you can correct with the computer or with filters in the darkroom.

As sunset approaches, the sky takes on its most flamboyant corals and oranges. You can silhouette subjects against this richly colored background. If you want to avoid a silhouette but still use the sky's palette, try balancing your strobe with the early evening sky.

In this situation, your strobe would become the dominant light source for the subject. The ratio of strobe light to the sky light would be equal. Many photojournalists shoot portraits and fashion using this balanced-light technique.

After a three-hour drive followed by a mountain climb, the photographer, wearing protective gear, took this picture of a 600-acre grassland fire. He shot with ISO 100 transparency film to capture the rich detail of the sunset and the flames. Lying flat on a hillside and bracing the camera with his elbows, he shot at 1/2 sec. and used a 20mm lens.
(Photo by Kent Porter, the *Santa Rosa Press Democrat*.)

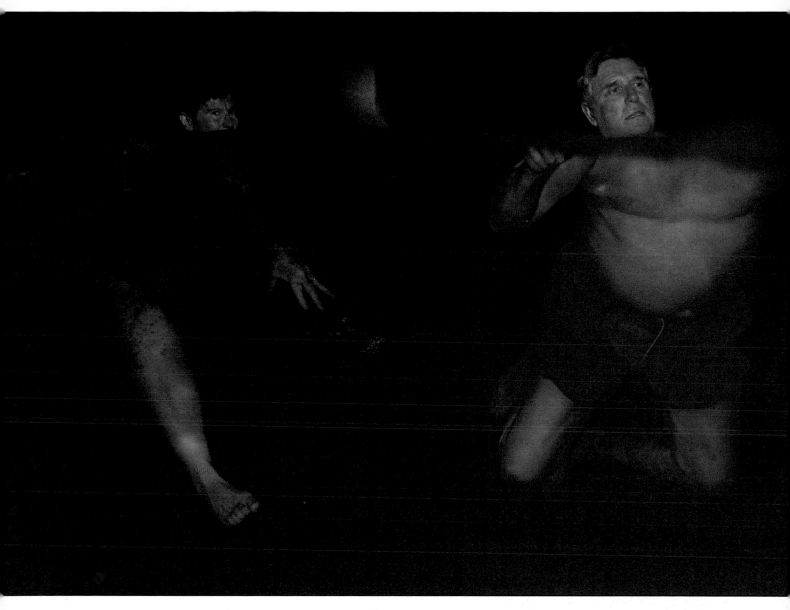

Evening

Evening light is cold and blue. Sometimes streets and buildings that look as bland as white bread during the day look haunting by night. Don't overlook the possibility of flash to illuminate the foreground and a long shutter speed to pick up any ambient light in the background. Also, tungsten film turns the nighttime sky a rich blue.

■ COLOR VS. BLACK-AND-WHITE

Can you imagine Van Gogh painting sunflowers without knowing whether his yellows would be seen as shades of gray? Or Ansel Adams photographing "Moonrise over Hernandez" in color and black-and-white—just in case? Yet this is what editors ask of photographers, who must visualize the scene simultaneously—with and without color. They try to take pictures that work both ways.

While many outlets today run all their photos in color, others have all assignments shot in color, which they convert to black-and-white, if necessary. So photographers face the challenge of shooting pictures that might run in either color or black-and-white.

Some scenes, however, have strong light but monotone hues. Others are awash with vivid hues, but the light is flat and uninteresting. You can't convert every color photo to black-and-white and expect to get equally good images. Photographers faced with this problem usually choose to shoot for one medium or the other and hope that editors in the office don't second-guess the decision.

■ COLOR FOR COLOR'S SAKE?

When the *St. Petersburg* (Fla.) *Times and Independent* began using color in the 1960s, editors often would send a photographer to

The water, acting like a filter, absorbed the long wavelengths of light, leaving a predominantly blue cast to the lower part of the picture. Notice also how the water acts like a lens, enlarging the bodies of the swimmers compared to their heads above the water line. (Photo by Greg Lehman, *Walla Walla* (Wash.) *Union-Bulletin.*)

Shooting a Story with Color Negative Film
Julie: Lifestyle of a Punk

Donna Terek spent nine months "just hanging out" with punks—getting accepted into the group, looking for an appropriate angle, and convincing someone to reveal his or her lifestyle to the mainstream press.

Although she began the project for her master's thesis, Terek was a part-time staffer for the *Minneapolis Star-Tribune* by the time she started shooting Julie. After six weeks of actual shooting, Terek wrote the story herself for the paper's Sunday magazine because the punks felt they'd get a raw deal from anyone else.

Negative film allowed Terek to shoot candidly under changing light sources and lighting conditions. The only additional lighting she needed was on-camera bounce flash. These pictures are just a few from her extensive project.

(Photos by Donna Terek, *Detroit News.*)

► Of the tattoo on Julie's skull, her mother says, "The one redeeming feature is that her hair will cover it."

◄ Says Julie's boyfriend, Al, "I'm against everything, just about. It's all against me. What is there to be for?"

◄ Julie says she doesn't care "if I look good or not, just so long as I look cool. Something really off the wall, something nobody else does. That's cool."

▲ Julie's parents live in a ranch-style house. Both parents work day jobs, while Julie works a graveyard shift. The family eats dinner and watches a few hours of TV together.

Missing the jump, the horse rammed into the rail and fell onto the jockey. The rider lived, but the horse was put away. Readers were furious that the paper ran the graphic picture, particularly with the horse's gushing red blood, on the front page. (Photo by Jeff Vendsel, *Santa Rosa* (Calif.) *Press Democrat.*)

the beach to photograph a pretty woman with a brightly colored beach ball for the Monday morning color project.

Thane McIntosh, a long-time shooter for the *San Diego Union-Tribune*, says he thinks editors are still in the "comic book era" of picking bright colors. In an interview for the National Press Photographers Association's "White Paper on Color," McIntosh observed, "Sure, in the old days, you had to go for those bright colors, but I still hear editors picking pictures for color, not for content. And I find myself, when setting up pictures, adding color to make the scene more 'complete.'"

Barry Fitzsimmons, another *San Diego Union-Tribune* veteran, recalls the old days: "For many years, color pictures were picked for bright colors. If it wasn't bright, they wouldn't use it." He remarked that photographers carried on location red clothing, which they included in the pictures so that later the pressmen could match the reds when they adjusted the inks.

Today, Fitzsimmons says, "It's with news that editors and readers have a hard time with color. It shows the reality . . . while black-and-white covers it up. In black-and-white, blood can just blend in with the street. In color (the blood) jumps out, and the editors are left to deal with it more than ever before (see opposite page and above). Same goes for fires. In color they're unbelievable, but black-and-white they're practically nonexistent."

While editors should not use photos just because they are as multi-hued as Joseph's proverbial coat, neither should they forget that color carries a great deal of information that would be lost on black-and-white film. Journalists are in the information business. Giving readers more information usually adds to their understanding of a story. ∎

Color in this picture carries a layer of information unavailable with black-and-white film. Color information is important for some photos, but not all. (Photo by Ken Kobré for Mercury Pictures.)

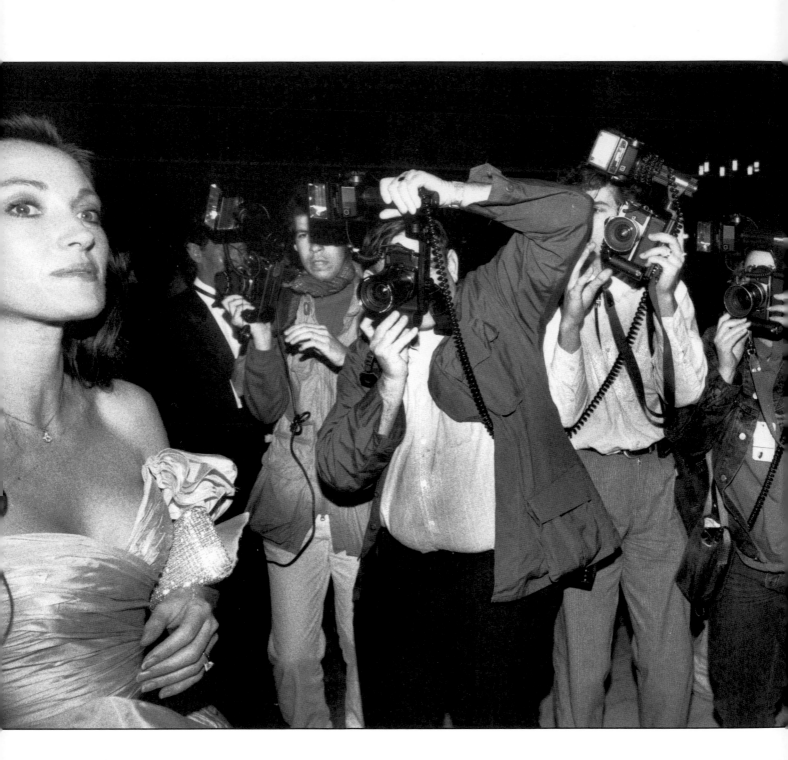

Strobe

Originally, photographers were limited to picture-taking only when the sun was out. Not all news, however, happens in the light of day. From flash powder through flash bulbs to electronic flash, photojournalists have searched for a convenient light source that would enable them to take pictures under any circumstances. Today, possessing a compact strobe is similar to having a pocketful of sunshine at

Photographers covering the Academy Awards use the strobe light's quick duration to catch the celebrities as they enter and leave the pavilion. (Photo by Deanne Fitzmaurice, *San Francisco Chronicle.*)

your fingertips. In the 1970s, manufacturers brought out miniaturized, lightweight, high-powered strobes. With a thyristor (energy-saving)

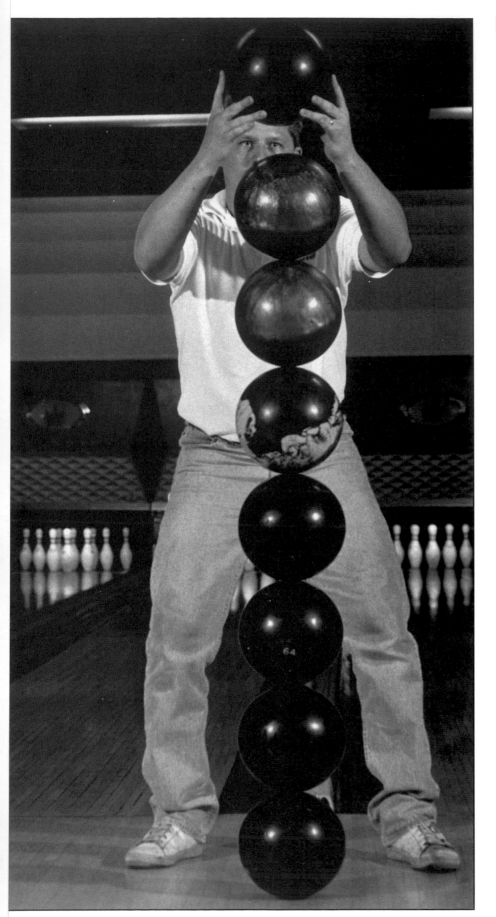

For this shot of a man who balances bowling balls, the photographer used strobes positioned on either side of the subject to separate him from the background. The highlights from the strobe also help to add definition to the black bowling balls.
(Photo by Keith Philpott, for *People* magazine.)

SELECTING THE SHUTTER SPEED
■ STOPPING ACTION

The super short flash duration of the strobe appears to freeze a subject's movement, no matter how fast the person is running or jumping. The strobe freezes the gymnast as she leaps in mid-air, the motorcyclist as he bends into a turn, or the skateboarder as he appears to hang, suspended in time and space.

In addition to stopping subject movement, because the flash is almost instantaneous, strobe light avoids blurry pictures caused by camera movement. Even if you are clicking pictures as you chase a city council member up the stairs of city hall, your pictures will come out sharp if you shoot with a strobe.

Sync Speed

Note, however, that a flash picture will not come out correctly if you set your shutter speed too fast. On some cameras, the upper limit is only 1/60 sec. Other cameras synchronize with the flash up to 1/250 sec. Some even sync as high as 1/4000 sec. If you use too fast a shutter speed, only part of the image receives the strobe's light. Some camera/strobe systems prevent the operator from using an incorrect sync speed. Check your camera instructions. (See demonstrations on pages 240–241.)

■ COMBINING FLASH PLUS AVAILABLE LIGHT

Each camera model does have an upper limit sync shutter speed. However, selecting a slower shutter speed often results in a more natural-looking flash photo. Indoors or outdoors at dusk, many photographers use slower shutter speeds to pick up available light from the environment and combine this with light from the flash. While the electronic flash light captures a moving subject in mid-air, the available light from the longer shutter speed lightens the background. Because the shutter stays open longer than the flash duration, the photographer can adjust the shutter speed to let in more and more available light. Up to a point, the greater the amount of available light the photographer lets in by slowing the shutter speed, the brighter will be the background behind the subject (see pages 240–241).

Beware, however, that some dedicated flash-camera combinations allow for limited or no variance in setting the shutter speed. Again, check your manual.

Many professional photographers also like the effect combining strobe and a slower shutter speed has on moving subjects. Although the strobe freezes the subject's movement for one instant, the long exposure also captures the subject's continuing movement, adding a ghost-like blur. The result is a sharp image combined with the blur of motion (see pages 240–241).

When Tom Duncan photographed a boxer in a dimly lit gym, he stopped the boxer's punch, with a strobe. So the gym wouldn't go black, he combined the strobe's light with ambient light, which he picked up by using a slow shutter speed. The combination of strobe and ambient light gives a sharp but natural-looking picture. The little bit of "ghosting" around the boxer adds to the feeling of movement and power in the picture.

While I was photographing a riot in downtown San Francisco, looters began breaking into store fronts and carting off armloads of leather coats and sporting goods through the broken plate glass windows. I used a strobe to light the looters but also used a slow shutter speed to pick up the light from inside the pillaged stores. (See page 242.)

DETERMINING APERTURE

Strobe manufacturers build their strobes in different ways. Hence a brief check of your instruction book will indicate how to operate your particular unit. Some basic principles, however, do apply.

■ MANUAL

To determine the aperture, measure the distance from the flash to your subject, and then check the distance scale on your strobe. Watch out. Some dials are marked in both meters and feet. Also, be careful to set the dial or read the scale for the particular film speed you are using.

■ AUTOMATIC EYE

The automatic sensor works well as long as the subject is neither exceptionally dark nor exceptionally light. The sensor adjusts the

The short duration of the strobe light stops the boxer's punch. A relatively slow shutter speed (1/15 sec.) lets in available light from the gym. The ghosting highlights give the picture its dynamic feel.
(Photo by Tom Duncan, the *Oakland* (Calif.) *Tribune*.

You can use the flash at any shutter speed at or below your camera's flash/sync speed. In these photos, the flash output remained constant. The flash was on manual.

For flash pictures, the f/stop is determined by the amount of light emitted by the flash that reaches the subject.

In this case, the photographer measured the amount of light with a strobe meter. THE F/STOP ON THE CAMERA REMAINED AT F/5.6. With the camera on a tripod, the photographer simply varied the camera's shutter speed from 1/500 sec. to 1 sec.

To demonstrate the full range of shutter speeds, the photographer shot at dusk. He also had the subject jump in every frame.

Notice how changing the shutter speed influences the picture. The choice of shutter speed controls the amount of available light reaching the film.

As the shutter speed slows, the background gets progressively lighter in each picture.

(Photos by John Burgess.)

• **1/500 sec.** You can see that most of the subject is dark. The focal plane shutter on this camera drops from top to bottom like a guillotine. The curtain on the shutter was about half open when the strobe fired. F/STOP STAYS AT F/5.6.

• **1/250 sec. (sync speed)** Here, the shutter's curtain was fully open when the flash fired. Some camera models sync with the strobe no higher than 1/125 sec. or 1/60 sec. The subject is correctly exposed, but the background is dark because at this exposure, the scene behind the subject is completely underexposed. The flash froze the subject in mid-air. F/STOP STAYS AT F/5.6.

• **1/125 sec.** The background lightens as the shutter speed lengthens. The subject remains frozen. F/STOP STAYS AT F/5.6.

• **1/60 sec.** The subject remains correctly exposed while the background gets yet lighter. By keeping the exposure on the subject constant and varying the shutter speed, you can control the background's brightness. F/STOP STAYS AT F/5.6.

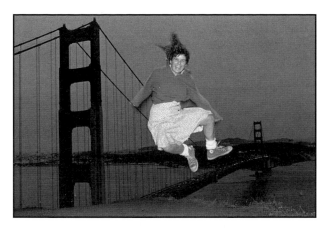

• **1/30 sec.** Here, the subject "pops" out of the background, which is about two stops darker but still readable. F/STOP STAYS AT F/5.6.

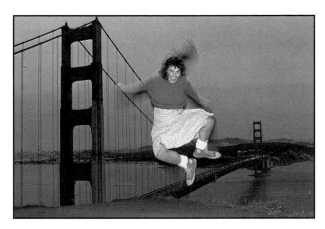

• **1/15 sec.** The moving subject produces two images, the sharp one frozen by the electronic flash, the other blurring in the available light. The strobe's light lasts only a split second, thereby freezing the subject in mid-air, while the available light remains constant—lighting the subject's motio —throughout the entire exposure. The "ghosted" blur from the available light becomes noticeable only when the subject is moving. When the subject is stationary, the strobe and available light images exactly overlap. F/STOP STAYS AT F/5.6.

• **1/8 sec. Strobe/available light balance point for this lighting situation.** As the shutter stays open longer, the available light image (the ghost) gets stronger. Here, the flash and ghost images become equal. At the point of equality, the picture is said to be balanced for flash and for available light. F/STOP STAYS AT F/5.6.

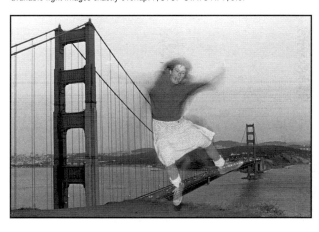

• **1/4 sec.** As the shutter speed slows further, the available light begins to overpower both the background and the subject. The available light is washing out the flash picture. F/STOP STAYS AT F/5.6.

• **1/2 sec.** At this exposure, the available light further overpowers the light from the strobe. The subject's face is starting to disappear. F/STOP STAYS AT F/5.6.

• **1 sec.** The flash exposure leaves just the subject's legs and dress. The darker image is the subject's body after the jump. F/STOP STAYS AT F/5.6.

To check the flash exposure, an assistant holds the incident strobe meter in front of the subject and points it back toward the camera.

strobe's light as if the subject were a neutral gray tone (18 percent gray).

The light meter in the camera and in the strobe function similarly. Both the strobe's sensor and the camera's light meter give correct readings most of the time because the average brightness of most subjects is equivalent to approximately 18 percent neutral gray. For the exceptionally light or dark subject, however, most strobes with automatic sensors require adjusting the f/stop on the lens to compensate for incorrect exposure information. The sensor on the strobe considers a small 5–10 percent angle of view in the center of the picture. The sensor eye is geared to read neutral gray correctly. If, for example, a subject is wearing jet black leotards while standing in front of a black brick wall, the sensor eye will be thrown off. To compensate, close down the lens' aperture one or two stops to avoid overexposed negatives. For a subject wearing wedding white, perhaps standing in front of a chalk-white chapel, the sensor eye will be misled once again. To compensate in this situation, open up one or two stops to avoid underexposed negatives. (See page 211 for examples where the camera's automatic light meter is fooled. Similar situations would fool the strobe's sensor.)

A new generation of strobes using 3D matrix metering, however, measures light reflected from the subject and compares this information with the subject's distance from the camera. If the through-the-lens (TTL) reading is wildly off the mark when compared with the subject's distance, the camera will use the preprogrammed distance exposure instead. If, for example, the subject is only a few feet away but is wearing black, the sensor would mistakenly direct the strobe to put out a lot of light, thereby overexposing the picture. However, with 3D matrix metering, the camera would recognize that, at this close distance, the light needed is much less than the reflected light meter reading is reporting. The strobe, instead, would deliver the appropriate amount of light for a correct exposure at the close distance. The sensor, in other words, is not fooled by a subject wearing extremely light or dark clothes or standing out of the frame's center.

■ THROUGH THE LENS (TTL)

With some dedicated strobe/cameras, the flash sensor is located in the body of the camera. With this setup, the flash is informed about the film's ISO automatically. The photographer can select almost any aperture on

As rioters broke into stores and shops and hauled out stolen goods, the photographer used a relatively slow shutter speed (1/30 sec.) to balance the strobe's light with that coming from the store's interior.
(Photo by Ken Kobré, Mercury Pictures.)

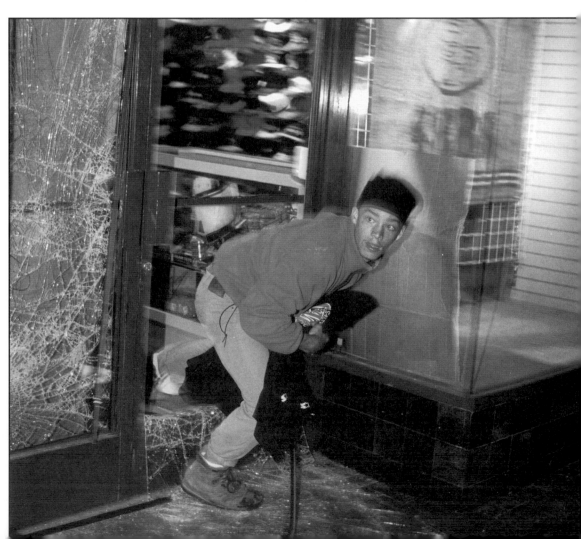

the camera because the sensor is located behind the lens. When the flash fires, the light returns through the lens' aperture and strikes the film. The light then bounces off the film, so when the internal sensor gets enough light, it will shut off the strobe. Also, because the sensor is in the camera and not in the strobe, the photographer can point the flash in any direction, and the sensor will record the amount of light that returns to the film.

■ HAND-HELD STROBE METER

Unlike standard light meters, strobe meters can measure the fantastically short burst of light emitted by a strobe. Often the meters are accurate to within one-tenth of an f/stop. Most strobe meters measure incident light—the light falling on the subject. You'll recognize an incident light meter by its white sphere that looks like a ping-pong ball cut in half. The photographer or assistant holds the meter about where the subject will be standing, pointing the meter back toward the camera. When the strobe is fired, the meter measures the light falling on the sphere—light that would have struck the subject. The meter indicates the correct f/stop for a particular film. Leaving the strobe on manual, the photographer adjusts the f/stop on the camera to the setting indicated by the light meter.

Using a strobe meter works fine if the subject is a celebrity sitting for a portrait, but the measuring device proves more difficult to use if the subject is a crook running down the courthouse steps. For fast-moving, slippery subjects, the internal sensor in the strobe or the through-the-lens sensor in the camera works best.

STROBE PROBLEMS TO AVOID
■ SHADOW ON THE WALL WITH DIRECT STROBE

The strobe mounted on the top or side of the camera produces a direct light aimed at the subject. At night, outside, or in a big gymnasium, direct strobe-on-camera works satisfactorily. Direct strobe-on-camera, however, creates a harsh shadow behind the subject in a normal-sized, white-walled room.

To get around the lurking black shadow problem, move the subject in front of a dark wall if possible. Now the black shadow created by the strobe will blend somewhat with the dark wall and be less prominent.

Or move the subject away from the wall. If you and the subject move away from the wall, keeping the same distance between the two of you, the subject will receive the same amount of light, but the wall behind will get less. Again, the wall will darken and the obtrusive shadow will merge with the darkened wall and disappear. (Note: diffusers alone will not eliminate these harsh shadows; see demo pictures on page 252.)

■ REFLECTIONS OFF GLAS

If you face someone wearing glasses to take a picture using strobe, often you will get an

annoying bright reflection off the subject's lenses. To avoid reflections of polished metal, glass, or eyeglasses, keep the strobe at an angle to the reflective surface you are shooting.

■ UNEVEN LIGHTING

Sometimes you must photograph a group of people with direct strobe. Flash on camera may overexpose group members nearest the light and underexpose those farthest from the light source. To avoid this problem, arrange the participants so they are approximately equidistant from the strobe light. When all the group's members are the same distance from the strobe, they will get

FRONT-LIGHTING. When the main light is placed close to the lens, few shadows are visible. Forms seem flattened and textures are less pronounced.

HIGH 45° LIGHTING. With the main light high and to the side of the camera, about 45°, shadows model the face, creating a more rounded shape. This is often the main light position used in commercial portrait studios.

SIDE-LIGHTING. A main light that is at about a 90° angle to the camera will light the subject brightly on one side and cast long shadows across the other side.

BACK-LIGHTING. Here the light is moved almost to the back of the subject. If the light were directly behind the person, her entire face would fall into shadow.

TOP-LIGHTING. The light is directly overhead and is casting dark shadows into the eye sockets and under the nose and chin. Few portrait purchasers would pick this lighting arrangement.

BOTTOM-LIGHTING. Lighting that comes from below looks distinctly odd in a portrait. This is because light on people outdoors or indoors almost never comes from below. This type of light casts unnatural shadows that often create a menacing effect.

the same amount of light and, therefore, be equally exposed.

■ INCOMPLETE COVERAGE AREA

Some strobes have automatic zoom heads that allow you to adjust the area the light covers to match the lens on the camera. These units change the light pattern to coincide with the wide-angle or telephoto lens you might have on the camera.

Most strobes, however, are designed to light only an area no wider than a 35mm lens. When you use a wider lens on your camera, you need to spread the light out farther. For telephoto lenses, it helps to focus the light on a smaller area. Some strobes do have an attachment that will spread the light so the scene will be evenly illuminated (down to 20mm-lens coverage) or focus the light so that it will be more efficient.

CREATING DIFFERENT EFFECTS
■ OFF-CAMERA LIGHTING FOR BOLD EFFECT

Sometimes lighting from the side with direct strobe can add drama to a picture. To achieve this effect, remove the flash from the top of the camera. Attach the flash to the camera with a PC extension cord or other remote trig-gering device (see page 255). Place the flash to the side of the subject. Moving the flash will dramatically change the picture's light.

On an assignment to photograph a young chess master playing in Boston, I found him practicing in a drably decorated, fluorescent-lit chess studio. I wanted the photograph to project the tension of the upcoming match. I decided to photograph the young player by placing a camera with a wide-angle lens on the playing board. With my left hand, I held out the strobe as far to the side as I could reach. The wide-angle lens, low vantage point, and side-lighting added punch to the picture that a straight, available-light portrait might have missed.

■ BOUNCE STROBE FOR SOFTER LIGHT

To avoid the harsh effects of direct strobe, a photographer can bounce the strobe's light off a room's ceiling, walls, or any other light-colored surface.

When the *Boston Globe*'s Joanne Rathe Strohmeyer accompanied sheriffs from a Drug Task Force on a raid, she needed the extra light provided by her strobe once inside the dark apartment. Crouched on one side of the room, she framed the picture to include a

The photographer used side-lighting and a wide-angle lens to achieve a dramatic effect.
(Photo by Ken Kobré for the *Boston Phoenix*, illustration by Ben Barbante.)

baby in the foreground, the sheriffs in the middle, and a man on the couch in the background.

Direct strobe on camera would have correctly lit either the child in the foreground or the adult in the background, but not both at the same time. So Strohmeyer bounced the light from her strobe off the ceiling, which provided even illumination so that the entire scene received the same amount of light.

When the light leaves the strobe, it comes out in a bundle of rays the size of the strobe face—about three inches in diameter, depending on the size of the flash.

The rays spread out as they head toward the ceiling. By the time they reach a typical ceiling, the rays cover an area about ten feet across. Because the surface of the ceiling is rough, the rays bounce off it in all directions, evenly lighting a much larger area below and leaving few shadows.

Bounce light has at least two advantages over direct strobe. Bounce light eliminates unattractive shadows, and it helps light a group of people evenly, removing the danger of burning out those in front or letting those in back go dark.

To photograph this drug search, the photographer used the light from a small portable strobe bounced off the ceiling. Bounce strobe spreads an even, almost shadowless light throughout the room.
(Photo by Joanne Rathe Strohmeyer, the *Boston Globe*.)

Not only can you bounce light off the ceiling, but you can also bounce light off a wall, partition, or any other large, opaque object. Light bounced off the ceiling results in a soft, relatively shadowless effect similar to that produced by fluorescent bulbs found in ceilings of most modern buildings. Light bounced off a wall or partition gives a more directional effect, such as the light that comes from a window. The directional effect becomes more prominent the closer the subject and the flash are to the wall.

Many photographers attach a small white card behind and up about a quarter of an inch from the top of the strobe head. This card picks up a little light when the strobe goes off and reflects this light into the subject's eye sockets. This reflected light from the white card avoids the raccoon look you can get with bounced light if you are standing near the subject.

While photographing a child lighting candles for Hanukkah, I could have taken the picture by the available light from the candles. I knew, however, that in the final print the candles in relation to the boy's face were so bright that they would wash out. The rest

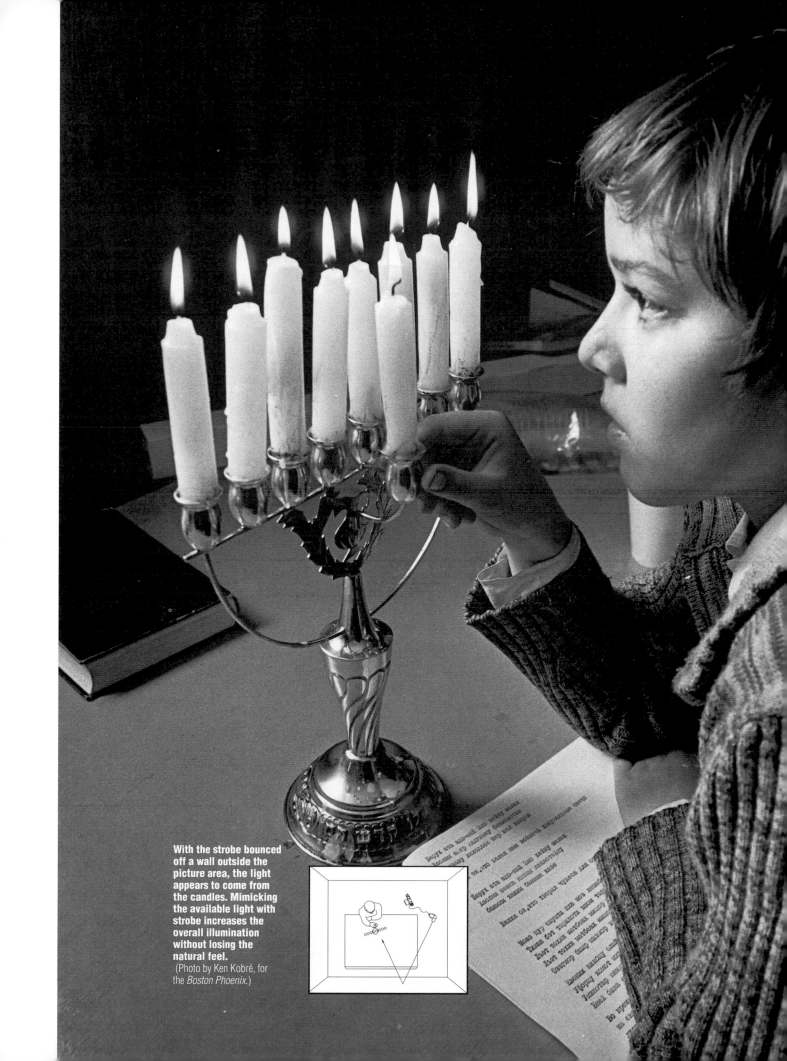

With the strobe bounced off a wall outside the picture area, the light appears to come from the candles. Mimicking the available light with strobe increases the overall illumination without losing the natural feel. (Photo by Ken Kobré, for the *Boston Phoenix*.)

of the picture would fall into deep shadow. I opted, instead, to bounce a strobe's light off a nearby wall. The bounced strobe light looks like it comes from the candles. The effect leaves both the candles and the young boy in sharp relief.

When I photographed Claude Caux, leader of a Houston mime troupe, I wanted to place a highlight on one side of his face. I didn't, however, want the shadow side to lose all detail. Also, I wanted a gradual fall-off between the highlight and shadow of the face.

Bouncing the flash off an umbrella satisfied these demands: the bounced light wrapped around the mime's face and allowed the highlights to blend into the shadows. (For more on umbrella, sees pages 249, 251, and 253.)

Caution with Bounce Flash

The light leaving the face of your strobe is spread over a much wider area when it reaches the bounce surface. When it strikes a ceiling, wall, or umbrella, the light is partly absorbed by the bounce surface. Finally, once reflected off that surface toward the subject, the light scatters in many directions. With bounce strobe, therefore, much less light reaches the subject than when you are using direct strobe. With bounce strobe, use caution:

- Save the bounce-flash technique for medium to small rooms.
- In an auditorium or gymnasium, the ceilings are usually so far away that not enough light will return from the ceiling to light up your subject adequately.
- Bounce your strobe off a light-toned surface. A dark wall, for example, will absorb the light rather than reflect it back toward your subject.
- Small, cigarette pack-sized strobes

don't put out enough power to produce an efficient bounce light in most rooms.
- With color film, don't bounce your strobe light off a pink, blue, or any other colored surface. The tint will color the strobe's light, giving the whole picture a color-cast that you may not like.
- When you bounce a strobe that has a sensor eye, make sure the eye remains pointed toward the subject. Don't try to bounce with a unit

that has a sensor that points only at the bounce surface.
- When bouncing, always set the strobe for its widest automatic aperture.

Bounce works perfectly with a medium to large portable strobe, in a normal room, with eight- to ten-foot high white ceilings and a subject standing within three to twenty feet of the photographer.

Aim Correctly ...

Strobe angle 90°

Strobe angle 75°

↑ When bouncing, aim the strobe carefully so that all the light bounces off the ceiling.

... or Pay the Price

Strobe angle 45°

◄ Do not aim the strobe too low, or direct light from the strobe's head will hit the subject, producing an uneven and unwanted lighting effect .

■ FILL-FLASH HANDLES HEAVY SHADOWS

At noon on a sunny day, the sun's harsh light can leave some subjects buried in shadow while others scorch in the sunlight. Shadowed eye sockets on faces turn into raccoon-like masks. Fill-flash to the rescue. The light from the strobe opens the shadow areas of subjects within ten or fifteen feet of the strobe.

With fill-flash, light from the strobe fills in the shadows without overpowering the highlights. You will find fill-flash particularly useful when you shoot color transparencies, which can record hue and texture in either brightly lit areas or deeply shadowed ones, but not both at the same time.

If important shadow areas meter more than one or two stops darker than highlight

To photograph this mime, the photographer bounced the light into an umbrella located to the side of the performer. The light from the umbrella wrapped around the face without leaving a harsh shadow line. (Photo by Ken Kobré for *Texas* magazine.)

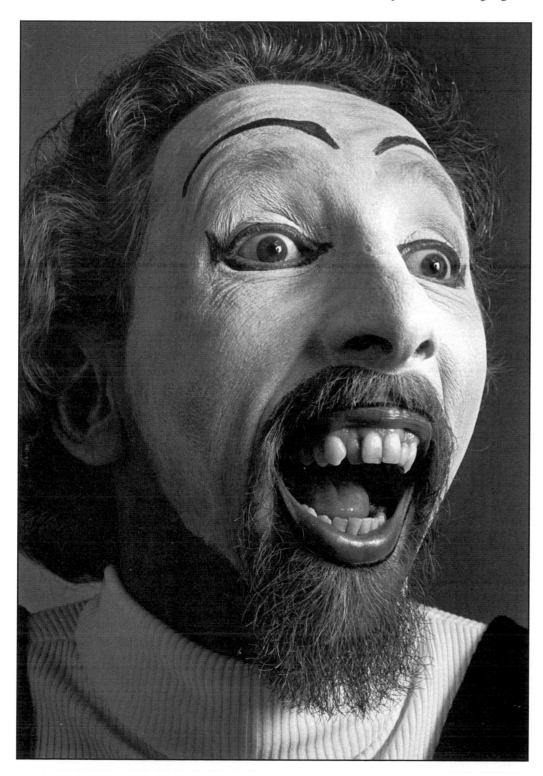

You can use strobe outdoors on a bright day to help fill in deep shadows on a subject if the person is within ten or fifteen feet from the camera. Some of the dedicated flash combinations will allow the photographer to select the ratio of fill-flash to available light. The camera and strobe do the rest automatically.

AVAILABLE LIGHT
left the subject's face obscured in shadow.

FILL-FLASH 1 STOP LESS
bright than the available light from the sun leaves open but delineated shadows as well as catch-lights in each eye. The subject looks well-lit but natural.

FILL-FLASH BALANCED
with the available light from the sun eliminates almost all shadows but looks overly lit in this situation.

areas, adding fill light will probably improve your picture. (See above.)

Many portable strobes today have a fill-flash setting that automatically balances the available and strobe light. In fact, some strobes allow you to dial in just the amount of fill-flash you might want to use. You can have the strobe balance or put out one to three stops less than the available light.

POWERING THE STROBE
■ SHOE-MOUNT STROBES

Most shoe-mount strobes are powered by AA batteries. Lithium batteries last the longest but are the most expensive choice. Alkaline batteries are easily available, but rechargeable alkalines are cheaper over the long haul.

Rechargeable nickel-cadmium batteries (NiCads), which store the least amount of juice, do provide a consistent recycle time before they completely and suddenly lose their charges. Lithium and Alkaline batteries, on the other hand, run down gradually, resulting in excessively long recycle times as they wear out. Note: always carry backup batteries. Nothing is more frustrating than waiting eons for dying batteries to recycle the strobe.

While Lithium, Alkaline, and NiCad batteries designed for shoe-mounted strobes are convenient, none provide enough electricity for more than a few rolls of 36-exposure film when the flash is used at full power. As Jon Falk says in his book *Adventures in Location Lighting*, "Throw away all whimpy AA and NiCad battery clusters." Many photojournalists who need power continuously over an extended time turn to external rechargeable batteries. You can recharge these external low- or high-voltage batteries repeatedly.

Some of these batteries fit on your belt, screw onto the bottom of the camera, or attach with velcro onto the strobe back. What they all have in common is the ability to provide 100 to 350 flashes at full power—some with less than a two-second delay between complete strobe recharge. These external batteries have become a mandatory part of most working pros' flash kits.

■ MEDIUM-POWERED STROBES

The typical battery-powered strobe most photographers use has a maximum output of 50 watt-seconds of light. For slow transparency films, many photographers have turned to more powerful portable strobes that can generate anywhere from 200 to 1200 watt-seconds.

While heavier and more costly, these strobes provide the needed light power for using umbrellas or soft boxes with slow films. With some of these medium-powered portable strobes, you can add on batteries for more power.

■ AC-POWERED STROBES

Using small portable strobes, you can't see the lighting effects until you have developed the film—hours or sometimes days later. With most AC-powered strobes, a modeling light is built into the strobe head, allowing the photographer to see where the light will fall.

Manufacturers have built AC-powered strobes with tremendous light output—an important consideration when working with slow color films.

Also, for large-format cameras like the 4"×5" or 8"×10" view camera, the photographer needs this quantity of light. Much of the photography shot in studios requires high-output power supplies.

When a wall or ceiling is not available for bouncing the strobe light, photographers use a number of other techniques and devices to soften the light and reduce shadows. Each device attempts to take the concentrated bundle of light coming from the strobe's face and broadens it before it heads toward the subject. The larger the effective light source, after it has been broadened, the softer will be the light that reaches the subject. (See demos on next page.)

DIFFUSERS ON THE STROBE.
Small devices placed over the strobe increase the effective light area somewhat. The Omnidome works like a bare tube. It combines the characteristics of direct and bounce light simultaneously. The indirect light bouncing off the ceilings and walls helps to soften the direct light coming straight from the dome. The Lumiquest Pocket Bouncer enlarges the effective light source by reflecting light off the angled hood. In addition, the angled hood helps to scatter light so that the rays will bounce off nearby surfaces and further soften the light on the subject.

UMBRELLA.
Because direct strobe light comes from a small light source, it produces a harsh effect on the subject. Light bounced off the ceiling is soft but produces somewhat featureless pictures. Many photographers use photographic umbrellas as alternatives.

The photographic umbrella is similar to a standard rain umbrella, only the inside is covered with a white or silver material, and the handle can easily be attached to a light stand. When the photographer aims the strobe into the center of the umbrella, out comes a soft white blanket of light that wraps around the subject.

Because the umbrella is on a light stand, the photographer can move it easily from side to side or up and down—allowing for total control of the light's direction. The nearer the photographer brings the light to the subject, the more the rays will encircle the person.

SOFT BOX.
The photographer attaches the strobe to a lightweight cloth box that contains diffusion panels to evenly spread the light. The result is a window-like light that is portable. Compared to reflecting light off an umbrella, the soft box gives a more defined edge to the light.

(Production photo by Deborah Whitney Prince. Photo by Chris Springman.)

You can buy an AC-powered strobe with 500, 1000, 2400, 4800 or more watt-seconds of light. The AC-powered units can drive two or more strobe heads at the same time.

Some newspaper and many magazine shooters regularly haul medium-sized AC units on assignment. These strobe units allow photographers to shoot color film at small apertures—and they also provide fast, dependable recycling. High-wattage strobes with modeling lights allow photographers to light a room and see where all the shadows will fall. While these strobes usually have more power than a portable strobe, they also require AC power and are consequently less convenient than their smaller counterparts. These strobes always operate on manual, so you'll always need a hand-held light meter to determine exposure.

Also, when shooting outdoors, photographers must remember to bring along either a long extension cord or a portable generator. However, the strobes' fast recycle times, practically limitless number of flashes, and powerful light output make them ideal for multiple-light photography.

PHOTOJOURNALISM GOES HOLLYWOOD

With the increasing use of color, photographers often are lighting scenes with several strobes. Fine-grain transparency film requires lots of light. And, as discussed earlier, transparency film cannot handle great brightness differences within a scene. Suppose you are taking pictures that include the corporate president inside his fifty-second floor office and the sun-drenched, spectacular view outside his window. Our eye has no trouble seeing both the wrinkles on the president's face and the sparkling bay outside. But your film cannot handle this brightness range. You may need to set up several lights to bring the two worlds into brightness balance.

Sometimes you may simply want more control of a scene than the light from one strobe can produce. You want to produce a special effect. Perhaps you seek to add a highlight to a person's hair, or you want to feature one member of a group more than the rest, or you want to use a light on either side of a dancer to emphasize the person's form.

Keith Philpott was assigned by *People* magazine to photograph the cast of a spooky movie. To get the horror-lighting effect he

INDOORS   INDOORS   OUTDOORS
no reflective surfaces

The harshest light comes from a camera-mounted strobe aimed at the subject. So photographers use a number of accessories to soften the light and reduce harsh, dark shadows behind the subject.

Generally, the larger the effective light source, the softer the light will be. The light from a 3'×4' soft box will produce softer light than the light from a 2"×3" direct strobe. When you bounce light off a ceiling, the effective light source becomes the wide spot on that ceiling. Photographic umbrellas, whether you are shooting through them or reflecting off them, also provide a relatively large light source, depending on their size.

Although smaller devices such as the Omnidome and Lumiquest Pocket Bouncer are not as effective as the larger light sources, many of the smaller items do work well indoors. In a light-colored room, some light rays bounce off the ceiling, walls, and floor. This extra scattered light helps soften the shadows when the devices are used within a small room.

However, outdoors or in a large ballroom or gymnasium, all the accessories work less well at softening shadows. The scattered light rays coming from the accessories have few surfaces to bounce off. Notice, in the outdoor series, that the shadow behind the model is darker in almost each situation. For these tests, the strobe was located nine feet from the subject.

DIRECT

BOUNCE

LUMIQUEST

OMNIDOME

THROUGH AN UMBRELLA

OFF AN UMBRELLA

THROUGH A SOFT BOX

NO CEILING
OUTDOORS

(Photos by John Burgess, *Santa Rosa* (Calif.) *Press Democrat*.)

TWO AND A HALF FEET FROM SUBJECT

SIX AND A HALF FEET FROM SUBJECT

ELEVEN FEET FROM SUBJECT

wanted, he placed one strobe below the actors' faces and a second light, remotely triggered, behind a tree to light up another actor. Taken at dusk to pick up some natural light, the picture had the desired scary look.

For a story about actors in a horror film, the photographer positioned one strobe at the feet of the couple in the foreground. A second strobe, hidden behind the tree and remotely triggered with an infrared slave eye (see page 255) signaled from the camera, lit the third actor for this just-past-dusk haunted house picture.
(Photo by Keith Philpott for *People* magazine.)

To handle complicated photo situations, you might set up several strobes on light stands and fire all of them simultaneously. The camera's sync cord can be connected to a three-way plug, and cords from strobes can be

attached to this plug. Then, when you trip the camera's shutter, all three strobes fire at once. With portable strobes, alternatively, you might use one of the cordless triggering devices. (See page 255.)

■ WHERE TO PLACE THE LIGHTS
Lighting a Whole Room
To light an entire room, you can set up several strobes around the room and bounce all of them off the ceiling or off umbrellas. Even if the room is not perfectly evenly lit—a common problem in this circumstance—you can still shoot freely by taking a reading with your hand-held strobe meter at different parts of the room ahead of time. With predetermined exposure readings, you can leave the lights in one place, and as you move from one area to another, adjust the

Whether the light is from an umbrella (like these examples) or from a soft box, the shadows it produces will be softer and less distinct when the source is near the subject, and sharper and more defined as the light source is moved away.
(Photos by Ron Bingham, *Edging West* magazine.)

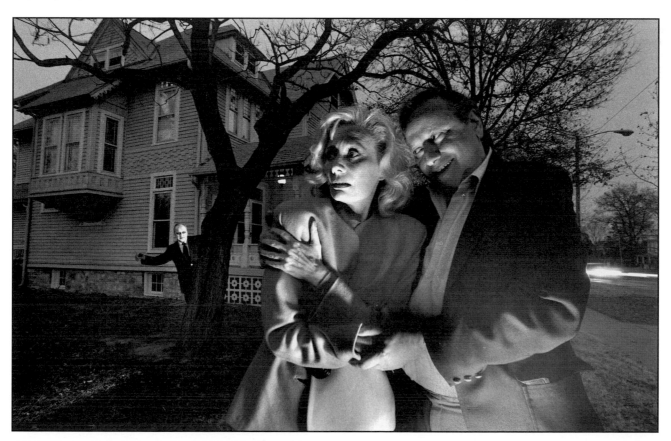

aperture for each section of the room. This technique of lighting and predetermining exposure allows you to shoot, in a relatively candid manner, with slow color film and multiple lights.

Multi-Light Setup

While you will find no two lighting situations identical, you often can use a basic lighting combination (see below) for shooting portraits: set up a main light and reflect it into an umbrella or through a soft box. Set the light about 45 degrees to one side of the camera. Bring the light as near as possible to the subject while still evenly lighting the person. Next, use a large reflector card to bounce light into the shadow side of the subject's face. Finally, attach a second strobe to a boom, a weighted arm that extends over the subject's head.

Using Multiple Lights

A soft box to the left of the conductor was the main light source in this picture. A fill card to the right bounced light from the main light source back toward the conductor and helped avert harsh shadows. A strobe on the end of a boom flooded the conductor's hair with light that helped separate him from the black background. The strobe heads were powered by a 1000-watt power pack. Each strobe head had a modeling light so the photographer could see where the shadows would fall. All lights fired simultaneously because they were hooked to one power supply.

(Photo by Ken Kobré for the San Francisco Chamber Symphony.)

Locate the strobe above and behind the subject to provide a hair light.

Photojournalists comment that setting up multiple lights can cause time delays and accidents caused by the cords running from the camera to the strobes. To eliminate the need for long cords between your camera and strobes, you can use a "photo slave." Attach the "slave" to your strobe either through the hot shoe or PC connection. Then put a second strobe on your camera. Now the light from the camera's strobe will activate the photo slave and trip the remote strobe.

Instead of a strobe on your camera, you can use an infrared trigger that functions like a strobe but puts out infrared light instead of strobe light. High-sensitivity photo slaves, such as those made by Wein, will pick up this infrared light and fire the remote strobe from distances as great as 500 feet.

Not only can you operate one remote strobe, but a photo slave allows you to fire as many strobes as you like, as long as you have a photo slave attached to each. You also can fire multiple strobes without cords by using a "radio slave," but I have found the infrared setup is more reliable.

On the camera is a small trigger that puts out an infrared light. The light activates the "slave" sensor located on the foot of the off-camera strobe. When activated, this "slave" trips the strobe. No cords are needed between the camera and strobe. On top of the strobe is an external battery called a Litepower that delivers 100 full-power flashes at a four-second recycle time.

One note of caution. The slave-eye, unless it has a special frequency, can be tricked. If any other strobe or flash in the area goes off, the slave eye might fire the remote strobes accidentally.

The setup works best when other pros are not firing their strobes and, even more irritating, when amateurs are not around using their instant cameras. ■

Eliminating PC Extension Cords

For the picture above, when the photographer tripped the shutter, a strobe mounted on top of the camera fired. In addition, a radio signal went out and fired a second strobe hooked to the receiver. The second strobe, the light from which you can see at the top left edge of the frame, was held by an assistant. A radio slave was used to avoid cords between the two strobes and so that no other flashes in the vicinity would activate the second light.

Digital Images

Associated Press staff photographer John Gaps III, based in Des Moines, Iowa, went 75 straight days without film. He was shooting exclusively with AP's digital camera. Nick Didlick of the *Vancouver Sun* used the same type of digital camera to cover the opening of the Commonwealth Games in Canada. "The moment the Queen passed by me, I clicked a picture. From then to the time the pictures

reached the newspaper was about fifteen minutes, including the seven-minute walk to the press center," Didlick notes. But the real field test of the

Taken with a digital camera under adverse weather conditions, this image of a mud-covered couple became the signature picture of the second Woodstock concert. The camera was reportedly in the same condition as the couple. (Photo by Stephen Savoia, Associated Press.)

digital camera came when the Associated Press used two digital bodies in addition to film-based cameras to cover the second Woodstock concert, twenty-five years after the original event. Recalls David Rocha, the AP's Northeast regional photo editor, "By Saturday there was mud like you have never seen before. Cameras and photographers were soaking wet." Yet the all-electronic cameras continued to click.

With film, you have to develop, edit, scan, and then transmit. Rocha estimates that film requires 25 minutes longer than a digital image to process and transmit. At Woodstock II, photographers came back to the AP trailer and downloaded their cameras' images into a computer. "We had the pictures to New York in five minutes," Rocha recalls. During the course of the three-day concert, AP transmitted approximately 120 pictures. Thirty percent had been shot with a digital camera. In terms of quality, Rocha says, he could not tell the difference between film-generated and digital pictures.

The signature picture, a mud-covered couple hugging, played on the front page of nearly every newspaper in the U.S. the next day—and was shot with the digital camera.

Digital Camera Features

With the filmless camera, the photographer doesn't have to change a roll of film to change the ISO (film speed) rating. Each frame can be shot at the ideal ISO for a given lighting situation. On some cameras, ISO ratings range between 200 and 1600.

Unfortunately, just like the increased grain that occurs with film at higher film speeds, increased "noise" in the pictures occurs with the electronic cameras at higher ratings.

Matt Rogers, a Kodak applications engineer, says that shooting with a digital camera is like shooting with a standard film camera with just a few exceptions. Although you're not using film, shooting in a situation of high contrast (a wide brightness range) requires thinking as if you're shooting with transparency—not color negative film. The camera, he says, can handle about a 4 1/2 stop range from highlight to shadow detail. With color negative film, the range would be seven to nine stops from the darkest area with detail to the lightest area with detail.

What does this limited dynamic brightness range mean in the field? Brian Whittier, a freelance photographer from Chapel Hill, N.C., tested Kodak's digital camera and reports that the camera handles the shadows fine but that it has a hard time with the highlights. Bob Cosway, Kodak Technical Support, confirms that the camera is "very sensitive to overexposure." You can underexpose pictures by a stop and get excellent results, he says, but you can overexpose by no more than a quarter stop and still hold detail. In other words, you need to meter for the highlights when using the digital camera.

When Whittier photographed a shrimping boat off the coast of North Carolina with Kodak's 420 digital camera, he also found it hard to "get really wide with the camera." This digital camera uses a chip that is smaller than the normal 35mm negative. Using a 15mm lens gives the effect of a 40mm lens. However, this change in effective focal length does not occur with all digital cameras.

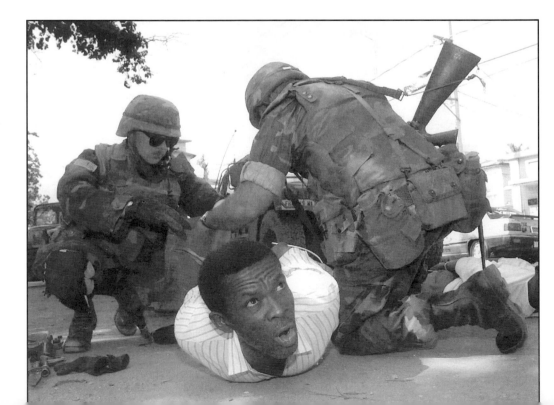

AP photographer John Gaps III covered the U.S. invasion of Haiti with a digital camera. While the NC 2000 camera is easy to use, highlights tend to bleach out. See the shoulder of the man's white shirt.
(Photo by John Gaps III, Associated Press.)

As for shooting, if you can use a 35mm camera, you can shoot with a digital camera. All the electronic flash, shutter speed, and light metering features found on the traditional camera work just the same.

■ ADVANTAGES OF ALL-DIGITAL PHOTOGRAPHY

Less Distortion

In the past, when a photographer transmitted photos using traditional equipment, storms or bad phones lines often resulted in poor-quality pictures because the images were being transmitted as continuous, modulating waves known as analog signals. However, the computer changes all information, pictures as well as words, into just ones and zeroes—electronic pulses (ones) and no pulses (zeros). Relaying ones (on) and zeroes (off) over the phone lines, it turns out, results in less distortion than transmitting continuous, modulating waves. Static and other line noises can distort a wave more than they can an on/off digital signal.

Greater Speed

Also, using the old analog wave system, color pictures used to take 24 minutes to transmit. A digital color picture, transmitted as ones and zeroes, takes only three to five minutes. Using a standard laptop computer with a fast modem (a device that sends computer information across telephone lines), the photographer can shoot, edit and send a picture from Berlin knowing that the image will arrive in the Big Apple intact and ready to roll on the waiting presses.

More Flexibility

When heading for an out-of-town assignment with standard 35mm film, the shooter often lugs not only a bag full of camera gear but also a rudimentary darkroom including chemicals, tanks, thermometers, mixing utensils—and more. Alternatively, the photographer might find a one-hour lab and persuade the owner to stay open for a late deadline. A digital camera allows the photographer to go from camera to computer. No muss. No fuss.

◄ Nick Didlick of the *Vancouver* (British Columbia, Canada) *Sun*, used the digital camera to photograph this skier. (Photo by Nick Didlick, *Vancouver Sun*.)

▼ Using a cellular phone, a laptop computer, a modem, and a digital camera, a photographer can send pictures immediately back to the office from almost anywhere. (Photo by Mike Blake, Reuters.)

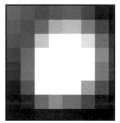

(Demonstrations by Jerry Wolford, *Greensboro* (N.C.) *News & Record*.)

Do you remember paint-by-number canvases from your childhood? So that you could paint a picture of the Eiffel Tower, the canvas would indicate a specific number for each color of paint. When a segment of the picture needed a blue sky, the canvas would call for a number five (blue). When a section of the tower needed to be red, the canvas would call for a number three (red). On the original canvas, the area representing the sky was covered with number fives, and the Eiffel Tower itself was filled with number threes. All you had to do was match the paint color on the little jar with the number printed on the canvas. Even if you didn't know what the canvas was supposed to show, you would eventually produce a painting of the Eiffel Tower if you painted in all the numbers correctly.

Now, imagine a paint-by-number canvas in which sections are of equal size, like graph paper, but smaller than the head of a pin. Computer techies refer to each tiny square as a picture cell—or pixel. Each picture cell (pixel) is assigned a number indicating its location and its brightness. Now, imagine if, instead of just a few jars in your paint set, your canvas called for 16.7 million jars, each a different shade, level of brightness, or saturation. Each square (pixel) on your graph paper could be any one of these sixteen million plus colors. If squares (pixels) are small enough and if you have enough paints, you can accurately represent in the computer any picture you might take.

Now you can appreciate how many numbers the computer is crunching whenever it deals with a color image. Basically, a computer is selecting from millions of jars of colors to paint by number with tiny, evenly spaced squares.

Dollar Savings

Using digital cameras translates into dollar savings, a fact few news outlets can ignore. Given the savings in film, chemistry, and paper, Glen Stubbe, director of photography for the *Washington Times*, estimates that his newspaper will pay back its initial investment in five years at the rate it uses film. Chris Ritter of the *Jonesboro* (Ark.) *Sun*, estimates that his paper, with three staffers all using the digital cameras, saves approximately $21,000 per year—reducing the payback time to about two years.

CONVERTING FILM TO DIGITAL IMAGES USING A SCANNER

OK. You don't have thousands of dollars to spend on your first digital camera.

You can still enter the digital revolution with your present camera and traditional film. You can take pictures with your trusty Nikon, Canon, Minolta, or any other camera using silver-based black-and-white or color films.

Once you have taken the pictures in the traditional way, you will need to develop the film as you have always done. Nothing new yet. Next, however, you will translate your negatives or slides into digital information that the computer reads. A scanner does the translation for you.

Scanners turn images into digital signals that the computer can use. The scanner acts just like a digital camera, although it doesn't photograph a scene. Instead, it takes a very precise picture of your negative, slide, or print and passes the digital image, now in the form of ones and zeroes, into the computer. Once the image is in the computer, the picture can be sent by telephone across the world (WAN—wide area network) or by a direct cable (LAN—local area network) to the presses in the backshop.

Many photographers today shoot with 35mm cameras and film, then process their film, often in a mini lab that develops the film dry-to-dry in twelve minutes, and then scan their negatives into the computer. The photo editor at the *Santa Rosa* (Calif.)*Press Democrat* assigned Annie Wells, a six-year veteran, to shoot the World Cup soccer match between Brazil and the United States. The match took place at Stanford University stadium, which, at 80 miles away, was too far to make the deadline. Wells shot her photos on color negative film, processed them at the stadium using a Fuji mini lab processor on site, and then scanned her negatives on a high-quality Kodak scanner controlled by her Apple PowerBook® computer. She initially scanned 10 pictures at low resolution to create small, contact-sized images. Then, using the computer's internal modem, she plugged into the telephone lines and sent the pictures back to the newspaper's computer. There, photo editor John Metzger viewed and selected the images that would run on the front page and on a picture page inside. Wells then transmitted only the selected photos, which she, in turn, had scanned at high resolution for high-quality, sharp reproduction. These high-resolution images ran in the *Press Democrat*'s next edition in color, five columns wide.

Since covering the World Cup and then the finals in Los Angeles, Wells has gone on to shoot stories about the Mexican election in remote parts of that country—transmitting the pictures back to Santa Rosa on deadline using her scanner and computer.

Scanning Considerations

Scanners and software packages vary, so the publication where you work will provide specific technical directions on how to get the best scanned images. However, for background purposes, there are two things to keep in mind.

The final resolution at which you scan depends on how the image will be reproduced in a publication—in traditional printing terms, it will depend on the fineness of the halftone dot screen. Newspapers, printed on coarse newsprint, traditionally used an 80- or 85-dot screen. The paper quality is such that finer screens don't produce finer reproductions. Magazines and books, which use smoother, often slickly coated paper, may use up to 150 or even 200 dots per inch to print fine reproductions. If the final printed image appears on newsprint, you are wasting time and computer storage space if you scan at a higher resolution. The image won't look any better, but it will take longer to scan and to print. And, the finer the scan, the more computer memory it will eat up.

The other important variable is the final size at which the image will appear on the page. Scan the picture either to size or to a size slightly bigger than you anticipate it may appear. If it's scanned and saved at a size equivalent to a two-column picture, for example, but it's run at four columns wide, it will look jagged and unattractive. In "computerspeak," there's not enough "information" for the image to be enlarged after the scan has already been completed. If you've scanned it to run four columns wide, but then it's only three, you're okay. All the information is available to run it at a larger size, so there will be enough information, as well, to

run it smaller. Your best bet is to provide a scanned image at exactly the size at which it will run. But, deadlines don't always allow the best of all worlds.

■ THE ELECTRONIC NEWSROOM

While the scanner and computer are convenient for travel, many newspapers have turned to this equipment for routine daily coverage. Throughout the United States, newspapers are replacing their chemical darkrooms and printing rooms with daylight mini labs, film scanners, and computers.

Not only does the film-to-computer process save time and money, but the technique also allows a news outlet to deliver its pictures directly to its computers. Traditionally, photographers handed an 8"×10" print to a layout editor at a newspaper or magazine. The editor then "dummied" the picture into a page-layout mockup that consisted of a rough sketch of the page, with a cross indicating the picture and squiggly lines indicating type. Only an experienced eye could discern from the dummy how the final page would look. With the dummy as a guide, the photograph and the story were assembled by production artists in the backshop before being sent to the presses.

Now, just as reporters use the computer to write and editors to edit stories, photographers can scan their pictures into the computer and photo editors can select and crop pictures in the computer. Layout editors can bring all the elements of a publication together, from headlines and photos and copy, to create pages on the computer. These fully designed electronic pages can be transmitted to a printer in the building or across town or in another state. Without putting a hand to

At the World Cup soccer match, the photographer shot the action on color negative film, processed the film normally, scanned the selected frame, and used a laptop computer and a modem to send the image over phone lines back to her newspaper. (Photo by Annie Wells, Santa Rosa (Calif.) Press Democrat.)

content or layout, the backshop prints the pages out as negatives or even as plates for the waiting presses.

■ THE DIGITAL DARKROOM

With the elimination of chemicals, enlargers, and photographic paper, the computer and its related photographic software are coming to be known as the digital darkroom.

Many photojournalists have become proficient in the digital darkroom with Adobe Photoshop, a photo editing software package widely used in the industry, by following the tutorial that comes with the program. Adobe also publishes *Photoshop in a Box*, a training course that includes a simple-to-follow book,

along with a CD-ROM (compact disc, read only memory) that contains helpful examples.

Photojournalists should know a few basics about using Adobe Photoshop. These include: how to control contrast and brightness, eliminate dust and scratches, dodge (lighten) and burn (darken), crop, and how to sharpen an image. I have described below some common steps, along with a few tips provided by Adobe's consultants.

Controlling Contrast and Brightness

Once the digital image comes on the screen, you will need to adjust its brightness and contrast. The book *Photoshop for Macintosh* (Weinmann and Lourekas), describes several

Controlling Contrast Using the Levels Option

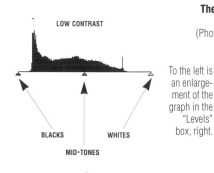

LOW CONTRAST

BLACKS
WHITES
MID-TONES

To the left is an enlargement of the graph in the "Levels" box, right.

The scan (RIGHT) produced a low-contrast image with no strong blacks or whites.
(Photo by Doug Kapustin, Patuxent Publishing Co.)

ADJUST SLIDERS TO ACHIEVE NORMAL CONTRAST

BLACKS
WHITES
MID-TONES

Moving the right-hand slider to the edge of the graph brings up the whites in the picture. Moving the one on the left increases the blacks. The middle slider controls the mid-tones. The graph is called a histogram.

methods for controlling brightness and contrast. Here are a few.

METHOD 1 From the "Image" menu, choose "Adjust," and then "Levels."

To increase contrast, brighten the highlights by moving the "highlights" slider to the left. (See page 262.) To darken the shadow, move the slider to the right. To decrease the contrast, go in the opposite direction. Moving the middle slider evens out the mid-tones. Click "OK."

METHOD 2 From the "Image" menu, choose "Adjust," and then "Levels." Click "Auto." Click "OK".

Tip: *If the picture is in black-and-white,*

Adobe product support engineer Rita Amladi recommends starting with "Auto," which she says does a fine job of adjusting the contrast and brightness for black-and-white images.

METHOD 3 Under the "Image" menu, choose "Adjust," and then "Levels." Click on the

white eye-dropper icon you'll see on the far right. Now click on a point in the picture that you consider to be the whitest area. Next, click on the black eye-dropper, then click on the part of the picture that you consider to be the blackest area. Photoshop will adjust the picture to the ranges you have indicated. Click "OK."

Tip: *With a color image, Adobe's Eric Thomas recommends against using the "Auto" option. Instead, he says, select the eye-dropper icons method described above.*

Tip: *If the contrast and brightness of your picture looks good from the start, don't do anything more. "Don't pick up a happy baby," Thomas advises.*

Eliminating Dust and Scratches

First, keep in mind that preventative maintenance is the best way to avoid dust and scratches on your negatives. Jim Johnson, professional image processor for the *Muskegon* (Mich.) *Chronicle*, recommends sleeving your film immediately after drying and before editing it. One pass of the film on the light table can produce minute scratches or even huge gouges. He also suggests using fresh stabilizer for each processing run. Gunk from this last step, he warns, gets on the negatives and dries into the emulsion.

Despite careful handling, your negatives may sometimes display imperfections.

Tip: *To just clean up scratches, you can select the "Dust-and-Scratch" option, located under "Noise" in Photoshop's "Filter" menu.*

Eliminating Dust and Scratches: Two Methods Demonstrated

To eliminate small specs, select the affected area with the "Lasso." Apply the "Dust & Scratch" filter as shown directly below.

To repair a large tear, use the "Rubber Stamp" tool to clone from around the tear. Photo illustration by John Burgess, *Santa Rosa* (Calif.) *Press Democrat.*) Color original.

(See page 263.) While this filter eliminates from the digital
image dust and scratches on the negative or slide, the filter does tend to blur the entire picture. Instead of applying the filter to the entire picture, first use the "Marquee" or the "Lasso" to select an area where you see the imperfections. Apply the "Dust-and-Scratch" filter only to the selected area, which will avoid blurring the rest of the picture. Then go under the "Filter" menu to "Sharpen" and select the "Unsharpen Mask" filter.

Tip: *Find a threshold setting that cleans the image with the least amount of correction, says Adobe's Rita Amladi. Once an area is blurry, you cannot bring it back to sharpness by using the "Unsharpen Mask" tool.*

Tip: *You can use the "Rubber Stamp" tool not only to eliminate dust and scratches but also to repair actual damage—by cloning*

segments from an unaffected area to a damaged area. (See page 263.) Johnson of the Muskegon Chronicle recommends using the "soft-edge brushes" option when working with the "Rubber Stamp" tool, although the "sharp-edged brushes" are better for flat areas like sky. Sharp-edged tools, he says, retain the surrounding grain structure better.

Tip: *"Remember this rule," Johnson admonishes. "Sample from an area exactly like the area you want to clone in. So if you want to remove a dust speck right from the edge of a brick wall, sample an area on axis, and exactly like the area you want to clone."*

Dodge, Burn, and Sponge

In a traditional darkroom, you could lighten or darken an image by dodging (blocking the light) or burning (adding additional light) to a section of the image when the negative was

---

Dodging for Detail the New-Fangled Way

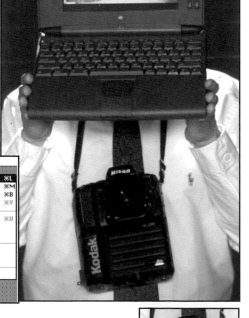

Use the "Lasso" tool to outline the area—like this camera—that needs to be dodged. Then use "Levels" option to adjust the detail in the black.
(Photo by Julie Iverson.)

Move the "white" and "mid-tone" sliders to the left to lighten the camera.

in the enlarger. You can still obtain similar results with the computer.

METHOD 1 Select the area to be dodged or burned with the "Lasso" tool from the Toolbox. As you did when adjusting contrast, go to the "Image" menu, to "Adjust," and then to "Levels." Move the sliders until the area lightens or darkens as needed. Click "OK."

METHOD 2 Double click the "Dodge/ Burn/Sponge" tool, which is located in the Toolbox. With the "Brushes" palette displayed, select a soft-edged brush. Stroke

on any area of the picture, pausing to allow the screen to redraw. Each stroke over the same area will intensify the effect.

Tip: *Master printers dodged and burned without leaving an obvious light or dark spot on the picture. In fact, photographers referred to an overly dodged or burned area on a print as leaving the "Hand of God" on the picture. Use your electronic tool sparingly, as well, because overworking an area will tend to cause streaks—an electronic touch from the "Hand of God."*

Tip: *Try a low exposure first (20 percent or 30 percent) so the tool won't bleach or blacken an area too quickly.*

Tip: *If you do dodge or burn an area too*

heavily, choose "Undo" from the "Edit" menu or "Revert" from the "File" menu. Don't use the "Dodge/Burn/Sponge" tool to repair your overzealousness. The effect will be uneven.

Cropping
To crop a picture, click on the "Cropping" tool, which is in Photoshop's Toolbox. Then mark the portion of the picture you wish to keep. (See below.) Position the pointer inside the marked area and then click with the "Scissors" pointer when it appears.

Tip: *To specify a height-to-width ratio, double-click the "Cropping" tool and enter values in the "Cropping Tool Options" dialog box that will appear.*

Sharpen Overall or Part of an Image
First, a warning: Adobe has labeled one filter with a misleading name. Called "Unsharpen Mask," this filter actually sharpens the picture to an extent and is many experts' filter of choice. The term "Unsharpen Mask" originally referred to a traditional darkroom technique in which technicians created masks for negatives. Though the mask's edges were "unsharp," they helped improve the apparent sharpness of the image when projected through an enlarger and onto printing paper. Adobe's engineers carried the term "unsharpen" forward to the world of electronics, where the label makes no sense as the filter accomplishes the opposite effect of its name.

Scanning your negative or print will cause it to lose some sharpness. Therefore, especially if you plan on reproducing your

Using the Cropping Tool

Use the cropping tool to eliminate parts of the image you don't want.
(Photo by Betsy Brill, for the *Houston Post*.)

pictures on newsprint, you'll want to apply "Unsharpen Mask," located under "Sharpen" under the "Filter" menu.

Unfortunately, if your original picture was not properly focused, you can't resurrect it electronically—regardless of which filter you use. With oversharpening, individual pixels lose their original color and brightness. The effect of oversharpening, called pixelation, gives the photo the look of a paint store color chart gone crazy. Blocks of unwanted, out-of-place colors start showing up in the picture. Sorry. Digital sharpening is no replacement for getting the picture focused correctly in the first place.

Tip: *Running "Unsharpen Mask" more than once at a lower setting will sharpen more smoothly than if you run the mask once* at a setting twice as high, note Linnea Dayton and Jack Davis in **The Photoshop Wow! Book.** *"You can apply the 'Unsharpen Mask' several times at a lower amount,"* they say, *"but if you sharpen too much or too many times, the photo pixelates." For best results, keep the threshold setting below 10 and the radius below three when using the "Unsharpen Mask."*

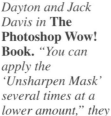

Tip: *You also can sharpen an individual segment of a picture by marking it with the "Marquee" or the "Lasso" and then using the "Sharpen/Blur" tool.*

Tip: *Use "Unsharpen Mask" only after an image has been cropped and sized, says the Muskegon Chronicle's Johnson. Also, he says, if you want to archive an electronic image, save a version that has* not *had this technique applied. If the image may be used later, it's best to start with an unaltered version.*

USING THE COMPUTER TO CREATE PHOTO ILLUSTRATIONS

Photo illustrations often involve combining parts of images from several pictures. (See Chapter 8, "Illustrations.") To combine images into one picture, photographers in the past had to either cut out each picture with scissors and then paste them together or try darkroom tricks such as multiple exposures or combining negatives. All these techniques were difficult, time-consuming, and usually somewhat obvious.

Today, computers allow photographers to combine images easily, quickly, and seamlessly. For photo illustration, photographers can take pictures in the field or in the studio

and scan them into the computer. The photographer can then vary the relative size of each image to correct or to distort proportions. Finally, the photojournalist can combine them in an infinite number of ways to make an editorial point or to illustrate a concept.

Jerry Wolford's illustration of a child standing atop the earth and reaching for the chocolate-covered cookie known as a "moon pie" is an example of combining seven separate images to form one.

Using other tools in Adobe Photoshop, you can twist images or make them look wavy or rippled. You can even change the apparent location and color of the original light source in the picture. The computer can free a photographer from the confines of reality and in mere seconds accomplish in many instances what could never have been achieved in the studio.

Keeping this in mind, see pages 270–273 for a discussion of ethics when manipulating photographs with the computer.

MEMORY, STORAGE, TRANSMISSION, AND OTHER MECHANICS
■ RANDOM ACCESS MEMORY

Like a human uses short-term memory, the computer uses its RAM—or random access memory—to do its number-crunching work. In other words, the computer uses RAM to do most of its thinking. The more RAM a computer has, the easier it can handle and manipulate large picture files. Unlike the human brain and its short-term memory, most computers' RAM can be expanded. To work with large color pictures, most

To illustrate a story about the saucer-sized, chocolate-covered sandwich cookies known as "moon pies," Jerry Wolford of the *Greensboro* **(N.C.)** *News & Record* **combined seven separate images. In the studio, he photographed a child with his hand raised (A) and then later used the computer to digitally erase the background (B). To achieve the proper perspective, he also digitally stretched the child's image at this point.**

Also in the studio, Wolford photographed the cookie (D) and later in the computer superimposed the moon's image onto the cookie's surface (E).

With photographs of the earth (C), sun (H), planet (I), and star-filled sky (G) in the computer, Wolford was ready to assemble all the parts. He manipulated the size of the cookie and placed it so that it appeared to be in the child's hand (F). He then added a dark area to the child's hand as if the cookie had cast the shadow. Using the software package Photoshop, Wolford was able to seamlessly combine all the elements into an eye-catching final image. The original was in color.

(Photo illustration by Jerry Wolford, *Greensboro* (N.C.) *News & Record*.)

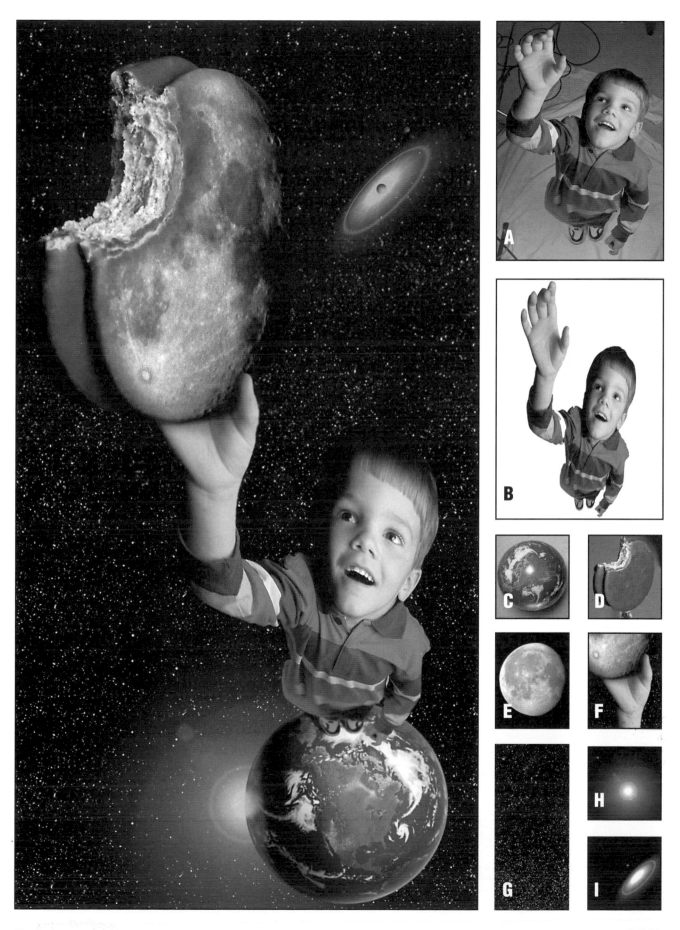

A

B

C

D

E

F

G

H

I

heavy-duty "power" users recommend a minimum of 8 megabytes of RAM, with 40 or more providing a more comfortable environment for picture manipulation.

■ STORING IMAGES

A hard disk drive for a computer is like a bank for your money. Both are relatively safe places to store your valuables. Remember that your scanned photographs are actually bits of data. Stored in files as electronic ons and offs, they will remain safe on a hard drive even when you turn off the electricity powering the computer. Sometimes the hard drive is located inside the computer. Other times, it is housed in a box alongside but connected by a cable to the computer.

While a thief can break into a bank and steal your money, your hard drive problems will generally come not from a two-bit criminal but from the hard drive itself. Sometimes hard drives stop working, jumble information, or just seem to lose things for unexplained reasons. Everything, including your favorite picture files, could be lost. Tech types call this a crash. For the best protection for your valuable photo data, copy your picture files onto yet a second drive or a floppy disk. Called "backing-up" your data, this procedure has saved many a photographer from an unhappy calamity. For even more permanent storage, some photographers transfer their images to a compact disc (CD).

Computer storage and money in the bank share at least one additional common characteristic: You can never have enough of either. Photographs, particularly large, sharp (high-resolution) color photographs, take up huge amounts of computer storage. One "high res" 8"×10" color photo can absorb around 128 megabytes of memory. Compare that to the fact that all the words in this book you are reading take up no more than 2 megabytes, and you can see how storage-greedy pictures can be. Although manufacturers are shrinking the physical size of hard drives while simultaneously expanding their capacity to store more numbers and thus bigger picture files, you just never seem to have enough storage when dealing with photographs.

You will probably always be in need of more storage to hold your digital pictures. For that reason, you may prefer to use a removable hard drive or an optical hard drive, both of which allow you to add more storage at less expense. Functioning a little like a blank tape on your VCR, a removable cartridge or optical disk allows you to add storage without buying a new hard drive each time you need more room. Adding additional storage units is much cheaper than continually upgrading to a larger, permanent hard disk drive. (Removable cartridges, however, do tend to be more prone to mechanical failure. Don't ever forget to back up your work with more backups!)

■ MAKING A PRINT FROM THE COMPUTER IMAGE

In the traditional darkroom, the photographer made a black-and-white or color print or sent a color slide to the backshop, which then rephotographed the prints through halftone screens to create screened negatives and then plates that would go on press. Because today's digital images are integrated right into page layouts that go straight to negatives or to plates, the necessity for an actual photographic print has been eliminated from the process. That doesn't mean you won't ever need a print, however.

To create an actual image for your portfolio, for your wall, or for a gift to a subject, you can still make a paper copy of your photo. A laser printer will produce an inexpensive but grainy black-and-white quick copy. For a beautiful continuous-tone black-and-white or color display print, a special dye sublimation printer would be the better choice. If the newspaper doesn't have one of these high-end printers, most commercial service bureaus do and can print out digital images at a still reasonable cost.

■ SENDING IMAGES BY TELEPHONE LINE AND SATELLITE

With a computer and modem anyone can send or receive pictures over telephone lines. A picture editor can search electronically through thousands of images in a digital photo library located in yet a different city. Suppose a Baltimore editor wanted a photo of a Chinese girl riding a bicycle for a story about transportation in China. Using Seymour, an on-line library with 265,000 digitized photos that is adding 15,000 more each month, the editor could search the picture collection by asking the computer to locate words in the pictures' captions like "Girl," "Chinese," and "Bicycle." Once the computer has searched for and found every caption that contains all three of these words, the editor would receive on his or her

The Associated Press sends an almost continuous stream of pictures to newspapers and magazines around the world. Editors can view many pictures at the same time on a computer screen called the Leaf Picture Desk. The small images on the screen are called thumbnails.
(Associated Press.)

computer a set of electronic thumbnail-sized images, much like a contact sheet, with photos matching the request. After selecting a particular picture, the editor could pay for it—electronically—and have a high-quality digital image sent in forty minutes across telephone lines to an office in Baltimore, Bakersfield, or Biloxi.

Rather than providing a library, the Associated Press and its service, Photo-Stream, offer continuous delivery of new digital images to its members.

The Kodak Picture Exchange, an on-line picture service, catalogs more than 100,000 images from 25 stock photo agencies, including Archive Photos, FPG International, and the Image Bank. With this service, the editor could seek pictures electronically and receive a thumbnail image and a proof image immediately over the computer but would have to order the reproduction-quality hard copy from the individual stock house rather than receive it directly by computer.

■ THE INTERNET: DELIVERING PICTURES TO VIEWERS WORLDWIDE

While newspaper circulation per household has declined steadily since 1953, the number of individuals owning computers has soared. At first, people used these home computers for writing, business analysis, and games. Each computer was a separate unit—independent and unconnected. This changed as people discovered that they could use telephones and modems to receive and to view information from all over the world at home on their computer screens. Using commercial services such as CompuServe, America Online, and Prodigy, computer owners began sending each other mail electronically. They also started leaving messages on electronic versions of bulletin boards for whole groups of people. The Internet, which was originally set up by the government to connect the computers of researchers at universities and military sites, became accessible to the public. Now, people worldwide use the Internet to communicate. Sitting before a monitor in San Francisco, Atlanta, or Houston, you can dial a local number to reach a computer that in turn is linked to a vast international network of computers in nearly every city in the United States and in almost every country in the world.

At first, the Internet provided people a way to exchange words. Hundreds of thousands—in fact, millions—of words on every possible subject. From astrophysics to alternative sex, the Internet has a place from which you can seek information or give your opinion.

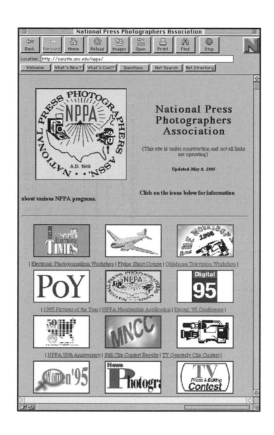

A World Wide Web page on the international network of computers known as the Internet can show text, graphics, and photos in black and white or in color. Individuals as well as news organizations are using the network to deliver pictures and stories directly to computers in your home. The address of this page is http://sunsite.unc.edu./nppa/.

To use the Internet in the past, however, you needed to know a programming language called UNIX, which only true computer buffs cared about. That was until the development of new software that allows information to be sent and received with a few clicks of a button. A "browser," as the new software is known, still uses the Internet to locate and exchange information, but rather than typing arcane commands, you click on highlighted words or pictures that then take you to different "sites" also created with the same simple-to-use software. Pictures is the key word for photojournalists. The new software allows the display and transfer of pictures, graphics, and typography—in a manner not unlike that in a printed publication.

In addition, anyone who has a computer and is connected to the worldwide network can create an electronic page referred to as a "home page" and display it for others connected to the Internet. Participants range from multimillion-dollar media corporations like the *San Francisco Examiner* to average individuals like ham radio buff Art Chandler, who maintains a page covering news about his hobby. The number of people with access to the Internet and, correspondingly, the number of "home pages" is growing.

As different people around the world have developed sites that take advantage of the easy-to-use software, the links they are creating among one another have become known as the World Wide Web (WWW). But you don't have to have a "page" yourself to visit the various sites. You just need the software and access to the Internet.

You might find yourself, for example, at the page called "Photojournalism: The Professionals' Approach," a site devoted to photojournalism. In addition to photographs and material that updates this textbook, you would find a reference to the National Press Photographers Association (NPPA). Clicking on the highlighted name of the organization would take you directly to the site maintained by NPPA, which includes workshop dates, contest deadlines, and organizational news. Just click on the words.

The World Wide Web and "home pages" being developed by individuals and organizations worldwide just may provide a supplement or alternative to print journalism. Sending pictures and words over the phone lines rather than via paper saves trees and eliminates the need for printing presses and delivery trucks. The Web also allows the instant transmission of news and pictures. All of these capabilities point to a new form of journalism and, consequently, to a new outlet for photojournalism.

ETHICS

Traditionally, the photographic profession has considered altering pictures through dodging and burning in the darkroom a perfectly acceptable practice. In fact, careful printing that involves dodging and burning is highly praised.

On the other hand, photojournalism professionals try to avoid retouching photos or combining photos. Many old photos were retouched because of poor reproduction, a practice basically eliminated since the 1970s. Combining photos into a composograph, a practice at the early tabloid, the *New York Daily Graphic*, (see Chapter 15, "History"), has been shunned by the "straight" press for many years. The *National Enquirer* and other modern tabloids have been more brazen in cutting-and-pasting photographs to create situations that never existed.

Photographers traditionally found extensive retouching with an airbrush or paints on black-and-white photos difficult, with results that usually looked obvious. Retouching color was even more difficult.

Recently, however, with the application of computer technology to photography, photographers and editors have discovered an easier way to manipulate picture elements so that the changes are undetectable. While a blessing for those working with photo illustrations, computer manipulation is a potential curse on the credibility of photojournalism.

■ COMPOSING PHOTOS ON THE ELECTRONIC LAYOUT TABLE

In a now-famous incident at the *National Geographic*, editors puzzled over what could have been a terrific cover shot of the great pyramids of Giza. Unfortunately, the foreground's camels and the background's pyramids were not lined up to fit correctly on the vertical cover. The answer: Send the picture to the scanner and computer. Through the magic of computer manipulation, the computer operator actually moved the pyramids in the photos. The final picture left no trails.

Rich Clarkson, who became director of photography at the *Geographic* after the incident, defended the magazine's digital alteration of the picture.

"It's exactly the same as if the photographer had moved the camera's position," he is quoted as saying in an article by Shiela Reaves in the NPPA special report, ***Ethics of Photojournalism***.

Clarkson's argument, however, made no distinction between acceptable and unacceptable methods to obtain a photo. Is fudging a photograph electronically really the same as moving the photographer—even if both methods result in photos that look the same?

As if moving pyramids was not enough, Collins Publishing Co., which published *A Day in the Life of America*, found moving the moon a necessity.

Reviewing their take from the shoot, editors decided that an evocative picture of a cowboy, tree, and crescent moon would make a perfect cover. Like the *Geographic*'s uncooperative photo, however, the horizontal shot would not fit on the full-bleed vertical cover—so a computer technician moved the cowboy and moon nearer to the tree and then finished composing the picture by adding branches and a bit of extra sky.

So, although more than one hundred photographers submitted thousands of frames of film, editors determined that only the picture of a cowboy who was too far away from a tree would succeed as a cover. And, instead of redesigning the cover to accommodate the photo, they redesigned the photo.

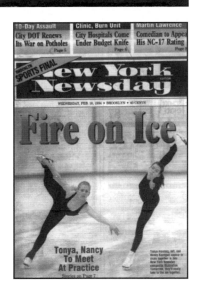

◼ ADDING OR SUBTRACTING ELEMENTS

Editors don't have to stop at moving the moon or just limit themselves to rearranging pyramids. They even can add or subtract elements from the original picture.

Some newspapers have used the computer to remove small distracting items from a picture, others to change the background color of the picture. *The St. Louis Post-Dispatch* removed a Coke® can from a portrait of its Pulitzer Prize-winning photographer. The *Orange County Register* increased the saturation of the blue sky in some of their prize-winning Olympics pictures. On a more mundane level, the *San Francisco Examiner* changed the color of a wall behind the mayor to enhance the appeal of a front-page picture.

Did these newspapers cross the ethical boundary between normal picture handling and doctoring photos?

Long Island's *Newsday* featured a picture of ice-skating rivals Nancy Kerrigan and Tonya Harding practicing together for the Olympics. The two athletes, however, did not really skate in practice together until the day after the paper ran the photograph on its front page. The computer-combined montage was a fake.

Newsday had one photo of Harding going through her routine and a separate picture of Kerrigan practicing. Fueled by public interest in the rivalry, in which Harding had been accused of engineering an attack against Kerrigan, editors used the computer to seamlessly meld the pictures of the two separate practices into one—and presented the result as if the two rivals were skating simultaneously. The decision was made against the protests of the photography department, and had editors

waited another day, the newspaper would have been able to publish a real picture of the two skaters on the rink together rather than printing a day-early but fake photo.

Texas Monthly went even further when it depicted then-governor of Texas Ann Richards in a white, leather-fringed outfit atop a Harley Davidson motorcycle. Although Richards does ride a motorcycle, the picture actually showed Richards' face melded onto a professional model's body. (Richards retorted that she was glad the magazine found a model with good thighs.)

Perhaps one of the most shocking instances of computer manipulation was when the *National Enquirer* used the computer to add bruises and a black eye to a photograph of Nicole Simpson, O. J. Simpson's murdered ex-wife. With the former athlete on trial for his ex-wife's murder, the *Enquirer* doctored the photo to "illustrate" how the victim would have appeared following an earlier instance of abuse by her ex-husband. Labeled as a computer manipulation, the image nonetheless stunned shoppers in grocery stores everywhere. How many people, do you suppose, knew what the *Enquirer* meant by computer manipulation?

◼ HOW FAR WILL MAGAZINE EDITORS GO?

Curiously, some magazines editors have shown little hesitation in altering cover photographs with the computer. "Magazines, I think, can get away with a little more," said Rocco Alberico of *Sports Illustrated for Kids.* "I mean they can fool around a little bit more than newspapers."

In her paper "Digital Alteration of Photographs in Magazines: An Examination

COVERS—LEFT TO RIGHT
The picture of Nicole Simpson is real, but the *National Enquirer* added the bruises.

The head on the woman in the picture is the former governor of Texas, Ann Richards. The body belongs to a model.

The competing ice skaters had not practiced together, so *Newsday* editors used the computer to combine two separate pictures (see below) for the page one picture above.

Reuters

Associated Press

While *Newsweek* ran an unaltered police "mug shot" of former football superstar and accused murderer O.J. Simpson, *Time* digitally darkened the photo and made him look more foreboding. Readers saw the two images side by side on newsstands and were shocked by *Time*'s decision.

of the Ethics," Shiela Reaves found that all 13 magazine editors and art directors she interviewed said emphatically that they would never digitally manipulate a news photograph. However, most had no problem in "cleaning up" a photograph by removing indistinguishable "blobs" or extending the sky or a background tone so a news photo could fit the layout.

Michele Stephenson, *Time* picture editor, noted that it was like cropping people out of a picture. "You crop a picture, there's a corner of an elbow, and somebody says 'We'd better take that out. It looks funny.' We do that sort of thing . . . everybody does that."

With specialized non-news magazines, the ethical line is even less distinct. "If your tagline (mission) is dedicated to the art of style, then I think you can do just about anything," said Diana La Guardia, art director of Conde Nast's *Traveler*.

As part of her survey, Reaves asked Bob Furstenau, director of magazine production for Meredith Corporation (publisher of *Better Homes and Gardens*) what kinds of things he would change in a picture. "Anything," he replied, "that interferes with the ultimate aesthetic of the picture—spots, telephone wires, people, whatever." He estimated that 45 of the 48 covers he had worked on at the time had been digitally manipulated.

Sports Illustrated for Kids featured one of the NBA's shortest basketball players dribbling through the legs of a large player. "We do a lot of that, especially on covers, but it's pretty obvious that they're basically fantasies," said Alberico, the magazine's art director. "That's such an obvious fake; kids know people that size really don't exist."

Do they?

Reaves found that newspaper picture editors were significantly less tolerant of digital manipulation of photographs. She also discovered that only 22 percent of the magazine editors had a photojournalism background, whereas 85 percent of those at newspapers had previous professional photojournalism experience. Perhaps this difference in background accounts for the stricter standards regarding digital picture manipulation held by daily newspaper photo editors.

■ LOSING CREDIBILITY?

What will happen as the public discovers that news outlets alter images electronically? Will the profession lose credibility? Will people believe photographs if they know that editors can easily alter images?

James Kelly and Diona Nace compared how much subjects believe a photograph before and after they were shown a video

demonstrating the techniques of computer manipulation. After watching the video, the subjects, perhaps surprisingly, maintained their trust in photos. Seeing the computer's wizardry does not automatically destroy the believability of the photographic image.

However, when readers saw a real-life comparison of altered and unaltered photos on newsstands, they reacted strongly and loudly. When *Time* magazine electronically altered a police mug shot of O. J. Simpson for its cover and called it a "Photo Illustration" the same week that *Newsweek* ran the untainted original, the American public joined a far-ranging debate about the use and misuse of digital alteration.

On every newsstand across the country, the two covers sat side by side—both showing the same image. But the covers looked quite different. *Time* had sent the photo to an illustrator who darkened the image and reduced the police identification numbers. *Time* editors thought they had ethically covered themselves by using the label "Photo-Illustration for *Time*" in the table of contents.

Shocked at public outrage—including 70,000 messages on America Online (a commercial on-line service) as well as articles in the *New York Times* and the Associated Press—a *Time* editor pondered, " . . . but we do illustrations all the time. Why is this different?"

While Kelly and Nace demonstrate that just knowing about digital manipulation does not cause readers to disbelieve photos, the reaction to the *Time* cover indicates that if people care about the event or the person, and if they can see both the altered and unaltered photos, they will respond—loudly.

■ GOING TOO FAR?

While few photographers object to dodging and burning a negative in the darkroom, most are outraged at digitally retouching a person into or out of a news picture. How far should electronic retouching go:
- remove a distracting branch behind a person's head?
- tone the sky to a deeper blue?
- smooth out wrinkles from a star's face?
- alter a news picture if the manipulation will produce a more telling picture?
- change a feature photo?
- electronically sharpen an image?

Digital manipulation has not been around long enough for the photojournalism community to form agreed-upon standards. In coffee shops, at national meetings, and in newsrooms, the topic has been hotly debated since *National Geographic* moved the pyramids for its 1982 cover.

Photojournalists who take the absolutist's position argue that editors should not digitally retouch or manipulate photos at all. They say that the final picture should look as near as possible to the original slide or negative. They maintain that the original is "truth" and any change from that is categorically wrong. Bob Gilka, who was the director of photography at *National Geographic* when the pyramids were moved, now argues that limited electronic manipulation is like a limited nuclear war. There isn't any such thing.

Others hold that editors should only make "global" changes—changes made to the entire photo similar to the way photographers in the field switch filters on the camera. This group says that shooters and editors should not electronically manipulate parts of the photo after it's been taken because photographers cannot do that in the field.

A less stringent position holds that editors should restrict manipulation of the photo to the same techniques practiced in the traditional darkroom—dodging, burning, lightening, darkening, and changing contrast. In an extensive survey of 511 picture editors, Shiela Reaves found that they were intolerant of computer alterations or manipulations, with the overwhelming majority disapproving any computer alterations other than burning and dodging.

One respondent summarized the feelings of most other editors by stating, "The philosophy at our newspaper is not to publish any image which we cannot produce in negative form. Thus, the only manipulation is lightening and darkening, boosting the colors, dodging/burning and spotting scratches and dust spots. No cloning pixels. No moving elements. No combining different negatives. No sanitizing images after the shutter has clicked."

John Long, a past president of National Press Photographers Association and a photographer for the *Hartford* (Conn.) *Courant*, falls into this category. He says there is nothing wrong with fixing flaws using the computer. "These are merely technical in nature and have nothing to do with the actual content or meaning of the photo." Dodging and burning, he says, are integral to the medium of photography—part of the "grammar" of how we communicate. "The public understands this (at least unconsciously), so it is not wrong." But Long argues that photographers should not try to whitewash a photo by eliminating even minor elements like distracting phone lines. Long uses this test, "Does the electronic change in the photo deceive the reader?"

Some editors are willing to go further than Long. They hold that the computer can be used to "clean up" a photo—to remove a distracting wire or a protruding telephone post from behind a subject, or close a pants zipper to save a subject from embarrassment.

Finally, some photographers argue that if the photographer could have taken the picture with a different lens or from a different angle, then manipulating the electronic image to get the same result passes muster. (See Rich Clarkson's comments earlier.)

■ WHO BENEFITS?

How should the profession resolve this dilemma? Perhaps photojournalists should consider who benefits by altering photos. The photographer? The editor? The reader?

Consider this. In the situations where *National Geographic* moved the pyramids and Collins Publishing Company moved the cowboy and the moon, editors and designers sought to fit a horizontal picture onto a vertical cover format. Could another picture have sufficed? Could the cover design have been changed to fit the shape of the image? Who benefited? Editors and designers. Was the reader any better off? Not really.

Removing a cola can from a picture cleaned up the image for an editor. But did the reader gain anything from this move? In all of these instances, electronic manipulation eased the jobs of either editors, designers, or publishers. None were carried out to benefit readers.

Combining the pictures of public figures or digitally "imagining" a victim's injuries goes beyond making jobs easy to simply fooling the reader because there's technology available that makes it easy to do so. Two separate pictures of the women run side-by-side would have conveyed the same message. Here, the reader not only fails to benefit but becomes the butt of a joke, as well.

■ FACILITATE, DON'T FOOL THE READER

On the other hand, when a photographer burns or dodges a print in the darkroom or similarly darkens or lightens the print in the computer, the reader benefits by seeing more clearly items in the picture that might have been missed with an unaltered picture. In the same way, the computer's ability to sharpen pictures or blur backgrounds to make the subject stand out more distinctly and legibly also benefits the reader.

Perhaps an ethical guidepost might read: "Electronically alter pictures only when doing so clearly benefits the reader. Avoid altering pictures when doing so fools the reader in any way." ■

The Law

CHAPTER 13

When people talk about "privacy," they usually mean the "right to be left alone." But privacy is simply not a broad constitutional right

basic to American citizens.

This chapter was revised with Dr. Michael Sherer, Department of Communication, University of Nebraska at Omaha.

The U.S. Constitution does not explicitly grant us this general right to be left alone. In fact, most analysts believe there never will be an explicit, expressed constitutional right of privacy similar to the right

A state trooper illegally tried to block the cameras of two photographers from the *Palm Beach Post* who were covering the arrest of an armed robber.
(Far left and top near left photos by Ken Steinhoff, bottom near left photo by C. J. Walker, the *Palm Beach Post*.)

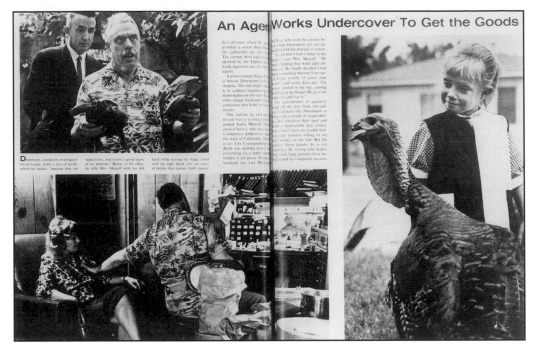

outlined in the First Amendment that protects and guarantees free speech and press.

Over the past ninety years, however, some commonly recognized principles of privacy have evolved, based on federal and state laws and court cases. These principles protect individuals from anyone:

- intruding by taking pictures where privacy could be expected.
- using a picture to sell a product without consent.
- unfairly causing someone to look bad.
- taking truthful but private or embarrassing photos.

At first glance, this list might appear somewhat intimidating. You may ask yourself, "May I ever take a picture of anyone, anywhere?" In practice, though, the courts have severely limited the meaning of each of the four principles of privacy.

■ INTRUDING WHERE PRIVACY COULD BE EXPECTED
Shooting Surreptitiously Inside Someone's Home
When do you need an invitation into someone's home to take pictures? Take the case of Antone Dietemann, a West Coast herbal medicinalist who had achieved a considerable amount of public recognition and was newsworthy, but declined to be photographed in his home-laboratory garden.

Life photographer Bill Ray posed as the husband of a patient and visited the medicinalist along with his wife-for-a-day, also a Life staffer. She complained of a lump in her breast and asked to be examined. With a hidden camera, the photographer snapped pictures of the herb man as he became engrossed in his therapy. Dietemann placed his hand on the patient's breast. He claimed that he could cure people by simply laying hands upon them. Bill Ray discreetly and quietly clicked off several frames. Life editors published the photos without the medicinalist's permission. Dietemann sued the magazine because he claimed his privacy was invaded. He won on the grounds that the photographer took the pictures surreptitiously. Dietemann had not given his permission for the pictures to be taken. Individuals do have privacy rights in their own homes.

Outside the House
The case of Ron Galella, self-styled paparazzo and pursuer of Jacqueline Kennedy Onassis for most of her public life, exemplifies the problem of intruding into someone's privacy outside the home. The former First Lady was newsworthy. Almost anything she did appeared in newspaper gossip columns. Any photo of Jackie a photographer could grab soon appeared on the cover of a national magazine.

Ron Galella is a full-fledged, full-time paparazzo who specialized in photos of Jackie. The word paparazzo means an Italian insect similar to a mosquito. In his movie *La Dolce Vita*, director Federico Fellini named the freelance photographers who covered the movie stars and other celebrities "paparazzo because they buzzed like mosquitoes."

Galella, who made his living buzzing after the stars, started tracking Jackie Kennedy Onassis in 1967. Galella hung around her

New York City apartment and waited for her to step outside the door. When she bicycled in Central Park, he and his camera were tucked into the bushes. As she peddled by, he would shoot her picture. When she shopped at Bonwit Teller's, he ducked behind a counter and snapped away. When she ate at a restaurant in New York's Chinatown, he hid behind a coat rack to get the first photographs of the former First Lady eating with chopsticks. He even dated her maid for a few weeks in an attempt to learn Jackie's schedule.

Onassis sued Galella, charging him with inflicting emotional distress. The court had to balance Onassis' right of privacy against Galella's right to take pictures.

The court found in Onassis' favor. Galella was restricted from coming closer than 100 yards of her home and 50 yards from her personally. This ruling was later modified to prohibit him from approaching within 25 feet of her. Note, however, that the court did not stop Galella from taking and selling pictures of the former First Lady, as long as the pictures were used for news coverage and not advertising. Few cases of this kind have arisen since the Galella-Onassis proceeding.

■ USING SOMEONE'S IMAGE TO SELL A PRODUCT

The law holds that you cannot publish a photo of a person for commercial purposes without obtaining consent from that individual. A company can't sell a product by identifying that product with someone without getting permission first.

Publishing someone's picture on the cover of a magazine or the front page of a newspaper is permissible if it is newsworthy. The court does not consider the newspaper or magazine itself a product. However, printing the same picture as part of an advertisement in a publication, without the subject's prior consent, is a violation of the person's right of privacy.

For instance, let's say that famous movie personality John Starstruck is driving down the street in a new Ford Thunderbird. As a photographer for the *Daily Sun*, you snap a picture of Starstruck, thinking your editor might want to use the photo, for no one knew Starstruck was in town. You were right. Your editor publishes, on the front page, the picture of Starstruck in his new car. No problem. You've done nothing wrong, nor has your editor done anything illegal.

Ford Motor Company, however, seeing the picture, recognizes its advertising value because the photo shows a famous movie star driving in a Thunderbird. The company, after legally obtaining a copy of the photo's negative from your newspaper, uses the picture in an advertisement. If the viewer can recognize Starstruck in the Ford advertisement, then

▼ After Marlon Brando broke photographer Ron Galella's jaw, Galella began wearing a football helmet to protect himself whenever he snapped pictures of the actor.
(Photo by Paul Schmulbach.)

◄ The late Jackie Kennedy Onassis sued Ron Galella, self-styled paparazzo photographer, for harassment, and she won. The court eventually restricted Galella from taking pictures within twenty-five feet of Onassis.
(Photo by Joy Smith.)

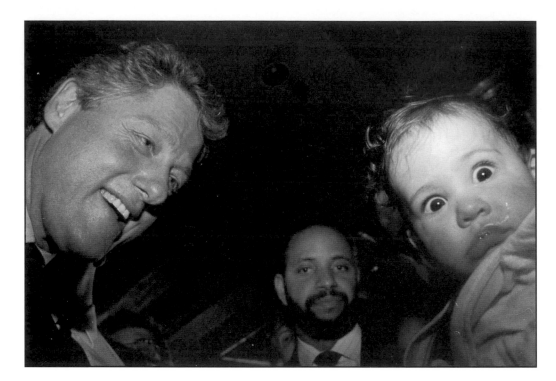

There are no problems publishing this picture of President Bill Clinton in a newspaper or magazine story. But without Clinton's written permission, the photo could not appear in an ad selling baby products.
(Photo by Larry Dailey, *Columbus* (Ga.) *Ledger-Enquirer.*)

the movie star's privacy—in the sense of commercial appropriation—is violated. Ford is using Starstruck's image to sell its cars. Starstruck may sue the Ford Motor Company, and unless Ford can produce a consent form in court, the movie star will win. The consent form, signed by the subject, gives the photographer or publication the right to use the photo in an ad.

Reserving the commercial use of a person's image is not limited to just the famous. All individuals have the right to protect themselves from this form of commercial exploitation. When you take a picture for the newspaper, you do not need a consent form from the subject, famous or unknown. But when you take a picture that you want to sell to a company for use in an advertisement, brochure, fund-raiser, and the like, then you must get a consent form signed, even if the subject is unknown.

■ UNFAIRLY CAUSING SOMEONE TO LOOK BAD

The law holds that people have the right of privacy not to be placed in a "false light." In other words, photos can't make a person look bad without cause. For example, a photographer photographed a child who had been struck by a car, and the picture appeared in a newspaper. No problem so far. Two years later, the *Saturday Evening Post* ran the same picture under the title, "They Asked To Be Killed," with a story about child safety. The original use of the picture was a legitimate publication of a newsworthy event. But when

the *Saturday Evening Post* used the headline with the picture, and placed the subhead "Do You Invite Massacre with Your Own Carelessness?" next to the photo, the parents claimed that the words and photo implied carelessness on their part. The words and photo gave the impression that the child had willingly run out in front of the car. The court decreed that the photo/headline combination placed the parents in a "false light." The parents won the lawsuit.

Saturday Evening Post editors used a picture from their old photo file to accompany this new story. They used the old picture as an illustration of a general, ongoing problem. Often, this use of file photos provides the grounds for later lawsuits.

In another such incident, John Raible even signed a consent form allowing *Newsweek* magazine to publish his picture with a story about "Middle Americans." The editors, however, chose the headline "Troubled American—A Special Report on the Silent Majority," and printed Raible's picture below the headline. Raible felt that the headline, associated with his picture, implied he was troubled, thus putting him in a "false light." He sued and collected damages.

Both the *Saturday Evening Post* and the *Newsweek* cases show a picture's meaning can be affected drastically by the words associated with it. Although the picture itself might have been legal when it was taken, after captioning or headlining, the photo-plus-word combination can be considered illegal. Robert Cavallo and Stuart Kahan, in their book *Photography: What's the Law?*, say that "Pictures, standing alone, without captions or stories with them, generally pose little danger of defamation. However, an illustration is usually accompanied by text, and it is almost always that combination of pictures and prose which carries the damaging impact."

The *Newsweek* case points up a second legal danger for the photographer to watch for. The consent form signed by Raible did not protect the photographer. The consent form is not a carte blanche; it is a limited authorization given by the subject to the photographer, warning the photographer to use the picture in an understood and agreed-on manner. A consent form does not give photographers or picture editors the right to use a picture in any way they see fit.

■ TAKING TRUTHFUL BUT PRIVATE OR EMBARRASSING PHOTOS

The right of privacy does include some restrictions on printing truthful but private or embarrassing information about a subject.

Generally, if the information is newsworthy and in the public interest, the press can photograph and publish the facts. The courts have liberally interpreted "public interest" to mean anything interesting to the public—and there are few things that won't interest some people.

Public but Embarrassing

The courts, however, have put certain limitations on the right of the public to know and see true but confidential facts about a person. Photographs, even if taken in a public place, should not ridicule or embarrass a private person unless the situation is patently newsworthy. The photos should not be highly offensive to a reasonable person and must be of legitimate concern to the public.

Ms. Graham went to the Cullman, Ala., county fair. After several rides, she entered a side-show fun house. In the fun house, she walked across a grate that blew up her dress. At that unlucky moment, a photographer from the *Daily Times Democrat*, Bill McClure, was on his first photo assignment for the paper—looking for "typical" features

Safety education in schools has reduced child accidents measurably, but unpredictable darting through traffic still takes a sobering toll.

They Ask to Be Killed
By DAVID G. WITTELS

Do you invite massacre by your own carelessness? Here's how thousands have committed suicide by scorning laws that were passed to keep them alive.

The parents of this child claimed that the combination of words and pictures implied that they were careless, thus placing them in a false light. When they sued the *Saturday Evening Post*, the court decided in their favor.
(Reprinted from the *Saturday Evening Post*, © 1949, The Curtis Publishing Co.)

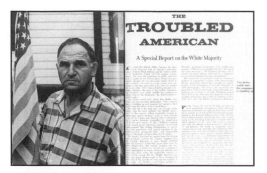

Special Children

You may take pictures of children; however, if the child is in a class for the retarded or handicapped, and you take a picture, his or her parents may consider that photo truthful but embarrassing. They could sue you and your newspaper. Getting the teacher's permission is not sufficient. To run the picture of the retarded or handicapped child, you must have the consent of the parent or legal guardian.

You can take and publish pictures of children in schools and public parks. You are open to suit only if the photo might be considered embarrassing or derogatory.

Hospitals

In 1942, an International News Photo photographer entered the hospital room of Dorothy Barber, who was in the hospital for a weight-loss problem. Without Barber's consent, the photographer took a picture of her, and *Time* magazine bought the photo and ran it under the headline "Starving Glutton." Barber sued the magazine, and Time lost the case. A Missouri court said, "Certainly if there is any right of privacy at all, it should include the right to obtain medical treatment at home or in a hospital without personal publicity."

Dorothy Barber had what the court considers a "private medical condition." Therefore, a photographer could not take her picture without her permission.

at the fair. With his Speed Graphic, he snapped Graham's picture just as her skirt blew up around her hips, exposing her underwear. After the picture was published, Graham called and complained. Getting no satisfaction from the photographer with an apology or retraction, Graham hired an out-of-town lawyer and successfully sued the *Democrat* for damages. The picture was truthful, but the jury found that the photo was embarrassing and contained no information of legitimate concern to the public.

Accidents

If someone is injured in an automobile accident or plane crash, falls out of a tree, nearly drowns, or is struck by lightning, that person would have a "public medical condition." In addition, if a person is shot by someone who is in the process of committing a crime, that person's condition would be considered "public." People who are victims of a crime, accident, or act of God are considered newsworthy, and they can be photographed outside the hospital.

If an accident happens on Pacific and Hyde, the photographer can begin taking pictures of the victim upon arriving at the scene because the victim has a public medical condition and is not in the hospital. As the rescue team places the victim on the stretcher and slides the body into the ambulance, the photographer is still within legal rights to continue to photograph.

Once the victim enters the emergency van, however, the individual is covered by the right of privacy and is off limits to photographers. The same off-limits rule inhibits photographers once the victim enters the hospital.

If a person's condition is newsworthy, interesting, and historic, but the condition is not caused by crime, accident, or act of God, the person's medical condition is considered "private." Barber's treatment was "private." The first heart and kidney transplants and the first test-tube baby were both "private medical conditions," even though they were newsworthy. Photographers could take pictures inside the hospital only if the patients involved granted permission.

■ THE LAW OF TRESPASS: THE HOME AS CASTLE

Without going onto a person's property, you may, from the street, photograph someone in his yard, on his porch, or even inside his house if you can see the person. You don't need the owner's permission. For instance, the courts consider people sitting on their verandas, mowing their lawns, or standing behind a picture window in their living rooms to be in "public view" and therefore legitimate subjects for photography.

The photographer still should be somewhat cautious when shooting onto private property, however, and should not step onto the grounds to get the picture. Nor should the photographer use an extremely long telephoto lens, which would capture more than the naked eye could see.

In fact, the court says you shouldn't go to any extra trouble to get this porch-sitting, lawn-mowing, or window-standing shot. You shouldn't even climb a tree to gain a better view. Although not all photographers follow these guidelines, all are limited essentially to the view of an average passerby, according to the courts.

■ NEWS EVENTS: ACCESS VS. TRESPASS

Cindy Fletcher, fourteen years old, died in a house fire in Jacksonville, Florida. Her mother, who was away at the time, learned about the tragedy in the next day's edition of the *Times-Union*. Alongside the story appeared a picture that showed where her daughter's burned body had left a silhouette scorched on the floor. Newspaper photographer Bill Cranford had entered the Fletcher home to take the photo. Mrs. Fletcher sued the Florida Publishing Co., owner of the *Times-Union*, on grounds that the photographer had invaded her home, hence her privacy.

This actual court case serves to illustrate the problem of access for the working photographer. Did the photographer, as a representative of the news media, have the right to enter the house? Which right comes first: the right of Mrs. Fletcher not to have someone trespass in her house or the right of the public to know what happened in that house? Would you have entered Fletcher's home if you were the photographer?

In *Florida Publishing Co.* (*Times-Union*) *v. Fletcher*, the court found in favor of the photographer. He had the right to enter the house and take the pictures. Yet, in other cases, the courts have recognized the right of private ownership over newsworthiness.

Trespass generally means entering someone's home, apartment, hotel, motel, or car without permission. This right of private ownership prohibits someone from walking

A photographer has the legal right to take this picture because the accident occurred on a public street. (Photo by Carolyn Cole for the *Sacramento* (Calif.) *Bee.*)

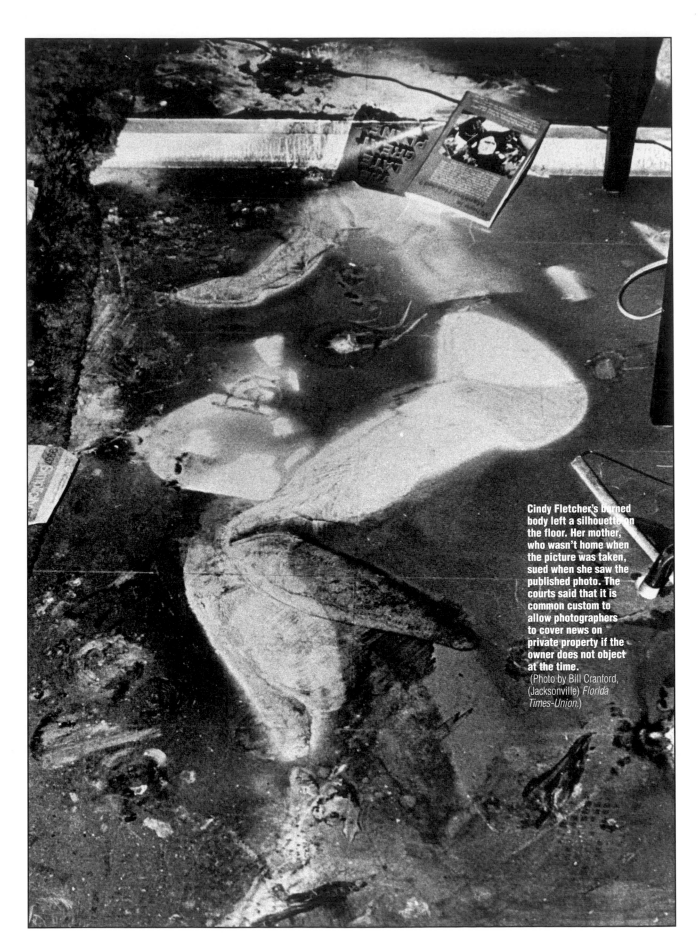

Cindy Fletcher's burned body left a silhouette on the floor. Her mother, who wasn't home when the picture was taken, sued when she saw the published photo. The courts said that it is common custom to allow photographers to cover news on private property if the owner does not object at the time.
(Photo by Bill Cranford, (Jacksonville) *Florida Times-Union*.)

in and taking pictures inside a house, without the permission of the resident.

Why, then, did the court find that the *Times-Union* photographer had the right to enter the Fletcher house and take pictures of the silhouette left from Cindy Fletcher's burned body?

Why was this not a case of trespass or invasion of privacy?

In the Fletcher case, the news photographer had been invited into the home by the police and fire marshal; no one objected to the cameraman's presence. In fact, the authorities had asked the photographer to take pictures because they needed the photos for their investigation, and the fire marshal's camera was out of film. Mrs. Fletcher's suit was dismissed because it was "common custom" for the fire department or the police department to permit the press onto private premises for the purposes of covering such newsworthy events.

Also, in the Fletcher case, no one had objected to the photographer's presence. Immediately, one asks, "How could Mrs. Fletcher object when she wasn't there?" That's the "Catch-22"—a legal dilemma. Had she been there and had she said "no," the photographer, despite official invitation, would have been trespassing. But Mrs. Fletcher did not say "no," and the fact that she couldn't say "no" wasn't relevant, according to the courts at the time.

A more recent court finding, however, calls into question the "common custom" of the Fletcher case (*Tawa Ayeni v. CBS Inc.*, and *United States of America v. Anthony Sanusi, et al.*).

The facts. A CBS camera crew was shooting an episode for "Street Stories," a real-life cop show, when police invited the news team to participate in a raid on a suspect's home. The police were looking for evidence of credit card fraud.

However, the suspect was not at home when the raid occurred. Only the suspect's wife, Tawa Ayeni, and her small child were on hand when the law enforcement officials pushed their way into the apartment—with the CBS video crew right behind them. The woman, clad only in her nightgown, implored the all-male crew, "Please don't take my picture."

She cowered, covered her face with a magazine, and directed her preschool son not to look at the camera. "Why do you want to take a picture?" she asked. When the raid was over, law enforcement officials found nothing they had sought, but the CBS crew had footage of the raid, including shots of personal letters and paycheck stubs.

Tawa Ayeni sued CBS and won at both the trial level and in the Federal Court of Appeals. Judge Jack Weinstein wrote, "Allowing a camera crew into a private home to film a search-and-seizure operation is the equivalent of a rogue policeman using his official position to break into a home in order to steal objects for his own profit or that of another."

Although law enforcement officials generally have a right to enter private property to conduct a reasonable search, Judge Weinstein maintained that this privilege does not extend to photojournalists invited along for the affair. Judge Weinstein wrote that inviting a camera crew into a private home is an unreasonable violation of the Fourth Amendment, which protects private citizens against the state conducting unlawful searches.

This finding runs counter to the "common custom and practice" concept that was established in the Fletcher case, where fire officials had invited the photojournalist into a private home to shoot the aftermath of a fatal fire. In the ruling against CBS, Judge Weinstein's views are more in line with contemporary court opinions that generally find little support for a police officer's "right" to invite photojournalists and other reporters onto private property.

Can you photograph a newsworthy event in a person's home if the owners do not object, and the police have not yet arrived? If you were riding down the street and heard a gunshot followed by a scream coming from a house, you could park your car, enter the house, and begin photographing the victim and the assailant.

If the homeowner realized what you were doing and didn't like it, the owner could ask you to leave. You would have to obey or be arrested for trespassing. Even if the police were there, you would have to leave if the homeowner objected to your presence.

The Florida Highway Patrol, after a strong protest from the *Palm Beach Post Times* about the harassment of two staff photographers (see opening spread of this chapter), issued a policy statement regarding "Journalists' Right of Access to Crime, Arrest or Disaster Scenes." The statement said, in part, "It is the long-standing custom of law-enforcement agencies to invite representatives of the news media to enter upon private property where an event of public interest has occurre . . . . "

"Invite," in this instance, does not mean literally to receive a formal invitation. Invite means to allow the photographer to enter. The common custom exists for photographers to cover news events and not be harassed or otherwise blocked by the police. The photographer should not wait for an engraved invitation from the cop at the scene before beginning to photograph.

The Florida Highway Patrol's policy statement goes on to say, "the presence of a photographer at an accident, crime, or disaster scene and the taking of photographs at the scene does not constitute unlawful interference and should not be restricted."

Unfortunately, this position is a policy statement of the Florida Highway Patrol, not a national or even a state law; therefore, the policy is not followed by police and firefighters in every state. In fact, only California has a specific law, stating, "accident and disaster areas shall not be closed to a duly authorized representative of any news service, newspaper or radio or television station or network." Even this law, however, does not protect the photojournalist if the police claim that the photographers will interfere with emergency operations.

■ **PRIVATE PROPERTY OPEN TO THE PUBLIC**

Do you have the right to take pictures on private property that is open to the public, such as a restaurant or grocery store? This area of the law is murky. Some authorities hold that you can take pictures unless the management has posted signs prohibiting photography or unless the owners object and ask you to stop. However, CBS was sued when its photographer entered the Le Mistral restaurant in New York, with cameras rolling, to illustrate a story about the sanitation violations of the establishment. The management objected, but CBS kept filming.

Although no signs prohibiting photography were posted, CBS lost the suit on the ground that the photographer had entered without the intention of purchasing food and was therefore trespassing. Although CBS was covering a legitimate news story in a private establishment open to the public, the network was found guilty of trespassing.

In a 1972 case (*Lloyd Corp., Ltd. v. Tanner*) the court ruled that "the public's license to enter a private business establishment is limited to engaging in activities directly related to that business and does not normally extend to the pursuit of unrelated business, e.g., news gathering."

Camera journalists have no right to enter the property, even in a spot-news situation, if they are prohibited by the owners of the establishment. Photographers must take their pictures from the public street, or they can be sued for trespass.

This means that, if a fire is raging inside a business, the management can exclude

photographers. If the management asks you to leave, you must comply with the request, or you can be arrested for trespassing. You can, however, still publish any pictures you have already taken. The proprietor can stop you from taking more pictures, but he can't restrict you from printing the ones you already have.

Retired California Appeals Court Justice John Racanelli points out that penalties for trespass are usually "nominal" if there is no intent to "do actual harm or injury."

Sometimes a manager will demand the film you have taken inside the store. On this point the law is clear. You do not have to give up your film. The owner or manager can ask you to stop taking pictures but can't take away your film. That film is your personal property, and you have every right to keep it.

■ **SHOOT FREELY IN PUBLIC PLACES**

You may photograph in public places and on public property. You can take pictures on the street, on the sidewalk, in public parks, as well as in the public zoo. You can photograph in a city-owned airport as well as in public areas of schools and universities. However, without the teacher's permission, you can't take pictures of a class in session.

You may take pictures of elected officials or private citizens in public places, such as the street or the park. The person may be the center of interest in your photo, or just part of the crowd. If a news event occurs on public property, then you may cover that event as long as you do not interfere with police or the flow of traffic.

There are times when bystanders or relatives try, by physical assault, to prevent a photographer from taking a picture. In such instances, the courts have generally stepped in to protect photographers when they shoot in public places, according to George Chernoff and Hershel Sarbin in their book *Photography and the Law*. They note that, some years ago, New York state even made it unlawful to damage the equipment of news photographers engaged in the pursuit of their occupation in public places.

Difficulties arise when police authorities inhibit photographers shooting on public property. In many situations, an overeager police officer may block a photographer's lens. In Iowa, photographers were once prevented by highway patrol officers and the National Guard from taking close-ups at the scene of a civilian airline crash. When airline officials arrived, photographers were given a free hand. In Philadelphia, police forcibly prevented photographers from taking pictures as officials bounced a heckler from a political rally. Philadelphia's city solicitor issued a formal opinion in which he told the police commissioner, "Meaningful freedom of the press includes the right to photograph and disseminate pictures of public events occurring in public places."

Police and fire officials have the right to restrict any activity of a photographer that might interfere with the officials' action. But taking pictures and asking questions do not constitute interference. Unfortunately, if a police officer stops a photographer at the scene of a breaking-news event, the photographer might find it hard to argue a fine point of law with an insistent cop. Photographers who disregard police directives can be arrested for disorderly conduct or for interfering with a police officer in the performance of duty, constituting a possible felony.

The National Press Photographers Association (NPPA) and some of its chapters have for years worked with fire and police academies to improve the graduates' understanding of the role of news in society. NPPA members have written police/press guidelines designed to reduce the conflict between working photojournalists and law enforcement officers. The Pennsylvania and the Philadelphia Press Photographers Associations were among the first to undertake such a program, beginning in the 1950s. The result has been improved cooperation between photographers and fire and police personnel.

■ GOVERNMENT BUILDINGS: PUBLIC BUT UNDER SPECIAL RULES

Although facilities may be publicly owned, a photographer does not have unlimited access to government buildings, such as the U.S. Senate and House of Representatives, the state legislature, or the chambers of the city council. The mayor's office and city hospital also fall under the special-rules category. In addition, military bases and jails are strictly controlled.

As mentioned above, hospitals, even if they are publicly owned, publicly supported, and publicly operated, occupy a special place under the law. It's true that the admission list to hospitals is public information, but that's about all. You might be allowed to photograph scenes in a hospital for, say, a feature story. But check your pictures. Are there people in the pictures? Yes. Are some of the people in the pictures patients? Yes. Are they identifiable? Yes. Do you have a release form? No. You say the people in the photo are "incidental"? For instance, a picture taken of a corridor or waiting room shows several people sitting and reading magazines.

Where and When a Photojournalist Can Shoot

	ANYTIME	IF NO ONE OBJECTS	WITH RESTRICTIONS	ONLY WITH PERMISSION
PUBLIC AREA				
Street	X			
Sidewalk	X			
Airport			X	
Beach	X			
Park	X			
Zoo	X			
Train Station	X			
Bus Station	X			
IN PUBLIC SCHOOL				
Preschool			X	
Grade School			X	
High School			X	
University Campus	X			
Class in Session				X
IN PUBLIC AREA—WITH RESTRICTIONS				
Police Headquarters			X	
Government Buildings			X	
Courtroom				X
Prison				X
Legislative Chambers				X
IN MEDICAL FACILITIES				
Hospital				X
Rehab Center				X
Emergency Van				X
Mental Health Center				X
Doctor's Office				X
Clinic				X
PRIVATE BUT OPEN TO THE PUBLIC				
Movie Theater Lobby		X		
Business Office		X		
Hotel Lobby		X		
Restaurant		X		
Casino				X
Museum		X		
PRIVATE AREAS VISIBLE TO THE PUBLIC				
Window of Home	X			
Porch	X			
Lawn	X			
IN PRIVATE				
Home		X		
Porch		X		
Lawn		X		
Apartment		X		
Hotel Room		X		
Car		X		

No matter. You must (a) get a release form; (b) don't run the picture; or (c) make the subjects unidentifiable in the darkroom.

The halls of the U.S. Congress are certainly public places, as are meeting rooms of state legislatures and city councils. But such places are generally run by their own unique rules. Even though the House of Representatives does allow television cameras limited access to debates, this legislative body will not allow photographers to take still pictures at a regular session of Congress. Politicians are afraid that the uncensored film of the still photographer will catch one of the members of this august body taking a nap, reading the newspaper, or, as is more often the situation, not present. Photographers are usually allowed in the U.S. House or Senate chambers only during ceremonial sessions, such as the opening day of Congress.

Photographers can snap legislators in committee meetings, elected officials in the halls of Congress, or legislators in their offices. Certain buildings—the Capitol and its grounds, all the House and Senate office buildings, the Library of Congress, and the General Accounting Office—are controlled entirely by the rules passed by Congress. The Constitution grants Congress the right to formulate special rules for operating these buildings. These rules are not subject to judicial review.

■ THE COURTROOM: ANOTHER SPECIAL SITUATION

The U.S. Supreme Court does forbid the presence of photographers in federal courtrooms but not in state courts. The effort of photojournalists to obtain access rights to both federal and state courtrooms has had a turbulent history.

A low-water mark in photographing in the courtroom occurred during the trial of Bruno Richard Hauptmann for the kidnapping and murder of Charles Lindbergh's infant child. Lindbergh had captured the imagination and admiration of the entire world for his nonstop solo trans-Atlantic crossing. The kidnapping and murder of his child attracted worldwide interest, and an estimated 700 reporters, including 129 photographers, came to the old courthouse in Flemington, N.J., to cover the trial. Photographers were allowed to take pictures in the courtroom only three times each

During Richard Hauptmann's trial for kidnapping and killing Charles Lindbergh's baby, the judge prohibited photographers from taking pictures while court was in session. On January 3, 1935, Lindbergh himself took the stand. Despite the judge's orders, a photographer snapped the picture during the trial. With only a few exceptions, after this trial cameras were barred from the courtrooms until the 1970s.

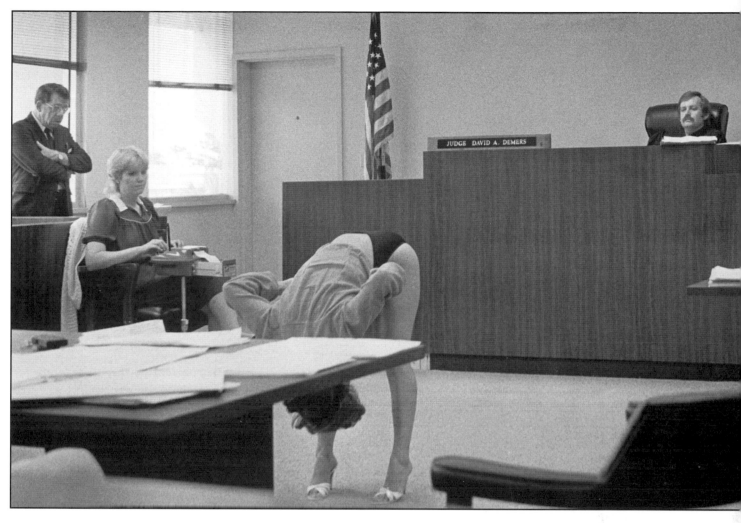

day; before court convened, at noon recess, and after court adjourned. Early in the trial, however, a photographer took unauthorized pictures of Lindbergh on the stand. The photographer claimed that he was "new on the job, having been sent as a relief man, and he did not know the rulings."

Another illegal picture was taken at the end of the trial. Dick Sarno of the *New York Mirror* concealed a 35mm Contax camera when he entered the courtroom on February 13, 1935, the day the verdict and sentence were announced. At the key moment of the proceedings, Sarno, who had wrapped his Contax in a muffler to conceal the noise, took a one-second exposure of the courtroom. Sarno later related, "As Hauptmann stood up and faced the jury, you could hear a pin drop. I tilted the camera, which I had braced on the balcony rail. The judge was directly in front and below me. If he looked up, I was sure he could see me." As the foreman of the jury stood to recite the verdict, Sarno recorded the instant.

Prejudicial press reports, contemptuous statements by trial attorneys and police, the rowdy behavior of the 150 crammed spectators and too numerous reporters added to the Roman holiday atmosphere of the proceeding, according to extensive research by Sherry Alexander, "Curious History: The ABA Code of Judicial Ethics Canon 35."

The three-ring circus atmosphere created by photographers and reporters covering the trial outside the courtroom as they mobbed each witness, as well as the indiscretions of the still and newsreel cameramen inside the courtroom, shocked a committee of the American Bar Association (ABA) that reviewed the legal proceedings in 1936.

Nevertheless, Alexander found, the original ABA Committee did not recommend a total exclusion of photography and broadcasting in the courtroom. Instead, it was the 1937 convention of the group that adopted a flat ban on cameras in court as the 35th Canon of Professional and Judicial Ethics. Many states, but not all, adopted these canons, effectively slamming the courtroom door shut on photojournalists for forty years.

Accused of bending over to "bare it all" during their show, exotic dancers demonstrated for the judge that their underwear covered up anything "illegal." Pictures are now possible in most courtrooms. The photographer in this instance got a tip that an interesting performance might take place in court.
(Photo by Jim Damaske.)

Restrictions easing

Florida's judicial system and legal code are viewed as the model by many states. Thus, in the late 1970s, when the Florida Supreme Court opened the courtroom to photographers and television equipment on a limited basis for a one-year period, the event was significant. The Florida test allowed nationwide broadcast of the Ronnie Zamora trial. Zamora, 15, was charged with killing his 82-year-old neighbor.

Zamora's attorneys tried to blame commercial television for the murder committed by their client. Noting that Ronnie had watched many episodes of "Kojak," a popular detective program, defense attorneys claimed that the boy was under "involuntary subliminal television intoxication."

While the defense proved unsuccessful, the experiment allowing photographers to cover the trial worked well. With modern fast films and compact electronic television cameras, photographers did not require excessive lighting, and their behavior did not interfere with the trial's progress.

Florida permanently opened its courts to the camera.

In 1980, the Supreme Court upheld the constitutionality of Florida's open courts law.

In *Chandler v. Florida*, two police officers convicted of burglarizing a restaurant claimed that the presence of TV cameras denied them a right to a fair trial because local stations broadcast only highlights of the prosecution's case.

But, when the Supreme Court considered the officers' appeal, the Justices ruled unanimously that states are not prohibited from allowing still and television cameras in their courts. The decision was a major victory for the First Amendment rights of photojournalists.

By 1995, all states except Indiana, Mississippi, and South Dakota had opened their courtrooms to the camera. There is even a cable television channel devoted to covering trials. Each state, however, continues to have unique and individual restrictions. Check your state's rules and regulations before you start shooting.

The federal court system remains closed.

LIBEL AND THE PHOTOGRAPHER

Libel is a printed, written, or pictorial statement that is defamatory to a person's character and reputation. The image must have been published or shown to another individual due to negligence on the part of the photojournalist or due to a willful disregard for the truth.

Since truth is a defense in libel cases, and since photos represent actual scenes and are truthful, it might seem that a person should not be able to win a libel suit against a photographer. However, a number of successful libel suits have been based on photographs, which can subject someone to ridicule, contempt, or hatred just as effectively as words can. Photographs can lie, or at least appear to lie, and photos in conjunction with print may form the basis for a libel suit.

Usually, a photo alone is not libelous, although such cases have happened. The most famous involved a Mr. Burton, who was paid for a cigarette endorsement. For the advertisement, Mr. Burton was photographed holding a saddle in front of him. In the photograph, quite by accident, the saddle's wide girth strap appeared to be attached to the man, giving, in the court's words, a "grotesque, monstrous, and obscene" effect. The photo was libelous.

In some situations, when words have been added to photos either in the form of headlines, cutlines, or stories, the photo/word combination has resulted in libel cases. The photograph itself may be harmless, but the caption or accompanying article may add the damaging element. For example, the *New York American* once printed a photograph of a wrestler, Sbyszko, next to that of a

Although truth is an absolute defense for libel, and this picture was "true," Mr. Burton sued when he saw what he looked like in this portion of a Camel cigarette ad. Burton had given permission for the ad, yet the court found publishing the picture was libelous.

gorilla, with the caption: "Not fundamentally different in physique." The photo-plus-word combination was libelous. As in cases involving privacy issues, photographers must be particularly careful how their pictures are associated with words.

Many photographic libel suits have involved individuals arrested as robbery suspects, according to Michael Sherer's report, "No pictures please: It's the law." Sherer notes that individuals allegedly involved in murder, illegal drugs, smuggling, police corruption, financial misdealing, illegal gambling, organized theft rings, and organized crime have sued for libel when their pictures appeared in print. In addition, he notes, people have sued because they felt photos of them implied sexual promiscuity or abnormal or illegal sexual activity.

To prove that a photo is libelous, the defendant must show that the photojournalist acted with willful disregard for the truth or was unprofessional. By relying on proper reporting procedures in gathering and publishing the photos, several media defendants have successfully defended themselves in libel litigation.

Sherer notes that problems arise when courts discover that proper reporting techniques were not used to obtain the photos. For instance, photographers failed to verify that individuals who were photographed during arrests were indeed suspects in the robberies or suspects accused of prostitution.

Finally, Sherer cautions that, if you have any doubt that the subjects pictured are not the same people as those mentioned in the accompanying caption or news story, find another way of illustrating the story.

PRESS CREDENTIALS USEFUL BUT LIMITED

Press credentials issued by the newspaper or magazine for which you work are a means of identification and nothing more. Press passes entitle you to nothing. Authorities use press credentials to determine if you are an official media representative and then may "invite" you to the scene of a crime or disaster.

Essentially, your press pass gives you no more rights than those held by the public. The press credential does not give you a right to break the law, even if you are in hot pursuit of a big news story. Sgt. Carl Yates of the Louisville (Ky.) police department characterizes the situation this way: "You have no more right of access than the general public. What you do have, and what you hope the police will recognize, is that you have more of a reason to be there than the general public."

Credentials issued by the highway patrol or the state police carry no legal weight other than providing proof you work for a newspaper or magazine. Official credentials can be ignored or recalled at any time by the law enforcement agencies that issued them.

On the other hand, authorities cannot discriminate against you or your newspaper at the scene of a crime or disaster. All reporters, photographers, and TV camera operators must have an equal opportunity to cover the story. The police cannot select one newspaper photographer and reject another. Nor can police choose to let in television camera crews and keep out still photographers. If the crime scene is crowded, however, they can ask photographers to cooperate and form a pool. One representative of the pool will photograph in the restricted area, and then share the pictures with the other photographers.

SUBPOENAS FOR NEGATIVES

A reporter for the *Louisville* (Ky.) *Courier-Journal* wrote a story about making hashish from marijuana. The article included a photograph of a pair of hands working over a laboratory table with the caption identifying the substance in the photo as hashish. After the article and photograph were published, the reporter was subpoenaed to appear before a grand jury and ordered to testify about whose hands had appeared in the photograph. The reporter claimed that both the First Amendment of the U.S. Constitution and a state law protected his confidential source of information. The U.S. Supreme Court said the reporter had witnessed a crime and that the sources did not receive special protection (*Branzburg v. Hayes*).

While a number of states have laws that, to some extent, shield reporters and photographers from courts subpoenaing negatives and notes, each state's laws are different. Unfortunately, the federal government has no shield statute that protects journalist/source confidentiality. And, existing state laws provide only limited protection, especially when the photojournalist witnesses a crime. As the Supreme Court ruled in the marijuana/hashish case, "The crimes of news sources are no less reprehensible and threatening to the public interest when witnessed by a reporter than when they are not."

A subpoena for negatives and prints, surprisingly, is the number one legal problem faced by news photographers, according to a survey of NPPA members by Michael Sherer of the University of Nebraska at Omaha. He found that 25 percent of the survey respondents had been subpoenaed for photographic materials in incidents similar to one faced by Richard Schultz after he photographed a street riot. Sherer recommends

Press credentials provide identification but do not supply any special legal rights.
(Wide World Photos.)

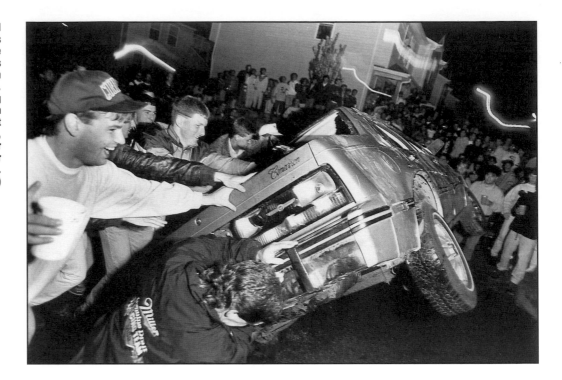

not complying with a subpoena without first consulting with a lawyer and your editor. Finally, he cautions against destroying photographs sought by a subpoena. Doing so, he points out, can result in a citation for contempt of court.

In the end, photographer Schultz did turn over his negatives because he feared a ruling against him would set a precedent in his state.

COPYRIGHT: WHO OWNS THE PICTURE?
■ WHEN THE EMPLOYER OWNS THE PHOTOS

When you are an employee, the copyright for your photos is owned by your employer. The employer holds the rights to the pictures and can reprint or resell the photos. Protecting those rights is the employer's concern. Usually the entire newspaper or magazine is copyrighted, including all material contained in each issue. For your company to own your work, you must be a full-time employee, and your employer must pay benefits as well as give you specific assignments. If you fit this definition of full-time employee, you have a "work-for-hire" arrangement with your employer.

You may, however, form other specific contractual arrangements with your employer. For example, when a company hires you for a staff position, you can agree to take the job with the stipulation that you own your negatives and transparencies, along with the rights to sell the photos after the company has published the originals.

In fact, you can negotiate any contract you like with your employer as long as you arrange the details before you sign on the dotted line.

The right to sell pictures, which you took originally for your employer, to other outlets differs among companies. Some organizations keep the negatives and prints permanently. When an outlet sells a picture to another organization, they retain the profits but usually give the photographer a credit line. Others give the photographer a percentage of the profits from any resales. Some give the negatives to the photographer after a fixed period of time; others let the photographer retain the negatives and prints immediately after publishing the photos the first time. As a freelancer, if you accept an assignment and agree in writing to a "work-for-hire" contract, your employer can reuse or resell the photos without your permission.

■ WHEN YOU RETAIN THE COPYRIGHT

If you are not a full-time employee, however, and have not signed a "work-for-hire" agreement, the company does not own the copyright to your photos. Unless you make a special agreement, you retain the copyright. When you accept an assignment from a newspaper, magazine, a CD-ROM manufacturer, or any kind of company, you are not an employee of that organization. When you turn over your photos to the assigning editor, you are granting one-time rights. The pictures can be published or used only once. Any other use the company wants to make of the photos is up to you—and all slides, negatives, and prints should be returned to you.

If you take pictures on your own without an assignment, you own the negatives and the copyright. When you sell a picture that was shot on your own time with your own film, you can form several arrangements with the organization buying the picture—as long as you form the agreement at the time of the sale. You can sell one-time rights. After the photo appears, you can resell the picture to another outlet.

In a second type of arrangement, you can sell the picture along with exclusive rights to the picture for a specified period of time. In a third type of agreement, for a lot more money, hopefully, you can sell your copyright. This means that only the agency or publication has the right to distribute and sell the photo. You no longer have that right.

Remember, if you formed no specific agreements when you sold the picture, you automatically retain your copyright. The agency or publication has first rights, but you can resell the photo to other outlets later.

■ COPYRIGHTING YOUR OWN PHOTOS

If you don't work for a paper or are not on a magazine assignment, how do you protect yourself from someone reprinting your photos and not giving you credit or paying you? How do you prove the printed photo is yours if it does not carry your credit line?

To protect your rights, put your copyright notice on the back of each print with either of the following notations: ©, or the word "Copyright," with your name and the date. Although not required, it is a fairly common practice to include a statement that reflects the concept of "all rights reserved" or "permission required for use."

After you've put the copyright notice on the back of the print, you can immediately register the print with the U.S. Copyright Office in Washington, D.C., by filling out a form, sending two copies of the print, and paying a fee, or, after the photo is published, by sending two sheets from the publication issue and paying a fee. But you do not have to register the print with the Copyright Office immediately, as long as you mark the photo with a copyright notation.

In fact, you never have to register the photo with the Copyright Office unless someone prints your picture without paying you, and you want to sue. Registration of the copyright is not necessary to maintain your rights, only to defend against infringement of them.

If you feel that someone is using your pictures in a manner that constitutes infringement, you must register your work as a prerequisite to filing an infringement suit. The advantage to registering your material as

close to the original publication date as possible lies in the fact that the type of damages you can collect is tied to the registration date. For infringement prior to the registration date, the law allows only the award of actual damages and an injunction barring further infringement. However, for proven infringement after registration date, the law allows for the assessment of additional statutory damages and legal fees. Regardless of whether you decide on immediate or delayed registration, remember that registration must occur within five years of original publication and no suit may be filed and no damages collected without registration.

■ RESPECTING THE COPYRIGHTS OF OTHERS

Finally, the ease of scanning images and incorporating them into photo illustrations makes it easy to forget that some other photographer or artist enjoys the same copyright protection that you do. Remember not to employ "found" images from newspapers, magazines, or the Internet without obtaining express permission to do so. ■

Law References

Barber v. *Time*, 1 Med. L. Rep. 1779 or 159 S.W. 2d 291 (Mo. 1942).

Branzburg v. *Hayes*, 408 U.S. 665 (1972).

Burton v. Crowell Publishing Co., 81 Fed. 154 (2d Cir. 1936).

Chandler v. *Florida*, 449 U.S. 560 (1981).

Daily Times Democrat v. *Graham*, 276 Ala. 380 162S. 2d 474 (1964).

Dietemann v. *Time*, 449 F. 2d 245.

Estes v. *Texas*, 381 U.S. 532, 536.

Florida Publishing Co. v. Fletcher, 340 So. 2d 914.

Galella v. *Onassis*, 487 F. 2d 986.

Le Mistral v. *Columbia Broadcasting System*, N.Y. Sup. Ct., N.Y. L.J. 6/7/76.

Leverton v. Curtis Publishing Co., 192 F. 2d 974 (3d Cir. 1951).

Lloyd Corp. Ltd. v. Tanner, 407 U.S. 551, 92 S. Ct. 2219, 33 L. Ed. 2d 131 (1972).

People v. *Berliner*, 3 Med. L. Rep. 1942.

People v. *Zamora*, 361 So. 2d 776.

Raible v. Newsweek, Inc., 341 F. Supp. 804 (1972).

Sbyszko v. *New York American*, 1930: 239 NYS, 411.

Tawa Ayeni v. CBS Inc., 848 F. Supp. 362 (E.D. N.Y. 1994).

United States of America v. Anthony Sanusi, et al., 813 F. Supp. 149 (E.D. N.Y. 1992).

Author's note

Laws differ from state to state. States pass new laws and drop old ones as courts set precedents. These laws and precedents are fairly clear about what is restricted, but they are usually unclear about what is permissible. Therefore, no chapter on photojournalism law is totally comprehensive or definitive. This chapter should be read as a guide to your rights as a photojournalist. For more specific information about the laws in your state, check with a media specialist from your local bar association.

Ethics

Photojournalism as a profession imposes a set of responsibilities. Some are fairly routine and fall neatly into the "daily duties" category: get to the scene, frame and focus the shot, collect the caption info, and so forth.

Beyond—or perhaps beneath—these functional tasks lie broader ethical considerations. And, confronting these issues is often more challenging than the assignment itself. At times, these ethical issues pit the photographer's professional duties against his or her own conscience, that internal barometer that guides behavior and

To protest the South Vietnamese government in 1963, a monk set himself afire after notifying the news media. Should the photographer have tried to stop the monk from committing suicide? Should American newspers have run the picture? (Photo by Malcolm Browne, Wide World Photos.)

ultimately maintains social order. Photographers may, in the course of completing their assignments, be forced to choose between how they might act as individual citizens and how they feel they should act as visual journalists.

This dilemma—personal choice versus professional responsibility—is certainly not unique to photojournalism. Consider, for example, the plight of the public defender charged to represent a rapist who he knows is guilty. Or the doctor who has the resources and training to artificially prolong the life of a suffering patient. In these examples, the Constitution and the Hippocratic oath, respectively, are compelling codes, but what about the individual rights of the attorney? Or the private conscience of the physician?

Now consider the less dire but still clouded situation of a photographer shooting a story about suburban high schools. While scanning a clattering lunchroom scene, the photographer spots a trio of students exchanging twenty-dollar bills for bags of white powder.

Does the photographer, acting as a genuinely concerned citizen, try to stop or at least to disrupt the deal? Does he or she report the incident to the principal and offer a description of the players? Or, does the photographer take the picture and publish it?

Almost every day, photojournalists face decisions of morality—ranging from removing a distracting item from a photograph to taking a gruesome picture at a murder site.

But a looming deadline or the logistical challenge of a six-site assignment sheet can pressure the photographer into making snap judgments about even the most morally delicate situations.

Thus, thinking about issues ahead of time may allow the photojournalist to avoid a crisis on the scene or regret after a picture has been published.

Photojournalists use several arguments to explain their decisions to shoot or print controversial pictures. One argument, which sometimes fails to distinguish between practices and standards, relies on the familiar "Other Guy" argument: "I did it because that's the way other photojournalists do it."

These photographers are comparing their actions with a perceived industry "standard." Whether the action is inherently right or wrong is irrelevant to their argument: "This is the way everyone does it." While such a decision-making strategy might reflect professional practices, it does not create a standard grounded in the norms of ethical decision-making.

■ FOUNDATIONS OF ETHICAL DECISION-MAKING

Many photographers, whether they realize it or not, turn to an established ethical framework to try to guide their decisions.

Utilitarian
That framework includes the "utilitarian" principle as defined by ethicists. Here the overriding consideration is "the greatest good for the greatest number of people."

The utilitarian position recognizes that photojournalism provides information critical to a democratic society. Photography might show the horrors of war, the tragedy of an accident, or the hardship of poverty. Therefore, it is right to take and publish pictures. Without information, in general, and pictures, specifically, voters cannot make informed decisions. Seeing accident pictures, for example, might cause voters to pass laws requiring air bags in every car.

Absolutist
However, the utilitarian principle of "the greatest good . . ." bumps up against a competing ethical principle that says, "Individuals have certain rights . . . ," among them, the right to privacy. These rights are absolute and inviolable regardless of the benefits to society, says this principle.

Taking a picture of the distraught parents of a drowned child and then publishing it might cause others to be more cautious, but invading the privacy of their grief—regardless of the benefits—is not acceptable, according to the absolute rights argument.

The Golden Rule
Another of the ethical cornerstones is the Judeo-Christian rule, "Do unto others as you would have them do unto you." This rule, too, sometimes conflicts both with professional standards and with actions that might benefit a democratic society in need of information.

In the last example, if you put yourself in the place of the grieving parent, you might not want your picture taken. On the other hand, if you are trying to save children from drowning in the future and think that running the picture might caution parents or affect funding for extra lifeguards, you might run the photo, anyway.

Without providing a behavioral prescription for the photographer, this chapter will lay out some of the ethical

The young boy in the body bag had just drowned. His parents and siblings were grief-stricken. Might running the picture in the paper help prevent future drownings?
(Photo by John Harte, Bakersfield, Calif.)

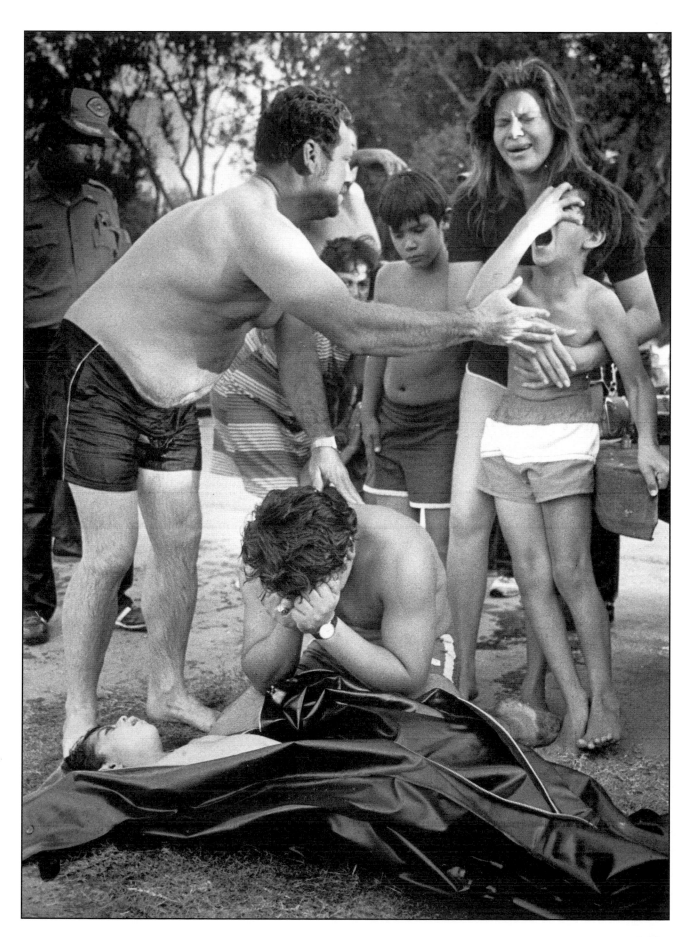

dilemmas faced by the professional photo-journalist and the picture editor. Rather than deal with cases of obvious fraud, fakery, and patent sensationalism, the chapter tackles the gray area between right and wrong—the zone that troubles photographers on an almost daily basis.

SET UP OR JUST CLEAN UP?

I once saw the well-known photo editor of a national magazine—and one of the most respected elders in the business—remove a Coke® bottle to improve the scene before he took a picture. While removing a pop bottle is a fairly trivial act, the incident does illustrate a basic ethical question: when can the photographer alter the scene without altering the message and creating an untruth? When does a comment become a stage direction? And, if some set-up is permissible, when does "some" become too much?

Would it be wrong to stage-manage a picture like this? Do readers care? (Photo by George Rizer, the *Boston Globe*.)

■ WHEN DO PROFESSIONALS POSE PICTURES?

In a precedent-setting study in 1961, Walter Wilcox, then-chairman of the Department of Journalism at the University of California, Los Angeles, designed a study to determine the attitudes of readers, photographers, and editors toward staging news pictures. He sent questionnaires to three groups of subjects: general readers, working photographers, and managing editors.

On a three-level scale, each group evaluated sample situations a photographer might face as "definitely unethical," "doubtful," or "not unethical." Here are three sample situations from Wilcox's study:

Murder trial: *A photographer attempts to get a shot of a defendant, but she consistently evades him by shielding her face or ducking behind her escorting warden. The photographer spots another woman who looks like the defendant and by diffusing the light and adjusting the focus, he gets a striking picture, which no one will challenge as being fake.*

Ground-breakers: *A photographer covers a ground-breaking ceremony for a new church. Local dignitaries have already turned the first bit of earth before the photographer arrives. He asks that the ceremony be repeated. The dignitaries cooperate, and he gets his picture.*

Cricket plague: *A plague of crickets is devastating the hinterland. A photographer goes out to cover the story, but he finds the crickets are too far apart and too small to be recognizable in a photograph. He thinks he could get a better picture if the crickets were shown in a mass, and, to that end, he builds a device that brings crickets through the*

narrow neck of a chute. He gets his shot of closely massed crickets on the march.

Wilcox found that the general public, managing editors, and working photographers agreed to a remarkable extent on what was ethical and what was not. In the survey, 92 percent of the public, 93 percent of the photographers, and 99 percent of the editors said the court photographer was wrong to photograph one person and claim it is another, even if the two look similar.

By comparison, 83 percent of the public, 88 percent of the photographers, and 94 percent of the managing editors said it was not unethical to re-stage the ground-breaking ceremony.

Thus it seems that these three groups operate within the same ethical framework that allows "set-up" pictures but rules out clearly faked photos.

The third scenario, however, in which the photographer collected and choreographed the crickets, sparked disagreement within each of the three groups. The general readers were almost evenly divided along the three-point ethics scale: 29 percent considered the photographer's actions "definitely unethical," 39 percent considered it "doubtful," and the remaining 32 percent considered it "not unethical." Managing editors were similarly split between definitely unethical (23 percent), doubtful (34 percent), and not unethical (44 percent).

Photographers, however, who probably have faced similar problems, were much more likely to consider amassing the crickets part of a photojournalist's routine job. Only seven percent of the photographers polled felt the photographer in the example was definitely unethical; 30 percent considered his behavior doubtful; but a whopping 63 percent said that the cricket photographer was not wrong. One could assume that two-thirds of the photographers polled would have rigged the shot if faced with the same situation.

In a 1987 study for the National Press Photographers Association (NPPA), Ben Brink found that re-creating a situation was acceptable to more than a third of the professional photographers he surveyed. However, staging a scene from scratch was acceptable to only 2 percent of the working pros.

The staging-from-scratch vignette: *A photographer is assigned to cover the aftermath of a big storm. She notices a phone booth turned over in about two feet of water. She asks a child riding a bike in the water next to the phone booth to pick up the phone and pretend to make a call. The photographer hands in the photo without telling the editor it was a set-up photo.*

Only 2 percent of the photojournalists responded that this situation was acceptable. On the other hand, 91 percent said they would definitely not stage this picture without telling their editors.

The re-creation scenario in the NPPA study produced a different result, however. *A photographer is doing a picture page on a visiting nurse in a rural farming community. The one element she lacks to tell the story is a shot of the nurse walking across the field to the farm house. The photographer has seen her walk across the field before, but she's never been at the right place at the right time to get the shot, so she asks the nurse to meet her at the house and walk across the field just as she normally would do. She has the nurse repeat the scene a couple of times to make sure she gets just the right shot.*

The survey results, based on the responses of 116 professional photographers, indicated that 38 percent would re-create the scene. On the other hand, 28 percent of the respondents were not sure how they would handle the situation. Another 34 percent indicated that they definitely would not have the visiting nurse walk across the field just for the camera.

Changing Values

In fact, photojournalists' ethics are changing. In 1961, Wilcox found that none of the pros he surveyed were bothered by repeating a ground-breaking ceremony for the camera. Twenty-six years later, Brink, in the NPPA survey quoted above, found that a third of the photographers he sampled would not repeat or re-create a picture. While the two vignettes, the repeated ceremony and the nurse crossing the field for the camera, are not identical, the radical difference in photographers' responses over time does suggest a shift in photojournalistic ethics. Re-creations of picture situations that were acceptable to every pro in the 1960s were anathema to a large segment of the photojournalistic community by the 1980s.

Whose Responsibility?

Surprisingly, many photographers felt that telling their editors absolved them of ethical responsibility in the Brinker study.

In a follow-up question to the staging vignette, the study showed that 33 percent of the photographers no longer found staging the picture unethical if they explained the facts to their editors. Telling a higher authority seemed to eliminate feelings of responsibility on the part of these pros.

Can photographers avoid ethical decisions this easily?

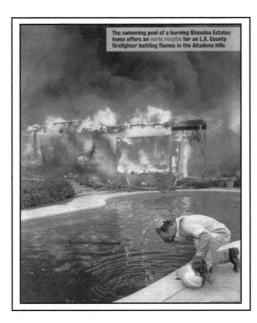

The swimming pool of a burning Kinneloa Estates home offers an eerie respite for an L.A. County firefighter battling flames in the Altadena hills

DO READERS BELIEVE THEIR EYES?

Below a headline in the *New York Post* that read NUKE LEAK AT INDIAN POINT, a picture ran showing a woman holding a child covered by a blanket. The mother appeared to be trying to protect her child from radiation from the atomic energy plant. The picture was published not only by the *Post* but also by *Time*, and was carried by the Associated Press and United Press International.

When several newspapers in the northwest printed the photograph, the editor and publisher of the *Centralia* (Wash.) *Chronicle*, Jack Britten, attacked the picture's integrity in an editorial.

"Come on," the editorial demanded. "Who do they think they're conning? Any discerning reader could quickly see that the photo is very likely staged . . . the photo is an obvious put-on, a misrepresentation of the actual situation, and the editors should have known it. If they didn't know it, they shouldn't be editors."

In fact, photographer Martha Cooper and *Post* reporter Deborah Orin actually found the woman as she was leaving her house, her baby covered with a blanket. Orin interviewed the woman, who had been worried about her year-old daughter's exposure to radiation. She had been ready to climb into her car and leave the area when the *Post* team found her. Cooper took the pictures during the interview. In a follow-up story in the *Washington Star*, columnist Mary McGrory confirmed the photo's authenticity.

If a seasoned newspaper editor questioned the photo's truthfulness, how often do readers wonder whether what they see in newspapers, magazines, and computer screens really

Mike Meadows, of the *Los Angles Times,* was covering a major wild fire sweeping southern California. His picture of a fireman cooling himself off from the water in a pool ran not only in the *Times* but also nationally.

Prior to submitting the photograph for a contest, however, the newspaper's editors contacted the fireman, who said he had been asked by the photographer to go over by the pool and splash water on his head. The photographer responded that "I may have been guilty of saying 'this would make a nice shot,' but I did not directly ask him to do that."

What Meadows did not understand was that even a suggestion to a subject in a news situation is a form of interference—and thus out of place on the continuum of control. The unfortunate photographer was suspended without pay, booted from editorial into administration, and his picture withdrawn from competition. He was lucky compared to another photographer (see pages 300–301) who didn't change with the times. (Reproduced from *Newsweek*.)

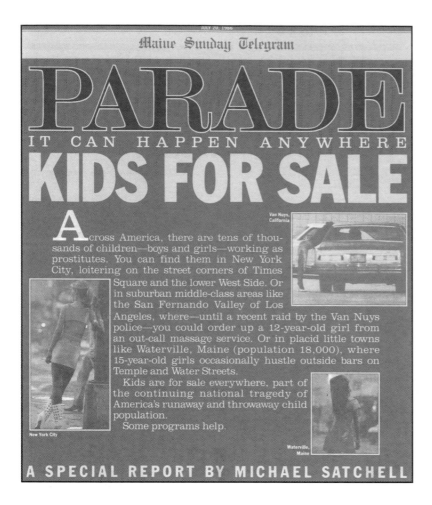

On this cover, two of the girls are models. One is not. How would the reader know which is candid and which is set up? Would a reader have known what "photo illustration" means had the disclaimer been included?
(©Parade.)

took place? After all, people watch professional photographers pose pictures at class reunions, bar mitzvahs, and weddings. While such photographers are not photojournalists, how many readers make the distinction?

■ WHEN FACTS CONFLICT WITH PICTURES

Just how widespread is disbelief in photojournalism? No one knows for sure, but the disbelief extends at least to Waterville, Maine.

"Kids for sale," shouted the July 20, 1986, cover of *Parade* magazine. "It can happen anywhere."

Three small color photos of unidentified and unidentifiable, sultry adolescent "girls of the street" dotted the text-dominated black cover, which announced a "special report" on child prostitution.

Anywhere, according to the picture identification, included New York City, Van Nuys, Calif., and "placid little towns like Waterville, Maine."

Fortunately, a local Maine newspaper challenged the story. Reporters discovered that the Attorney General's office in the Maine jurisdiction had prosecuted only two cases of prostitution in Waterville, none

involving teen-agers—and that the young Waterville "prostitute" in the photo was actually a model.

When freelance photographer Dean Abramson was unable to find an actual street-walking teen in Waterville, his *Parade* magazine editors told him to hire a model. Abramson complied and eventually snapped the posed picture.

Although *Parade* editors initially denied the subterfuge, later they recanted, saying that an explanatory line of type had been omitted. In a follow-up article for *News Photographer* magazine, they further rationalized the situation by telling writer Betsy Brill that they routinely used models for stories involving minors.

In interviews with other photographers on the project, however, Brill discovered that, despite editors' claims, only two of the three pictures had been set up with models for the *Parade* cover. A third photographer captured an actual candid moment.

Camera 5 freelancer Neal Preston verified that his assignment from *Parade* had been to find and photograph actual teen-age prostitutes (not models). He had done so in Van Nuys, California.

"I could have saved a lot of time and film if I had hired a model," he told Brill, when he learned the other photos had been set up. "I'm proud that my picture was the one that was real."

Award-winning photojournalist Eddie Adams, who photographed the New York City set-up, told Brill that concern over the staged photos was "a lot of bullshit." He said that the hiring of models for stories involving children is done "all the time"—not just by him, he said, and not just by *Parade*, but by all magazines, especially for cover stories.

"There's a difference," Adams said, "between an illustration and a straight picture." (See Chapter 8, "Illustrations.") Yet, he admitted, the reader has no way of knowing the difference without words.

Adams, however, begged the ethical question and relied on the familiar "everybody does it" argument.

The question is not "Do photographers hire models regularly when taking pictures of children?" The real question is: "Should photographers use models—and pose them so that they look as though they're in real situations?"

Whether you're a magazine reader in Waterville or a newspaper reader in New York City, your belief in pictures drops when you discover that some of the images you are seeing are figments in the imaginations of photo editors and not records of reality.

CONTINUUM OF CONTROL

Between moving an obstructing Coke® bottle and hiring a model to impersonate a teen-age hooker lies a large, gray ethical chasm. This gray zone, with its myriad shadows and shadings, can challenge even the most clear-sighted photographer. Are all situations alike?

Do the same rules apply to features, portraits, and illustrations, as well as to hard news? Far from being a fixed commodity, the photographer's level of control is variable, logistically and ethically. A photojournalist's weekly assignment sheet is likely to represent a continuum of control—from strictly hands-off to complete manipulation. Photojournalists cover subjects ranging from a war in the Middle East to a fashion shoot in midtown. Like the fashion shoot, some pictures require complete control. Other situations, like accidents or arrests downtown, require the hands-off, fly-on-the-wall approach.

Any time you take pictures, you are affecting the scene to some degree. According to noted physicist Werner Heisenberg, observation itself alters the object being observed. This principle applies to photography as surely as it does to the subatomic world.

For instance, whether a subject consciously thinks about the photographer or not, that person's behavior changes in the presence of a camera. Some subjects exaggerate their behavior; others shy away from the camera. Even thinking a camera might be present can alter some people's behavior.

Even though photographers and their cameras have some influence on the scene they are photographing, the question the working pro must ask is: "When should the photojournalist remain an observer, removed as much as possible from the scene? When should the photographer intervene?"

- **Hidden cameras.** On the extreme end of the continuum, consider the security camera at the First National Bank. The camera automatically snaps a picture at regular intervals, regardless of who is standing at the teller window. The bank camera, which exercises no control over the

(Photo courtesy Bank Security.)

subject, represents the farthest end of the control continuum—no control at all. Despite its passivity, however, even the bank camera alters the scene being observed: most criminals would take different precautions if robbing a bank under constant photographic surveillance.

- **Sports photography.** Next, consider the sports photographer shooting action along the sidelines of a track event. A hurdler races down the track. Even if she wanted to, the sports photographer could have little influence on the athlete. She would not tell the runner to run to the right for a better picture. The sports photographer has virtually no control over the subject but does select the moment to release the camera's shutter.

- **Hard news.** Elsewhere along the continuum you will find the news photographer covering a riot. Most photographers would hesitate to direct a demonstrator or tell a policeman to stand aside to improve a photograph's composition. The photographer could initiate control but refrains in a true hard-news situation.

- **Features.** When shooting the feature picture, the continuum becomes slippery. Here, photographers disagree about when to intervene and when to merely observe. The action is touching, but the light is not great. If you asked the subject to move over a few feet, you could get perfect back-lighting. Would that be acceptable? Different photographers have determined different points where they will draw the control line when faced with a feature assignment. Some photojournalists would not hesitate to ask the subject to move. Other shooters would never consider disturbing the moment, even if leaving the situation untouched meant that they would not get a superb picture.

- **Portraits.** Taking portraits usually requires some direction on the part of the photographer. If the assignment is to take pictures of the president of the local university, the photographer usually must tell her where to sit and what to do with her hands. The photographer might ask the president to look directly at the camera. This way the reader will know that the administrator was aware of the photographer and won't think the picture is a candid photo. An unwritten but probably accurate rule holds that, if the subject is looking straight at the photographer (i.e.,

(Photo by Michael Meinhardt, UPI.)

(Photo by Charlie Fellenbaum, the *Hemet* (Calif.) *News*.)

(Photo by Juanito Holandez, *Long Beach* (Calif.) *Press-Telegram*.)

(Photo by Pat Crowe, *Wilmington* (Dela.) *News Journal*.)

(Photo by Bob Farley, *Birmingham (Ala.) Post-Herald.*)

the reader), the subject is aware of the camera.

- **Photo Illustrations.** Now let's analyze the extreme, full-control end of the continuum: photo illustrations. Photojournalists manufacture every aspect of an illustration—including editorial concept photos, food photos, studio and location fashion shoots. The photojournalist arranges the props, perhaps builds the set, and hires and even dresses the models. In fact, the only real element in the picture is the film. The viewer has no illusions about the photo or the photographer's role. If the photographer has been careful, the created photo cannot be mistaken for real. Through the use of exaggerated size, seamless backgrounds, and other visual devices, the photojournalist can assure the reader that the picture is constructed and not a slice of real life. (See Chapter 8, "Illustrations.") With photo illustrations, the photographer exercises complete control.

■ CONCLUSION

For photojournalists, the issue of posing often centers on a photographer's role as reporter versus his or her role as an artist with a camera, says Sheila Reaves in her article "Re-examining the Ethics of Photographic Posing: Insights from the Rank-and-File Members of ASMP (American Society of Media Photographers)." Editors in particular and the profession in general convey a double message, she observes. The message reads "produce both a truthful picture and one that demonstrates artistic merit." Observe an event—*and* be inventive and creative. Sometimes those two distinct roles come into conflict.

The key to making an ethical decision is to know which professional role is required in a given situation. If the assignment from the food editor requests a photo illustrating hot dogs as the quintessential American food for the Fourth of July, the photographer's creative juices need to flow. With the studio's seamless backdrop as a canvas, the photographer becomes an artist bringing together hot dogs, American flags, and sparklers into a pleasing and story-telling composition. On the other hand, if the scanner radio broadcasts that a murder/suicide in a college dorm has just occurred, the photographer's purely observational skills need to kick in. No

One Photographer Who Didn't Change With the Times

Not long after the Janet Cooke affair (see page 302, one *St. Petersburg (Fla.) Times* staff photographer selected a spot on the continuum that proved out of sync with changing times. The results were disastrous for him.

The incident began with a routine assignment for 61-year-old Norman Zeisloft, a veteran photographer and past president of his regional NPPA chapter. He had been shooting for the *St. Petersburg Times and Evening Independent* for more than seventeen years.

HELPING ALONG A FEATURE

Zeisloft had been assigned to cover a baseball game between Eckerd and Florida Southern Colleges. "It was quite a nothing event," he recalled for Jim Gordon, who later wrote a comprehensive story about the incident for *News Photographer* magazine.

Spotting three bare-soled fans with their feet up, Zeisloft approached them and said it would be "cute if you had 'Yea Eckerd' written on the bottom of your feet."

They agreed, and Zeisloft pulled out a felt-tip pen and began writing on the soles of one man's feet. Zeisloft found that his pen was dry and the spectator's feet were too dirty to accept writing. Meanwhile, one fan left the stands, washed his feet and reappeared with "Yea, Eckerd" on his soles. Zeisloft took the photo, and it ran two days later in the *Evening Independent.*

"It was just a whimsical thing, just for a little joke," Zeisloft recounted. "It was just a little picture to make people smile rather than an old accident scene."

But nearby was Phil Sheffield, a *Tampa (Fla.) Tribune* photographer since 1974 and a photographer for Miami's Associated Press bureau before that. Almost instinctively, Sheffield said, he snapped one frame as Zeisloft originally applied pen to sole.

Posted as a joke on the bulletin board of the *Tampa Tribune*, the photo eventually found its way to the presinvention should be needed as the police bring out the stretcher and dormmates cry. No studio, no props. No direction. Recording reality will suffice. The photographer's role is to record, not to influence. Of course, the problem lies with assignments that fall between these two extremes.

As they go from assignment to assignment, most working pros find themselves at different points on the continuum of photographic control. Generally, photojournalists find decisions about how to handle the ends of the continuum fairly easy. How the photojournalist approaches a sports event or five-alarm fire is quite different from how that person handles a fashion or portrait assignment. Photojournalists set up some pictures but not others. The question that each photographer must ask is: Where should I be on the continuum of control? At any given time, what part of the continuum should I choose? Which spot along the continuum is appropriate for this assignment?

KEEPING UP WITH SHIFTING STANDARDS

The decision regarding control is a choice based more on a photographer's time in history than on any established guidelines.

Photojournalism has no Bible, no rabbinical college, no Pope to define correct choices. And, while surveys like those by Wilcox and Brink help establish current practices in the field, professional values do not remain fixed in time. Not only are professional standards changing, so also are readers' expectations. Staying abreast of professional standards and evaluating decisions with an eye to the ethical foundations described at the beginning of this chapter should be helpful when faced with difficult moments.

Keep in mind that setting up feature pictures used to be perfectly acceptable to most newspaper photojournalists. In his book *Spot News Photography*, written in the early 1950s, *New York Post* photographer Barney Stein proudly described as a routine photojournalistic activity how he went about setting up feature pictures of a cowboy performing for crippled kids or of a Dalmatian firedog wearing the chief's hat.

John Faber, historian for the National Press Photographers Association (NPPA), told of traveling around the country as Kodak's professional representative, teaching newspaper photographers how to create imaginative feature pictures.

---

ident and editor of the *St. Petersburg Times*—Norm Zeisloft's boss, a judge on the Pulitzer committee that had been caught in the web of Janet Cooke's dishonesty.

STANDARD PROCEDURE OR GROUNDS FOR DISMISSAL?
Zeisloft was fired on his first day back from vacation.

Later, in an administrative appeal hearing over denied unemployment benefits, Zeisloft explained that news photographers often set up pictures about society and club news, recipe contest winners, ribbon-cutting and ground-breaking ceremonies, awards and enterprise features.

He took to the hearing pictures that had won professional contests, some from the old *Life* "Speaking of Pictures" department. Others, he explained, had gone "nationwide via AP and UPI wire services. The pictures had won awards plus applause from editors.

"These pictures were not intended to bamboozle the public or to 'distort' the news. They were shot with good humor and were merely designed to give the reading public a good chuckle. They were harmless and entertaining. That and nothing more," Zeisloft said.

"To me," Zeisloft said, "it seemed like cruel and unusual punishment to be fired after seventeen and a half years of faithful service on the basis of one photo that was designed merely to bring a chuckle to our

readers. There was not one phone call or letter from our reading public in regards to the picture.

"If a cop shot a person he'd get a suspension. Doesn't seventeen and a half years count for anything?" he asked.

A CONTINUUM TEMPERED BY TIME
Unfortunately, Norm Zeisloft had selected a spot on the control continuum that was not professionally acceptable for the time and place he was working. Ten years earlier or at another newspaper or magazine, the set-up feature might have been perfectly accepted by the profession and even by the public. Zeisloft found himself out of register with the current dividing line between acceptable and unacceptable practice on the continuum of control.

Because the place acceptable to fellow professionals and the public on the continuum shifts with time and events, all photojournalists should re-evaluate their own set points. Do theirs coincide with other members of the profession, with editors, and with the public?

Finally, even if a practice is acceptable in the field, the photographer must answer a more difficult question: is the behavior ethically right? Should I do this even if all my peers are doing it? While photographers should be aware of standards in the field, they should also deal with the more basic question of right and wrong.

In his 1961 survey, Wilcox found that no photojournalist objected to restaging a ceremony for a photo. Yet, today, according to the Brink survey, at least a third of the photographers who are NPPA members would object to restaging a situation.

W. Eugene Smith, the famous *Life* magazine photographer, wrote in 1948, "The majority of photographic stories require a certain amount of setting up, rearranging and stage direction to bring pictorial and editorial coherency to the pictures." Smith notes, however, that if the changes become a perversion of the actuality for the sole purpose of making a "more dramatic" or "salable picture," the photographer has indulged a "poetic license."

Howard Chapnick, in his book ***Truth Needs No Ally***, points out that in the 1990s the "changes in camera and film technology have made it a truism that anything we can see we can photograph." He argues that now there is no excuse for the photojournalist to manipulate people in real-life situations.

■ JANET COOKE

What has caused this change in standards for the profession? Many observers point to one incident as the pivot-point for journalists.

In 1981, Janet Cooke, a reporter for the *Washington Post*, won a Pulitzer Prize based on a story she wrote about a 6-year-old drug addict. After the prize was awarded, investigators discovered that the child had never existed. The young addict was a figment of Cooke's imagination—a "composite" of characters and incidents she had come upon in her research. The journalism profession threw up its arms in outrage and began a hard, soul-searching re-examination of its ethical practices. Professional groups sponsored seminars, authors wrote books, and universities initiated classes in journalism ethics. And, the public's view of the press, its practices, and its prizes dropped to a new low.

The outgrowth of this examination was an increased sensitivity, even vigilance, to how the profession performs its work. The profession began to question some of its accepted standards. The spotlight on the Cooke case also heightened sensitivity toward ethical standards within the photojournalism community.

■ MONITORING ETHICAL STANDARDS

For the neophyte photographer or the seasoned pro, the profession does not provide a fixed yardstick, a definitive set of guidelines, or a regular measure of what other photojournalists in the trade are thinking and doing.

In fact, photojournalists disagree among themselves about the correctness of many choices. Craig Hartley, in a national survey of professionals for his thesis on photojournalistic ethics, found that, of nineteen hypothetical problems presented to working pros, almost half the questions resulted in a wide split among respondents. On nine questions, at least a third of the photojournalists did not agree with their other responding colleagues. Clearly photojournalists do not think as a monolithic block when the topic turns to ethics.

Interested photographers can, however, use the trade media and other resources to monitor the thoughts of their fellow journalists and shape their own ethical touchstones. *News Photographer* magazine, the trade publication of the National Press Photographers Association, reports on controversial issues. Read, in particular, the magazine's "Letters to the Editor" column to check the pulse of the working pro. In addition, magazines such as *Columbia Journalism Review*, *American Journalism Review*, and *Photo District News* report on changing professional standards. *Journalism Quarterly* also publishes research on this topic.

In addition to magazines, workshops such as NPPA's Flying Short Course and the organization's on-line computer bulletin board can help provide valid insights into photojournalism's shifting standards.

■ A GENERAL RULE

What if you're not abreast of current standards, and you find yourself in a touchy situation on assignment? You might use this test of your own honesty, originally suggested by Elisabeth Biondi, who has been a photo editor for *Geo*, *Vanity Fair*, and *Stern* magazines. She suggests that photographers test their ethical decisions by considering whether they would feel comfortable writing a note to the reader explaining how the picture was taken. For example, would the photographer mind explaining, "I brought these clothes for the subject to wear, and then I told him to make that crazy face"? If the photographer is willing for the reader to know how the picture was constructed, what props were added, and what direction was given, then, Biondi says, the photo is probably ethically acceptable. However, if the photographer would feel uncomfortable revealing to the reader his or her methods, then the picture likely falls on the unethical side of the line.

COVERING TRAGEDY AND GRIEF

When injuries occur at a car crash, a hotel fire, or a natural disaster, bystanders and relatives often block a camera reporter from taking pictures. Understandably these people are upset. John L. Hulteng, in his book ***The Messenger's Motives***, writes, "Photographers have acquired the reputation of being indifferent to the human suffering they frame in their viewfinders."

While the law gives the photographer the right to take a picture, the law is an institution, not a human being who has just lost a son or daughter.

Using the utilitarian principle of ethical decision-making, on the other hand, photographers have a moral responsibility to their readers to picture the world accurately, showing both its triumphs and its tragedies. A democracy in which citizens must be informed to vote intelligently depends on information. Photos provide information. In the long run, individuals cannot make informed decisions without a balanced and accurate picture of the world. This argument says that people will benefit from seeing both the good and bad, the happy and sad, the joyful and tragic elements that comprise our world.

However, does this case for the "common good" supersede the rights of the grief-stricken individual? Does the photographer have the right—or the obligation—to record

moments of individual loss? These issues are complex, but there is one clear tenet to guide the photographer's behavior in traumatic situations: the photographer has a responsibility not to inflict greater suffering than necessary on survivors of a tragedy. "Than necessary" is obviously a troublesome phrase here, one defining that difficult gray zone. Unfortunately, there is no clear measure of necessity.

In the end, the photographer must balance the harm to an individual subject caught in the jaws of tragedy with the long-range needs of society to see an unvarnished picture of the world.

Pictures of grief personalize the news. Statistics about car accidents, wife beatings, murders, and accidental drownings distance the reader from the event. Seeing a picture of a particular person who was hit by a drunk driver gives the issue a face. No matter how large the numbers, issues remain abstract. From "Thousands die on the road every year" to "Katy Smith was struck by a Honda yesterday and here is what she looked like," photographs transform an otherwise abstract issue into a personal event. The reader is more likely to care about Katy than all the thousands of other people who died last year.

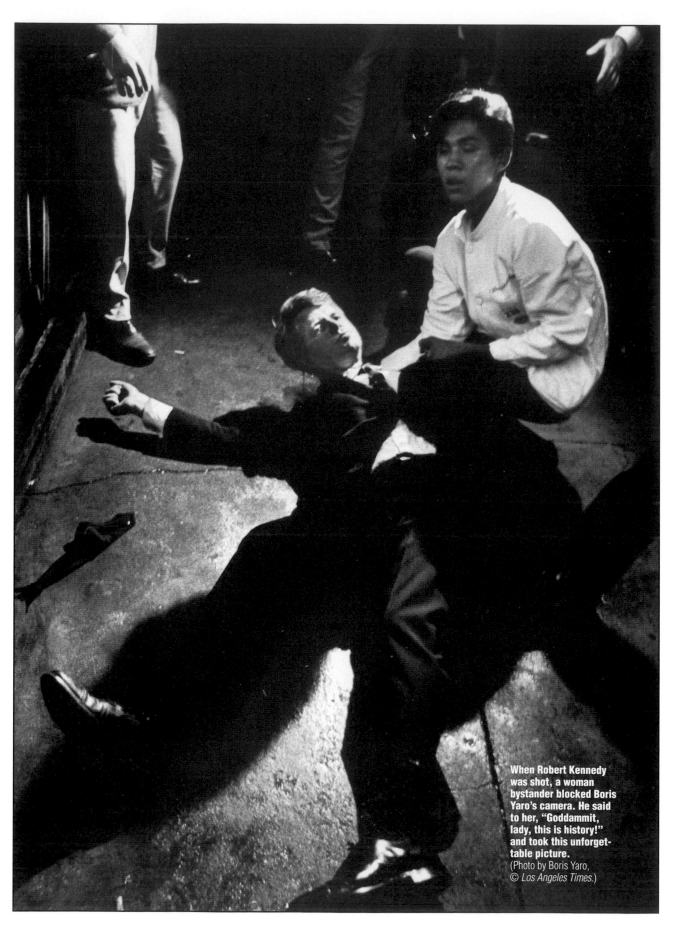

When Robert Kennedy was shot, a woman bystander blocked Boris Yaro's camera. He said to her, "Goddammit, lady, this is history!" and took this unforgettable picture. (Photo by Boris Yaro, © *Los Angeles Times*.)

Pictures can actually help the victim and the family. Some families understand that running the picture of a tragedy may prevent the same thing from happening to others. The published pictures give the family some rationale for a terrible calamity. In his book *Lessons in Death and Life*, Dave LaBelle observes, "Although many cry foul when photographs of grieving subjects are published, often the subjects themselves are helped to deal with their grief." He notes this story: "Two days after the *Albuquerque* (N.M.) *Tribune* published graphic pictures of a burn victim, Sage Volkman, it ran a letter from the girl's parents explaining why they thought the public needed to see the photos. 'We would like you to be aware of her struggle from when she was first burned and almost through death's door to her return to us as a 6-year-old girl with feelings who sees life in terms of Barbie dolls and her Brownie troop. When you come upon her unexpectedly in a store or restaurant, your first reaction may be one of sadness. But if you do run into her, we hope you will see her as we do—as a brave little girl.'" Publication of the pictures helped raise more than $50,000 toward Sage's medical bills.

■ DO ALL TRAGEDIES NEED PHOTO COVERAGE?

If you are familiar with your equipment, you can usually take a few quick, available-light, candid shots nearly unnoticed at any accident scene. Beyond these photos, you must weigh the short-range pain of your presence versus the long-range value of your potential photos—a difficult judgment each photographer must make. Neither photographers at the scene nor editors back at the office are clairvoyant. Neither can look into a crystal ball and predict a picture's effect.

Photojournalists must maintain a belief in the overriding long-range importance of photos and the specific contribution of their particular photo. With emotion-laden events, this balancing act proceeds cautiously and continuously.

Eddie Adams, who won the Pulitzer Prize for his photograph of a Viet Cong suspect being assassinated in the streets of Saigon (see page 316), told me about a photo he didn't take while covering that war:

"On a hilltop in Vietnam, I was pinned down with a Marine company. Machine guns were going off. Dead bodies were lying on either side of me. Rocket fire seemed to be coming from everywhere. I was lying on the ground five feet away from an 18-year-old marine. I saw fear on that kid's face like I had never seen before. I slid my Leica, with

its preset 35mm lens, in front of me. I tried to push the shutter, but I couldn't. I tried twice more, but my finger just would not push the button. Later, I realized that I was just as scared to die as that kid was. I knew my face looked exactly like his, and I would not have wanted my picture seen around the world. I think his and my face said WAR, but I still think I did the right thing by not taking that picture."

Adams chose to invoke the "do unto others . . ." Golden Rule. However, the photographer might also have considered the possible value to society from seeing the censored image. Adams' Pulitzer Prize-winning picture of the Vietnamese colonel executing a suspected Viet Cong did help to change the course of the Vietnam war. In the execution situation, society's greater good was served by photographing the scene.

Adams' hesitation at taking pictures on the hilltop in Vietnam was rare. Most professional photographers don't hesitate to take pictures when faced with a gut-wrenching accident or tragic murder.

In fact, many photographers say that, because the critical moment is fleeting, they shoot instinctively. They point out that you can always decide not to use the picture, but you can't revisit the moment. The consequences of taking someone's picture, the momentary disturbance or embarrassment, is relatively minor. Publishing the picture, which will be seen by friends, colleagues, and strangers, has a different and perhaps longer lasting impact on the subject. Finally, hesitating to take pictures can conflict with the professional role of the photojournalist. In most circumstances, professional standards would support the "shoot now—edit later" approach.

Boris Yaro, a *Los Angeles Times* photographer, had no trouble making the decision to take pictures when he photographed Senator Robert Kennedy's assassination at the Ambassador Hotel. Later he told the story to John Faber, author of *Great News Photos*.

"I was trying to focus in the dark when I heard a loud Bang! Bang! I watched in absolute horror. I thought, 'Oh my God it's happening again! To another Kennedy!' I turned toward the Senator. He was slipping to the floor. I aimed my camera, starting to focus, when someone grabbed my suit coat arm. I looked into the dim light, seeing a woman with a camera around her neck screaming at me. 'Don't take pictures! Don't take pictures! I'm a photographer and I'm not taking pictures!' she said." For a brief instant, Yaro was dumbfounded. Then he told her to let go of him. "I said,

'Goddammit, lady, this is history!'" He took the photographs.

■ SUGGESTIONS FOR PHOTOGRAPHING TRAGIC MOMENTS

In an article for *News Photographer* magazine, Michael D. Sherer collected comments from photographers who had covered tragic events. Here are their guidelines:

- **On conduct.** Be early, stay out of the way, and don't disrupt what's going on. Be sensitive to your subjects and the situation. Be compassionate. Do not badger or chase subjects to the point of annoyance. "How would I feel if I were the person being photographed?" asked Jim Gehrz, of the *Worthington* (Minn.) *Daily Globe*, invoking the Golden Rule.
- **On equipment.** In sensitive situations, carry as little gear as possible, leave the motor drive behind, and use the longest lens possible. Don't become a spectacle.
- **On selectivity.** Pick your shots carefully— look for angles and subjects that will not offend subjects' and readers' sensitivities.
- **On dress.** Wear "appropriate" clothing. "Dress is an important part of the way the public perceives us and in their acceptance of us in times of stress," said Mark Hertzberg, of the *Racine* (Wisc.) *Journal Times*. "I think many of us can dress better day-to-day without having to wear a three-piece suit."
- **Afterward.** Dave Nuss of the *Salem* (Ore.) *Statesman-Journal* suggests, "Consider contacting the subjects sometime after publication to discuss the reason for, and reaction to, publishing the image."

■ RESPECTING PRIVACY AT FUNERALS

Funerals are sad, stressful, and emotionally draining. They provide a context for grief and a forum for sharing sorrow among family and friends—not photographers. As well, sometimes they are also newsworthy.

The decision to cover a funeral generally rests with an editor, but once that decision is made, it's the photographer's responsibility to complete the assignment. And, it's the photographer, not the editor in the office, whom mourners notice, resent, and berate.

Photographers and the public have widely differing views about professional ethical conduct at these ceremonies. Craig Hartley surveyed NPPA members and citizens of Austin, Texas. He wanted to find out how each group viewed a number of ethical situations, one of which involved the funeral of a slain police officer, an event that an uninvited photographer attends and photographs even after being asked to leave.

Hartley found that, while 63 percent of the news photographers he surveyed found the photojournalist's behavior at the funeral "ethical," 85 percent of the public found the behavior "unethical." Readers, who vehemently denounced the actions of the photojournalist at the funeral, did not perceive the picture's value as meriting this intrusion into the private ceremony.

With such reader reactions in mind, Mary Lou Foy of the *Washington Post* offers suggestions for funerals:

- **Make arrangements ahead.** When you get a funeral assignment, contact the family or close friends to let them know you are coming. Express your sincere sympathy by simply saying you are sorry about their loss. If you are unable to speak with a family member or friend, the funeral director is your next best choice.
- **Dress soberly.** Photographers must dress as if attending the funeral. This means a suit or dress in dark color.
- **Be early.** Then you will be situated and are a part of the scene when everyone else arrives.
- **Limit the motor drive.** Don't unload with your motor drive. Even if the family has said okay, you'll offend those who are also grieving and who don't know you have family permission.
- **No lights, please.** Avoid using strobes. Nothing is more offensive than a strobe flashing in the face of a crying person during a funeral service.

PROFESSIONAL VS. GOOD SAMARITAN

When should the photographer act as a professional photojournalist, and when should the cameraperson act as a responsible citizen? What happens when the roles conflict? Consider these scenarios:

You are driving along the street and see a man running out of a pawn shop carrying a television set under his arm with the proprietor in hot pursuit. Do you try to stop the thief with the intent of holding him for the police, or do you take a picture of the whole scene as the criminal escapes around the corner?

Later in the day, you see an accident by the side of the road. A child, stuck behind the car's dashboard, cries inconsolably. Do you take the little girl's picture, or sit and comfort her?

A terrorist group has agreed to let you photograph their activities. They take you on a secret mission to plant a bomb. Do you take their pictures or try to stop them from activating the explosive? How would you handle the situation if you were photographing a similar raid, only this time the group was a U.S. army unit, not a terrorist gang?

The argument for professionalism often parallels the utilitarian principle of ethics. The photojournalist has a role in society just as a doctor or lawyer has. That role is to inform the public. Information allows this country's citizens to make intelligent decisions. By actually seeing what is going on—including a thief in the act of stealing a television set, terrorists planting a bomb, a person committing suicide, or even the agony of a child caught in a car wreck—citizens can perhaps learn enough—or be moved enough—to prevent such things from happening to others in the future. Information can lead to changes in public policy, laws, funding, or perhaps just improved behavior.

A photographer's job is to record the news, not to prevent it or to change it. Like an anthropologist observing a foreign culture, the photojournalist should look, record, but not disturb what is going on.

The Good Samaritan argument, on the other hand, is absolutist: a photojournalist is, first and foremost, a human being. A photojournalist's primary responsibility is to the human being needing immediate help. Journalism comes second. No one can measure the ultimate good a photo will do later, but you can see the immediate needs of the present.

Joe Fudge, of the *Newport News* (Va.) *Daily Press/Times Herald,* had no problem making the ethical choice between being Good Samaritan and professional photojournalist when he saw smoke pouring from the third floor of a house.

First asking the newspaper office via two-way radio to notify the fire department, Fudge then charged into the burning house and alerted residents that their attic was ablaze. "I went into the house and found three people sitting around eating. They didn't know that a fire was burning off the top of their house. The woman said, 'Oh, my God, my husband is asleep in the third-floor bedroom.' By this time, the flames were coming through the ceiling of the third floor. We went up and woke him up. Then all of us escaped."

When Fudge jumped out of his car after spotting the fire, he did not take in his cameras. Later, he returned for his equipment for a picture of the dad saving the family dog. Rather than photograph the burning house, Fudge decided to save lives first.

■ SUICIDE: A SPECIAL CASE?

When he worked for the *Oregon Journal*, photographer William T. Murphy, Jr., faced the dilemma of taking pictures or trying to help a woman stop her husband from killing himself. He tried to do both—by taking five shots as he attempted to talk the man out of jumping one hundred feet into the Columbia River and as he yelled at another motorist on the bridge to go for help. But the man soon struggled free from the desperate grip of his wife and jumped to his death in the swirling river.

Few readers sympathized with Murphy's ethical dilemma. According to "Ethics of Compassion," an article by Gene Goodwin in *Quill* magazine, many readers complained about Murphy's photo of the suicide, which went out over the UPI wires.

"Don't the ethics of journalism insist that preservation of human life comes first, news second?" asked a reader from Philadelphia. A New York reader wrote, "He let a man die for the sake of good photograph."

Murphy replied to the criticism: "I don't know what I could have done differently. I am a photographer, and I did what I have been trained to do. I did all I could."

A Suicide for the Media

At a press conference called by Bud Dwyer, Pennsylvania's state treasurer, he proclaimed himself innocent of a kickback scandal and then killed himself. No photographer could have stopped him. Should these pictures have been published?
(Photos by Gary Miller (LEFT) and Paul Vathis (BELOW), Associated Press.)

Suicide as a Form of Protest

No one attempted to stop a Buddhist monk who set himself on fire protesting the 1963 Diem government in South Vietnam. The shocking picture showed readers dramatically and convincingly how serious the country's problems were. The monk used his death as the ultimate form of political expression. (See page 292.) Peter Arnett of the Associated Press, who reported the event, said that he could have prevented that immolation by rushing at the monk and kicking the gasoline away. "As a human being I wanted to; as a reporter I couldn't."

One person's private turmoil resulted in a national issue when Pennsylvania State Treasurer R. Budd Dwyer called a press conference just hours before he was to be sentenced for his conviction in a $300,000 kickback scandal. Dwyer, 47, was facing up to 55 years in prison. After thirty minutes of proclaiming his innocence to reporters and photographers, Dwyer picked up a large manila envelope and pulled out a long-barrel, blue-black handgun. He placed the gun in his mouth and pulled the trigger.

Could photographers, reporters, or TV camera crews have stopped Dwyer? The consensus was no. Once the gun was out of the envelope, only 15 seconds elapsed before Dwyer shot himself. Also, Dwyer had built a barricade of chairs and tables between himself and the press.

Should photographers have stopped Budd Dwyer if they had the opportunity? Was Dwyer making a political statement?

In any case, are the pictures so upsetting to the public that they cause the reader to look away rather than consider the underlying issues?

At least on the front page, according to one study, almost every editor surveyed (95%) thought that the photo of Dwyer's body slumping after he fired the shot was too shocking for their readers. Robert Kochersberger surveyed newspapers in three states to see how they used the photos. He found that most newspapers (66%) used the photo of Dwyer holding out his hand, but exercised restraint by not publishing either the photo of the pistol in Dwyer's mouth or the one of his body slumping to the floor.

Suicide as Mental Illness

Beyond the political question of suicide as a form of expression, photographing suicide raises the issue of documenting severe mental problems.

In Wichita Falls, Texas, a former mental patient committed suicide with a 12-gauge shotgun. In this situation, the photographer had no chance to stop the man. Don James, the executive editor of the normally conservative *Record News*, explained the picture to readers by saying, "We felt the story leading up to the suicide illustrated a shocking failure on the part of our system."

In the United States, mental illness remains hidden behind closed doors. Yet half the deaths by gunshot are a result of suicide. Rarely does the problem of mental illness become photographable. The relatively rare pictures of someone in the act of suicide might help to call attention to the failure of mental health policies in the United States.

MORAL DILEMMAS OF A PICTURE EDITOR
■ GRUESOME PICTURES: SEEN OR SUPPRESSED?

Editors who deal with pictures are also on the ethical firing line. A photographer at the scene of an accident or disaster does not have the time to determine if a particular picture is too gruesome or horrible to appear on the paper's front page. Only when the film has been processed can the photographer and the editor study the images with an impartial eye toward deciding if the photos are too indecent, obscene, or repulsive for publication.

The reader, with the morning edition of the *Republican-Democrat* neatly folded between his coffee and his oat bran, might gag on a gory front-page accident photo (ultimately tossing both the paper and his cereal). Editors sometimes refer to this as the "breakfast test" for hard-to-digest pictures.

Yet editors must not whitewash the world. Murders, accidents, wars, and suicides happen. Eliminating violence presents readers with a false view of their community and the world. (See Chapter 9, "Editing.")

In fact, totalitarian dictators always try to

A former mental patient shot himself with a 12-gauge shotgun. Do the pictures help call attention to the problems of the mentally ill?
(Photo by Peter Bradt, *Wichita Falls Time Record News*.)

muzzle the press in order to suppress information and hide truth. Despite the best of intentions, the press also self-censors with written or unwritten guidelines. Newspapers at the beginning of World War II, for example, never showed dead American soldiers, because editors wanted to keep morale high on the homefront. Until *Life* magazine ran a

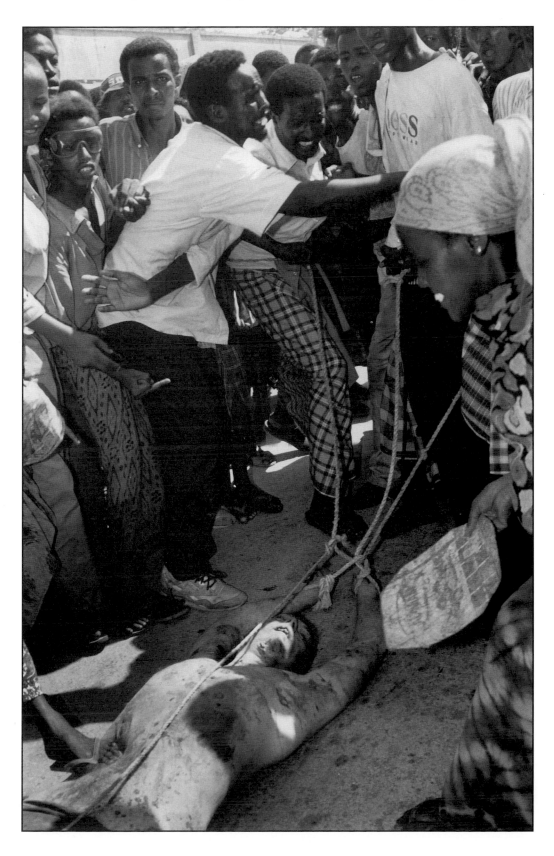

On a mission in Africa to provide food for starving Somalians, an American soldier was killed and then dragged through the streets of the city of Mogadishu. The picture was so powerful that it helped to change U.S. policy toward involvement in Somalia.
(Photo by Paul Watson, *Toronto Star*.)

photo showing dead American soldiers strewn on a beach, the public was sheltered visually from some of the war's impact. Is it right or even responsible for the press to protect the public in this way? Is it possible that, by withholding these scenes, the press actually prevented Americans from developing a healthy outrage about events in Europe, a fury that perhaps could have fueled the war effort? (See "Hiding Dead Bodies," on the following page, and Chapter 15, "History.")

The corpseless photos were not inaccurate per se. They were merely incomplete. Arbitrarily editing out death—or any other sign of violence or tragedy—gives readers a false sense of their own security and a skewed view of their world.

Sebastian Balic, a stringer for the Associated Press, shot a grisly set of pictures of youths stoning, then stabbing, and finally setting a man on fire in Soweto, South Africa. The *New York Daily News* ran the photograph of the stoning. Referring to the pictures in an article by Sue O'Brien, Jeff Jarvis, the newspaper's Sunday editor, said, "I don't think the breakfast test works for the '90s." Mike Zerby, photo editor at the *Minneapolis Star Tribune*, agreed. "The standard line," he said, "is 'we don't bleed on your eggs,' but I think at this particular newspaper we've grown past that."

Northwestern University's Curtis MacDougall, author of **News Pictures Fit to Print . . . Or Are They?**, recalled that, when he was a reporter on the old *St. Louis Star Times*, the managing editor once spent a full hour soliciting the opinions of everyone in the newsroom regarding the propriety of using a picture of a lynching. The photograph showed a corpse slumped at the base of the "hanging tree." MacDougall recalled the photo and the incident: "No facial expression was visible; nevertheless the decision was made to black out the body and substitute an artist's drawn 'X' to mark the spot."

This conservatism was typical of American editors through a century of brutal torture and murder of African Americans. According to MacDougall, plenty of photographs were available to document this inhuman treatment; however, when those photographs reached the newsroom, they were relegated to the paper's files rather than to its news pages.

Of another lynching picture described as "shocking and unnecessary," Ernest Meyer wrote in the *Madison* (Wisc.) *Capital Times*, "So was the crime. The grim butchery deserved a grim record. And those photographs were more eloquent than any word picture of the event."

At the time, newspaper editors argued that lynching pictures were too grisly to print. However, during that same era, editors did play up horrible pictures of blood-soaked, maimed car-accident victims. Editors rationalized that accident pictures served as a warning to careless drivers and thus improved highway safety. (The same logic today prompts driver's ed teachers to screen a bloody crash site film for novice drivers.) Sadly, no one thought to add that lynching pictures might also have a positive benefit by stirring up moral outrage against mob rule.

Today, the number of accident photos has decreased. Because accidents have become so common, they are less newsworthy. Accident photos, too, are often more difficult to get because the police remove bodies promptly. But the underlying moral question remains: does the sight of mutilated victims in a mangled car frighten readers into caution when they drive their cars? And, should this type of picture be published?

The *Akron* (Ohio) *Beacon Journal* said in an editorial about accident coverage:

"The suddenness and finality of death, the tremendous force of impact, are vividly depicted in crushed, twisted bodies and smashed vehicles. The picture implants in the minds of all who see it a safety lesson that could not be equally well conveyed in words alone. How long the shock value of such a picture persists, varies. But one can be sure that a majority of those who see photographs of traffic accidents are more concerned with their safety than they had been before seeing the picture. 'This can happen to you!' is the unwritten message of every picture of an accident."

■ READER COMPLAINTS

In Craig Hartley's survey comparing photojournalists' and general readers' reactions to ethical situations, he found that the two groups differed widely in their reactions to shooting and transmitting gruesome pictures.

Hartley found that 58 percent of the professionals he surveyed considered ethical the actions of a photojournalist who photographed the removal of a famous actress' body from an automobile crash and the editors' subsequent decision to send the pictures over the wires. However, nearly three-fourths (71 percent) of the public disapproved of the journalists' actions.

Note, however, that readers' approval rating does not always coincide with their curiosity rating. Regardless of their opinion, drivers routinely slow down to "rubberneck" a highway accident.

When editors select and publish strong,

compelling, but perhaps hard-to-look-at pictures that include mangled bodies, blood, or victims' or bystanders' tearful reactions, readers often complain.

From an economic point of view, editors certainly care what readers do and don't want to see on page one. However, most readers today subscribe to their newspaper rather than buy a copy on the street. Single-copy sales and, therefore, individual front-page pictures no longer control circulation sales as they did in the days when competing tabloids would run shocking pictures for the sole purpose of attracting readers. Editors are looking for a sustained readership, not a one-day circulation boost. From the ethical perspective, however, should editors make decisions based on reader preferences? Do editors have a responsibility that supersedes the likes and dislikes of their audience?

The "Distance" Rule

For stories involving tragedy, journalists sometimes make conflicting decisions regarding the play of written stories compared to photos. For written stories, geographic proximity is one of the determining criteria in assessing news value—the closer the event, the more importance and, therefore, more prominent play it is given. Yet, because readers are more likely to complain about gruesome local pictures than those from far away, editors often will play down or suppress strong pictures that involve hometown residents but run revealing pictures of atrocities in other parts of the world. In fact, some newspapers, like the *Tampa Tribune*, even have policies mandating this practice. Denise Costa of the *Tribune* says that she wants to "protect the people involved more than she would want to run the photo." This attitude toward photography is counter to traditional news criteria for print stories—top among them, proximity. Editors, however, don't like fielding calls from irate readers.

■ HIDING DEAD BODIES

When to run and when to hold a photo often comes up when editors must deal with a picture containing a dead body. Readers of the *Detroit Free Press*, for instance, were jolted by a front-page photograph of a Detroit firefighter carrying a dead child from a home in which seven brother and sisters locked alone inside had died in a fire. In Detroit tradition, doors and windows in the house were barricaded or barred to keep burglars out.

Initially, readers complained about the picture, shot by stringer Bill Eisner. But, within a few days, calls and letters supporting the paper's decision started coming in.

The response was about 50 percent positive, director of photography Mike Smith reports, and about 50 percent negative.

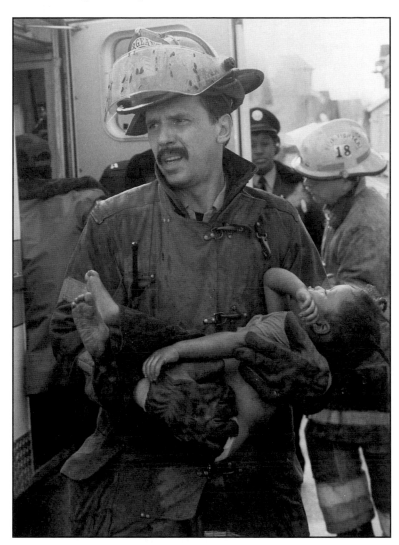

Initially, readers objected to this picture of a fireman carrying the lifeless child who had been trapped in a building with locked burglar bars on the windows. Many papers will not run any picture that shows a dead body.
(Bill Eisner, stringer, *Detroit Free Press*.)

Detroit Free Press columnist Susan Watson wrote: *"Callers—some callers, not all—found the picture disgusting. Sickening. Inappropriate. The paper was accused of overstepping the bounds of good taste.*

"Well, it's a good thing that I don't make the final call—or any call, for that matter—on what runs on page one.

"If I did, I would have spread that picture across the entire page. Heck, I wouldn't have stopped there. I would have made a huge poster out of it and hung the poster from the top of this building and city hall and even the Capitol in Lansing.

"I would have done it as a chilling reminder of the ungodly price we pay when we take risks with our children. . . . It screamed, loudly and rudely, that we have to stop endangering our loved ones to protect our belongings."

' Joan Byrd, a *Washington Post* ombudsman, summarized the counterargument: *"the family should not have to see news photos of someone killed in an accident or a crime. Families of victims have said that years later something haunts them every single day: the picture of the body at the scene, the description of the person in the newspaper. Images on TV are here and gone. Still photos in the newspaper last."*

The two columnists eloquently summarize conflicting ethical points of view. Running the picture, the *Detroit Free Press* columnist argues, helps the most people and hurts the fewest. The *Washington Post* ombudsman, on the other hand, takes an absolutist position by pointing out that if the picture hurts just a few relatives and friends, it is wrong to run the picture because the media must protect those few from more pain.

Similar reactions and arguments apply to pictures of drowned children, like John Harte's photo in the *Bakersfield Californian*. (see page 295.) Harte's photograph of lifeless 5-year-old Edward Romero, lying partially exposed in a plastic body bag and surrounded by grieving family members, is a powerful image. The paper received 400 phone calls, 500 letters, and a bomb threat. The editor subsequently ran an apology to the readers for running the photo.

The number of drownings in the Bakersfield area, however, dropped from fourteen in the month previous to the picture's publication to just two in the month after the paper printed the photo.

In another instance, Jonathan Adams photographed rescuers carrying a dead 6-year-old child to an ambulance after the child had fallen off a pier and been under water for 45 minutes. The *Muskegon Chronicle* editor, Gunnar Carlson, had two reporters take the photo to the family and ask if they minded if the paper published the photo. When they objected, the paper spiked the picture.

In other situations, editors make decisions by guessing how a family will react but never checking out their assumptions. Based on the "do unto others as you would have them do unto you" principle, editors act in a way they suppose families would want them to. Sometimes, however, relatives or friends of a victim recognize that publishing a picture may be one of the only beneficial outcomes of a tragic situation. When a child fell through the ice and drowned in a pond in Columbia, Missouri, the *Columbia Missourian*, after much discussion regarding the family's feelings, ran a picture showing rescuers recovering the child's body. The next day, the child's mother came to the office, where she picked

up extra copies of the newspaper after thanking the editors for running the photograph. She said she hoped that the front-page picture of her child would help deter others from playing on the thin pond ice.

Perhaps news outlets should routinely call victims' families to warn them that an emotional photograph will run. This procedure would diminish a family's shock at seeing the image but would still allow the wider public to be informed in the strongest way possible about the news event. (See material on war censorship in Chapter 15, "History.")

Trouble Ahead

In his book *Photojournalism: An Ethical Approach*, Paul Lester constructed a list of warning signs for editors to help signal when a shocking picture might elicit a controversial reaction from readers. The list includes: photos taken for a local story; photos taken by a staff photographer; images printed in a morning paper; images printed on the front page, images with no accompanying story; images that show subjects overcome with grief; pictures containing dead bodies, pictures portraying mutilated bodies; pictures run in color; and photos containing nudity. Lester argues that if five or more of these conditions apply, editors should prepare themselves for reader reactions before the firestorm hits.

■ PHOTOGRAPHY CAN MAKE A DIFFERENCE

Stanley Forman's photo of a collapsing fire escape during a blaze—a woman plunging to her death along with a falling child who miraculously survived—was printed on more than a hundred front pages across the country. Later, telephone calls and letters to newspapers charged sensationalism, invasion of privacy, insensitivity, and tasteless display of human tragedy for the purpose of selling newspapers.

Hal Buell, who was AP's assistant general manager for news photos at the time, said he received more reaction to the Forman picture than to any other news photo. Buell wagered that if the woman had survived, there would have been very little reaction. "The pictures would not have changed, but the fact of death reached into the minds and feelings of the readers," he said.

Most of the nation's editors published Forman's picture on their front pages. Yet, in a survey taken by the *Orange County Daily Pilot* in Costa Mesa, Calif., 40 percent of its readers did not approve of that paper's publishing the photo. Wilson Sims, editor of the *Battle Creek* (Michigan) *Enquirer and News*, defended publishing the picture: "The essential purpose is not to make the reader feel pain or to bring the reader happiness. It is to help the reader understand what is happening in the world. Therefore, we ran the picture."

Forman's photograph of the falling woman and child not only won a Pulitzer Prize, but it is also a classic example of how photography can bring about change. That shocking image contributed to a change in fire safety laws in Boston. Forman's editor, Sam Bornstein, said, "Without the picture, the word-story would have been 'page 16.'

Only pictures of this magnitude would have resulted in something being done by the safety agencies."

Sometimes pictures not only can change a state's laws but can alter a country's foreign policy. In response to the starvation of Somalians in Africa, the United States sent its troops to help United Nations peace keepers quell fighting and distribute food in that country. Despite the presence of U.S. troops, war lords continued to pillage. At one point a U.S. soldier was killed by the followers of General Aidid, one of the war lords. At great

This fire escape collapsed during a fire, plunging a woman to her death; the child miraculously survived. After the picture ran on hundreds of front pages around the country, telephone calls and letters deluged newspapers, charging sensationalism, invasion of privacy, insensitivity, and tasteless display of human tragedy—all to sell newspapers. Would you have printed this picture? (Photo by Stanley Forman.)

personal danger, the *Toronto Star*'s Paul Watson photographed the yelling and screaming crowd as they dragged the almost nude body of the soldier through the city streets. The horrifying picture of the body of an American soldier being desecrated in the streets of a country halfway around the world was so shocking to the U.S. public that the administration quickly reversed policy and pulled U.S. troops out of Somalia. (See page 309). While a single picture alone probably did not change American foreign policy, this image, which generated immediate reaction from the public, commentators, and legislators, certainly played a significant role in hastening the withdrawal of U.S. troops.

■ MATTERS OF TASTE

Nudity in pictures generates more disagreement among editors than even the most gruesome picture. An editor's judgment about nudity in pictures generally reflects his or her understanding of readers' attitudes and of mores in the host community. In most cases, the standards for pictorial nudity are more a matter of taste than a question of ethics. With the advent of *Hustler* and other "skin" magazines, almost no part of the human anatomy is reserved for the imagination. Yet, most American newspapers and magazines refrain from printing nudity on their pages. AP's Hal Buell says that the wire service won't carry frontal views of nude men or

women, except in extreme cases. "Such a story has yet to occur," he observes.

Professionals and the public again disagreed in Hartley's ethics survey when he turned to the question of nudity. Here is the hypothetical situation: *Two women athletes collide in a volleyball game, with one falling in such a way that her shorts are pulled down and her bare buttocks are exposed.*

While a majority of the professionals surveyed endorsed sending out a photo of the athlete's derriere, a whopping 75 percent of the public turned thumbs-down on the bottoms-up picture.

Robert Wahls, who was a photo editor for the *New York Daily News*, avoided running nudes except under unusual circumstances. Despite the *Daily News*' reputation as a genuine tabloid, Wahls felt that, while nudity is acceptable in film and theater, "it is inappropriate when you can sit and study it." The photo editor made an exception when there was an overriding news value to a picture. The photos from the original Woodstock, a massive outdoor rock concert in 1969, showed members of the audience frolicking in the muddy field without their clothes on. The sheer size of the audience—300,000—gave the activities news value.

Wahls, however, pointed out that, even if nude pictures help push up the circulation of a newspaper, the gain might be useless if advertisers start to consider the paper porno-

Taken by their staffer at the 25th anniversary of Woodstock, editors of the *Washington Times* refused to run this photo. Later, the photo generated so much controversy as a contest winner that the paper finally did publish the picture—with a demurely placed black box over offending body parts.
(Photo by Kenneth Lambert, the *Washington* (D.C.) *Times.* For publication in this book, the following special credit note was required by the editor-in-chief, "This photograph did not run in the *Washington Times* due to reasons of taste.")

graphic. "A newspaper's job is to inform, not to titillate," said Wahls.

Twenty-five years later, the *Washington Times*' Ken Lambert photographed Woodstock's silver anniversary, which, like the original, gave kids an excuse to party, wear tie-dye, and "get naked." Although only a few got naked this time around, Lambert took a funny picture of a young woman glancing disapprovingly at a long-haired "hippie" wearing nothing but his birthday suit. The picture was too dicey for the *Washington Times*, whose editor, Josette Shiner, called the *Times* "a family newspaper."

The photo, however, was not too spicy for judges of the White House News Photographers Association (WHNPA) photo contest, who awarded the picture a first place for features. The controversy did not end there, however.

The president of the WHNPA, Ken Blaylock, who was personally offended by the picture, tried to block its exhibition with the other winners in a Library of Congress show and in the group's yearbook. The ensuing outcry of censorship caused the *Washington Times* to write a story about its own photographer and the photo they had originally refused to print.

This time, the paper published the picture—but with a black bar placed strategically to cover offending body parts. Finally, after all the publicity, the president of the White House News Photographer's Association relented and allowed the photo

to take its place among the winners in the exhibit—without cropping the picture or running a black bar (the modern equivalent of the Victorian fig leaf) to protect the innocent.

"Innocent" readers also might disapprove of photos showing obscene gestures. With the exception of the *New York Times*, however, few news desk editors refrained from printing the picture of then-Vice President Nelson Rockefeller "giving the finger" to a crowd of hecklers at an airport. In this situation, news value overruled matters of taste.

FAIR AND BALANCED REPORTING

The experienced professional reporter continues to dig up the facts of a news story until he or she feels prepared to write an unbiased, balanced report of the event. News reporters might write articles in which several paragraphs explain the position of each conflicting party.

Many stories have no clear heroes or villains; hence, the reporter simply extends copy to explain the complexities of the situation. The writer has not only the advantage of several paragraphs, but the subtlety and precision of the English language, with its great store of adjectives and adverbs. These modifiers enable the writer to emphasize an idea or soften a phrase.

Listen to the difference between the words "the suspect stared at me" and "the criminal glared at me."

The photographer has no adjectives or adverbs, no pictorial thesaurus to refine an image. A single picture captures only one moment in time, one set of circumstances, one expression or action. If the newspaper's managing editor has allotted space for just one picture to illustrate a complicated story, then the photo editor is faced with a task as difficult as if the writer had to tell a multifaceted story in one monosyllabic sentence. Of the two hundred or so exposed frames shot on an assignment, which single picture tells the whole story?

The Vietnam War presented a constant challenge for photo editors. Each day they had to sum up a complicated, tragic event in a few pictures. Eddie Adams won a Pulitzer Prize for a shocking photo of a South Vietnamese colonel executing a suspected Viet Cong on a Saigon street (see above). During this war, the South Vietnamese were our allies. The overwhelming message of the picture, however, spoke of the cruelty of the South Vietnamese officer. To balance this view of the war, many editors chose to run, on the same day, another picture portraying the terrorism of our enemies, the Viet Cong. The photo, although not as dramatic as Adams' picture, showed a soldier leaving a civilian house recently bombed by the Viet Cong. Do the two photos really explain both sides of the conflict? Can any two pictures be balanced?

■ SELF-CENSORSHIP

Censorship often occurs before the shutter is ever released or a print ever made. For a variety of reasons, photographers decide not to take or publish photographs. A

photographer might not photograph two men holding hands, for fear the community "is not ready to deal with homosexuality" or that "my paper won't run that." A photographer might not want to "embarrass the person."

In addition to gays and lesbians, newspapers traditionally have ignored various groups over the years. Through neglect or, perhaps, in deference to a predominantly white readership, newspapers have overlooked large segments of the American population—African Americans, Hispanics, and other ethnic groups. Through self-censorship on a conscious or subconscious level, photojournalists can create an artificial reality for their readers. Each journalist must look at his or her biases.

Who is being protected by not taking or running a picture?

Are you sure your editor won't publish a picture? Are the regulations about acceptable subjects and topics written down or just unofficially passed on to new members of the staff? Are you responding to your own fears and prejudices when you hesitate to release the camera's trigger or turn in a print? Have you challenged your publication's written or unwritten policy?

The message: examine your own motives. Scrutinize your actions for patterns that may reveal your own prejudices. Are elements or groups from your community consistently absent from your shots? Is it coincidence— or choice—that your pictures display these patterns? Then apply the same vigilance to your editor and your organization. A responsible journalist must remain alert to even the most subtle signs of prejudice, at all levels. If you discover that prejudice is part of the "corporate culture" at your paper, you have three options: accept it, change it, or quit. Each carries a price.

REMEMBER THE READER

Photojournalists don't take pictures for contests, editors, or other members of the profession. They take pictures for readers—pictures that provide information about sad moments as well as happy ones. Without complete and well-rounded reporting, including both written and visual facts, a democratic society cannot function.

Therefore, when faced with a tough ethical question, try phrasing the problem in this way:

First, faced with this problem, what do other professionals in the field do? What is the professional standard for this action?

Next, are the actions of other professionals right or wrong? To borrow an apt phrase from mothers everywhere, "Just because everyone else does it doesn't mean you have to."

Then ask yourself, "Will taking or running a photo serve the greatest good for the greatest number of people?" Although you will find it hard to predict exactly a photo's effect, can you hypothesize a positive outcome from readers seeing the photo? What is the negative impact if readers don't see the picture?

If you decide the photo has potential social significance, you should next ask, "Who will be hurt by taking or running the picture? Is this a situation in which an individual's rights supersede those of society?" You might ask, "How would I feel if I were the person in the photo?" Can you soften the hurt with a phone call informing relatives about what they will see in the next day's paper?

Finally, while some individual rights are absolute, some are not. Keep in mind that you must weigh an individual's rights against society's need for correct and complete information.

■ LOOKING FOR A YARDSTICK

Not all pictures showing dying and death help readers or society. A picture of a man dying at home of natural causes does not provide information that society can use to change anything. No laws can prevent this death. Readers would not be shocked by the passing of another elderly man. No public policy issues are at stake. Pictures of a death that could not have been prevented are not necessarily news or newsworthy. On the other hand, pictures of a drowned child or one falling from a poorly maintained fire

escape graphically highlight either behavior that individuals could prevent or laws that should be enacted.

In his book *News Pictures Fit to Print . . . Or Are They?*, Curtis MacDougall struggled to find a common rule to help editors decide when to splash a controversial picture on the front page or when to file the picture in the bottom desk drawer. "My yardstick is the public interest," said MacDougall. "I would run any picture calculated to increase the public's understanding of an issue about which the public is able to act."

MacDougall's yardstick, however, does not take into account competing claims like privacy, which in certain circumstances must also be considered.

While each editor will use his or her own yardstick of public versus private interest, photographers should not rely on editors to shoulder the ethics burden. Photographers must determine for themselves what they find valuable about taking and then publishing photos. The photographer provides the first line of ethical defense and, finally, the photographer's name runs under the photo. The photographer must take responsibility for the printed image. ■

Sometimes photographers don't take pictures like these of two elderly gay couples because they assume their papers won't run the photos. Through conscious or unconscious self-censorship on the parts of news outlets, groups such as gays, disabled people, and others tend to remain invisible to the public eye.
(Photos by Pavlos Simeon for his M.A. Thesis, "Older Gay Couples.")

History

CHAPTER 15

Written with Julie Levinson, assistant professor, Babson College.

On a balmy April day in 1877 the staff of the *New York Daily Graphic*, the first illustrated daily newspaper in the United States, conducts business as usual. Reporters labor to complete their copy in time for the morning deadline. Artists put the finishing touches to their drawings, which will comprise three and a half of the tabloid's eight pages.

The first "portable" strobe for the news photographer was perfected and manufactured by Edward A. Farber for members of the *Milwaukee Journal* photo staff. (*Milwaukee Journal.*)

In a makeshift darkroom, where a janitor stores mops and brooms, a lone photog-rapher places 5"×7" precoated, dry glass plates into light-tight holders. The photographer is so engrossed in the delicate operation that he barely hears the sudden commotion in the newsroom. The commotion's cause is a passing fire engine. For the staff of the *Daily Graphic*, whose every sense is attuned to such signals, the fire engine's clanging bell tolls news.

Several reporters drop what they're doing, grab pencil and paper, and dash out to cover the late-breaking story. Someone remembers to inform the photographer about the fire alarm. He, too, puts aside his work and carefully balances his cumbersome view camera and tripod on one arm and a case containing twelve previously prepared glass plates on the other arm. The *Graphic* cameraman sets off with his unwieldy load.

By the time he reaches the site of the blaze, it is raging full force. He sets up his tripod and camera as quickly as possible, points his lens at the action, and takes his first exposure. Normally he would take only one exposure, or perhaps two, of a given event. Because this is such a huge fire, however, he decides to expose several of his glass plates. He has only one lens, so if he is to get different perspectives on the action, he must change his position, pick up his bulky equipment, lug it to the new spot, and take the time to set up again. He then covers his head and the back of the camera with a black focusing cloth. Next he opens, focuses, closes, and sets the lens. Following this he loads the plate holder into the rear of the camera body and removes the dark-slide. Finally, he takes the picture.

Before he can make the next photo he must replace the dark slide and carefully put the holder back into his case. If he accidentally knocks the holder too hard, the glass plates will shatter. Unfortunately, the crowd continually jostles him as he works.

He attracts much attention because a news photographer is still a curiosity. But the *Graphic* photographer doesn't mind; he is particularly excited about the challenge posed by this event. Usually his assignments limit him to photographing portraits of famous people or carefully posed tableaux. Because of the technical limitations of his slow film (equivalent to ISO 24 by today's standards), he can photograph only under optimum conditions, with bright light and minimal subject movement. On this day, he is able to get some action shots by carefully panning his camera with the movement of a late arriving horse-drawn fire engine.

After several hours, the *Daily Graphic* photographer finishes making his twelve exposures, and by the time he packs his case,

camera, and tripod, the firemen finally have the blaze under control. But as the photographer heads back to the newspaper office, weary from his physical exertion, his own ordeal has just begun. Now he must develop his pictures in chemicals he mixes from a formula he found in a copy of the *Philadelphia Photographer*, one of the country's first photo magazines.

Enlargers are not used commonly. The 5"×7" negative is of sufficient size for reproduction when it is simply contacted on photographic paper. More than an hour after returning from the fire, the photographer has his first picture. After all that work, however, the photo can't be printed in the newspaper.

The photographer now hands his pictures over to an artist, who draws replicas of them. Unfortunately, the artist often changes details from the original if he thinks the new variations improve the picture. The artist, in turn, gives his drawings to an engraver, who reproduces them onto a zinc plate. The plate is then printed on a Hoe rotary press.

As may be imagined, a good deal of time elapses between the hour of the fire and the moment when these line-drawn renderings of the photographs appear in the newspaper. Yet the drawings receive front-page play.

■ EVOLUTION OF THE CAMERA REPORTER

How did the photographer of 1877 evolve into the photojournalist of the 1990s? Two major factors contributed to this development. First, the technical innovations: the invention of roll film, smaller cameras, faster lenses, and the introduction of portable light sources enabled the photographer to shoot pictures more easily and get better results. The invention of the halftone process for reproducing photos and the improvement of printing presses led to better reproduction. Meanwhile, with the expansion of the wire services and the development of picture transmission devices, photos could be sent across the nation and the world almost instantaneously.

The technological leaps made in photography since 1877 enable today's resourceful photographer to reach virtually any action anywhere and bring home a picture to the newspaper- and magazine-reading public. Because of these scientific and engineering discoveries, photographers can capture events previously impossible to shoot on film: night pictures, fast action, and successive motion now can all be recorded with the camera.

But technological strides are only half the answer to this evolutionary question. Photographers broadened the scope of news pictures by introducing feature and sports

THE DAILY GRAPHIC

An Illustrated Evening Newspaper

39 & 41 PARK PLACE

VOL. XIII | All the News, Four Editions Daily. | NEW YORK, MONDAY, APRIL 16, 1877 | $12 Per Year in Advance Single Copies Five Cents | NO. 1275

SCENES AT THE BURNING OF THE SOUTHERN HOTEL, ST. LOUIS, LAST WEDNESDAY MORNING.
(FROM SKETCHES BY MR. G. JUMP.)

In 1877, the *New York Daily Graphic*, the first U.S. illustrated daily newspaper, devoted an entire front page to five fire pictures. The *Daily Graphic*'s hand-drawn sketches were often based on photographs taken at the news scene.
(New York Public Library.)

This is an enlargement of a halftone dot pattern showing an eye.

pictures to the newspaper. Photographers sought candid photos that revealed natural moments rather than the posed, frozen images typical of early photo reportage. Photographers today do more than just record the news. They have become visual interpreters of the scene by using their cameras and lenses, sensitivity to light, and keen observational skills, to bring readers a feeling of what the event was really like.

The ingenuity of individual photographers in taking photos also laid the foundations of modern photojournalism. From the days of the *Daily Graphic* to the present, photographers first have had to figure out a way to get to the news event no matter where it is located—skyscraper or coal mine. They often must work around obstacles, both physical and human. Once photographers have the picture, they face the pressure of the deadline. Whether they transmit electronic images or develop film in a darkroom, they still must deliver the picture in time for the next edition. The daring and cleverness of the early photojournalists are the kinds of traits successful photographers have exhibited throughout the history of photojournalism.

Thus, technical advances and the imagination and resourcefulness of the photographer have gone hand-in-hand. The two have had complementary developments, each contributing to the gradual evolution of reportorial photography.

HALFTONE SCREEN REPRODUCES PHOTOS
■ SCREENS FIRST USED IN 1880

In 1877, our *Daily Graphic* photographer had little way of knowing that he stood on the threshold of a new age in photography. The next twenty years would see several rapid technological advances that would revolutionize the field of pictorial journalism: light, hand-held cameras; faster lenses; improved shutter mechanisms; and roll films. But perhaps the most momentous technological occurrence in the history of photojournalism was the development of the halftone printing process.

Before the introduction of the halftone process, there was no practical way to transfer the photograph directly onto the printed page. An ordinary press could print only blacks and whites—full tones—and was incapable of rendering the intermediate shades of gray, the halftones. As such, newspaper illustrations, based on artist's original sketches or photographs, consisted of black-and-white line drawings, hand-carved on wood blocks or etched on zinc plates.

After years of experimentation, experimenters found a method that could reproduce the full tonal range of photographic images. Still employed today, this process involves the use of a screen with an ordered dot pattern. This screen is held rigidly against a sensitized film in the engraver's camera. The engraver's camera copies the original photo through the screen, which breaks up the photo's continuous tones into a series of tiny dots of varying sizes. The darkest areas of the original photo translate into a series of large dots. As the tones in the picture change from black to gradations of gray and white, the dots get progressively smaller.

The engraver develops the film and contact prints it onto a metal plate. The pattern of dots is chemically transferred onto this printing plate. On the press, the dots transfer the ink onto the paper. Where they are largest and closest together, the image is darkest, and where they are smallest and farthest apart, the image is lightest. Thus the resulting printed image duplicates the shadings of the original photograph.

How much detail can be reproduced depends upon the fineness of the screen and the quality of the paper. By holding a magnifying glass up to any newspaper or magazine picture, you can easily see the tiny dot pattern of the halftone screen. A newspaper generally uses an 85-dots-per-inch screen. This book uses 133 dots per inch.

■ THE FIRST HALFTONE: SHANTYTOWN

The *Daily Graphic* published the first halftone on March 4, 1880: a picture of Shantytown, a squatter's camp in New York City. Stephen H. Horgan, the photographer in charge of the *Daily Graphic*'s engraving equipment, produced the halftone. Although Horgan had been perfecting this process for several years, his successful experiment in 1880 did not immediately affect the look of the daily newspaper. His halftone invention, however, did encourage further experimentation.

■ OPPOSITION TO PHOTOS

In 1893, four years after the demise of the *Daily Graphic*, Horgan was working as art editor for the *New York Herald* when he again recommended the use of halftones to James Gordon Bennett, the paper's owner. After a brief consultation with his pressmen, Bennett pronounced the idea unfeasible.

Similarly, Joseph Pulitzer, who had been publisher of the *New York World* since 1883, initially expressed reluctance to print halftones. In fact, Pulitzer feared that widespread use of any pictures, including line drawings, would lower the paper's dignity, so he tried to cut down on the extensive use of woodcuts, which already had made his paper famous. When circulation fell as a result, Pulitzer reconsidered his decision and reinstated the drawings.

As Pulitzer realized the paper-selling potential of such illustrations, he began to increase their size from the original one-column to four- and five-column spreads. When the halftone was finally perfected, the *World* was one of the first newspapers to make liberal use of the new process. The daily's circulation rose rapidly. Other publishers and editors soon jumped onto the pictorial bandwagon. One such newsman, Melville Stone, investigated the potential of newspaper illustrations for the *Chicago Daily News*. He ultimately concluded, "Newspaper pictures are just a temporary fad, but we're going to get the benefit of the fad while it lasts."

Today we know that newspaper pictures were neither temporary nor faddish, but, in the closing years of the nineteenth century, the halftone continued to struggle for legitimacy. By the late 1890s, the process had yet to achieve daily use, although the *New York Times* did print halftones in its illustrated Sunday supplement begun in 1896. Skeptical publishers still feared that their readers would lament the substitution of mechanically produced photographs for the artistry of hand-drawn pictures; also, artists and engravers were well-established members of the newspaper staff. Thus, long after the halftone was perfected, carefully drawn copies of photos continued to appear in many

papers. Gradually, however, papers adopted the halftone process. By 1910, hand engraving was becoming obsolete and the halftone, in turn, became a front-page staple.

THE MAINE BLEW UP, AND JIMMY HARE BLEW IN

While these technological strides were taking place in the latter part of the nineteenth century, several photographers were setting photojournalistic precedents. Jimmy Hare, one of the most colorful of the pioneer photojournalists, wrote the handbook for future photographer-reporters. During his career, Hare covered nearly every major world event, from the wreckage of the U.S. battleship Maine in Havana harbor during the Spanish-American War in 1898 to the closing days of World War I in Europe. His ingenuity and his no-holds-barred attitude when it came to getting the picture set a standard for the new profession of photojournalism.

London-born Hare, whose father crafted hand-made cameras for a living, came to the United States in 1889. One magazine, the *Illustrated American*, committed itself to using halftone photographs. From 1896 to 1898, Hare worked as a freelancer, supplying the magazine with photos ranging from presidential inaugurations to sporting events. A month after he left the *Illustrated American*, the battleship Maine exploded, thus signaling the start of the Spanish-American conflict. The ever enterprising photographer promptly

The first photograph reproduced on a printing press using the halftone process: on March 4, 1880, this photograph of Shantytown dwellings appeared in a special section of the *New York Daily Graphic*. Notice that this first halftone used different sized lines to create shades of gray rather than the varying-sized dots of modern halftones.
(Henry J. Newton, *New York Daily Graphic*, courtesy of the New York Historical Society, New York City.)

presented himself to the editors of _Collier's Weekly_, and offered to take pictures of the wreckage. Twenty years after the Maine episode, then-editor Robert J. Collier was to recall, "The Maine blew up and Jimmy blew in! Both were major explosions!" Jimmy continued "blowing in" to important world events for the next several decades.

So successful were his pictures of the Maine and of Cuba, where American soldiers fought the Spanish in the Spanish-American War, that the publisher named Hare special photographer for _Collier's_, thus beginning a long and productive association.

Whether trekking over Cuban countryside, touring battlefields with Stephen Crane, author of _Red Badge of Courage_, or following Teddy Roosevelt's Rough Riders, Hare with his camera remained intrepid and resourceful in his coverage of the Spanish-American War. Hare made use of the new folding cameras (with lenses as fast as f/6.8) and of roll film (with twelve exposures per roll). His lightweight equipment gave him more mobility than his competition, who were shooting with fragile glass plates and awkward 5"×7" Graflexes, the popular news cameras of the day.

Regardless of the reduced weight of his folding camera, Hare still had to get to the middle of the action to take a picture. In one battle during the Spanish-American conflict, a soldier spotted Hare snapping away as wounded bodies dropped all around him. "You must be a congenital damn fool to be up here! I wouldn't be unless I had to!" the soldier shouted. Hare's even-handed reply: "Neither would I, but you can't get real pictures unless you take some risks."

In addition to the Spanish-American War, Hare's photographic escapades brought him to the combat lines of the Russo-Japanese War, the Mexican Revolution, the First Balkan War, and the First World War. Hare described these experiences as "one-sided adventures in which it was always my privilege to be shot at but never to shoot." But shoot he did—with his camera, that is—and his pictures contributed greatly to _Collier's_ rapidly rising circulation and national prominence.

■ HARE COVERS FIRST FLIGHT

Not all of Hare's exploits took place on the battlefield. The story of how Hare managed to record on film the experiments of the Wright brothers in 1908 is indicative of his tenacity and his skill. The Wrights' first successful flight had taken place in 1903 but, five years later, the public remained unconvinced that men had actually flown. Rumors abounded but no one had documented proof of any flight. The brothers refused to allow reporters to witness their experiments at Kitty Hawk.

Hare was determined to check out the rumor for Collier's, however, and, along with four reporters from various newspapers, he secretly went to the Wright brothers' testing area. The five intrepid men spent two days hiking over the sands of Kitty Hawk, North Carolina. Approaching the site of the rumored flights, the newsmen took cover in a clump of bushes and anxiously waited for something to happen. Covered with mosquito bites and tired of lugging his camera, Hare was tempted to dismiss the rumors as false and head back home. But suddenly an engine noise was heard, and, as the reporters watched in disbelief, an odd-looking machine glided across the sand and gradually rose into the air. Hare ran out of the bushes and managed to snap two photographs of the airborne machine. The party of reporters then sneaked back to their base and prepared to reveal their booty to the world.

Because Hare was far away from the plane, the image in his photo was small and indistinct. But Collier's was proud to publish the picture in its May 30, 1908, issue. The photo proved at last that man could indeed fly. Hare had the distinction of taking the first news photograph of a plane in flight.

Hare began chronicling his world during photojournalism's infancy. When Collier's first published his photos, editors considered pictures mere embellishments of the text. But through his dogged efforts to capture, with his camera, a sense of immediacy and excitement, Hare served as a catalyst in the growth of the photographer into a full-fledged "reporter with a camera."

WOMEN ENTER THE FIELD

Since 1900, female photojournalists have made their mark in the newsroom. Frances Benjamin Johnston, an indomitably spirited woman, managed to transcend the constraints usually imposed on Victorian women. She documented early educational methods in black, white, and Indian schools. She shot a series of photographs on the activities in the White House and on the visits of foreign dignitaries. Then Johnston sold her pictures to the newly formed Bain News Service, and became its photo representative in Washington, D.C. Bain suggested that she photograph Admiral George Dewey aboard

his battleship after his successful takeover of the Philippines. With great ingenuity she made her way to Italy, where Dewey's ship first docked, and covered the story. She managed to endear herself to the crew and, when it came time to fill out an enlistment record, she earned five out of five possible points for everything from seamanship to marksmanship, but only a "4.9" for sobriety.

Jessie Tarbox Beals was another photojournalistic pioneer. She started out as a school teacher but soon discovered the lure of photography. In 1902 the *Buffalo Inquirer and Courier* hired her as a press photographer. During her two years with them, and later in St. Louis and New York, she exhibited an important skill of the photojournalist—the "ability to hustle," as she once put it. Before her career ended, Beals sneaked photographs through a transom at a murder trial, rode the gondola of a balloon above the St. Louis World's Fair for a photo, and photographed Mark Twain.

THE CAMERA AS A REFORMER'S TOOL

Social documentary photographers, notably Jacob Riis and Lewis Hine, demonstrated that the camera could provide not only a record of events but could also serve as a potent tool for social change. Hine once summarized his goals as a concerned photographer: "There were two things I wanted to do. I wanted to show the things that had to be corrected. I wanted to show the things that

Frances Benjamin Johnston, an early photojournalist around 1900, represented the Bain News Service in Washington, D.C. (Library of Congress.)

had to be appreciated." As America moved into the new century, crusading photographers chose to concentrate on the former aim, the social objective. Riis and Hine were among the first to press the camera into service as an agent for social awareness.

Their photographic pleas for reform placed them in the ranks of such social muckrakers as Upton Sinclair, Lincoln Steffens, and Ida Tarbell. Together with these writers/reformers, the camera journalists probed the underside of city life, exposing the unimaginable, and bringing out into the open what had previously been shielded from view. The tradition Riis and Hine helped to establish carried through to the 1930s with the photographers of the Farm Security Administration, who used their cameras to record the faces of Depression-ridden America.

■ RIIS EXPOSES SLUM CONDITIONS

Neither Riis nor Hine, in fact, began as a photographer. The Danish-born Riis started in the 1870s as a carpenter and then got a job as a reporter for the *New York Sun*. He wrote first-hand accounts of the indignities and inequities of immigrant life. When he was accused of exaggerating his written descriptions of life in the city slums, he turned to photographs as a means of documenting the human suffering he saw.

For Riis, the photograph had only one purpose: to aid in the implementation of social reform. Pictures were weapons of persuasion that surpassed the power of words and the absolute veracity of the photographic image made it an indispensable tool. As Riis stated, "The power of fact is the mightiest lever of this or any other day."

But Riis was up against many obstacles as a photographer. The crowded tenements were shrouded in darkness and shadows. To show the perpetual nighttime existence in the slums, Riis pioneered the use of German Blitzlichtpulver—flashlight powder—which, although dangerous and uncontrollable, did sufficiently illuminate the scene. Lugging a 4"×5" wooden box camera, tripod, glass plate holders, and a flash pan, Riis ventured into the New York slums with evangelical zeal. With a blinding flash and a torrent of smoke, he got his pictures. The scenes he recorded of immigrant poverty shocked and goaded the public into action for reform.

The Riis pictures are remarkably poignant glimpses of ghetto life. Grim-faced families stare at the camera with empty eyes. Shabbily clothed children sleep amid the garbage of a tenement stoop. A grown man stands in the middle of the street and begs for someone to buy one of his pencils. An immigrant sits on his bed of straw. In a coal bin, a newly arrived American citizen prepares for the Sabbath.

Unfortunately, when Riis was photographing, the halftone had yet to achieve widespread use. Consequently, his actual pictures were not directly reproduced in printed sources and so were seen by only limited numbers of people, such as those attending his lantern-slide shows. At these talks, he used his pictures to buttress his plea for attention and reform.

When his first book, *How the Other Half Lives*, was published in 1890, it consisted of seventeen halftones and nineteen hand drawings modeled on his photographs. The halftones were technically poor—somewhat fuzzy and indistinct—but the pictures exerted a powerful influence that drew attention to slum conditions, and they remain moving documents of human suffering.

■ HINE'S PHOTOS HELP BRING ABOUT CHILD LABOR LAWS

Lewis Hine began as an educator and, like Riis, turned to photography as a means of exposing "the things that had to be corrected." In turn-of-the-century urban America, a great many conditions begged to be noticed and changed. The influx of immigrants into the cities and the simultaneous growth of industrialism were important characteristics

of the new century. With the reformer's commitment, Hine set out to catalogue how people survived in this new way of life.

In 1908, the magazine *Charities and the Commons* published a series of his pictures of immigrant life. The series included some of Hine's most famous pictures: portraits of newly arrived immigrants at Ellis Island. The power and eloquence of these pictures attracted much attention. With the further refinement of the halftone, Hine, unlike Riis before him, published his work in books and magazines and gained a good deal of public exposure for his social issues.

That same year, Hine began to work as an investigator and reporter for the National Child Labor Committee. His work took him everywhere, from St. Louis slums to California canneries. To get past the doors of the offending factories and mines, Hine posed as every type of worker, from a fire inspector to a Bible salesman. One time he packed his camera in a lunch pail, filed with the workers into a clothing factory, and surreptitiously snapped pictures of the sweatshop conditions. Hine juxtaposed the diminutive children against the huge machines. The weary stares of young knitting mill operators and seamstresses spoke more eloquently than words. The impact of these photographs, along with others he took,

Lewis Hine photographed the soot-blackened faces of children who worked in the coal mines. In part because of Hine's photos, Congress passed protective child labor laws.
(Photo by Lewis Hine, Library of Congress.)

such as the soot-blackened faces of child coal-miners, helped the committee get the new Child Labor Laws restricting exploitation of youth passed by Congress.

National Geographic did not start out as a picture magazine. In fact, its first issue in 1888 contained no photos. It wasn't until 1903 that *National Geographic* magazine ran its first halftone—a photo of a Philippine woman at work in the rice fields.

Not until 1905 did the magazine try a photo spread unbroken by text. As it happened, the photo display was unintended.

On the day the magazine was scheduled to go to the printer, the editor, Gilbert Grosvenor, was faced with eleven open pages and no material whatsoever to fill the space. By coincidence, he had received that same day a package of photographs from the Imperial Russian Geographic Society.

These pictures of the previously unphotographed Tibetan city of Lhasa had been taken by two Russian explorers and were being offered to the *Geographic* for publication. Grosvenor, fascinated by the photographs, decided to take a risk. He laid them out as an eleven-page spread—all pictures and almost no text—and sent them to the printer.

Grosvenor was sure he would be fired for having made this unprecedented and expensive editorial decision. Instead, readers stopped him in the street to congratulate him.

Although Grosvenor had run the Lhasa pictures primarily to fill up empty pages, he repeated the experiment after seeing the stir they created. In April 1905, he ran thirty-two consecutive pages of 138 photographs of the Philippines—a turning point in the magazine's history.

National Geographic contributed many photographic firsts, including the first nighttime nature shots ever published, shot by George Shiras III in 1906.

The magazine's first color photos, in 1910, were not color photos at all. In fact, they were hand-painted black-and-white pictures by William C. Chapin, showing scenes of Korea and China. Coloring black-and-white pictures continued until 1916, when the Autochromes Lumieres, real color photos, made their debut in the magazine's pages.

The first series had no particular theme other than that they were all natural-color photographs. Since those early Autochromes, the magazine has published color photos from every part of the world as well as from the bottom of the sea and from outer space.

Happy Accident at the *National Geographic*

(IMMEDIATE RIGHT)
On deadline at *National Geographic* and faced with eleven open pages, editor Gilbert Grosvenor used free pictures from Lhasa, Tibet, to fill the space for the magazine's first extensive photo layout.
(Photos courtesy of *National Geographic*.)

(IMMEDIATE RIGHT)
George Shiras III took the first night nature photos for *National Geographic*.

(FAR RIGHT) Readers were so delighted with the magazine's first picture layout that editor Grosvenor ran 32 pages of pictures about the Philippines in the following issue.

■ ROTOGRAVURE
AND THE PICTURE PAGE APPEAR

In 1914, the *New York Times* began publishing the first Sunday rotogravure section, and several other newspapers soon followed. The rotogravure process, which usually used a dark sepia ink, offered a cheap printing process that could print sixteen pages simultaneously and an unlimited number of screened photos.

That same year, the *Times* also started the *Mid-Week Pictorial War Extra* to absorb the rash of World War I pictures pouring in from Europe. In spite of severe censorship, picture agencies managed to obtain photos of the trench warfare, poison gas, and wholesale destruction of small towns taking place in Europe.

Photographers were explicitly forbidden to visit the battlefield. In fact, censorship was so severe that the Allied command attached an officer to each correspondent to control what the journalist saw and what scenes were photographed. Photographers covering the war employed their best ingenuity to circumvent the censors. Consequently, many of the photographs that finally appeared in print were taken by soldiers at the front who happened to be amateur photographers. By 1916, the *New York Times* expanded the coverage of the *Mid-Week Pictorial*, sold it for 10 cents, and dropped the words War Extra.

A highlight occurred in 1924 when the magazine reproduced autochrome photographs of Tutankhamen's treasure. Reproduction of color was rare for that time, although color roto had appeared as "tintogravure" in Joseph Pulitzer's *Sunday World* in 1923. *Mid-Week Pictorial* took pride in its exclusive photographs, touting "the first photography" whenever possible. Tremendous coverage was given to Charles A. Lindbergh's solo nonstop trans-Atlantic flight in 1927. To show readers the magazine's concern with timely news coverage, one photographic caption read, "A Radio Photograph. . . This picture was taken, was then carried to London by airplane and flashed across the ocean to New York by Radiograph."

The magazine, however, ran far more features than news. Through the 1920s, pictures of movie and theater stars, fashion, sports and high school beauty queens regularly filled its pages. One had to look below or alongside the oval, circular, and odd-shaped photographs to find minimal cutline information. Overall, according to Keith R. Kenney and Brent W. Unger's study titled "The *Mid-Week Pictorial*: Forerunner of American News-Picture Magazines," the

1920s began a period of slow decline for the *Mid-Week*. With faster and faster picture transmission and higher quality newspaper reproduction, the best photographs had begun appearing in daily newspapers. Circulation for *Mid-Week Pictorial* fell every year until 1937, when America's first modern picture magazine folded.

Picture Pages

Presses of the period were technically incapable of interspersing pictures with print and still achieving good halftone reproduction throughout the paper. Therefore, almost all the photos were grouped together on one single page. Printers achieved this improved reproduction by putting a specially designed ink blanket on the press cylinder that carried the halftone engravings. Thus a page-one story would have its corresponding picture printed inside on this special "Picture Page."

TABLOIDS: THRILLS AT THREE CENTS A COPY
■ IMMIGRANTS UNDERSTAND PICTURES

The immigrants who Hine and Riis photographed couldn't read English very well, but they could understand pictures. At a time when the country was teeming with non-English-speaking immigrants, photographs became a universal language and, along with movies, a visual handle on the new world. Also, because of the new industrialism, people had more leisure time to spend reading newspapers and magazines. With the wiring of the city for electricity, families could study published pictures long after dark.

In the late 1910s, another journalistic phenomenon caught the public's fancy: the tabloid, a half-the-standard-size newspaper that the commuter could easily read on the trolley or subway. The tabloid was designed for the less-educated masses and newly arrived immigrants.

The first twentieth-century tabloid in the United States was the *New York Illustrated Daily News*, launched in 1919. Circulation of the heavily illustrated *Daily News* soared rapidly, and it became one of the most remarkable success stories in journalism. The name of the paper was changed to *The News, New York's Picture Newspaper*, and survives to this day.

In its early days the *News'* stock and trade was titillation—with crime and sex scandals—vicarious thrills for only three cents a copy. One of the most famous stories, illustrating the lengths to which the *Daily News* would go to get a provocative picture, involved the electrocution of Ruth Snyder in January of 1928. In what was dubbed "the crime of the decade," a jury found Snyder,

The *New York Daily News*, a tabloid, hired Thomas Howard to get a picture of murderess Ruth Snyder's electrocution in 1920. He strapped a miniature glass-plate camera (above) to his ankle and released the cable as he hiked his trouser leg. He exposed the plate three times, once for each electric shock administered to Snyder.
(ABOVE: Smithsonian Institution; RIGHT: Photo by Thomas Howard, *New York Daily News*.)

Average net paid circulation of THE NEWS, Dec., 1927:
Sunday, 1,357,556
Daily, 1,193,297

DAILY ● NEWS EXTRA EDITION
NEW YORK'S ● PICTURE NEWSPAPER

Vol. 9. No. 173 56 Pages   New York, Friday, January 13, 1928   2 Cents

DEAD!

—Story on page 3

(Copyright: 1928: by Pacific and Atlantic photos)

RUTH SNYDER'S DEATH PICTURED!—This is perhaps the most remarkable exclusive picture in the history of criminology. It shows the actual scene in the Sing Sing death house as the lethal current surged through Ruth Snyder's body at 11:06 last night. Her helmeted head is stiffened in death, her face masked and an electrode strapped to her bare right leg. The autopsy table on which her body was removed is beside her. Judd Gray, mumbling a prayer, followed her down the narrow corridor at 11:14. "Father, forgive them, for they don't know what they are doing?" were Ruth's last words. The picture is the first Sing Sing execution picture and the first of a woman's electrocution.—*Story p. 3; other pics. p. 28 and back page.*

with the aid of her lover, guilty of murdering her wealthy husband. The *Daily News*' editor felt the public was entitled to see Snyder's execution, but photographers were barred from the actual scene. The editor devised a plan to sneak a cameraman into the room. Thomas Howard, a news photographer from the *Chicago Tribune*, sister paper of the *Daily News*, was brought in for the occasion.

He strapped to his ankle a prefocused miniature glass-plate camera. The camera had a long cable release running up Howard's leg into his pants pocket. Howard aimed his camera simply by pointing his shoe and hiking his trouser leg. To get sufficient light to the film, Howard, when the time came, exposed the plate several times—one for each shock administered to the body of Ruth

Because they couldn't take a picture inside the courtroom during the sensational Rhinelander divorce trial, the *Evening Graphic* staged the courtroom scene at the newspaper office with actors playing the parts of real individuals (ABOVE). Faces of actual participants were pasted on later. The new technique was dubbed a "composograph"—and repeated many times.
(Harry Grogin, *New York Evening Graphic*.)

Snyder. The following day, Friday the 13th, the picture ran full page with a single-word headline: "DEAD!"

■ THE COMPOSOGRAPH

If the *News* was "a daily erotica for the masses," it still paled in comparison to its fellow scandal monger, the *Evening Graphic*, commonly known as the "Porno Graphic." In the *Evening Graphic*, the composograph, the first staged and faked news photo, was born. The occasion was the Kip Rhinelander divorce trial. Alice Jones, an African American, was sued for annulment by Rhinelander.

The husband maintained he had married her without knowing her race. The wife's defense attorney had her strip to the waist as proof the husband should have known.

Barred from the courtroom, newspaper photographers brought back no pictures of the sensational display.

The *Graphic*'s assistant art director, Harry Grogin, shed no tears. "Hell with photographers," Harry is said to have muttered. "What we need 'em for?"

He began tearing pictures. He had pictures of Alice, of the Judge, of opposing counsel, of the stolid, forlorn Rhinelander, of Alice's mother, of Rhinelander's lordly father.

The pictures were put through a process by which they would come out in proper proportion. Meanwhile, Harry sent for Agnes McLaughlin, a showgirl, and got her to pose as he imagined Alice Rhinelander had stood before the lawyers and the judge.

For the photo, the art director had the actress wear as little as possible.

The *Evening Graphic's* staged hanging (LEFT) nearly cost the life of the art department assistant when he accidentally kicked over the stool on which he was posing for a composograph.
(Harry Grogin, *New York Evening Graphic*.)

Grogin tinted Agnes McLaughlin's skin, faintly, to give the effect of being light-colored. He used twenty separate photos to arrive at the one famous shot, but for the *Graphic*, it was well worth the effort.

The picture was believable. You feel you are looking in on the judge's chambers. With Alice in the foreground, one of the lawyers points at the husband, as if to say, "He knew it all the time!"

Emile Gauvreau, the managing editor, and the City Desk went wild; what to call it? Headline, maybe: ALICE UN-DRESSES? They settled for ALICE DISROBES IN COURT TO KEEP HER HUSBAND.

So the *Graphic* Composograph was born. The *Graphic*'s circulation rose from 60,000 to several hundred thousand after that issue.

The composograph was a *Graphic* depiction, posed in the art department, of a sensational real-life scene that, for one reason or another, could not be photographed. It was officially called a "Composograph" in the paper and identified as having been made in the art department.

As might be expected, the *Graphic* continued to exploit the popularity of the composite picture, while admitting in tiny print at the bottom of the composograph that the pictures were faked. Later, while staging a phony hanging of thief Gerald Chapman, Grogin called upon one of his assistants to pose with a noose around his neck, bound hands and feet, and a mask over his head. The man stood on an empty box that later would be blocked out of the picture. Just as the picture was about to be snapped, the stand-in victim accidentally kicked the box away. Luckily, Grogin acted with lightning reflexes and caught the suspended man seconds before the would-be hanging became a real one.

Of course, not all of the tabloid pictures were composographs. If a real-life picture was gruesome and lurid enough to satisfy the thrill-hungry public, the *Graphic*, the *Daily News*, and other tabloids were more than happy to run the photo.

Weegee (Arthur Fellig) (ABOVE) intuitively understood people's fascination for crime, which attracted the attention of both the bystander at the scene and the reader at home. Weegee was the first photographer to use a police radio to get early tips about gangland shootings.
(BELOW: Photo by Arthur Fellig.)

WEEGEE: KING OF CRIME PHOTOGRAPHERS

The most famous photographer to capitalize on the tabloid mentality and concentrate his energies on the seamier side of city life was Arthur Fellig, universally and simply known as "Weegee." Weegee acquired his name because, like the Ouija board, he supposedly had an uncanny ability to predict what would happen when and where, and he would miraculously be there often ahead of the police. However, because he was a poor

speller he wrote his new name phonetically "Weegee." His news sense, of course, was a helpful quality for a photojournalist and, with the advantages of his police radio and strategically located living quarters near the police station, Weegee managed to keep on the scent of the city's assorted crimes, auto crashes, and fires. The city was his working space, the night was his time, and violence was his specialty. Too independent to be tied to any one publication, Weegee remained a freelancer and a free spirit for most of his career. He cruised the city streets nightly in his car, always ready to cover the happenings of urban nightlife.

Weegee poked his inquisitive camera into every dark corner of the city, photographing life as he saw it—stark and uncensored. His book, **Naked City**, was later made into a movie and then a television show. Its title is an apt summation of his style and his subject. In his pictures, the city was indeed naked, unadorned, and exposed.

Weegee knew not only how to get a picture but how to sell it as well. He explained his technique, "If I had a picture of two handcuffed criminals being booked, I would cut the picture in half and get five bucks for each." For a photo of a bullet-ridden corpse, he had an entrepreneur's price scale. Weegee's going rate: $5 per bullet! Never one for modesty, he would stamp the back of his pictures, "Credit Weegee the Famous." The stamp was hardly necessary, though, as his direct, unflinching style of photography identified him as much as his signature or his omnipresent cigar.

Weegee reveled in his role as a special character and he played it to the hilt. With his chewed-up cigar, crushed felt hat, and bulging eyes, he sometimes looked like the popular stereotype of a crime photographer. He gloried in beating the cops to the scene of the action. Rushing from his car he would point his camera at the subject without bothering to focus or adjust the f-stop—ten feet at f/11 with flash covered most situations.

Besides covering violent scenes, Weegee also shot ordinary life—people relaxing at Coney Island, fans at Frank Sinatra concerts, children sleeping on a fire escape. Later in his career he photographed many Hollywood stars.

In Weegee's work the flash bulb's explosion intruded on the night's protective darkness, violating its cover and exposing the startling scenes that he was a party to. In all of his photos, the flash bulb is a real presence. It is evident in the strong tonal contrasts from the harsh light of a flash used on the camera. Somehow, in Weegee's world, everyone looks like a victim, caught unaware by the insistent light of the camera's flash.

SEARCH FOR A CONVENIENT LIGHT SOURCE
■ DANGERS OF FLASH POWDER

Although Weegee had to replace the flash bulb after each exposure, flash bulbs proved infinitely more convenient than the flash powder used in Jacob Riis' day. Horror stories about flash powder are legion. Flash photographers in the old days wore special cuffs so the powder wouldn't roll down and burn their arms when the chemical was ignited. Eddie McGill, a *Chicago Tribune* photographer, suffered a skull fracture when a big flash pan bent as it fired. Another Chicago photographer, Nick McDonald, of the *Chicago Herald-Examiner*, lost a hand from exploding powder as he poured it from a bottle onto a hot flash pan. When several photographers were on the scene, they had to decide which one would set off the flash powder. Once the substance was lit, smoke filled the room, eliminating the possibility of anyone taking a second picture. An additional problem, of course, was the subjects gasping for air, sometimes between curses. Needless to say, photographers and their flash pans were not exactly welcome in most places.

Three kinds of flash lamps were available for the photographer: the Caywood, the Imp, and the Victor. The Caywood flash was used for indoor portraits and group pictures. The Imp lamp, manufactured by the Imperial Brass Co., worked well for large groups indoors. Outdoors, at night, when lots of light was needed, the news photographer used a long Victor flash pan.

A photojournalist could choose between three types of flash powder manufactured by the Excel Fire Works Company. Powder in the red label can burned the fastest (1/25 sec.), so it was selected for sports. Yellow-labeled powder fired slower but brighter. Blue-labeled powder, used for portraits, burned the slowest but gave off the most light.

Photographers always filled the flash pan with four times as much powder as needed to make sure they would have enough light, recalls Frank Scherschel, who was a news photographer in those days. He says that, besides packing his camera and plates, he always carried a tube of Unguentine in case he burned his hands. With the lens set at f/16 the news photographer fired the flash lamp and prayed.

■ FLASH BULBS: SAFE BUT INCONVENIENT

Although smokeless flash powders were developed over the years, it was not until 1925 that a superior method of lighting was found. In this year Paul Vierkotter patented the flash bulb—a glass bulb containing an inflammable mixture that was set off by a weak electric current. Four years later, the flash bulb appeared in an improved form, with aluminum foil inside. Although these bulbs were infinitely preferable to the smoky, noisy, and dangerous flash pans, the flash bulbs still were inconvenient for the press photographer. Some of the biggest bulbs were close in size to a football. Static electricity or electromagnetic energy could cause them to fire. In addition, the bulbs had to be replaced after each shot, a delay that could cause the photographer to miss important pictures.

Marian Fulton, in her book *Eyes of Time*, points out that the flash bulb gives an artificial quality to the photo. The light coming from the on-camera flash is always bright. The flash tends to flatten the subject in the foreground, separating it from the rest of the scene, which becomes a separate, darker background. She notes that all flash pictures, regardless of content, tend to take on the same "look."

■ EDGERTON DEVELOPS THE ELECTRONIC FLASH

Although it did not change the character of the light, the electronic flash was far more convenient than the flash bulb. The forerunner to the modern electronic flash was designed by Harold Edgerton (see p. 332) of the Massachusetts Institute of Technology in the early 1930s. While investigating motors, Edgerton developed an electronic stroboscope that flashed at repeated fixed intervals, synchronizing with the moving parts of the machine. Edgerton later used his stroboscope to take single and multiple-image photos, not only of moving machine parts but also of tennis players, golfers, and divers, as well as hummingbirds in flight. Basically, his electronic flash worked by discharging a high voltage from a capacitor through a gas-filled tube, producing an extremely brief burst of light. The light was powerful enough for photography despite the relatively insensitive films available at the time. Though an observer would not be aware of it, the light from the electronic flash exceeded the combined output of 40,000 50-watt bulbs.

Edgerton designed his electronic flashes for research. George Woodruff, a photographer with the International News Photos (INP), heard about Edgerton's invention and dropped by the scientist's M.I.T. lab. Woodruff asked if the electronic flash had any use in news photography. Edgerton

Flash powder fired in a pan left the room filled with smoke, unfortunately delaying the possibility of taking a second photo. Here, Harry Rhodes demonstrates his flash technique. Rhodes, we hope, never inhaled at the wrong time.

Flash bulbs, which replaced flash powder, were smokeless and safe, but cumbersome and awkward.

Ed Farber of the *Milwaukee Journal* modified the electronic flash, making it portable and convenient for news photographers.

(Photos above from the files of the National Press Photographers Association, courtesy of John Faber.)

answered by helping Woodruff lug three flash units to the circus playing in town that night.

Each strobe—all of which are still in use, according to Edgerton—had a large capacitor that put out 4000 volts (9600 watt-seconds). The flash duration lasted less than 1/50,000 of a second. On successive nights, the pair tried their strobe set-up at a variety of sporting events. With Woodruff on camera and Edgerton on strobe, the team of photographer and scientist managed to stop the action of runners, boxers, and swimmers in their natural environments.

While working for the *Milwaukee Journal*, photojournalist Edward Farber designed an electronic flash that could be synchronized with the common shutter found on most press cameras. Farber's first working electronic flash weighed ninety pounds and had oil capacitors and an AC power supply. The *Journal* sent Farber back to the lab to design a more portable model.

By October 1940, Farber had the flash's weight down to twenty-five pounds. Powered by a motorcycle battery, it also had a plug for household current. In the fall of 1941, Farber found a lighter battery, and around it he built a "dream" portable flash weighing only 13½ pounds. In the 1950s, the electronic flash design was sold to Graflex Inc., in Rochester, New York, and remained for many years a standard piece of equipment for the news photographer.

About the time the flash bulb was perfected, another invention was being developed that allowed pictures to be taken in dim indoor light without any artificial illumination at all. The candid camera, as it came to be known, was to change the course of news photography and redefine the role, as well as the potential, of the photojournalist.

■ GRAFLEX USED UNTIL 1955

At the beginning of the century, the most widely used press camera was the Graflex and its German counterpart, the Ica. These cameras were portable, although still heavy; they used either a 4"×5", 4"×6", or 5"×7" glass plate. Because of the large size of the negative, the resulting print was of high quality and had adequate detail.

The Graflex looked like a large rectangular box with a hood on top. To view through this oversized single-lens reflex camera, the photographer would look down the hood at an angled mirror that would reflect what the lens saw—except that the image was reversed left to right. The photographer could attach a 40-inch telephoto lens for shooting sports from the press box. When the Graflex carried the telephoto, the seventy-pound combination was affectionately known as Big Bertha. The large negative produced by the Graflex meant that photographers did not have to frame perfectly on every play—they

Edgerton (FAR RIGHT) inventor of the electronic flash, took pictures with local photojournalists at the circus to demonstrate how his equipment could be used to cover events outside the lab.
(Courtesy, MIT Museum.)

were secure in the knowledge that if they captured the action on at least part of the film they could make a usable blow up. James Frezzolini, a news photographer, modified the Big Bertha with a notched lever for rapid focusing between first, second, and third bases at a baseball game. According to John Faber, a former historian for the National Press Photographers Association, some photographers continued to shoot with the Graflex at sports events until 1955.

■ SPEED GRAPHIC: A NEWS PHOTOGRAPHER'S BADGE

For general news, the Speed Graphic, introduced in 1912 by Folmer and Schwing (a division of Eastman Kodak), replaced the Graflex by the 1920s. The front of the Speed Graphic folded down to form a bed with tracks. The lens slid out on these tracks. A bellows connected the lens to the box of the Graphic and expanded or contracted as the photographer focused. The film was carried in holders, two shots to a holder. Whereas a range finder came attached to the side of the camera, a seasoned pro often removed this device and just guess-focused. While the camera could be used with a tripod, it was more conveniently hand-held. The 9½-lb. camera could take intensive pounding, and even after the development of the small 35mm camera, many news photographers continued to shoot with Speed Graphics.

Bob Gilka, who later became director of photography for the *National Geographic*, was picture editor of the *Milwaukee Journal* in 1955, when he issued a memo that read in part, "This 35mm stuff may be okay for magazines . . . but we might as well face the facts. We are wasting our time shooting the average news assignment on 35mm."

Robert Boyd, a past president of the National Press Photographers Association, was once asked what the press camera could do that the 35mm couldn't. Boyd put the big camera on the ground and sat on it.

The days of the Speed Graphic, however, were numbered.

■ LEICA LIGHTENS THE LOAD

The earliest miniaturized camera was the Ermanox, a German-designed small camera that took single glass plates and had an extra-fast lens. The lens, at f/1.8, had an almost incredible light-gathering capability for the period. The manufacturer of the Ermanox lens proudly claimed, "This extremely fast lens opens a new era in photography and makes accessible hitherto unknown fields with instantaneous or brief time exposures without flash-light. . . ."

He was right that the lens opened a new era in photography. But unfortunately, one major drawback aimed the Ermanox for extinction. The camera used only individually loaded 4.5×6 cm glass plates—an obvious

To view through the Graflex camera, the photographer looked down into the hood on top of the box. The bulky camera used glass plates.
(Files of the National Press Photographers Association, courtesy of John Faber.)

The Graflex camera in the foreground, nicknamed "Big Bertha" when fitted with a telephoto lens, was used by many papers to cover sports until the mid-1950s.
(Photo courtesy of the Associated Press.)

The 4"x5" Speed Graphic was the standard news camera of the business from the 1920s to the 1950s. Experienced photographers didn't focus: they just guessed the distance. Old Speed Graphic users claimed the camera had only three distance settings: here, there, and yonder.

The early Leica camera.

inconvenience for news photographers. Still, the Ermanox was important in that it was the forerunner to the camera that would revolutionize photojournalism.

Oskar Barnack, a technician at the E. Leitz factory in Germany, invented the Leica. Like the Ermanox, the Leica had an extremely fast lens but, rather than glass plates, the Leica used a strip of 35mm motion picture film with as many as forty frames per roll possible in the original models. Barnack continually worked on his design and, in 1924, the first Leicas were put on the market. By 1932, Leitz mass-produced the camera in fully refined form with extremely fast, removable lenses and a built-in range finder.

The implications of this handy, small-format camera were wide ranging.

Now, with existing light, the photographer could snap pictures without having to bother with flash bulbs. The Leica's lightness, ease of handling, and fast lens allowed the photographer to move freely, unencumbered by heavy camera accessories, flash attachments, clumsy tripods, or glass plates.

Because the film could be rapidly advanced, photographers could make exposures one after another, thus enabling them to capture an unfolding event without stopping between pictures.

The Leica gave the news photographer unprecedented mobility and the ability to take a picture unobtrusively. The photographer no longer had to stop life in its tracks to snap a picture; people no longer posed for the camera's lens. Now, subjects could be more relaxed and natural, leaving the photographer free to concentrate on atmosphere and composition rather than on technical

matters. These new capabilities did nothing less than change the relationship between photographers and the world. Because they could use available light and remain unobtrusive, press photographers could imbue their pictures with a new sense of realism, of life in the making.

ERICH SALOMON: FATHER OF CANDID PHOTOGRAPHY

The man who first exploited this photographic impression of life was Erich Salomon. Often called "the father of candid photography," he was probably the person who coined the term photojournalism to describe what he was doing. Salomon began his photography career in 1928 with the new Ermanox camera. Salomon's arenas of action were diplomatic gatherings and government functions; his subjects were the foremost statesmen and political personalities of Europe. When he initially tried to penetrate these carefully guarded events, the officials refused to let him in, claiming that flash powder and large cameras would disrupt the orderly proceedings. But when Salomon demonstrated the capabilities of his unobtrusive camera, he was not only given entry into these private quarters but he also became a habitué of diplomatic circles, causing French Prime Minister Aristide Briand to remark, "There are just three things necessary for a conference: a few Foreign Secretaries, a table, and Salomon."

Even the ingenious Salomon, however, could not charm his way into all top-level, top-secret meetings. When barred from an important conference, the dapper photographer would don his top hat, white gloves, and

The man pointing had just learned that press photographers were not being allowed in. The politician said he doubted that and wagered that at least one would be there. Slowly, he peered around the room until he discovered Erich Salomon just as the photographer was taking a picture of him. Salomon was the first photographer to use extensively the Ermanox miniature camera to catch candid photos. Salomon specialized in diplomatic gatherings and governmental functions. If Salomon couldn't get in openly, he hid his camera in the crown of his hat, in a temporary sling around his arm, or in a hollowed-out book.
(Photo by Erich Salomon, Magnum.)

tails and set to work concocting some scheme to allow him entry into this private world. The ruses that Salomon used are legendary. He once managed to take pictures in a courtroom, which was off-limits to photographers. He shot his film by cutting a hole in the crown of his hat and hiding his camera there. Following the success of this technique, he used a similar ploy to photograph a roulette game in Monte Carlo. He hollowed out several thick books and hid his camera inside. While Salomon appeared absorbed in the game, he was actually busy clicking away with his concealed camera.

The urbane, multilingual Salomon moved with ease among dignitaries and heads of state, capturing with his camera the personalities of the people who shaped history and the atmosphere of their inner sanctums. With the Ermanox, and later with the Leica, he penetrated the masks of the public personae to reveal those very human characteristics that lay underneath—of dozing diplomats, bored-looking royalty, down-to-earth movie stars.

There is a remarkably intimate quality to Salomon's work. Because his camera enabled him to catch these prominent people off guard, his pictures give the impression that the camera, rather than being an intruder, is simply a watchful observer who happens to be present at the scene. Salomon's candid photography attracted a good deal of attention, and he numbered among his subjects such luminaries as Albert Einstein, Herbert Hoover, and Marlene Dietrich.

Salomon later died in one of Hitler's concentration camps. As one of the first to demonstrate the possibility of recording events with the candid camera, Salomon truly deserves the title of "father of candid photography."

THE PHOTO ESSAY

Salomon's candid-camera style proved that current events could be captured pictorially. The impact of this discovery was felt strongly in Germany, where in such picture magazines as the *Muncher Illustrierte Presse,* *Berliner Illustrierte Zeitung* and in England in the *Illustrated London News*, the photo essay first appeared in embryonic form. Stefan Lorant, editor of the *Muncher Illustrierte Presse*, developed the notion that there could be a photographic equivalent of the literary essay. Previously, if several pictures appeared together, they were arranged either arbitrarily or sequentially, with little regard for the conceptual logic of the layout, captions, cropping, or picture size. Lorant and his colleagues began experimenting with a new photographic form, in which several

pictures appeared—not in isolation, but as a cohesive whole.

Illustrated magazines were not a new phenomenon in the United States. As early as the nineteenth century, *Leslie's Illustrated Newspaper* and *Harper's Weekly* relied on drawings to elucidate their articles. After the invention of the halftone, such publications as *McClure's, Cosmopolitan,* and *Collier's* continued the tradition of adding pictures to supplement their stories.

The difference between these early magazines and the great American picture magazines that followed lay not only in the number of pictures used but also in the way they were used. In the new magazines, several pictures were grouped together with an overall theme and design, and picture editors discovered truth in the old adage, "The whole is worth more than the sum of the parts." Accordingly, the role of the picture editor became all-important; along with the photographer, the picture editor shaped the story and, with the aid of shooting scripts, mapped out the photographer's plan of attack.

■ *LIFE* COMES TO LIFE

Life was the brainchild of Henry Luce, the publisher of *Time* and *Fortune* magazines. Spurred by the success of similar European ventures, Luce and his colleagues felt the time was ripe in the United States for a new, large-format picture magazine. Hence, *Life* came to life in the 1930s. In its manifesto, the new magazine stated its credo:

> *To see life, to see the world; to eyewitness great events; to watch the faces of the poor and the gestures of the proud; to see strange things—machines, armies, multitudes, shadows in the jungle and on the moon; to see man's work—his paintings, towers and discoveries; to see things a thousand miles away, things hidden behind walls and within rooms, things dangerous to come to; the women that men love and many children; to see and to take pleasure in seeing; to see and be amazed; to see and be instructed.*

For the first issue, November 23, 1936, *Life*'s editors dispatched Margaret Bourke-White to photograph the construction of a WPA dam in New Deal, Montana. In the 1920s Bourke-White had made a name for herself as a freelancer and later as a top-notch industrial photographer on the staff of *Fortune* magazine. Her pictures celebrated the burgeoning machine aesthetic of the time, and her expertise in capturing on film structural and engineering details made her the perfect candidate for the assignment.

The first cover of *LIFE* magazine taken by Margaret Bourke-White (ABOVE) showed a WPA dam in New Deal, Montana.
(© 1936 Time Inc., courtesy of Time Incorporated.)

When she returned with her pictures, however, the editors of *Life* were in for a surprise. Not only had she captured the industrial drama of the dam under construction, but she took it upon herself to document the personal drama of the town's inhabitants, as well. Bourke-White turned her camera on the details of frontier life—the hastily erected shanty settlements, the weather-beaten faces of the townspeople, the Saturday night ritual at the local bar—and enhanced her story by adding the human dimension.

On the cover of the first issue of *Life* is a picture of the huge dam in all its geometrical splendor. And inside is Bourke-White's photo essay: nine pages of carefully laid-out, strategically chosen pictures of the New Deal's people. The first issue was a sell-out. The editorial offices of *Life* in New York were besieged by phone calls and telegrams asking for more copies. The presses were restarted to meet the demand. "During the first year you had to hurry to the news stands on publication day to grab up a copy before they were all gobbled up," according to Arthur Goldsmith in an article about the magazine.

The photo essay of Peck Dam became the prototype for a form that flourished in the pages of *Life*, a form that expanded the scope of photojournalism and redefined the way we see. The first four photographers who appeared on the magazine's masthead, besides Margaret Bourke-White, were Peter Stackpole, known for his photographs of the construction of the Golden Gate Bridge;

Thomas McAvoy, an expert on the use of the 35mm for political candids; and Alfred Eisenstaedt, a specialist in the new German style of candid photography.

During its first few years, *Life* had the reputation of a magazine that ran sensational pictures. The magazine's first real shocker was titled "How to undress in front of your husband." The story, tame by today's standards, was supposed to be "sophisticated satire," but many readers let it be known they thought it indecent. Several issues later, *Life* ran an article titled "Birth of a Baby." The feature ran four pages and showed in drawings how the unborn child grows in the womb and the progress of the baby from the mother's body. In the actual birth pictures the only things visible in the frame were the baby's head, the doctor, and masses of sterile dressing. After publication, a furor broke out. The magazine was banned in 33 cities and Canada and publisher Roy Larsen was arrested for selling indecent literature.

The complicated career of W. Eugene Smith

Perhaps the most influential, controversial, and well-remembered photographer ever to work for *Life* was W. Eugene Smith—who quit the magazine twice. He signed a contract with *Life* magazine in 1939, and subsequently shot many photos and photo essays for the magazine. Smith resigned in 1941 because he felt he was in an assignment rut at *Life*. He referred to his pictures at this time as having "a lot of depth-of-field but not much

W. Eugene Smith's landmark essay "Spanish Village," for *LIFE* magazine, opens with a young girl preparing for confirmation and closes with a wake for a dead villager.
(*LIFE*, April 9, 1951.)

depth-of-meaning." He covered World War II at first for Ziff-Davis Publishing Company and then was rehired by *Life*.

Obsessed with the gap between the reality of war and the comfortable headlines of war seen by the people back home, the 24-year-old correspondent hurled himself into the front lines, trying to catch on film the horror of killing. Smith followed thirteen invasions, taking memorable pictures of the war—a tiny, fly-covered, half-dead baby held up by a soldier after being rescued from a cave in Saipan; a wounded soldier, bandaged, stretched out in Leyte Cathedral; a decaying Japanese body on an Iwo Jima beach. Then, while shooting a story on a day in the life of a soldier, Smith was hit by a shell fragment that ripped through his left hand, his face, and his mouth—critically wounding him. Two years of painful convalescence followed.

In 1947, Smith resumed his work for *Life* magazine. During the next seven years, he produced his best-known set of photo essays: the exhausting dedication of a country doctor; the poverty and faith in a Spanish village; the pain of birth, life, and death being eased by a nurse midwife, Smith's own favorite essay (see pages 118–129). "In many ways, shooting these photos was the most rewarding experience photography has allowed me," said Smith of the midwife essay.

According to Jim Hughes' extensive biography, ***Shadow and Substance***, Smith himself was not an easy photographer to work with. While most *Life* staffers shot their assignments and shipped the film back to New York, Smith developed his own negatives and then held on to them. With control of his negatives, Smith could threaten to withdraw a story if he felt the editors were not going to play the photos accurately.

In 1954 Smith photographed the essay "Man of Mercy," about Dr. Albert Schweitzer and his leper colony in Africa. After carrying the Schweitzer essay back to America, Smith quarreled with *Life*'s editors about it. In a futile attempt to affect the use of pictures and captions, and to expand the Schweitzer layout, Smith resigned from *Life* for the second time.

Smith, in the latter part of his life, and with the help of his wife Eileen, photographed a moving story about mercury poisoning in Minamata, Japan, which was published first in *Life* and eventually appeared as a book.

■ COMPETITION FOR *LIFE*
Look Based on Survey
The astounding success of *Life* was matched by that of its fellow picture magazine, *Look*. *Look* was founded by the Cowles brothers, a Minneapolis newspaper publishing family who commissioned George Gallup to discover what part of the newspaper was most widely read. When Gallup's poll revealed that the picture page was most popular, the brothers founded *Look*, which first appeared in January 1937, a few months after *Life* began. *Look* quickly developed a reputation for sensational stories. One description at the time claimed that *Look* was a combination of "gall and honey." Cowles answered, "*Look* has been criticized as sensationally thrilling. My only reply is that life itself is thrilling . . . "

Look toned down its sex-and-violence image to concentrate on feature stories. Known for its writer/photographer team approach, *Look* hired many outstanding shooters including Arthur Rothstein, Paul Fusco, and Stanley Tretich.

SEE, PEEK, CLICK, SCOOP
The rapid rise in *Life*'s and *Look*'s circulation persuaded other publishers to start picture magazines. Within two years of *Life*'s first issue, the picture magazine field was crowded with thirteen periodicals sporting one-word, punchy names like *See, Click, Peek, Pix, Picture*, and *Scoop,* and boasting a combined circulation of 16 million per issue. The magazines' content ranged from "girlie" pin-ups to the social ills of drinking. Stories included the "Truth about cremation" and "How you should tell your child about sex." Most stories in these *Life* and *Look* imitators were highly scripted with few candids. Each represented a little melodrama, and sometimes actors even played parts in the photos. The proliferation of picture magazines, starting in 1936 and continuing through the 1940s and 1950s, has caused historians to call the period before television's dominance the "golden age of photojournalism."

PHOTOGRAPHERS COMPETE
■ RIVAL PHOTOGRAPHERS WERE MANY
The success and style of the picture magazines had some important effects on newspaper photojournalism. The photo essay layout influenced many newspapers to adopt a similarly simple and direct arrangement of pictures about one subject. Likewise, newspapers began running more feature stories and using larger pictures.

Philadelphia boasted 20 daily newspapers during the 1920s and more than 200 press photographers. During the depression, however, many papers died. While newspapers competed for readers, press photographers competed for scoops. Photographers were not above sabotaging one another. Joe Costa, who worked for the *New York Morning World*

The success of *Life* and then *Look* spawned many picture magazines in the days before television.

and later the *New York Daily News*, recalled that photographers never let their camera bags out of their sight. He called it a "dog-eat-dog" business. A competitor might expose the film in a fellow photographer's holders or simply switch holders: the exclusive picture would be in the opposition's newspaper the next day!

Using the basic 4"×5" speed graphic, photographers of this period covered gangland slayings and bootlegged booze all without the aid of an exposure meter. Photographers determined most exposures by "guesstimations." The effective film index at this time was around ISO 25.

Guessing lighting exposures was just one of the shooting techniques photographers learned from one another because few went to school to learn photojournalism. In fact, almost no universities prior to the 1940s offered photojournalism as a major. News photographers often got started as copy boys on newspapers. If they expressed a leaning toward pictures, they could start an apprentice program in which they mixed chemicals and loaded film holders in the darkroom—progressing then to developing film and printing. They also carried equipment for photographers in the field. Moving from printing in the lab to covering news in the street was a major hurdle that took some photographers five years or more to leap, according to Sam Psoras, who started with International News Photos before joining the *Philadelphia Daily News*.

One newspaper that maintained a large photographic staff was the *Milwaukee*

Journal. Historically, the *Journal* staff worked under a unique setup. They were a part of the engraving department rather than the editorial department. Because they were part of the production team, the engraving department management was not shocked by large capital outlay expenses for equipment. As a result, the photo department instigated many technological advances, including the early use of the 35mm camera. Staff photographer Brownie Rowland brought back a Leica from Germany, and Frank Scherschel was interested enough to borrow the little camera and try it out. History books credit Bob Dumke with inventing a synchronizing switch for his Speed Graphic that allowed him to shoot flash pictures in daylight. Ed Farber developed the portable electronic strobe for covering news events. The *Journal* continued to experiment with running four-color pictures throughout the paper during the depression.

Another newspaper noted for its outstanding use of pictures was the *Des Moines Register and Tribune*. In 1928, to transport pictures from rural areas of Iowa, the paper bought an airplane and hired a pilot. In the latter half of the 1930s, *Quill and Scroll*, a trade journal, ranked this paper first in the number of pictures carried.

■ A PROGRESSIVE VISUAL NEWSPAPER

PM, a short-lived, liberal tabloid, exhibited the most progressive and modern use of pictures by a newspaper. Founded in 1940 by Ralph Ingersoll, who previously had helped edit *Time* and *Life,* the paper combined the word approach of the newsweekly with the visual approach of the picture magazine in a daily, tabloid newspaper. The squarish-format tabloid hired the best photographers of the day, including Weegee (Arthur Fellig) and Margaret Bourke-White. The paper was beautifully printed with a special ink and stapled so that the pages would not fly apart. Its sections with eight consecutive pages of full-page pictures were an approach unheard of in its day and, in fact, rarely if ever seen since. The crusading paper used photographs to document its exposés, including one series on the unsanitary conditions in the New York poultry market.

Cindy M. Brown, in her study of the newspaper titled, "*PM*: Just Another Picture Paper?," found that, not only did *PM* run more pictures than its New York rivals—including the *Post, Sun,* and *Mirror*—but it ran them larger and grouped them in a more storytelling way. In fact, the paper approached a 50/50 picture/text split, unheard of in today's newspapers. Brown wrote that *PM* not only ran more visually

PM combined a news-magazine's approach to writing and a picture magazine's approach to photos into a strikingly different daily newspaper.
(Collection of Sidney Kobré.)

interesting pictures, but the pictures had stronger compositional elements than its rivals. In fact, every Sunday, *PM's Weekly*, the paper's Sunday edition, featured a gallery of full-page photographs. Unfortunately, relying on newsstand sales and subscriptions alone, the paper eventually died, because it contained no advertising and thus lacked sufficient revenues to survive.

WAR CENSORSHIP

World War II produced corpses in abundance. Nonetheless, during the war, American citizens saw few dead soldiers. When they did, it was the U.S. government's attempt to influence public opinion. This censorship was not new. During the entire nineteen months of American involvement in World War I, the government prohibited publication of any photographs of dead American soldiers. A similar prohibition lasted for the first twenty-one months of American involvement in World War II.

Unlike World War I, in which the government tried to completely restrict photographers' access to front lines, photojournalists during World War II could move freely on battlefields and accompany naval assaults. During the war, accredited photographers submitted exposed film to field censors. Photographers could shoot where, when, and what they wanted, but all exposed film was screened by two layers of censors—one in the field and another in Washington. Early in the war, censors placed all photographs of dead and badly wounded Americans in a secret Pentagon file known to officials as the "Chamber of Horrors."

Initially, censors were worried that if the population saw pictures of dead American soldiers they would press for a compromise settlement with Germany and Japan. Later, as government leaders became concerned about public complacency brought on by Allied victories, they released some of these photographs of war's brutality. For instance, *Life* published George Strock's photograph of three American soldiers lying dead on Buna Beach in new Guinea. After almost two years of the war, this photo was the first released that showed dead American soldiers. The *Washington Post* said it was time that the government treated Americans as adults, and that photographs "can help us to understand something of what has been sacrificed for the victories we have won." Yet even the *Post* went on to say that "an overdose of such photographs would be unhealthy."

But, until the war's end and after, the government continued to censor photographs of mutilated or emotionally distressed American soldiers, even though more than a million soldiers suffered psychiatric symptoms serious enough to debilitate them for some period. The censors held back any pictures showing racial conflicts at American bases, and other visual evidence of disunity or disorder. In George Roeder's book ***The Censored War***, he tells how American opinions about World War II were manipulated both by wartime images that citizens were allowed to see and by the images that were suppressed.

At the beginning of the Korean War, photographers were under a system of voluntary censorship. However, on November 2, 1950, American troops came into direct contact with Chinese forces as the Chinese Communist army entered the war in full strength. What followed was a long and difficult retreat covered by the media.

This World War II photo of a frozen American soldier with a stake driven through him was censored by the U.S. government for fear of discouraging citizens on the home front.
(Photo courtesy of the National Archives.)

Embarrassed personally, General McArthur ended the voluntary censorship system and imposed a full military censorship on news.

Before the general attached the clamp of military censorship, photographers covered all aspects of the Korean War. Despite relatively free access, and limited only by self-censorship, fewer than 5 percent of the photos published by *Life, Newsweek*, and *Time* were actual combat photos.

The same reticence about showing soldiers under fire did not hold true for America's next war. During at least part of the Vietnam War, 40 percent of the published pictures run by *Life, Newsweek*, and *Time* portrayed soldiers in the heat of battle, according to a study by Michael Sherer. The American public saw more of the brutal side of combat during the Tet offensive in Vietnam than during major battles in Korea. During the Vietnam War, images of dead and wounded, plus photographs of people in immediate, life-threatening situations, were offered to the public on a regular basis.

PHOTOGRAPHERS ORGANIZE

Because the public began to recognize such names as Margaret Bourke-White and Alfred Eisenstaedt, photographers began to achieve parity with writers. Originally, the photographer was a second-class citizen in the newsroom. According to one common story, when a news photographer's job opened up, the editor would find the nearest janitor and hand him a camera, telling him to set the lens at f/8 and shoot. Photographers were thought of as the people who chased fires and took cheesecake pictures. Taking cheesecake pictures involved meeting the incoming steamship to take snaps of pretty women with "lots of leg showing."

Along with steamships, cheesecake pictures slowly went out of vogue. Editors began acknowledging the contribution of pictures as a means of reporting the news. The photographer's status gradually rose.

In 1945, Burt Williams, a photographer with the *Pittsburgh Sun-Telegraph*, started organizing a professional association for photographers, The National Press Photographers Association. According to Claude Cookman in his history of the organization, *A Voice Is Born*, Williams obtained financial backing from the Cigar Institute of America for the organization and began the groundwork with a ten-city coast-to-coast telephone conference in which leaders in press photography took part. At a meeting in New York City on February 23 and 24, 1946, the group adopted a constitution and elected officers: Joseph Costa, *New York Daily News*, president; Burt Williams, *Pittsburgh Sun-Telegraph*, secretary; and Charles Mack, Hearst Metrotone News, treasurer.

Today the organization holds an annual meeting, runs a traveling education seminar, and publishes an attractive, well-written magazine, *News Photographer*, which is edited by Jim Gordon. With more than 9,000 members, including pros and students, the association also administers a photo contest and sponsors educational programs in photojournalism and electronics.

More and more college graduates enter the field of photojournalism each year. The first college grad to work on the picture side of a newspaper was Paul Thompson, who graduated from Yale in 1902.

Today many schools offer courses and even degrees in photojournalism. More than ninety colleges offer at least one class in

Bain News Photographic Service provided a steady supply of photos, including light feature pictures like this one, to member papers around the country.
(Bain Collection, Library of Congress.)

news photography. Some universities even grant a Ph.D. in journalism or communications with an emphasis in photojournalism.

DISTRIBUTING PICTURES ACROSS THE LAND
■ BAIN CREATES A PICTURE SERVICE

In 1898, a newspaper writer and photographer, George Grantham Bain, started the Bain News Photographic Service in New York City. As manager of the Washington, D.C., United Press office in the 1890s, Bain realized that he could accumulate pictures and sell them to subscribers. After Bain left the United Press, he began his own photo service. He catalogued and cross-indexed photographs he had bought from correspondents or newspapers that subscribed to his service. From newspapers throughout the country, he received pictures, copied them, and sent the copies to his list of subscribing newspapers. Bain's business expanded rapidly and, by 1905, he had acquired a million news photographs. Many of his pictures were the first of their kind, including the first federal courtroom pictures, the first photos of the Senate in session, and the first automobile race. Although a massive fire in 1908 completely destroyed Bain's archives, he immediately set about rebuilding his collection.

Other picture services developed, including Underwood and Underwood, who started out making stereoscopic pictures. Newspaper editors would call on the Underwoods for pictures to illustrate stories about remote countries where the Underwoods had operators. The Brown brothers, too, saw the possibilities of selling news pictures from their experience as circulation managers on *Harper's Weekly*. Soon the Underwood, Brown, and Bain photographers were all competing for scoops.

By 1919 the Hearst organization formed International News Photos (INP); Wide World Photos followed. In 1923 Acme News Pictures appeared. The Associated Press News Photo service began in 1927. These services sent their pictures by train, giving a tip to the porter to hand-deliver the package of photos for extra-quick service. Acme and INP later combined into United Press International (UPI), and Wide World Photos became part of the Associated Press (AP).

■ PICTURES TRANSMITTED INSTANTLY

Ever since newspapers began publishing pictures, the search was on for a way to transport the images over long distances. As early as 1907, Professor Alfred Korn of the University of Munich, Germany, had demonstrated an electrical system using a photocell, which would transmit and receive a picture over a telegraph wire. His basic principle remains in use today. In the same year, *L'Illustration* of Paris and the *London Daily Mirror* inaugurated a cross-channel service that later included other capitals of Europe.

Not until 1925 was there a permanent transmission line set up in the United States. In that year the American Telephone and Telegraph Co. (AT&T) opened a commercial wire between New York, Chicago, and San Francisco. It was first come, first served and cost $60 to send a picture coast-to-coast. AT&T sold the wire to the Associated Press in 1934. The AP bought the Bell Lab equipment, leased AT&T wire, and set up twenty-five stations. On January 1, 1935, the AP serviced an aerial picture of a plane wreck in the Adirondack Mountains, and the age of rapid wire transmission began in the United States. Soon other picture services, including International News Photos and Acme, started their own wire photo transmission networks.

For a long time, such uncontrollable factors as weather conditions would influence the quality of pictures sent on long-distance transmission lines. But today, because of digital techniques, the wire services can send photos instantaneously all over the world, with the quality of the final product looking as good as that of the original.

The development of electronic cameras, portable scanners, high-speed modems, laser transmission, as well as the improvement in fast lenses and the introduction of lighter cameras and more sensitive film, have freed the photojournalist from many of the earlier technical limitations. The improvement in technology has led to a greater range of photo styles and subjects for the news photographer. Instead of cheesecake and composograph photos taken with flash-on-camera, the new journalist can produce creative and expressive photos. These in-depth pictures, taken with available light or light from portable strobes, on color film or with an electronic camera, can attain a candid look that was impossible in the days of the *New York Daily Graphic*. ■

Transmitters like this Associated Press machine did for photographers in the 1930s what the telegraph had done for writers prior to the Civil War. The device allowed photographers to send pictures by wire across the country and eventually around the world.
(Photo courtesy of the Associated Press.)

In addition to listings from previous editions of *Photojournalism: The Professionals' Approach*, this bibliography includes articles and books derived from searches of a number of different electronic databases. Barbara Taber conducted the searches through Spring 1995.

Assignment

"Beyond the Killing Fields." *News Photographer* (April 1992): 27-31.

Bilker, Harvey L. *Photojournalism: A Freelancer's Guide.* Chicago: Contemporary Books, 1981.

Bissland, James H. and Kielmeyer, David. *Bypassed by the Revolution? Photojournalism in a Decade of Change.* Bowling Green, OH: School of Mass Communication (Bowling Green State University), 1992 [a paper presented to the Visual Communication Division Association for Education in Journalism and Mass Communication Annual Conference, Montreal, 8 Aug. 1992].

Bissland, James H. *Life in a Professional Ghetto: the Situation of Photojournalists.* Bowling Green, OH: School of Journalism (Bowling Green State University), 1984 [a paper presented to the Visual Communication Division Association for Education in Journalism and Mass Communication, Gainesville, FL, 7 Aug. 1984].

Bissland, James H. "The News Photographer's Career Ladder." *An NPPA Special Report* (also appears in the Oct. 1984 issue of *News Photographer*).

Brecher, Ellie. "Reporter-Photographer Relationships and How to Improve Them." *4Sight* (Nov.-Dec. 1993): 12-13. NPPA Region 4 magazine.

Byrne, Howard. *Without Assignment: How to Freelance in Photography.* New York: Pelegrini and Cudahy, 1952.

Durniak, John. "The New Wave of Picture Agencies." *Popular Photography* (Nov. 1980): 95-101, 146-47.

"Getting Started in Photojournalism Takes More than Technical Know-How." *Rangefinder* Winter 1991: 30-34.

Jacobs, Louis, Jr. *Free-lance Magazine Photography.* New York: Hastings House, 1970.

McDonald, Michele. "The Hard Way: Know What You're Doing Before You Sell Your Photos, It's a Tough World Out There." *News Photographer* (April 1987): 13-15.

McNamara, Michael J. "Digital Photography Comes of Age." *Popular Photography* (Sept. 1994): 33-40.

Rotkin, Charles E. *Professional Photographer's Survival Guide.* New York: American Photographic Book Publishing, 1982.

Camera and Film

Brown, Cindy M. "Color's Influence on the Content and Origin of Newsphotos." [paper]

Brown, Cindy M. "How the Use of Color Affects the Content of Newspaper Photographs." [paper presented at the Annual Meeting of the Association for Education in Journalism and Mass Communication, Washington, D.C., 1989]. ERIC, ED308525.

The Camera. Rev. ed. Alexandria, VA: Time-Life Books, 1981.

Cioffi, Ron. "*USA Today*: Its Influence on the Color, Design, Graphics and Photography of Daily U.S. Newspapers." MA thesis, Michigan State University, 1986.

Covert, Douglas C. "Color Preference Conflicts in Visual Compositions." *Newspaper Research Journal* 9 (Fall 1987): 49-59.

Denton, Craig L. "Supercharged Color: Its Arresting Place in Visual Communication." [paper presented at the Annual Meeting of the Association for Education in Journalism and Mass Communication, Gainesville, FL, 1984]. ERIC, ED244292.

Doughtie, Daniel H. "Have the Technical Problems Associated with Color Changed the Shooting Style of News Photographers?" MS thesis, Ohio University, Athens, 1988.

Garcia, Mario R., and Fry, Don. *Color in American Newspapers.* St. Petersburg, FL: The Poynter Institute for Media Studies, 1986.

Gilbert, Kathy, and Schleuder, Joan. "Effects of Color Complexity in Still Photographs on Mental Effort and Memory." [paper presented at the Annual Meeting of the Association for Education in Journalism and Mass Communication, Portland, OR, 1988]. ERIC, ED298579.

Horenstein, Henry. *Color Photography: a Working Manual.* Boston: Little, Brown and Co., 1995.

Kodak Datalines: an Exclusive Report from Kodak for the Photojournalist, Rochester, NY: Eastman Kodak Company (Issue No. 1 1989).

Smith, Ron F. "How Design and Color Affect Reader Judgment of Newspapers." *Newspaper Research Journal* 10 (Winter 1989): 75-85.

Sweers, George, ed. *A White Paper on Newspaper Color: A Special Report.* Durham, NC: National Press Photographers Association, 1985.

Tell, Judy. *Making Darkrooms Saferooms. A National Report on Occupational Health and Safety.* Durham, NC: National Press Photographers Association, 1988.

Weinberg, Adam D. *On the Line: The New Color Photojournalism.* Minneapolis: Walker Art Center, 1986.

Weintraub, David. "Ektapress Gains Popularity." *Photo District News* (April 1989): cover.

Editing

Adams, R. C., Copeland, Gary A., Fish, Marjorie J., and Hughes, Melissa. "Effect of Framing on Selection of Photographs of Men and Women." *Journalism Quarterly* 57 (1980): 463-67.

Baxter, William S., Quarles, Rebecca, and Kosak, Herman. "The Effects of Photographs and Their Size on Reading and Recall of News Stories." [paper presented at the Annual Meeting of the Photojournalism Division, Association for Education in Journalism. Seattle, WA, 1978]. ERIC, ED159722.

Bergeman, Rich. "Photo Editing: A Neglected Art." *Community College Journalist* 15 (Winter 1987): 18-20.

Bernt, Joseph P. and Greenwald, Marilyn S. *Tolerance of Senior Daily Newspaper Editors for Photographs of People with AIDS and Gays and Lesbians.* [presented to the Visual Communication Division of the Assn. for Education in Journalism and Mass Communication, Montreal, 5-8 Aug. 1992].

Blackwood, Roy E. "The Content of News Photos: Roles Portrayed by Men and Women." *Journalism Quarterly* 60 (1983): 710-14.

Blackwood, Roy E. "International News Photos in U.S. and Canadian Papers." *Journalism Quarterly* 64 (1987): 195-99.

"Changing Face of America: Gay Teens Project Wins Sabbatical." *News Photographer* (June 1993): 2, 4, 8.

Chapnick, Howard. "Markets and Careers: American vs. European Picture Editing." *Popular Photography* (Dec. 1986): 38-39.

Chapnick, Howard. "Markets and Careers: Changing Views on Picture Editing." *Popular Photography* (Dec. 1986): 38-39.

Chapnick, Howard. "Markets and Careers: Photographic Captions." *Popular Photography* (Feb. 1979): 42, 64, 127, 143.

Chapnick, Howard. "Markets and Careers: Words Tell the Reader what Pictures Can't; They Make a Photographer a Photojournalist." *Popular Photography* (Feb. 1979): 40, 64, 127, 143.

Einsiedel, E. F., and Murray, A. "Content Analysis of the Use of Front-Page Photographs: *Akron Beacon Journal* 1936-1976." [paper presented at the meeting of the Photojournalism Division, Association for Education in Journalism, Madison, WI, 1977].

Evans, Harold, ed. *Pictures on a Page: Photo-Journalism, Graphics and Picture Editing.* New York: Holt, Rinehart and Winston, 1978.

Fedler, Fred; Counts, Tim; and Hightower, Paul. "Changes in Wording of Cutlines Fail to Reduce Photographs' Offensiveness." *Journalism Quarterly* 59 (1982): 633-37.

Finberg, Howard I., and Itule, Bruce D. *Visual Editing: A Graphic Guide for Journalists.* Belmont, CA: Wadsworth Publishing Co., 1990.

Fosdick, James A., and Shoemaker, Pamela J. "How Varying Reproduction Methods affect Response to Photographs." *Journalism Quarterly (*Spring 1982): 13-20.

Frascella, Larry. "The Searchers: Four of Today's Most Committed Picture Editors Talk About How They Hunt Out the Best Photographs, Where Visual Style is Headed, and Why Photographers Need to Be More Original." *American Photographer* (Dec. 1989): 48-51.

Gentry, James K., and Zang, Barbara. "Visual Editing: Graphics and Photo Editors Are Finding Their Place in the Newsroom." *MGR* [insert in *News Photographer*] (April 1989): 1-3.

Golden, Anthony R. "The Effect of Quality and Clarity on the Recall of Photographic Illustrations." [paper presented at the Annual Meeting of the Association for Education in Journalism and Mass Communication, San Antonio, TX, 1987]. ERIC, ED287162.

Halliday-Levy, Tereza. "The Connotation Dimension of News Photographs." [paper presented at the Annual Meeting of the Association for Education in Journalism, Athens, OH, 1982]. ERIC, ED217475.

Harrower, Tim. *The Newspaper Designer's Handbook*. Portland, OR: Oregonian Publishing Co., 1989.

Heyman, Ken, and Durniak, John. *The Right Picture: A Photographer and a Picture Editor Demonstrate How to Choose*. New York: Amphoto, 1986.

Huh, Hyun-Joo Lee. "The Effect of Newspaper Picture Size on Readers' Attention, Recall and Comprehension of Stories." [paper presented to the Visual Communication Division of the AEJMC 1993].

Hunter, Jefferson. *Image and Word: The Interaction of Twentieth-Century Photographs and Texts*. Cambridge, MA: Harvard University Press, 1987.

Hurley, Gerald D., and McDougall, Angus. *Visual Impact in Print: How to Make Pictures Communicate; A Guide for the Photographer, the Editor, the Designer*. Chicago: American Publishers Press, 1971.

Jett, Anne. "Diversity and a Local Newspaper: When Photojournalism Becomes Public Relations." Minneapolis, MN: University of Minnesota, 1994. [student paper presented to Visual Communication Division of AEJMC].

Kalish, Stanley E., and Edom, Clifton C. *Picture Editing*. New York: Rinehart, 1951.

Kenney, Keith. "Forces Affecting Selection of Photos and TV Stories." *News Photographer* (Feb. 1992): 51-52.

Kenney, Keith. "How Groups of People are Portrayed." *News Photographer* (Jan. 1992): 43-46.

Kerrick, Jean S. "Influence of Captions on Picture Interpretation." *Journalism Quarterly* 32 (1955): 177-184.

Kerrick, Jean S. "News Pictures, Captions and the Point of Resolution." *Journalism Quarterly* 36 (1959): 183-188.

Lang, Wendy. "Sequences: Conceptual Relationships." *Peterson's Photographic Magazine* (June 1979): pp. 88-99.

Leggett, Dawn and Wanta, Wayne. "Gender Stereotypes in Wire Service Sports." *Newspaper Research Journal* Vol. 10, #3 (Spring 1989): 105-114.

Lester, Paul, and Smith, Ron. "African-American Picture Coverage in *Life*, *Newsweek*, and *Time*, 1937-1988." [paper presented at the Annual Meeting of the Association for Education in Journalism and Mass Communication, Washington, DC, 1989]. ERIC, ED310460.

Lester, Paul. "Use of Visual Elements on Newspaper Front Pages." *Journalism Quarterly* 65 (1988): 760-63.

Luebke, Barbara F. "Out of Focus: Images of Women and Men in Newspaper Photographs." *Sex Roles* 20 (1989): 121-33.

MacLean, Malcolm S., Jr. "Communication Strategy, Editing Games and IQ." In *Science, Psychology and Communication*. Edited by Steven R. Brown and Donald J. Brenner, 327-44. New York: Teachers College Press, 1972.

MacLean, Malcolm S., Jr., and Hazard, William R. "Women's Interest in Pictures; The Badger Village Study." *Journalism Quarterly* 30 (1953): 139-162.

MacLean, Malcolm S., Jr., and Kao, Anne Li-An. *Editorial Predictions of Magazine Picture Appeals*. Iowa City, IA: School of Journalism, University of Iowa, 1965.

MacLean, Malcolm S., Jr., and Kao, Anne Li-An. "Picture Selection: An Editorial Game." *Journalism Quarterly* 40 (1963): 230-232.

Mann, Maria. "Great Expectations: Trying to Gain an Equal Foot in the Decision Making Process." *MGR* [insert in *News Photographer*] (April 1989): 1, 4.

Matthews, Mary L., and Reuss, Carol. "The Minimal Image of Women in *Time* and *Newsweek*, 1940-1980." [paper presented at the Annual Meeting of the Association for Education in Journalism and Mass Communication, Memphis, TN, 1985]. ERIC, ED260405.

McDougall, Angus, and Hampton, Vieta Jo. *Picture Editing and Layout: A Guide to Better Visual Communication*. Columbia, MO: Viscom Press, 1990.

Noble, Edward R. "Credible Cutlines." *Editor and Publisher* (17 Feb. 1979): 9.

O'Brien, Sue. "Eye on Soweto: a Study of Factors in News Photo Use." Boulder, CO: the University of Colorado, 1991. [paper presented to the Visual Communication Division, AEJMC Annual Convention, Boston, MA, Aug. 1991].

Pasternack, Steve and Utt, Sandra. "A Study of America's Front Pages: a 10 Year Update." [paper presented to the Visual Communication Division of the AEJMC Atlanta Convention, Aug. 1994.].

Peterson, John. "Reader Response to Newspictures by Photographic Type." [Unpublished paper.]

Peterson, John C. "Toward a Theory of Picture Editing and Use in Printed Publication." [paper presented to the Visual Communication Division of the AEJMC, Boston, MA, 8 Aug. 1991].

Rich, Kathy. "Contact Sheet: Responses of Leading Picture Editors to a Survey to Determine How They Choose Pictures." *Camera 35* (April 1979): 34.

Roark, Virginia, and Wanta, Wayne. "Response to Photographs." *VCQ* (Spring 1994): 12-13.

Roche, James M. "Newspaper Subscribers' Response to Accident Photographs: The Acceptance Level Compared to Demographics, Death Anxiety, Fear of Death, and State Anxiety." [paper presented at the Annual Meeting of the AEJMC, Corvallis, OR, 1983]. ERIC, ED234386.

Schlagheck, Carol. "Handling Critics and Controversy: How Some Editors and Ombudsmen Have Dealt with Negative Reader Response." [NPAA Management Report] *News Photographer* (July 1993): 17-25.

Sentman, Mary Alice. "Black and White: Disparity in Coverage by *Life Magazine* from 1937 to 1972." *Journalism Quarterly* 60 (1983): 501-508.

Sherer, Michael D. "Comparing Magazine Photos of Vietnam and Korean Wars." *Journalism Quarterly* 65 (1988): 752-56.

Shoemaker, Pamela J., and Fosdick, James A. "How Varying Reproduction Methods Affects Response to Photographs." *Journalism Quarterly* 59 (1982): 13-20, 65.

Singletary, M. W. "Newspaper Photographs: A Content Analysis, 1936-76." *Journalism Quarterly* 55 (1978): 585-89.

Swanson, Charles. "What They Read in 130 Daily Newspapers." *Journalism Quarterly* 32 (1955): 411-21.

Tannenbaum, Percy H., and Fosdick, James A. "The Effect of Lighting Angle on Judgment on Photographed Subjects." *Audio Visual Communication Review* 8 (1960): 253-262.

Ungero, Joseph M. "How Readers and Editors Judge Newspaper Photos." *APME Photo Report* (15 Oct. 1977).

Unity '94. *News Watch: a Critical Look at Coverage of People of Color*. San Francisco: SFSU Center for the Integration and Improvement of Journalism, 1994.

Vitray, Laura, Mills, John Jr., and Ellard, Roscoe. *Pictorial Journalism*. New York: McGraw Hill, 1939.

Walters, Basil L. "Pictures vs. Type Display in Reporting the News." *Journalism Quarterly* 24 (1947): 193-196.

Wanta, W. "The Effects of Dominant Photographs: An Agenda-Setting Experiment." *Journalism Quarterly* 65 (1988): 107-11.

Wanta, Wayne, and Leggett, Dawn. "Gender Stereotypes in Wire Service Sports Photos." *Newspaper Research Journal* 10 (Spring 1989): 105-14.

White, Jan V. *Editing by Design: Word and Picture Communication for Editors and Designers*. New York: R.R. Bowker, 1974.

Whiting, John R. *Photography Is a Language*. New York: Ziff-Davis, 1946.

Wilkins, Lee. *Envisioning the Blind in Film and the News: Moving from Cultural Stereotype to Reality*. Columbia, MO: University of Missouri, 1994. [paper presented to the Visual Communication Division AEJMC, Atlanta, GA, Aug. 1994].

Willem, Jack M. "Reader Interest in News Pictures." In *Graphic Graflex Photography*, edited by Morgan and Lester. New York: Morgan & Lester, 1946.

Wolf, Rita, and Giotta, Gerald L. "Images: A Question of Readership." *Newspaper Research Journal* 6 (Winter 1985): 30-36.

Woodburn, Bert W. "Reader Interest in Newspaper Pictures." *Journalism Quarterly* 24 (1947): 197-201.

Ethics

Adams, Jonathan. " . . . They Should Have Published It." *4Sight* (NPPA region 4 magazine) (Nov.-Dec. 1993): 17.

Baker, Robert L. "Portraits of a Public Suicide: Photo Treatment by Selected Pennsylvania Dailies." *Newspaper Research Journal* 9 (Summer 1988): 13-23.

Barney, Ralph D., and Black, Jay. *Journal of Mass Media Ethics* 2 (Spring/Summer 1987).

"Bearers of Bad News Examine Roles." *News Photographer* (May 1987) (series of articles): 20-44.

Brecheen-Kirkton, Kent. "Visual Silences: How Photojournalism Covers Reality with the Facts." *American Photojournalism* (Winter 1991).

Brill, Betsy. "Town Protests Staged Photo, Hooker Image." *News Photographer* (Sept. 1986): 4-8.

Brink, Ben. "Question of Ethics: Where Does Honesty in Photojournalism Begin? 'The Foundation Is Basic, Simple Honesty,' an Editor Says." *News Photographer* (June 1988): 21-22, 23-33.

Brown, Jennifer E. "News Photographer and the Pornography of Grief." *Journal of Mass Media Ethics* 2 (Spring/Summer 1987): 75-81.

Bryant, Garry. "10-50 P.I.: Emotion and the Photographer." *Journal of Mass Media Ethics* 2 (Spring/Summer 1987): 32-39.

Chapnick, Howard. "Markets and Careers: Getting the Pictures is only the First Worry for Photojournalists; how it Affects Subjects is the Other." *Popular Photography* (Aug. 1983): 40, 93.

Chapnick, Howard. "Markets and Careers: Today's Ethics in Photojournalism." *Popular Photography* (Aug. 1983): 40, 93.

Coleman, A. D. "Private Lives, Public Places: Street Photography Ethics." *Journal of Mass Media Ethics* 2 (Spring/Summer 1987): 60-66.

Dick, David B. "'What Did Mr. Dwyer Do, Daddy?' 'Well, As You Could See, He Committed Suicide, Darling.'" *The Quill* (March 1987): 18-20.

Diehl, Michael. "Viewer Response to Contrivance in Journalistic Photography." [paper presented to the Graduate Office of Journalism, University of Texas at Austin, Autumn 1981].

"Fake Photo Wins 'Prize' for Magazine." *News Photographer* (Dec. 1992): 27.

Farsai, Gretchen Jeanette. "A Review of Moral Standards Used to Select News Photographs." MA thesis, California State University, Long Beach, 1985.

Floren, Leola. "The Camera Comes to Court." Columbia, MO: Freedom of Information Center, 1978. ERIC, ED163559.

Foster, D. Z. "Photos of Horror in Cambodia: Fake or Real?" *Columbia Journalism Review* (March 1978): 46-47.

Foy, Mary Lou. "Photojournalism: Covering the Worst and Best." *News Photographer* (May 1993): 14-15.

Goldberg, Vicki. *The Power of Photography: How Photographs Changed Our Lives.* New York: Abbeville Press, 1991.

Goodwin, Gene. "The Ethics of Compassion: 'Hard-nosed, Macho' Journalism Is Turning Off Readers and Viewers." *The Quill* (Nov. 1983): 38-40.

Gordon, Jim. "Death of a Photograph: Assaults on Credibility or Much Ado about Nothing?" *News Photographer* (April 1994): 4.

Gordon, Jim. "Judgment Days for Words and Pictures: To Print or Not to Print." *News Photographer* (July 1980): 25-29.

Gordon, Jim. "Question of Credibility: A Western Editor Raises Issue." *News Photographer* (Oct. 1979): 20-22.

Gordon, Jim. "Zeisloft Incident: Foot Artwork Ends Career." *News Photographer* (Nov. 1981): 32-36.

Gross, Larry, Katz, John Stuart, and Ruby, Jay, eds. *Image Ethics: The Moral Rights of Subjects in Photographs, Film, and Television.* New York: Oxford, 1988.

Hagen, Charles. "Robert Doisneau Dies at 81; Photos Captured Gallic Spirit." *NYT* 2 (April 1994): 9.

Hartley, Craig H. "Ethical Newsgathering Values of the Public and Press Photographers." *Journalism Quarterly* 60 (1983): 301-4.

Hartley, Craig. "Photographers, Public View Practices: Ethics and Photojournalism Today." *News Photographer* (Jan. 1982): 23-25.

Hartley, Craig, and Hillard, B.J. "The Reactions of Photojournalists and the Public to Hypothetical Ethical Dilemmas Confronting Press Photographers." MA thesis, University of Texas, Austin, 1981.

Hazard, William R. "Responses to News Pictures: A Study in Perceptual Unity." *Journalism Quarterly* 37 (1960): 515-524.

Hulteng, John L. *The Messenger's Motives: Ethical Problems of the News Media.* 2nd ed. Englewood Cliffs, NJ: Prentice-Hall, 1985.

"Intern Puts Photos on Hold, Helps Save Drowning Child." *News Photographer* (Sept. 1993): 10.

Johns, David. "All about Boo-Boos: Is It Ethical to Photograph Embarrassing Moments? Is Prominence Enough Justification?" *News Photographer* (July 1984): 8.

Junas, Lil. "Ethics and Photojournalism: Code of Ethics: Yes or No?" *News Photographer* (July 1984): 6-7.

Junas, Lil. "Ethics and Photojournalism: Photographer Qualities and Picture Selection." *News Photographer* (June 1984): 24.

Junas, Lil. "Ethics and Photojournalism: Posed, Set Up, Faked, Controlled or Candid?" *News Photographer* (March 1982): 19-20.

Junas, Lil. "Ethics and Photojournalism: Techniques and 'Bring Back Something'." *News Photographer* (June 1982): 26-27.

Kenney, Keith. "Ethical Attitudes." *News Photographer* (Nov. 1991): 12-14.

Kenney, Keith. "Follow-Up: Ombudsmen under Glass." *News Photographer* (Oct. 1993): 40-41.

Kochersberger, Robert C. "Survey of Suicide Photos Use in Newspapers in Three States." *Newspaper Research Journal* 9 (Summer 1988): 1-12.

LaBelle, David. *Lessons in Life and Death.* Durham, NC: NPPA Bookshelf, 1993.

Lester, Paul. "Computer Aids Instruction in Photojournalism Ethics." *Journalism Educator* 44 (Summer 1989): 13-17.

Lester, Paul. *Photojournalism: an Ethical Approach*. Hillsdale, NJ: Lawrence Erlbaum Associates, Publishers, 1991.

Lewis, Michael. "What's so bad about Posing Firemen?" *The New Republic* (28 Feb. 1994).

MacDougall, Curtis D. *News Pictures Fit to Print ... Or Are They?* Stillwater, OK: Journalistic Services 1971.

Mallette, Malcolm F. "Ethics in News Pictures: Where Judgement Counts." [paper presented at Rochester Photo Conference, George Eastman House, Rochester, NY, 1975].

Mallette, Malcolm F. "Should These News Pictures Have Been Printed? Ethical Decisions Are Often Hard but Seldom Right." *Popular Photography* (March 1976): 73-75, 118-120.

Manion, B. C. "Faking It! Omaha Daily Fabricates Photo." *News Photographer* (June/July 1981): 30-31.

Martin, Edwin. "Against Photographic Deception." *Journal of Mass Media Ethics* 2 (Spring/Summer 1987): 49-59.

Mundt, Whitney R., and Broussard, E. Joseph. "The Prying Eye: Ethics of Photojournalism." [paper presented at the Annual Meeting of the Association for Education in Journalism, Houston, TX, 1979]. ERIC, ED173863.

Murphy-Racey, Patrick. "Pictures of the Month-January: A Case of Situation Ethics." *News Photographer* (May 1988): 30-31.

"News Views: *Milwaukee Sentinel* Photographer Helps Firemen in Rescue." *News Photographer* (March 1988): 4.

"News Views: Texas Tragedy, Suicide Coverage a Jolt in Newspaper, on TV." *News Photographer* (June 1983): 4-5,8.

Padgett, G. E. "Let Grief Be a Private Affair." *Quill* 76 (Feb. 1988): 13, 27.

Peters, Greg. "Ethics: Covering the Klan: Are the Sensational Photos Accurately Portraying the Event?." *4Sight*, NPPA Region 4 magazine (Nov.-Dec. 1993): 10-11.

Peters, Greg. "Ethics: It's Time for NPPA to Put Some Teeth in its Ethical Policies." *4Sight,* NPPA Region 4 magazine (July-Aug. 1994): 8-9.

"A Public Suicide: Papers Differ on Editing Graphic Images." *Associated Press Managing Editors (APME) Report: Photo and Graphics.* New York, 1987.

"A Question of Ethics." (multiple article anthology). *News Photographer* (July 1983).

Reaves, Shiela. "Re-Examining the Ethics of Photographic Posing: Insights from the Rank-and-File Members of ASMP." Madison, WI: University of Wisconsin, 1993. [paper presented to the Visual Communication Division of the AEJMC, Kansas City, MO, July 1993].

Reaves, Shiela. "The Vulnerable Image: a Hierarchy of Codes among Newspaper Editors toward Digital Manipulation of Photographs." Madison: University of Wisconsin, 1992. [paper presented to the Visual Communication Division of the AEJMC, Montreal, 7 Aug. 1992].

Remole, Mary K., and Brown, James W. "Ethical Issues for Photojournalists: A Comparative Study of the Perspectives of Journalism Students and Law Students." [paper presented at the Annual Meeting of the Association for Education in Journalism, Boston, MA, 1980]. ERIC, ED191022.

Russial, John and Upshaw, Jim. "See No Evil? Differing Responses to an Awful Picture." *CJR* Vol. 32, No. 5 (Jan./ Feb. 1994): 9-11.

Sherer, Michael D. "Photojournalism and the Infliction of Emotional Distress." *Communications and the Law* 8 (April 1986): 27-37.

Stein, Barney. *Spot News Photography.* New York: Verlan Books, 1960.

Stone, Steve. "When Two Worlds Collide: Public Press, Private Lives, Crash Head-On." *News Photographer* (Aug. 1986): 14-18.

"Suicide." (multiple article anthology). *News Photographer* (May 1987): 20-32, 34-43, 62.

"To Publish? Pro and Con." *News Photographer* (May 1993): 12-17.

Trussell, Robert C. "Press Image 'Under Fire': Recent Movies Fuel Public Debate Over Journalistic Ethics." The *Kansas City Star* (6 Nov. 1983): 1F,13F.

"Why Do They React? Readers Assail Publication of Funeral, Accident Photos." *News Photographer* (March 1981): 20,22-23.

Wilcox, Walter. "Staged News Photographs and Professional Ethics." *Journalism Quarterly* 38 (1961): 497-504.

Wischmann, Lesley. "Dying on the Front Page: Kent State and the Pulitzer Prize." *Journal of Mass Media Ethics* 2 (Spring/Summer 1987): 67-74.

Digital

"Altering Photo Brings Lab Tech's Resignation." *News Photographer (*March 1994): 11.

Bossen, Howard. "Zone V: Photojournalism Ethics and the Electronic Age." *Studies in Visual Communication* 11 (Summer 1985): 22-32.

"Debut: Associated Press, Kodak Introduce Digital Camera." *News Photographer* (March 1994): 22.

"Digital Technology." *ASMP News* (May/June 1994); entire issue.

Dozier, Steve. "Concentrate on Photo Content Development, not on Computers." *Editor Publisher* Vol. 125, No. 16 (18 April 1992): 32, 45.

Fraser, Bruce. "Seven Steps to Superior Scans." *MacUser* (Jan. 1995): 103-105.

"The Future of Photography." *American Photo* (May/June 1994).

Goldsmith, Arthur. "Reinventing the Image: As We Edge Uncertainly Into the Electronic Age, Does Photojournalism Have a Future?" *Popular Photography* (March 1990): 48-53.

Gordon, Jim. "Nothing but the Real Thing: No Playing with Pixels—including the Front Cover." *News Photographer* (March 1994): 4.

Hodges, Lou. "Chemical to Digital Manipulation: the Moral Imperative for Photojournalists." *Protocol* (July 1991): 7-8.

Hubbard, Tom. "Small State, Big Ideas in Digital Image." *News Photographer* (Jan. 1994): 42-43.

Humphrey, Dana. "Stock Photography Develops Online." *Online Access* (Jan. 1995): 62-65.

Kelly, James D. and Nace, Diona. "Digital Imaging and Believing Photos." *VCQ* (Winter 1994): 4-5, 18.

Kenney, Keith. "Photojournalism Research: Computer-Altered Photos: Do Readers Know them when they See them?" *News Photographer* (Jan. 1993): 26-27.

Lasica, J. D. "Photographs That Lie: The Ethical Dilemma of Digital Retouching." *WJR Washington Journalism Review* (June 1989): 22-25.

Lewis, David M. *"Electronic Cameras and Photojournalism: Impact and Implications."* MS study, Ohio University, Athens, 1983.

Morse, Michael L., ed. *The Electronic Revolution in News Photography.* Durham, NC: National Press Photographers Association, 1987.

Noack, David. "Newspapers online: the Big Rush to Cyberspace." *Online Access* (Sept. 1994): 42-47.

Parker, Douglas. "Ethical Implications of Electronic Still Cameras and Computer Digital Imaging in the Print Media." *Journal of Mass Media Ethics* 3 (Fall 1988): 47-59.

"Photo CD." *Photographic* (Sept. 1992): 16-24.

Reaves, Shiela. "Digital Retouching: Is There a Place for It in Newspaper Photography?" *Journal of Mass Media Ethics* 2 (Spring/Summer 1987): 40-48.

Reaves, Shiela. "Digital Alteration of Photographs in Magazines: An Examination of the Ethics." [paper presented at the Annual Meeting of the AEJMC, Washington, DC, 1989]. ERIC, ED310444.

Reaves, Shiela. "Photography, Pixels and New Technology: Is There a 'Paradigm Shift'?" [paper presented at the Annual Meeting of the AEJMC, Washington, DC, 1989]. ERIC, ED310388.

Reaves, Shiela. "What's Wrong with this Picture? Daily Newspaper Photo Editors' Attitudes and their Tolerance toward Digital Manipulation." *Newspaper Research Journal* Vol. 13 & 14 No. 4 & 1 (Fall/Winter 1993): 131-155.

Ritchin, Fred. *In Our Own Image: the Coming Revolution in Photography*. New York: Aperture Foundation, 1990.

"The Sixth Electronic Times." *News Photographer Magazine* Vol. 6, No. 1 (Sept. 1994): 1-40. (a series of articles to supplement *News Photographer*)

Steele, Bob. "Protocols for Ethical Decision-Making in the Digital Age." *Protocol* (1991): 13-17.

Suger, James. "Photojournalism and Computers." *International Designers Network* Vol. 1, No. 6: 85-89.

"Tennessee Photographers Willing to Learn New Technologies, Research Finds." *Digital Digest* (March 1992): 36.

Terry, Danal and Lasorsa, Dominic L. "Ethical Implications of Digital Imaging in Photojournalism." [paper presented at the Annual Meeting of the Association for Education in Journalism and Mass Communication, Washington, DC, 1989]. ERIC, ED310397.

Wilder, "The Internet Pioneers." *Informationweek* (9 Jan. 1995): 38-44.

Features

Armor, Terry. "'Enterprise' Art: When Should You Pitch It?" *News Photographer* (March 1988): 20,22,25. Converse, Gordon N. *All Mankind: Photographs.* Boston: Christian Science Pub. Society, 1983.

Converse, Gordon N. *Reflections in Light: The Work of a Photojournalist.* Boston: Christian Science Monitor, 1989.

Kunhardt, Philip B., Jr. *The Joy of Life.* Boston: Little, Brown, 1989.

Kobré, Ken *How to Photograph Friends and Strangers.* Sumerville, MA: Curtin and London, 1983.

LaBelle, David. *The Great Picture Hunt.* Bowling Green Kentucky: Western Kentucky University, 1989.

Welsch, Ulrike. *Faces of New England: Special Moments from Everyday Life.* 2nd ed. Chester, CT: Globe Pequot Press, 1981.

Welsch, Ulrike. *The World I Love to See.* Boston: Boston Globe/Houghton Mifflin, 1977.

General News

Gans, Herbert J. *Deciding What's News: A Study of CBS Evening News, NBC Nightly News,* Newsweek *and* Time. New York: Pantheon, 1979.

Grace, Arthur. *Choose Me: Portraits of a Presidential Race.* Waltham, MA: University Press Of New England, Brandeis, 1989.

Kobré, Sidney. *Behind Shocking Crime Headlines.* Tallahassee, FL: Florida State University, 1957.

Kobre, Sidney. *News Behind the Headlines: Background Reporting of Significant Social Problems.* Tallahassee, FL: Florida State University, 1955.

Kobre, Sidney. *Press and Contemporary Affairs.* Tallahassee, FL: Florida State University, 1957.

Lukas, Anthony J. "The White House Press 'Club'." *New York Times Magazine* (15 May 1977): 22, 64-68, 70-72.

Moriarty, Sandra E., and Garramone, Gina M. "A Study of Newsmagazine Photographs of the 1984 Presidential Campaign." *Journalism Quarterly* 63 (1986): 728-34.

Musi, Vincent J. "'Racist' Tag on Richards Won't Hold." *News Photographer (*July 1994): 30-31

Mydans, Carl. *Carl Mydans, Photojournalist.* New York: Abrams, 1985.

Nachtwey, James. *Deeds of War: Photographs.* New York: Thames and Hudson, 1989.

Pierce, Bill. "Photography Down and Dirty: Tips from White House Press Photographers on How to Grab Those Candid, Travel and News Pictures That Everybody Else Misses." *Popular Photography* (Nov. 1975): 88-91,130-133.

Rhode, Robert B., and McCall, Floyd H. *Press Photography: Reporting with a*

Camera. New York: Macmillan, 1961.

Streitmatter, R. "The Rise and Triumph of the White House Photo Opportunity." *Journalism Quarterly* 65 (1988): 981-85.

Tames, George. *Eye on Washington: The Presidents Who've Known Me.* New York: Harper & Row, 1990.

History

Abramson, Howard S. *National Geographic: Behind America's Lens on the World.* New York: Crown Publishers, 1987.

Ades, Dawn. *Photomontage.* London: Thames and Hudson, 1986.

"Albany, N. Y., Paper Outraged by Assault." *News Photographer* (Jan. 1995): 12, 14.

Alland, Alexander. *Jacob A. Riis.* Millerton, NY; Aperture, 1974.

ASMP: 1944-1994 50th Anniversary Bulletin Vol. 13, No. 12 (Dec. 1994). Princeton: The American Society of Media Photographers, 1994.

Auer, Michael. *The Illustrated History of the Camera: From 1839 to the Present.* Translated & adapted by D.B. Tubbs. Boston: New York Graphic Society, 1975.

Barrett, Wayne M. "Margaret Bourke-White: New Vistas in Photojournalism." *USA Today* Vol. 118, No. 2523 (Sept. 1989): 55-63.

Baynes, Ken. *Scoop, Scandal and Strife.* New York: Hastings House, 1971.

Bessie, Simon Michael. *Jazz Journalism: The Story of the Tabloid Newspapers.* New York: E.P. Dutton, 1938.

Bethune, Beverly, ed. *Women in Photojournalism.* Durham, NC: National Press Photographers Association.

Bourke-White, Margaret. *Portrait of Myself.* New York: Simon & Schuster, 1963.

Brill, Charles. "The Early History of the Associated Press Wire Photo: 1926-1935." [paper presented at the meeting of the Photojournalism Division, Association for Education in Journalism, Madison, WI, 1977].

Brown, Cindy M. "*PM*: Just Another Picture Paper?" Bloomington, IN: Indiana University, 1994 [paper presented to Visual Communication Division of AEJMC, 12 Aug. 1994].

Brown, Theodore M. *Margaret Bourke-White, Photojournalist.* Ithaca, NY: Andrew Dickson White Museum of Art, Cornell University, 1972.

Callahan, Sean, ed. *The Photographs of Margaret Bourke-White.* Boston: New York Graphic Society, 1972.

Carlebach, Michael Lloyd. "The Origins of Photojournalism in America, 1839-1880." Ph.D. diss., Brown University, 1988.

Carnes, Cecil. *Jimmy Hare News Photographer: Half a Century with a Camera.* New York: Macmillan, 1940.

Cohen, Lester. *The New York Graphic. The World's Zaniest Newspaper.* Philadelphia: Chilton, 1964.

Cole, Bernard, and Meltzer, Milton. *The Eye of Conscience: Photographers and Social Change.* Chicago: Follett, 1974.

Cookman, Claude. *A Voice is Born: The Founding and Early Years of the National Press Photographers Association Under the Leadership of Joseph Costa.* Durham,

NC: National Press Photographers Association, 1985.

Costa, Joseph. Collected Papers. George Arents Research Library. Syracuse University: Syracuse, NY.

Costa, Joseph, ed. *The Complete Book of Press Photography.* New York: National Press Photographers Association, 1950.

Daniel, Pete. *Official Images: New Deal Photography.* Washington, DC: Smithsonian Institution Press, 1987.

Daniel, Pete and Smock, Raymond. *A Talent for Detail: Frances Benjamin Johnston.* New York: Harmony Books, 1974.

Durniak, John. "Focus on Wilson Hicks." *Popular Photography* (April 1965): 59.

Faber, John. *Great News Photos and the Stories Behind Them.* 2nd ed. New York: Dover Publications, 1978.

Faber, John. "On the Record: The Atomic Bomb, Hiroshima." *News Photographer* (July 1980): 30.

Faber, John. "On the Record: Birth of *Life* Magazine." *National Press Photographer* (Aug. 1958).

Faber, John. "On the Record: Development of the Electronic Flash." *National Press Photographer* (March 1959).

Faber, John. "On the Record: Development of the Halftone." *National Press Photographer* (Feb. 1957).

Faber, John. "On the Record: History of the Photo Syndicates." *National Press Photographer* (Dec. 1958).

Faber, John. "On the Record: Sacrificial Protest of Quang Duck." *News Photographer* (July 1983): 10.

Faber, John. "On the Record: Wire Transmission of Photos." *National Press Photographer* (April 1958).

Faber, John. "This is How NPPA Came into Being." *National Press Photographer* (June 1960).

Faber, John. Telephone Interview with author. Sept., 1988.

"Fifty Years and Counting... Series on the history of photojournalism ." *News Photographer* (Supplement).

Fulton, Marianne, ed. *Eyes of Time: Photojournalism in America.* Boston: Little, Brown, 1988.

Gidal, Tim N. *Modern Photojournalism: Origin and Evolution, 1910-1933.* New York: Macmillan, 1973.

Goldberg, Vicki. *Bourke-White.* East Hartford, CT: United Technologies, 1988.

"The Golden Age of the Picture Magazine." *Photographic Journal* 126 (March 1986): 104-8.

Gould, Lewis L. and Greffe, Richard. *Photojournalist: The Career of Jimmy Hare.* Austin: University of Texas Press, 1977.

Gramling, Oliver. *AP, the Story of News.* New York: Farrar and Rinehart, 1940.

"Great News Photos." *Photographic Journal* 119 (Dec. 1979): 384-85.

Gutman, Judith Mare. *Lewis W. Hine: Two Perspectives.* New York: Viking Press, 1974.

Hamblin, Dora Jane. *That Was the Life.* New York: W.W. Norton, 1977.

Harris, John. *A Century of New England in News Photos.* Chester, CT: Globe Pequot

Press, 1979.

Heller, Steven. "Photojournalism's Golden Age (Through the Great Picture Magazines of the '20s and '30s)." *Print 38* (Sept./Oct. 1984): 68-79, 116, 118.

Hine, Lewis. *America and Lewis Hine: Photographs 1904-1940.* Millerton, NY: Aperture, 1977.

Hurley, Forrest Jack. *Portrait of a Decade: Roy Stryker and the Development of Documentary Photography in the Thirties.* 1972. Reprint. New York: Da Capo, 1977.

Jaubert, Alain. *Making People Disappear: An Amazing Chronicle of Photographic Deception.* Washington: Pergamon-Brassey's International Defense Publishers, 1989.

Juergens, George. *Joseph Pulitzer and the New York World.* Princeton, NJ: Princeton University Press, 1966. Kaplan, Daile.

Lewis Hine in Europe: The Lost Photographs. New York: Abbeville Press, 1988.

Kenney, Keith R. and Unger, Brent W. "The *Mid-Week Pictorial*: Forerunner of American News-Picture Magazines." *American Journalism* Vol. 11, No. 3 (Summer 1994): 201-216.

Kenney, Keith. "*Mid-Week Pictorial:* Pioneer American Photojournalism Magazine." [paper presented at the Annual Meeting of AEJMC, Norman, OK, 1986]. ERIC, ED271767.

Kobre, Sidney. *Development of American Journalism.* Dubuque, IA: Wm. C. Brown, 1969.

Kobre, Sidney. *Modern American Journalism.* Tallahassee, FL: Florida State University, 1959.

Kobre, Sidney. *The Yellow Press and Gilded Age Journalism.* Tallahassee, FL: Florida State University, 1964.

Kodak Milestones: 1880-1980. Rochester, NY: Eastman Kodak, 1980.

Leslie, L. Z. "Newspaper Photo Coverage of Censure of McCarthy." *Journalism Quarterly* 63 (1986): 850-53.

Lewinski, Jorge, comp. *The Camera at War: A History of War Photography from 1848 to the Present Day.* London: W.H. Allen, 1978.

Lewis, Charles W. "*From Brady to Bourke-White: An Examination of the Foundations of American Picture Magazine Photojournalism, 1860-1940.*" MA thesis, Mankato State University, MN, 1986.

Lewis, Greg. "A Tribute to W. Eugene Smith." *The Rangefinder* (Dec. 1978): 35.

Life 50, 1936-1986: The First Fifty Years. Boston: Little, Brown, 1986.

Life, the First Decade, 1936-1945. London: Thames and Hudson, 1979.

Life, the Second Decade, 1946-1955. Boston: Little, Brown, 1984.

Life, Through the Sixties: An Exhibition and Catalogue. New York: Time, 1989.

Liotta, Louie and Wadler, Joyce. "Candid Cameraman: After 50 Years of Shooting for the Front Page, News Photographer Louie Liotta Spills." *Time* (11 Dec. 1989): 171.

Mallen, Frank. *Sauce for the Gander. [The New York Evening Graphic].* White Plains, NY: Baldwin Books, 1954.

Martin, Rupert, ed. *Floods of Light: Flash*

Photography, 1851-1981. London: Photographers Gallery, 1982.

Meltzer, Milton. *Dorothea Lange: A Photographer's Life.* New York: Farrar, Strauss, Giroux, 1978.

Meredith, Roy. *Mr. Lincoln's Camera Man Mathew B. Brady.* 2nd rev. ed. New York: Dover, 1974.

Morgan, Willard D. *Graphic Graflex Photography for Prize Winning Pictures.* 11th ed. New York: Morgan and Morgan, 1958.

Morris, Joe Alex. *Deadline Every Minute: The Story of the United Press.* Garden City, NY: Doubleday, 1957.

Newhall, Beaumont. *The History of Photography from 1839 to the Present Day.* Rev. & enlgd. ed. New York: Museum of Modern Art, 1964.

"News Views: Edward Farber, Portable Strobe Inventor, Dead." *News Photographer* (April 1982): 3.

Paine, Richard P. *The All American Cameras: A Review of Graflex.* Houston: Alpha Publishing, 1981.

Permutt, Cyril. *Collecting Old Cameras.* New York: Da Capo Press, 1976.

Pollack, Peter. *The Picture History of Photography.* New York: Abrams, 1969.

Pozner & Pomeyrol. *Leica Story*. Publisher and date of publication unknown.

Rayfield, Stanley. *How Life Gets the Story: Behind the Scenes in Photojournalism.* Garden City, NY: Doubleday, 1955.

Riis, Jacob. *How the Other Half Lives.* New York: Scribner, 1904.

Roeder, George H. *The Censored War: American Visual Experience during World War Two.* New Haven, CT: Yale University Press, 1993.

Rogers, Madeline. "The Picture Snatchers." *American Heritage* Vol. 45, No. 6 (Oct. 1994): 66-73.

Salomon, Erich. *Erich Salomon, Portrait of an Age.* New York: Macmillan, 1967.

Schuneman, R. Smith. "The Photograph in Print: An Examination of New York Daily Newspapers, 1890-1937." Ph.D. diss., University of Minnesota, 1966.

Six Decades: The News in Pictures: A Collection of 250 News and Feature Photographs Taken from 1912 to 1975 by the Milwaukee Journal Co. Staff Photographers. MN: Milwaukee Journal Co., 1976.

Smith, C. Zoe. "Black Star Picture Agency: *Life's* European Connection." *Journalism History* 13 (Spring 1986): 19-25.

Smith, C. Zoe. "Dickey Chapelle." *VCQ* (Spring 1994): 4-9.

Smith, C. Zoe. "Great Women in Photojournalism." Parts 1-3. *News Photographer* (Jan. 1985): 20-21; (Feb. 1985): 26, 28-29; (April 1985): 22-24.

Spruill, Larry Hawthorne. "Southern Exposure: Photography and the Civil Rights Movement, 1955-1968." Ph.D. diss., State University of New York at Stony Brook, 1983.

Squiers, Carol. "Seeing History As It Happened: A Century and a Half in the Life of the World, As Recorded by Its Most Daring Witness." *American Photographer* (Oct. 1988): 33-44.

Stettner, Louis. *Weegee.* New York: Alfred A. Knopf, 1977.

Stettner, Louis, and Zanutto, James M. "Weegee." *Popular Photography* (April 1961): 101-102.

20 Years with AP Wirephoto. New York: Associated Press, 1955.

Walter, Paulette H. *"A History of Women in Print Photojournalism."* MS thesis, University of Ohio, Athens, 1987.

Watkins, Patsy G. "The Power of Editorial and Historical Context: a Photo History Interprets WWII for Americans." Fayetteville, AK: University of Arkansas, 1993. [paper presented to the AEJMC National Convention, Kansas City, KS, Aug. 1993].

Weegee. *Naked City.* New York: Essential Books, 1945.

Weegee. *Weegee by Weegee: An Autobiography.* New York: Ziff-Davis, 1961.

Weegee. *Weegee's People.* 1946. Reprint. New York: Da Capo Press, 1975.

Welling, William. *Photography in America: The Formative Years 1839-1900, a Documentary History.* New York: Crowell, 1978.

Law

Alexander, S. L. "Curious History: The ABA Code of Judicial Ethics Canon 35." [paper presented at the Annual Meeting of the Association for Education in Journalism and Mass Communication, Portland, OR, 1988]. ERIC, ED296422.

Cavallo, Robert M., and Kahan, Stuart. *Photography: What's the Law?* 2nd ed. New York: Crown Publishers, 1979.

Chernoff, George, and Sarbin, Hershel B. *Photography and the Law.* 5th ed. Garden City, NY: Amphoto, 1975.

Costa, Joseph. "Cameras in Court: A Position Paper." Muncie, IN: Journalism/Public Relations Research Center, Ball State University, 1972.

Craig, R. Stephen. "Cameras in Courtrooms in Florida." *Journalism Quarterly* 56 (1979): 703-10.

Culver, Kathleen B. "An Open Door with a Big Spring: Cameras in Federal Courts." *VCQ* (Spring 1994): 17-18.

Dow, Caroline. "Prior Restraint on Photojournalists." *Journalism Quarterly* 64 (1987): 88-93, 118.

Dow, Caroline. "Privacy Law As It Affected Journalism, 1890-1978: Privacy Is a Visual Tort." [paper presented at the Annual Meeting of AEJMC, Memphis, TN, 1985]. ERIC, ED262399.

Dow, Caroline. "The Response of the Law to Visual Journalism, 1839-1978." Ph.D. diss., Michigan State University, 1985.

Dykhouse, Caroline Dow. "Privacy Law and Print Photojournalism." [paper presented at the Annual Meeting of the Association for Education in Journalism, Seattle, WA, 1978]. ERIC, ED1655144.

Dykhouse, Caroline Dow. "Shuttered Shutters: The Photographic Statutes and Their Faithful Companion, 18 USC 1382—An Examination of Photographic Access to Military Areas." [paper presented at the Annual Meeting of the Association for Education in Journalism, Athens, OH, 1982]. ERIC, ED218678.

Galella, Ron. *Jacqueline.* New York: Sheed and Ward, 1974.

"Guidelines: Suggestions for Police/Press Relations Prepared by the National Press Photographers Association, Inc." *News Photographer* (Dec. 1981): 12.

Hoyt, James L. "Cameras in the Courtroom: From Hauptmann to Wisconsin." [paper presented at the Annual Meeting of AEJMC, Seattle, WA, 1978]. ERIC, ED158307.

Huttenstine, Marian L., and Reddin, Debra D. "Let's Keep Photographers Out of Court: A Legal Primer for Photographers." [paper presented at the Annual Meeting of AEJMC, Boston, MA, 1980]. ERIC, ED192368.

Kendall, Robert. "Photo 1978: Some Provisions of the 1976 Copyright Act for the Photojournalist." [paper presented at the meeting of the Photojournalism Division, Association for Education in Journalism, Madison, WI, 1977].

Kielbowiez, Richard B. "The Making of Canon 35: A Blow to Press-Bar Cooperation." [paper presented at the meeting of the Photojournalism Division, Association for Education in Journalism, Houston, TX, 1979].

Middlebrooks, Donald M., Jones, Clarence, and Shrader, Howard. "Access: Scope of Privilege in Gathering News Is Vague and Narrow, Scope of Liability Is Far More Certain." *News Photographer* (Dec. 1981): 10-11, 13-16, 18-19.

"Negative Reaction: when Work was Subpoenaed, Indiana University Student Faced Tough Court Decision." *4Sight* (Jan.-Feb. 1991): 8-9.

Reed, Pat. "Paparazzo, Meet Ron Galella. Nemesis of Jackie O., Brando, etc." *Houston Chronicle Texas Magazine* (15 April 1979): 20.

Sherer, Michael D. *No Pictures Please: It's the Law.* Durham, NC: National Press Photographers Association, 1987.

Sherer, Michael D. "Photographic Invasion of Privacy: An Old Concept with New Meaning." [paper presented at the Annual Meeting of the International Communication Association, Dallas, TX, 1983]. ERIC, ED236626.

Sherer, Michael D. "The Photojournalist and the Law: The Right to Gather News Through Photography." Ph.D. diss., Southern Illinois University at Carbondale, 1982.

Sherer, Michael D. "Photojournalists and the Law: A Survey of NPPA Members." *News Photographer* (Jan. 1988): 16, 18.

Sherer, Michael D. "The Problem of Libel for Photojournalists." *Journalism Quarterly* 63 (1986): 618-23.

Sherer, Michael D. "Your Photos or Mine: An Examination of the Laws Governing Warranted Searches and Subpoenas for the Photojournalist's Work Product." [paper presented at the Annual Meeting of AEJMC, Corvallis, OR, 1983]. ERIC, ED236610.

Sherer, Michael D. "A Survey of Photojournalists and Their Encounters with the Law." *Journalism Quarterly* 64 (1987): 499-502, 575.

Sherer, Michael D. "What You Cover Today May Affect Coverage Tomorrow." *News Photographer* (July 1993): 42-45.

Thayer, Frank. "Legal Liabilities for Pictures." *Journalism Quarterly* 24 (Sept. 1947): 233-237.

Yates, Carl. "What to Do when the Law Says, 'No Pictures, Please!" *News Photographer* (Nov. 1993): 19.

Photo Illustration

Brill, Betsy. "Pictures Don't Lie. . . or Do They?" Master's Thesis, University of Missouri, 1988.

Bryant, Michael. "The Problem with Illustrations." *News Photographer* (July 1987): 36.

Geraci, Phillip C. "Newspaper Illustration and Readership: Is *USA Today* on Target?" *Journalism Quarterly* 61 (1984): 409-13.

Halsman, Phillipe. *Halsman on the Creation of Photographic Ideas*. New York: Ziff-Davis, 1961.

Heartfield, John. *Photomontages of the Nazi Period*. New York: Universe Books, 1977.

Heller, Steven, and Chwast, Seymour, eds. *Sourcebook of Visual Ideas*. New York: Van Nostrand Reinhold, 1989.

Herde, Tom. "Editorial Illustration." *News Photographer* (July 1979): 28-29.

Hinds, Geff. "Giving Computer-Aided Illustration Respect it Deserves." *News Photographer* (Nov. 1992): 44-45.

Kobré, Ken. "Something Different for the News Photographer: Illustrations Solve Problems." *News Photographer* (July 1979): 28-30.

Newcomb, John. *The Book of Problem Solving: How to Get Visual Ideas When You Need Them*. New York: R.R. Bowker, 1984.

Poppy, John. *The Persuasive Image: Art Kane*. New York: Crowell, 1975.

Professional Photographic Illustration. Rochester, NY: Eastman Kodak, 1989.

Stern, Bert. *Photo Illustration: Bert Stern*. New York: Crowell, 1974.

Wedding, George. "Illustrative Photojournalism." [paper presented at San Jose Graphics '88 Conference, CA, April 30, 1988].

Wolf, Henry. *Visual Thinking: Methods for Making Images Memorable*. New York: American Showcase, 1988.

Photo Story

Cohen, Stuart. "Focusing on Humanity: The Life of W. Eugene Smith." *Boston Phoenix* (31 Oct. 1978).

Deschin, Jacob. "W. Eugene Smith Recalls Brutal Beating While Documenting a Poison Scandal." *Popular Photography* (Oct. 1973): 14,20,212.

Dobell, Byron. "The Picture Story." *Popular Photography* (June 1959): 49.

Dykhouse, Caroline Dow. "The Detroit Workshop, 1949-1951: Robert Drew and the *Life* Photojournalism Essay Formula." MA thesis, Michigan State University, 1980.

Edey, Maitland. *Great Photographic Essays From Life*. Boston: New York Graphic Society, 1978.

Girvin, Robert E. "Photography as Social Documentation." *Journalism Quarterly* 24 (Sept. 1947): 207-220.

Hart, Russell and Zwingle, Erla. *William Albert Allard: the Photographic Essay*. Boston: Little, Brown and Company, 1989.

Hughes, Jim. "The Nine Lives of W. Eugene Smith." *Popular Photography* (April 1979): 116-117,135-141.

Hughes, Jim. *W. Eugene Smith, Shadow & Substance: The Life and Work of an American Photographer*. New York: McGraw-Hill, 1989.

Kaplan, John "Was It Simply a Case of Kill or Be Killed? Rodney's Crime." *The Pittsburgh Press Sunday Magazine* (6 Nov. 1988).

Kobré, Ken. "Last Interview with W. Eugene Smith on the Photo Essay." [paper presented at the Annual Meeting of AEJMC, Houston, TX, 1979]. ERIC, ED178948.

Maddow, Ben. *Let Truth Be the Prejudice: W. Eugene Smith, His Life and Photographs*. Millerton, NY: Aperture, 1985.

Mark, Mary Ellen. *The Photo Essay*. Washington, D.C.: Smithsonian Institution, 1990.

Martin, Peter. "Gene Smith As 'The Kid Who Lived Photography.'" *Popular Photography* (April 1979): 130,149-150.

Mich, Daniel D., and Eberman, Edwin. *The Technique of the Picture Story*. New York: McGraw-Hill, 1945.

Pierce, Bill. "W. Eugene Smith Teaches Photographic Responsibility." *Popular Photography* (Nov. 1961): 80-84.

Richards, Eugene. *50 Hours*. Text by Dorothea Lynch. Long Island City, NY: Many Voices Press, 1983.

Richardson, Jim. *High School: U.S.A.* New York: St. Martin's Press, 1979.

Rothstein, Arthur. *Documentary Photography*. 3rd ed. Boston: Focal Press, 1987.

Smith, W. Eugene. "Country Doctor." *Life* (20 Sept. 1948): 115-126.

Smith, W. Eugene. *W. Eugene Smith: His Photographs and Notes*. Millerton, NY: Aperture, 1969.

Smith, W. Eugene. "A Man of Mercy." *Life* (15 Nov. 1954): 161-172.

Smith, W. Eugene, and Smith, Aileen M. *Minamata*. New York: Holt, Rinehart and Winston, 1975.

Smith, W. Eugene. "Nurse Midwife." *Life* (3 Dec. 1951): 134-145.

Smith, W. Eugene. "Pittsburgh." *1959 Photography Annual* (1958): 96-133.

Smith, W. Eugene. "Saipan." *Life* (28 Aug. 1944): 75-83.

Smith, W. Eugene. "Spanish Village." *Life* (9 April 1951): 120-129.

Smith, W. Eugene. *W. Eugene Smith, Master of the Photographic Essay*. Millerton, NY: Aperture, 1981.

Smith W. Eugene. "W. Eugene Smith Talks About Lighting." *Popular Photography* (Nov. 1956): 48.

Stott, William. *Documentary Expression and Thirties America*. New York: Oxford Press, 1973.

Turnley, David C., and Cowell, Alan . *Why Are They Weeping? South Africans Under Apartheid*. New York: Stewart, Tabori and Chang, 1988.

Webb, Alex. *Hot Light/Half-Made Worlds: Photographs from the Tropics.* New York: Thames and Hudson, 1986.

Webb, Alex. *Under a Grudging Sun: Photographs from Haiti Libere 1986-1988.* New York: Thames and Hudson, 1989.

Photojournalism—General

Angeli, Daniel, and Dosset, Jean-Paul. *Private Pictures: Photographs*. New York: Viking Press, 1980.

Arnold, Edmond C. *Modern Newspaper Design*. New York: Harper & Row, 1969.

Barnes, Fred. "Where Is It Leading?" *News Photographer* (April 1979): 28-29.

Barnhurst, Kevin G. *Seeing the Newspaper*. New York: St. Martin's Press, 1994.

Benson, Harry. *Harry Benson on Photojournalism*. New York: Harmony Books, 1982.

Bergin, David P. *Photojournalism Manual: How to Plan, Shoot, Edit and Sell*. New York: Morgan & Morgan, 1967.

Best of Photojournalism. Philadelphia: Running Press, 1977-1995. [Annual.]

Bethune, Beverly M. "Profile of Photojournalists on Two Metropolitan Newspapers." *Journalism Quarterly* 58 (1981): 106-8.

Bethune, Beverly M. "A Sociological Profile of the Daily Newspaper Photographer." *Journalism Quarterly* 61 (1984): 606-14, 743.

Bethune, Beverly. "Under the Microscope: A Nationwide Survey Looks at the Professional Concerns and Job Satisfaction of the Daily Newspaper Photographer." *News Photographer* (Nov. 1983).

Bowden, Robert. *Get That Picture*. Garden City, NY: Amphoto, 1978.

Bowditch, Tom, and Gay, Jerry. "Stress." *News Photographer* (Feb. 1979): 11-13.

Bowermaster, J. "Eyes on the Prize (How a Photographer and a Newspaper Turned Iowa's Farm Crisis into a Pulitzer Prize)." *American Photographer* (Jan. 1988): 60-69.

Boyle, Patrick. "Standard for Photography's Cutting Edge." *Washington Journalism Review* Vol. 14, No. 9 (Nov. 1992): 12.

Brauchli, Marcus. "Prize Under Glass... Chance, Ingenuity, Violence Often Cited as Key Factors in Pulitzer Winners." *News Photographer* (June/July 1981): 20-23.

Brisco, Debbie. "Photojournalism: the Inside View." *Editor & Publisher* Vol. 125, No. 11 (14 March 1992): 26-28.

Buell, Hal, and Pett, Saul. *The Instant It Happened*. New York: Associated Press, 1975.

Burnett, D. "Seven Voices." *Columbia Journalism Review* (Nov./Dec. 1986): 57-59.

Capa, Cornell. *The Concerned Photographer*. New York: Grossman Publishers, 1968.

Cartier-Bresson, Henri. *The Decisive Moment*. New York: Simon & Schuster, 1952.

Cartier-Bresson, Henri. *The World of Henri Cartier-Bresson*. New York: Viking Press, 1968.

Chapnick, Howard. "Looking for Bang Bang: Photojournalists are Flocking to Trouble Spots Like El Salvador, and Too Many Are Not Returning Alive. Are the Results of War Photography Today Really Worth the Risks?" *Popular Photography* (July 1982): 65-67, 99, 101-102.

Chapnick, Howard. "Photojournalism Should Work On More Than One Level—and Its Images Should Be Clear, Simple, and Spontaneous." *Popular Photography* (Sept. 1984): 36-37.

Chapnick, Howard. *Truth Needs No Ally: Inside Photojournalism*. Columbia, MO: University of Columbia Press, 1994.

Crawley, Shirley. *1988 Scholarship Compendium for Communication and Photojournalism Majors: Scholarships, Essay Contests, Loans, Fellowships, Internships.* Washington, DC: Crawley, 1986.

"Creative Fulfillment: Kennedy Urges Photographers to Help Themselves." Florida News Photographers Association (pg. 3-5, 16) (Excerpts from Kennedy's speech titled "Pictures from the Heart.")

Davidson, Bruce. *Subway.* New York: Aperture, 1986.

Duncan, David Douglas. *Self Portrait: U.S.A.* New York: Abrams, 1969.

Dunn, Philip. *Press Photography.* Sparkford, UK: Oxford Illustrated, 1988.

Durham, Michael S. *Powerful Days: the Civil Rights Photography of Charles Moore.* New York: Stewart, Tabori & Chang, 1991.

Dykhouse, Caroline Dow. "Public Policy's Differential Effects on News Photographers." [paper presented at the meeting of the Photojournalism Division, Association for Education in Journalism, Seattle, WA, 1978].

Edom, Clifton Cedric. *Photojournalism: Principles and Practices.* 2nd ed. Dubuque, IA: W. C. Brown Co., 1980.

Evans, Harold. *Eyewitness: 25 Years Through World Press Photos.* London: Quiller Press, 1981.

Evans, Harold. *Eyewitness 2: 3 Decades Through World Press Photos.* Updated ed. London: Quiller Press, 1985.

Feinberg, Milton. *Techniques of Photojournalism.* New York: John Wiley & Sons, 1970.

Finberg, Howard I., ed. *Through Our Eyes: The 20th Century as Seen by the San Francisco Chronicle.* San Francisco: Chronicle Publishing Co., 1987.

Fincher, Terry. *Creative Techniques in Photojournalism.* London: Batsford, 1980.

Fisher, Andrea. *Let Us Now Praise Famous Women: Women Photographers for the U.S. Government, 1935-1944.* New York: Pandora Press, 1987.

Fosdick, James A., and Tannenbaum, Percy H. "The Encoder's Intent and Use of Stylistic Elements in Photographs." *Journalism Quarterly* 41 (1964): 175-182.

Fosdick. James A. "Stylistic Correlates of Prescribed Intent in a Photographic Encoding Task." Ph.D. diss., University of Wisconsin, 1962.

Fox, Rodney, and Kerns, Robert. *Creative News Photography.* Ames, IA: Iowa State University Press, 1961.

Freeman, John. "Are Journalism Schools Teaching the Right Skills?" *News Photographer* March 1994: 23-24.

Gatewood, Worth. *Fifty Years in Pictures: The New York Daily News.* Garden City, NY: Doubleday, 1979.

Geraci, Philip C. *Photojournalism: Making Pictures for Publication.* Dubuque, IA: Kendall/Hunt, 1976.

Geraci, Philip C. *Photojournalism: New Images in Visual Communication.* 3rd ed. Dubuque, IA: Kendall/Hunt, 1984.

Germar, Herb. *The Student Journalist and Photojournalism.* New York: Richards Rosen Press, 1967.

Grossfeld, Stan. *The Eyes of the Globe: Twenty-Five Years of Photography from the Boston Globe.* Chester, CT: Globe Pequot Press, 1985.

Grossfeld, Stan. "Photo Opportunities: Local Photographers Go Global." *WJR Washington Journalism Review* (May 1986): 39-41.

Grossfeld, Stan *The Whisper of Stars: A Siberian Journey.* Chester, CT: Globe Pequot Press, 1988.

Hanka, Harold. *Positive Images: Photographs.* Willimantic, CT: Chronicle Print, 1982.

Haworth-Booth, Mark. *Donald McCullin.* London: Collins, 1983.

Heller, Robert. "Photojournalism Education: Contradictions for the Nineties." *Journalism Educator* Vol. 46 No. 1 (Spring 1991): 29-31.

Hicks, Wilson. *Words and Pictures: An Introduction to Photo-Journalism.* 1952. Reprint. New York: Arno Press, 1973.

Hightower, Paul Dudley. "The Influence of Training on Taking and Judging Photos." *Journalism Quarterly* 61 (1984): 682-86.

Horenstein, Henry. *Color Photography: a Working Manual.* Boston: Little, Brown and Company, 1995.

Horenstein, Henry. *The Photographer's Source: A Complete Catalogue.* New York: Simon and Schuster, 1989.

Horton, Brian. *The Associated Press Photo-Journalism Stylebook.* Reading, MA: Addison-Wesley, 1990.

Horton, Brian. *The Picture: An Associated Press Guide to Good News Photography.* New York: Associated Press, 1989.

Hoy, Frank P. *Photojournalism: The Visual Approach.* Englewood Cliffs, NJ: Prentice-Hall, 1986.

Hubbard, Jim. *Shooting Back: a Photographic View of Life by Homeless Children.* San Francisco: Chronicle Books, 1991.

Huyler, Jean Wiley. "Teach Photojournalism: Not Just Photography." *Communication: Journalism Education Today (C:JET)* 14 (Spring 1981): 4-7.

Images of Our Times: Sixty Years of Photography from the **Los Angeles Times.** New York: Abrams, 1987.

John, Alun. *Newspaper Photography: A Professional View of Photojournalism Today.* Marlborough: Crowood, 1988.

Jones, Bernard, ed. *Cassell's Encyclopedia of Photography.* 1911. Reprint. New York: Arno Press, 1974.

Kennedy, Thomas. "Content and Style: How Do Limited Expectations Affect the Creative Process?" *MGR* (insert in *News Photographer*) (Jan. 1989): 1-3.

Kenney, Keith. "Effects of Still Photographs." *News Photographer* (May 1992): 41-42.

Kerns, Robert. *Photojournalism: Photography with a Purpose.* Englewood Cliffs, NJ: Prentice-Hall, 1980.

Kessel, Dmitri. *On Assignment: Dmitri Kessel,* **LIFE** *Photographer.* New York: Abrams, 1985.

Kielmeyer, David A. "After the Graphics Revolution." *News Photographer* (April 1993): 37-44.

Kobré, Kenneth (photographs) and Brown, Tricia (writing) *L'Chaim: The Story of a Russian Émigré Boy.* New York: Holt, 1994.

Kobré, Ken. "Positive Negative: A critical look at our field." Column in *Visual Communication Quarterly*, a supplement in *News Photographer* magazine

"New York Times;" "*Defying Gravity: Development of the Newton;*" "*Life* Magazine;" "Censoring Somalia." Vol. 1 No. 1 (Winter 1994).

"Picturing Assisted Suicide;" "*USA Today Turns a Profit;*" "Holding a Mirror to a Town." Vol. 1 No. 2 (Spring 1994).

"Unearthing *Outtakes;*" "*Colo*rs." Vol. 1 No. 3 (Summer 1994).

"Rwanda: Witnessing a Holocaust;" "Not a '*Time*' for Illustration." Vol. 1 No. 4 (Fall 1994).

"*The New York Times* is Not What She used to Be." Vol. 2 No. 1 (Winter 1995).

"The Long Tradition of Doctoring Photos." Vol. 2 No. 2 (Spring 1995).

"Good Things Do Come In Small Packages." Vol. 2 No. 3 (Summer 1995).

Lamb, John, and Postle, Bruce. *Images of Our Time: 30 Years of News Photographs.* South Jarra, Victoria: Currey O'Neil, 1985.

Leekley, Sheryle, and Leekley, John. *Moments: The Pulitzer Prize Photographs.* Updated ed. 1942-1982. New York: Crown, 1982.

Lewis, Greg. *Content and Technique.* Dubuque, IA: Wm. C. Brown, 1990.

Livingston, Jane. *Odyssey: The Art of Photography at* **National Geographic.** Charlottesville, VA: Thomasson-Grant, 1988.

Loengard, John. **Life** *Classic Photographs: A Personal Interpretation.* Boston: New York Graphic Society Books, 1988.

Loengard, John. *Pictures Under Discussion.* New York: Amphoto, 1987.

Logan, Richard, III. *Elements of Photo Reporting.* Garden City, NY: Amphoto. 1971.

Loosley, A.E. *The Business of Photojournalism.* New York: Focal Press, 1970.

Lopes, Sal. *The Wall: Images and Offerings from the Vietnam Veterans Memorial.* New York: Collins, 1987.

Lyons, Nathan, ed. *Photographers on Photography.* Englewood Cliffs, NJ: Prentice-Hall, 1966.

MacDougall, Kent A. "*Geographic*: From Upbeat to Realism." *Los Angeles Times* (5 Aug. 1977): 1,8-10.

Magmer, James, and Falconer, David. ***Photograph + Printed Word.*** Birmingham, MI: Midwest Publications, 1969.

Manchester, William Raymond. ***In Our Time: The World as Seen by Magnum Photographers.*** New York: American Federation of the Arts with Norton, 1989.

Markus, David. "Moving Pictures: How Photographers Brought the Ethiopian Famine to Light in the Shadow of Television." *American Photographer* (May 1985): 50-53.

McCullin, Donald. ***Hearts of Darkness.*** London: Secker & Warburg, 1980.

McDonald, Duncan. "Staff Employment: A Tie That Binds?" *News Photographer* (May 1980): 26-29.

Meijer, Emile, and Swart, Joop, eds. ***The Photographic Memory: Press Photography: Twelve Insights.*** London: Quiller Press, 1988.

Mili, Gjon. ***Gjon Mili: Photographs and Recollections.*** Boston: New York Graphic Society, 1980.

Moeller, Susan D. ***Shooting War: Photography and the American Experience of Combat.*** NY: Basic Books, 1989.

Moments in Time: 50 Years of Associated Press News Photos. Rev. ed. North Ryde, Aust.: Angus & Robertson, 1984.

Morris, Desmond. ***Manwatching: A Field Guide to Human Behavior.*** New York: Abrams, 1977.

Morrow, Lance. "Imprisoning Time in a Rectangle." *Time* (Fall 1989): 76

Morton, Robert, ed. ***Images of Our Times: Sixty Years of Photography from the* Los Angeles Times*.*** New York: Harry N. Abrams, Inc., 1987.

Nilson, Lisbet. "Paper Tiger: As an Associate Editor at the *Boston Globe*, Stan Grossfeld Has Advised Something Few Photojournalists Ever Get Their Hands On—Power in the Newsroom." *American Photographer* (Oct. 1988): 46-55.

Norback, Craig T., and Gray, Melvin, eds. ***The World's Great News Photos, 1840-1980.*** New York: Crown Publishers, 1980.

Nottingham, Mary Emily. "From Both Sides of the Lens: Street Photojournalism and Personal Space." Ph.D. diss., Indiana University, 1978.

Ohrn, Karin Becker. "How Photographs Become News: Photojournalists at Work." [paper presented at the Annual Meeting of AEJMC, Corvallis, OR, 1983]. ERIC, ED232191.

O'Mara, Richard. "In a World of Moving Images, Does the Book Have a Future?" *The Sun* 26 (June 1994): Section E.

Peattie, Peggy. "Photojournalism in the '80s: Special Report, Part I: Can Serious Newspaper Documentary Photography Survive the Economic Crash, Quick-Read Presentation and the Photo-Illiterate Paginator?" *News Photographer* (Nov. 1988): 57-60.

Phillips, John. ***It Happened in Our Lifetime: A Memoir in Words and Pictures.*** Boston: Little, Brown, 1985.

"Photography in Newspapers Issue." Pullout Section. *Editor and Publisher* (24 Feb. 1990): 1P-52P.

Photojournalism. Rev. ed. Alexandria, VA: Time-Life, 1983.

Ratcliff, Carter. "The Image Makers." *Picture 20* (1982): 12-56.

Riboud, Marc. ***Marc Riboud: Photographs at Home and Abroad.*** Translated by I. Mark Paris. New York: Abrams, 1988.

Robaton, John and Smith, Harris. ***Photojournalism Basics: an Introduction to Photography for Publication.*** Ipswich, MA: Upper River Press, 1994.

Rodger, George. ***Magnum Opus: Fifty Years in Photojournalism.*** London: Nishen, 1987.

Rolling Stone, the Photographs. NY: Simon & Schuster, 1989.

Rothstein, Arthur. ***Arthur Rothstein, Words and Pictures.*** New York: Amphoto, 1979.

Rothstein, Arthur. ***Photojournalism.*** Garden City, NY: Amphoto, 1979.

Salgado, Sebastiao. ***Other Americas.*** New York: Pantheon, 1986.

Schiffman, Amy. "Keeping Tabs on Photojournalism." *American Photographer* (Sept. 1984): 18.

Schiffman, Amy. "Through the Loupe: Schiffman's Ten Rules of Photojournalism." *American Photographer* (Aug. 1984): 14.

Schrage, Michael. "And Now, a Remake of Your Life, Brought to You by Kodak." *Los Angeles Times (*24 Nov. 1994): D-1.

Schuneman, R. Smith, ed. ***Photographic Communication: Principles, Problems and Challenges of Photojournalism.*** New York: Hastings House, 1972.

Schwartz, Donna. "To Tell the Truth: Codes of Objectivity in Photojournalism." *Communication* Vol. 13 (1992): 95-109.

Sherer, Michael D. "Invasion of Poland Photos in Four American Newspapers." *Journalism Quarterly* 61 (1984): 422-26.

Sherer, Michael D. "The Problem of Trespass for Photojournalists." *Journalism Quarterly* 62 (1985): 154-56, 222.

Sidey, Hugh, and Fox, Rodney. ***1,000 Ideas For Better News Pictures.*** Ames, IA: Iowa State University Press, 1956.

Spina, Tony. ***On Assignment, Projects in Photojournalism.*** New York: Amphoto, 1982.

Spina, Tony. ***Press Photographer.*** Cranbury, NJ: A.S. Barnes, 1968.

Spremo, Boris. ***Twenty Years of Photojournalism.*** Toronto: McClelland and Stewart, 1983.

Steichen, Edward. ***The Family of Man.*** New York: Simon & Schuster, 1955.

Szarkowski, John. ***The Photographer's Eye.*** New York: The Museum of Modern Art, 1966.

Szarkowski, John. ***Photography Until Now.*** New York: Museum of Modern Art, 1989.

Szarkowski, John. ***From the Picture Press.*** New York: The Museum of Modern Art, 1973.

Time: 150 Years in Photojournalism. New York: Time, 1989.

Townsend, Jerry. "Photojournalists Need Reporting Skills, Too." *Community College Journalist* 8 (Winter 1980): 8, 29.

Wheeler, Chris. "Do We Best Serve the Public Interest by Covering the Ku Klux Klan?" *Rangefinder* (Summer 1992): 11.

"Women in Photojournalism." *News Photographer* (Dec. 1984): 16-17; (Feb. 1985): 25-29; (April 1985): 22, 24.

Woo, Jisuk. "Journalism Objectivity in News Magazine Photography." *VCQ* (Summer 1994): 9.

Wooley, Al E. ***Camera Journalism.*** South Brunswick, NJ: A. S. Barnes, 1966.

Portraits

Edwards, Owen. "A Mover Among the Shakers: Arnold Newman's Photographs Are a Tribute to the Staying Power of a Good Idea." *American Photographer* (Nov. 1985): 68-73.

Eisenstaedt. Alfred. ***The Age of Eisenstaedt.*** New York: Viking Press, 1969.

Eisenstaedt, Alfred. ***Eisenstaedt on Eisenstaedt: A Self-Portrait.*** New York: Abbeville Press, 1985.

Eisenstaedt, Alfred. ***Eisenstaedt—Germany.*** Edited by Gregory A. Vitiello. New York: Abrams, 1981.

Eisenstaedt, Alfred. ***Eisenstaedt: Remembrances.*** Boston: Little, Brown, 1990.

Eisenstaedt. Alfred. ***People.*** New York: Viking Press, 1973.

Eisenstaedt. Alfred. ***Witness to Our Time.*** New York: Viking Press, 1966.

Goldsmith, Arthur. "A Lesson in Portraiture From a Master: A Look Over Arnold Newman's Shoulder as He Photographs Dr. Francis Crick for His Notable 'Great British Series.'" *Popular Photography* (Dec. 1979): 100-107, 123-25.

Harwood, Philip J., and Lain, Lawrence B. "Mug Shots and Reader Attitudes toward People in the News." *Journalism Quarterly* Vol. 69, No. 2 (Summer 1992): 293-300.

Karsh, Yousuf. ***Portraits of Greatness.*** New York: Thomas Nelson & Sons, 1959.

Lain, Laurence B. "How Readers View Mug Shots." *Newspaper Research Journal* 8 (Spring 1987): 43-52.

Lange, George. "Feature: Riding Shotgun with Annie (Leibovitz)." *American Photographer* (Jan. 1984): 56, 59.

Leibovitz, Annie. ***Annie Leibovitz: Photographs.*** New York: Rolling Stones Press, 1983.

Lester, Paul Martin. "Front Page Mug Shots: A Content Analysis of Five U.S. Newspapers in 1986." *Newspaper Research.*

Marcus, Adrianne. ***The Photojournalist: Mary Ellen Mark and Annie Leibovitz.*** Los Angeles: Seskog with Crowell, 1974.

Muchnic, Suzanne. "The Lost Art of Portraits." *Los Angeles Times* (21 Aug. 1994): Calendar pg. 6.

Newman, Arnold. ***Arnold Newman, Five Decades.*** San Diego: Harcourt Brace Jovanovich, 1986.

Newman, Arnold. ***Artists: Portraits from Four Decades.*** London: Weidenfeld and Nicolson, 1980.

Newman, Arnold. ***The Great British.*** London: Weidenfeld and Nicolson, 1979.

Newman, Arnold. ***One Mind's Eye.*** Boston: New York Graphic Society, 1974.

Shames, Laurence. "Profile: On the Road with Annie Leibovitz, The Queen of Celebrity Photographers Is Quite a Character Herself." *American Photographer* (Jan. 1984): 38-55.

Sobieszek, Robert A. *Arnold Newman.* Englewood Cliffs, NJ: Prentice-Hall, 1982.

Solomon, Deborah. "Newman at Work." *American Photographer* (Feb. 1988): 44-55.

Souza, Pete. *Unguarded Moments: Behind-the-Scenes Photographs of President Ronald Reagan.* Fort Worth, TX: The Summit Group, 1992.

Sports

Brown, Susan L. "Shooting Sports: John Iacono Shows Us How He Captures Sizzling Action." *Popular Photography* (Oct. 1983): 72-75, 146, 166.

Callahan, Sean, and Astor, Gerald. *Photographing Sports: John Zimmerman, Mark Kauffman and Neil Leifer.* Los Angeles: Alskog, 1975.

Campbell, Bryn. *Great Action Photography.* New York: Amphoto, 1983.

Cappon, Massimo, and Zannier, Italo. *Photographing Sports.* Translated by Maria Piotrowski. Chicago: Rand McNally, 1981.

How to Catch the Action. Alexandria, VA: Time-Life Books in association with Kodak, 1983.

"How to Shoot Sports: It's the Action and Emotions That Count. Here's How the Pros Get Their Great Shots." *Popular Photography* (Aug. 1980): 77-83.

Hurter, Bill. *Sports Photography: Breaking into the Field, How to Capture the Action.* Los Angeles: Petersen, 1978.

Iooss, Walter. *Baseball.* New York: Abrams, 1984.

Iooss, Walter. *Sports People.* New York: Abrams, 1988.

Leifer, Neil. *Sports!* Text by George Plimpton. New York: Abrams, 1983.

McQuilkin, Robert. *How to Photograph Sports and Action.* Tucson, AZ: HP Books, 1982.

McQuilkin, Robert, and Landers, Clifford. "How to Photograph Sports and Action." *Darkroom Techniques* (Sept./Oct. 1984): 41.

McQuilkin, Robert. *Outdoor Sports Photography Book.* Mountain View, CA: Runner's World Books, 1982.

Rabinowitz, Allen. "Marlene Karas: in a League of Her Own." *News Photographer* (April 1993): 1216.

Rabinowitz, Allen. "Super Bowl: All the Action's Not on Georgia's Dome Field." *News Photographer* (March 1994): 19-21.

Rigger, Robert. *Man in Sport.* Baltimore, MD: Baltimore Museum of Art, 1967.

Sahadi, Lou, and Palmer, Mickey, eds. *The Complete Book of Sports Photography.* New York: Amphoto, 1982.

Self, Charles. *How to Take Action Photographs.* Garden City, NY: Dolphin Books, 1975.

Turner, Richard. *Focus on Sports: Photographing Action.* Garden City, NY: Amphoto, 1975.

Spot News

"Associated Press." *Camera 58* (July 1979): 52-53.

Associated Press News and Photo Staff, eds. *One Day in Our World.* New York: Avon Books, 1986.

Blumenfeld, Harold. "The Wire Services That Want You." *Popular Photography* (Jan. 1974): 88-89.

Bork, Charles. "On War Photography." *National Review* (12 Sept. 1986): 34-38.

Buell, Hal. "The Associated Press Behind the Scene." *Camera 58* (July 1979): 4-6, 15-16.

Chapnick, Howard. "Markets and Careers: Keeping News Pictures Meaningful." *Popular Photography* (March 1983): 18, 130.

"Covering the Flood of '93." *News Photographer* October 1993: 42-47. (series of articles under the heading, written by various authors)

Dorfman, Ron. "Journalists Under Fire: This Year's 'Absence of Malice' Will Make Even More Trouble." *The Quill* (October 1983): 12.

Garcia, Mario R. and Stark, Pegie. *Eyes on the News.* St. Petersburg, FLA: The Poynter Institute for Media Studies, 1991.

Loundy, Mark. "Producing Earthquake Extra by 9 a.m. " *News Photographer* (June 1994): 20-21.

Pasternack, Steve, and Martin, Don R. "Daily Newspaper Photojournalism in the Rocky Mountain West." *Journalism Quarterly* 62 (1985): 132-35, 222.

Pearson, Bob. "AFP Mobilizes Staffers to Cover Quake." *News Photographer* (June 1994): 19-20.

"Photographers of the Vanguard: Front-line Journalism is a Matter of Life and Death." *News Photographer* (Sept. 1981): 13-26.

Pizac, Doug. "A Long Week's Work in Quake Aftermath." *News Photographer* (June 1994): 16-17.

"The Process of Recording Conflict" (five article anthology). *Aperture* 97 (Winter 1984): 6-77.

Prouser, Fred. "Reuters Covers Damage." *News Photographer* (June 1994): 17-18.

Tsang, Kuo-Jen. "News Photos in *Time* and *Newsweek.*" *Journalism Quarterly* 61 (1984): 578-84, 723.

Strobe

Edgerton, Harold E. *Electronic Flash/Strobe.* 3rd ed. Cambridge, MA: M.I.T. Press, 1987.

Edgerton, Harold E., and Killian, James R., Jr. *Moments of Vision: The Stroboscopic Revolution in Photography.* Cambridge. Massachusetts: M.I.T. Press, 1979.

Falk, Jon. *Jon Falk Presents Adventures in Location Lighting.* Rochester, NY: Eastman Kodak, 1988.

"Sixteen Great Flash Pictures and How You Can Make Them." *Popular Photography* (Feb. 1995): 42-57.

Spitzing, Gunter. *The Photoguide to Flash.* Garden City, NY: Amphoto, 1974.

(Photo by Tom Levy, San Francisco.)